CLAIMING THE REAL

CLAIMING THE REAL

The Griersonian Documentary and Its Legitimations

BRIAN WINSTON

BFI PUBLISHING

First published in 1995 by the
British Film Institute
21 Stephen Street
London W1P 2LN

The British Film Institute exists to promote appreciation, enjoyment, protection and development of moving image culture in and throughout the whole of the United Kingdom. Its activities include the National Film and Television Archive; the National Film Theatre; the Museum of the Moving Image; the London Film Festival; the production and distribution of film and video; funding and support for regional activities; Library and Information Services; Stills, Posters and Designs; Research; Publishing and Education; and the monthly *Sight and Sound* magazine.

British Library Cataloguing-in-Publication Data
A catalogue record for this book is available from the British Library

ISBN 0-85170-463-8
      0-85170-464-6 pbk

Cover by Robert Harland Design

Front cover image: stills from
Man with a Movie Camera (Dziga Vertov, 1928)
and *Man of Aran* (Robert Flaherty, 1934)
Back cover: still from *Cane Toads* (Mark Lewis, 1994)

Typeset in Plantin by Goodfellow & Egan, Cambridge
Printed in Great Britain by St Edmundsbury Press,
Bury St Edmunds, Suffolk

For George Stoney and Penelope Houston
and in memory of Ralph Bond
and (of course) for
Adèle, Jessica, and Matthew

Il est l'idéologie bourgeoise même, le mouvement par lequel la bourgeoisie trans-forme la réalité du monde en image du monde, l'Histoire en Nature ... l'idéolo-gie bourgeoise sera scientiste ou intuitive, elle constatera le fait ou percevra la valeur, mais refusera l'explication: l'ordre du monde sera suffisant ou ineffable, il ne sera pas jamais signifiant.

Roland Barthes
(*Mythologies*, p. 250)

It is the bourgeoise ideology itself, the process through which the bour-geoisie transforms the reality of the world into an image of the world, History into Nature ... Bourgeois ideology is of the scientist or the intu-itive kind, it records facts or perceives values, but refuses explanations; the order of the world can be seen as sufficient or ineffable, it is never seen as significant.

(*Mythologies*, pp. 141–2)

A quotation from Barthes does not automatically carry the day.

David Bordwell
('Adventures in the Highland of Theory', *Screen* vol. 29 no. 1,
Winter 1988, p. 89)

Contents

Preface

This book has its origins in the Fifth Broadcasting Symposium at Manchester University in 1973, where for the first time I met both Colin Young, head of the recently founded National Film School of Great Britain (NFS), and George Stoney, a distinguished documentary film maker and a doyen of film teaching in the United States. I was then a producer at Granada TV.

After the symposium, Colin hired me to be general tutor at the school. Because I had worked on *World in Action* (and been trained by Tim Hewat) I became involved in teaching documentary production at the NFS. I now had the benefit of Colin's insights into the documentary, he having thought more thoroughly and, indeed, more academically about it than anybody I had yet encountered.

Three years later, when Stoney took a sabbatical to film his explication of Flaherty's *Man of Aran* (*Man of Aran: How the Myth Was Made*), I was honoured to take his chair at New York University (NYU) for the year. Now I had to teach not only documentary film production but also George's course on the history of documentary, 'The Documentary Tradition'.

Although I had seen the documentary canon (without it bowling me over, I must confess), my training and work had been in a distinctly journalistic environment; but I had lived through the era of professional hostility to the new equipment, with crews objecting to being asked to shoot handheld with available light and sound. I recall lab officials denying that film stocks could be 'cooked' to 1000 ASA even after we showed them American documentaries in which this had been done. I had even been taken by *World in Action*'s then lead camera, David Samuelson, to a special meeting at the National Film Theatre where André Coutant explained his brand-new Eclair camera with slides of its blueprints (very blue) covered with very small French labels. David did not think the thing would work, I seem to remember.

Before going to America, the only persons, apart from Young, with whom I had had any extended conversations about documentary were the late Alex Valentine (who had worked out the rules for himself) and Dick Fontaine (who was an early enthusiast for direct cinema and indeed got Granada to hire the Maysles brothers for a couple of *World in Action* projects).

Now, in a classroom in the basement of the NYU business school, I first began to put all these professional experiences and conversations into a formal context.

1

Upon my return to the United Kingdom and the National Film School in 1978, Colin Young and Gus Macdonald asked me to prepare a survey of all the previous year's documentary output on British television for the Edinburgh Television Festival. Since I had not seen any of it, having been in the United States, I was not perhaps in an ideal position to do this. However, helped by Jerry Kuehl and others, I managed to screen everything the trade deemed significant and I wrote a paper for the Festival which Penelope Houston kindly reprinted in *Sight and Sound*.

Some of the television documentarists at the festival claimed that they could not understand this paper. (It is amazing to me how intellectual workers in Britain, normally holding degrees from the older élitist universities, can think it an appropriate response to an argument to claim they cannot follow it.) Other practitioners, however, could, and I have benefited enormously from conversations with Roger Graef, Mike Grigsby, Philip Donnellan, Stuart Hood and John Wyver (among others) which have been of immense value to me over the years. Penelope Houston was also good enough to allow me to write further articles about the 'totemic ancestors' of the documentary for *Sight and Sound*.

And I continued to teach documentary. In that context I have gained much from my students at NYU and Penn State and my colleagues there and elsewhere – especially George Stoney (of course), Lynne Jackson, Bill Uricchio, Jay Ruby and Michael Renov (to whom I am additionally indebted as the source of my title here). It was with Roberta Pearson's help that I first came to grips with the issues of the documentary's formal structure.

I owe a special debt of thanks to Henry Breitrose, very much the instigator of this present volume without whose help it would not be appearing in its present guise. And I should thank Alan Rosenthal, not only for his sustained efforts on behalf of the documentary in general but also for having enabled me to return to documentary production in the 1980s.

The first half of this book is about older films, some so obscure that they are for the most part unavailable on videotape, seldom screened on television and not in general circulation. Without the help of Catherine Egan at New York University's Bobst Library, Bill Sloan and Charles Silver at the Museum of Modern Art and, over many years, Elaine Burrows at the British Film Institute in making them available to me I could not have written these chapters.

I am grateful to others at the British Film Institute: to Colin MacCabe for wanting this project, to Ed Buscombe for facilitating it and to Geoffrey Nowell-Smith for his informed and vigorous editing. *Il miglior fabbro* all right. Needless to say the book's faults are not his; nor, indeed, can they be laid at the door of anybody here mentioned, except myself.

And, finally, as usual, my thanks to my wife Adèle. This one nearly got away but, thankfully, it did not.

Cardiff, August 1993

PART ONE

THE CREATIVE TREATMENT OF ACTUALITY

1

The Documentary, Scitex and Harry

By the summer of 1993, the status of the photographic image as evidence was becoming somewhat tattered, at least among journalists. On 5 July the *UK Press Gazette*, the newspaper trade weekly, reported 'a growing concern at the ease with which photographs can now be electronically altered'. The tabloid *Sun*, for example, had manipulated a picture of a monk, 'said to be at the centre of a love tangle', and a woman by substituting a habit for the ordinary clothes he was actually wearing. The report continued: 'In an official statement, *The Sun* said: We have superimposed the monk's habit to make it clear to the readers that the story is about a monk.' Incidents of this sort were increasingly coming to light.

In an even more playful mode, British popular newspapers had for some years been running 'Spot the Difference' competitions using not drawings but photographs. For example, the *Sunday Mirror Magazine* of 23 June 1991 carried pictures of the Queen and Prince Philip which had been digitally retouched – clothing recoloured, the Garter Star removed, the hat remodelled, and so on. Digital technology was, even before the public was generally aware of its power, here deployed to *mock* the relationship of the photographic image to the reality of their majesties and the historic moments which the photographs supposedly memorialised.[1]

The technology for digital image manipulation is rapidly becoming a fixture in all newspaper and magazine offices. In the United States, the pioneering commercial device's brand-name, 'Scitex', is a synonym for the whole process, much like 'hoover'. As a verb it is already a term of art – 'to scitex', meaning to retouch digitally. The *St Louis Post Dispatch* scitexed a coke can out of the portrait photograph of one of its own photographers who had just won a Pulitzer prize for his work. The *Orange County Register* won a Pulitzer for its photographic coverage of the 1984 Los Angeles Olympics but every one of its outdoor images had scitexed azure blue skies. On another occasion the paper ran a news picture of a swimming pool that vandals had dyed red; but its own technicians scitexed the pool back to Southern Cal blue for publication, rendering the caption nonsense. *National Geographic* was caught, in 1982, repositioning one of the pyramids at Giza. A spokesperson promised: 'Scitex will never be used again to shift any of the Seven Wonders of the World' (Winston, 1990, pp. 30ff.).

Parallel technology for the moving image exists. To take an early instance, more interesting than 'simple' colourisation, music video director Ethan Russell spent six days with a Harry (video's equivalent of Scitex) altering 42 seconds'-worth of Hank Williams Senior's lips. In a unique 1952 telerecording, the only film of the man in performance, Williams sang 'Hey, Good Looking'. After Harry, with somebody else's lips digitally sutured into this image, Williams appeared to be singing 'Tears in My Beer'. (Give Russell enough time and money and Hank Williams will sing 'Nessun Dorma'.) In the world of Scitex, Harry and the technologies that produced such special effects masterworks as *Roger Rabbit*, Bette Davis can get to play Scarlett O'Hara after all – and will, if it is to the copyright holders' advantage so to arrange. Absolute undetectability, for the first time, is undermining the mimetic power of all photographic processes.

It seems to me likely that the implications of this technology will be decades working themselves through the culture. However, it is also clear that these technological developments, whatever else they portend, will have a profound and perhaps fatal impact on the documentary film. It is not hard to imagine that every documentarist will shortly (that is, in the next fifty years) have to hand, in the form of a desktop personal video-image-manipulating computer, the wherewithal for complete fakery. What can or will be left of the relationship between image and reality?

I know of no theoretical position, no definition of documentary that does not in some way reference that relationship – from the phrase coined by John Grierson, the founder of the British documentary film movement, who described it as the 'creative treatment [that is, image making] of actuality [that is pre-existing reality]', to Michael Renov's 'direct ontological claim to the real': 'Every documentary issues a "truth claim" of a sort, positing a relationship to history which exceeds the analogical status of its fictional counterpart' (Renov, 1986, p. 71). It is hard to see how the documentary, in all its current guises, can find a replacement for such 'truth claim' legitimations.

This danger is, in my view, markedly increased because almost no attention has been paid to documentary theory. This means that there is only a confused and partial understanding generally available of these existing legitimations, their sources and implications.

Public reception of the documentary still turns on an unproblematised acceptance of cinematic mimesis. Documentarists have, for years, obfuscated basic issues so that they could, at one and the same time, claim journalistic/scientific and (contradictory) artistic privileges. When they have paid attention, scholars, by and large, have avoided questions of definition. As a result, the documentary, unclear as to its legitimations and confused as to its *raison d'être*, is thus not in a good position to counter current threats.

Yet for all these failures there have also been some advances in the study of documentary in the last three decades or so. The long march through the paper archives has begun, as has the re-evaluation through close text readings of the films themselves. There has been one brilliant study of a documentary technician, the British film editor Stewart McAllister (Vaughan, 1983). The recovery of alternative radical documentary traditions in the 1930s has been a major historiographic effort. There has been a dribble of work in English on the non-English-speaking documentary. Ethnography and ethics are being considered. The great row occasioned by direct cinema and cinéma vérité thirty years ago brought us closer to fundamental issues than at any time since the LEF arena debates on these matters in the USSR forty years earlier; and there has been a modicum of more extensive theorising – notably by Nichols (1991).

It is in the light of all these developments that I am here trying to understand what the 'First Principles of Documentary' (as Grierson's 1932–4 manifesto puts it) actually were; where they came from; how they were legitimated; how these legitimations changed through time; and what, from time to time, their practical effects were, on the screen as well as politically and ethically. Therefore, this study does not propose a fresh forage through the primary sources. Its aim is more modest, merely an examination of the documentary idea, its sources, its practice, its development and its current state, with some thoughts as to its future possibilities.

It is also primarily a study of the realist documentary idea, and for three reasons. First, the realist documentary makes the greatest 'truth claims' for itself. Second, realist documentaries constitute the dominant tradition, not just in the United Kingdom and North America but also in the rest of Western Europe and all other parts where Griersonian realists trained local film-makers in the form. Finally, the contemporary realist documentary dominates world-wide because it is the preferred variant of the form on television.

In all candour, I do not see any easy solution to the radical difficulties the documentary now faces, except to seek in past and current practice some indicators as to what can be salvaged, or avoided, for the future. It is with that ambition that this book addresses itself to a single question: whence came and what were, are, and can be the legitimations for the realist documentary project?

2

The Documentary Film in 1914

'Documentary value' was the phrase John Grierson used in reviewing Robert Flaherty's *Moana* for a New York newspaper in 1926. This is usually credited as being the first occasion on which the word 'documentary' was applied, in English, to this specific sort of film. Grierson noticed, and, it must be said, dismissed as having secondary importance, the 'documentary value' of *Moana*, which he thought was a result of the film's 'being a visual account of events in the daily life of a Polynesian youth and his family ... But that, I believe, is secondary to its value as a soft breath from a sunlit island' (Grierson, 1981, p. 24). This is where conventional accounts of documentary begin. (See, for example, Ellis, 1989, p. 4; Jacobs, 1971, p. 25; Barsam, 1973a, p. 7; Winston, 1978, p. 2.)[2] Grierson's enormous abilities as a publicist, and his achievements in setting up a production unit systematically dedicated to producing 'documentary value', quite swept away other claimants to the honour (such as it is) of recognising documentary as a distinct type of film. For instance, not even the efforts of Erik Barnouw, in a standard history (1974, p. 26), and Jay Leyda in his work on compilations (1964, p. 15) could substitute Boleslaw Matuszewski for Grierson.

In *La Photographie animée, ce qu'elle est, ce qu'elle doit être*, published in Paris in 1898, Matuszewski saw film as an instructional medium, documenting history, daily life, artistic performances, even medical procedures.[3] Notwithstanding this, Grierson remains the documentary's Adam, presumably because Matuszewski is ruled out of court as he was a Pole writing in French and because Barnouw and Leyda offered no evidence of a connection between him and Grierson.

Edward Sheriff Curtis, however, is in a different case. Curtis worked as a photographer of native Americans for nearly thirty-five years. His 1,500 sepia-coloured prints are central to the collective photographic image of *The North American Indian*, his twenty-volume masterwork.

In 1914, Curtis made a movie, *In the Land of the Headhunters*. Virtually lost shortly after its release until the late 1940s, the film has now been restored with a Kwakiutl soundtrack and a new title, *In the Land of the War Canoes*.[4] When Curtis was preparing for this venture, he issued a prospectus for The Continental Film Company: 'Associated with several of Seattle's leading business men, Mr. Edward S. Curtis has formed a small company for the making of commercial motion pictures of the Indian and the Indian life' (Holm and Quimby, 1980, pp. 113ff.). The prospectus goes on to stress Curtis's extensive experience with the tribal peoples, and proposes a series of films on all the tribes of North and South

America. 'Exceptionally substantial dividends' are promised, not least as the proposed films will have, because of their historical and ethnological importance, increasing value, unlike the entertainment pictures which 'go to the junk pile' after six months. Then comes this:

> The question might be raised as to whether *the documentary material* would not lack the thrilling interest of the fake picture. It is the opinion of Mr. Curtis that the real life of the Indian contains the parallel emotions to furnish all necessary plots. ... All pictures made should be classed among the educational, and should be preserved as part of *the documentary material* of the country. ... In making such pictures, the greatest care must be exercised that the thought conveyed be true to the subject, the ceremony be correctly rendered, and above all, that the costumes be correct. It must be admitted that the making of such a series of pictures would be the most difficult thing attempted in motion photography, but it can be done, and will be one of the most valuable *documentary works* which can be taken up at this time. (my italics)

'Documentary material', 'documentary works' and a definition of the documentary film stressing authenticity; by 1914, at the latest, Curtis was using the term 'documentary work' in a clearly Griersonian sense.

Curtis was exploiting a minor vogue for melodramas set in exotic locales. For instance, one of Méliès's brothers produced two such South Sea dramas in 1913 (De Brigard, 1975, p. 18). The genre was well enough established in France to be named *documentaires romancés* and distinguished from *documentaires*, which were films of the locales without the melodrama, as it were. Curtis's contribution, beyond importing the term into English, was grounded in his photographic practice. Although after the fashion of the day *In the Land of the Headhunters* is a crude melodrama, Curtis worked hard to ensure that its setting and costumes were authentic, albeit of a previous age. His is a dramatic ethnographic film, a romance perhaps, but one which he saw clearly as containing 'documentary material'.

There is a connection, and a strong one, between Curtis and the Griersonian tradition, via Robert Flaherty. Flaherty was acknowledged by Grierson as a profound influence and worked with him in Britain in 1931. Curtis was interested in Flaherty's still photographs of the Inuit (Danzker, 1980, p. 15). There is also every reason for believing Curtis showed Flaherty *Headhunters*. Jay Ruby has examined Mrs Flaherty's diaries and, according to this source, on 9 April 1915 Flaherty and Curtis met in New York. On the 13th, they screened *In the Land of the Headhunters* and Flaherty's first footage of the Baffin Island Inuit, shot, as was the Curtis film, the previous year. At lunch, Curtis apparently gave Flaherty 'the benefit of his own personal experience in the moving picture world' (Ruby, 1980, p. 94; Holm and Quimby, 1980, p. 30). (The importance of Curtis's influence on the making of *Nanook*, and thereby the whole mainstream tradition, is examined below, p. 98.)

And another link – high on Grierson's list of Chicago 'attractions', when he went to that city on his Rockefeller fellowship in 1924, was the poet Vachel Lindsay. Lindsay's book *The Art of the Moving Picture* had been published in 1915, the year of Flaherty's meeting with Curtis. As one of the earliest books on cinema, it was noticed and reprinted in 1916 and

1922 (Wolfe, 1973, pp. 19ff.). The book cites *Headhunters*, for among Lindsay's notions about film was one that the cinema should be 'sculpture in motion'. 'The photoplay of the American Indian should in most instances be planned as bronze in action.' In Lindsay's view *Headhunters* 'abounds in noble bronzes' (Lindsay, 1915, p. 86).

More is at stake here than simple-minded firstism. For Matuszewski and Curtis there can be no question as to the ontological importance of mimesis for their vision of what the documentary might be. In this sense, although unacknowledged, it is their vision which informs the reception of documentary to this day. The application of the adjective 'documentary' to film (and the use of 'documentary' as a noun meaning a documentary film) most appositely flags the fact that, despite claims to artistic legitimacy ('creativity') and dramatic structuring ('treatment'), when dealing with this film form we are essentially and most critically in the realm of evidence and witness ('actuality').

3

The Documentary as the
Creative Treatment of Actuality

In English, the adjective 'documentary' was coined late, by 1802. The modern meaning of its source word 'document', as 'something written, inscribed, etc., which furnishes evidence or information', dates from only 1727. The word itself is derived from *documentum*, a lesson, and enters the language with that meaning by 1450. 'Document' in the sense of something written actually replaces 'muniment', 'a title deed preserved as evidence of rights and privileges', in use in that sense by the late Middle Ages.

Raymond Williams (1976, *passim*) taught us that words coined or acquiring new meanings during the last two centuries have particular significance for us. The new meanings or neologisms afford rich clues to the *histoire des mentalités*. The change from 'muniment' to 'document' is no exception. 'Muniment' is derived from the Latin for fortification. A 'muniment' *prima facie* afforded a lot more protection than does a 'document'. 'Document' speaks to the modern growth of legal rights grounded in contracts rather than rights arising from status. It also speaks to the swamping of the emerging industrial world in paper. The old particularities, 'muniment', 'affidavit', 'charter', 'memorandum', 'brief', 'writ', 'note' (also originally a legal term), 'letter', etc., are all subsumed in the new generic term – 'document'.[5] This whole group of words comes largely from the legal realm and binds writing and what is written to the common law, specifically to evidence before the law in both the pre-modern and the modern periods.

The contemporary use of 'document' still carries with it the connotation of evidence. This sense of document provided the frame, as it were, into which the technology of photography could be placed. The photograph was received, from the beginning, as a document and therefore as evidence. This evidential status was passed to the cinematograph and is the source of the ideological power of documentary film.

But when Grierson came in the late 1920s to expand his insight about 'documentary value' into a full-blown approach to the cinema, the evidential proved to be a two-edged sword. Clearly, documentary needed to make a strong claim on the real but at the same time Grierson did not want it to be a mechanical, automatic claim arising from nothing more than the very nature of the apparatus. He defined documentary therefore as 'the creative treatment of actuality' and thereby created a problem (Rotha, 1952, p. 70). For one does not have to be too much of a sceptic to spot the obvious contradiction in this formulation. The supposition that any 'actuality' is left after 'creative treatment' can now be seen as being at best naive and at worst a mark of duplicity.

11

Only in Ian Aitken's valuable examination (1990, pp. 24ff.) of Grierson's education can be found any reasonable explanation of what Grierson might have had in mind when he coined the definition.

Grierson attended Glasgow University after the First World War and there not only studied but also actively embraced idealist philosophy. Aitken's resolution of the contradictions in Grierson's definition turns on the distinction Grierson was taught to make between the 'real' and the 'phenomenal' or 'actual'. The 'real' is here taken to be 'abstract and general', whereas the 'phenomenal' is 'empirical and particular'. The 'real' is of greater significance but the 'phenomenal' offers the best means of understanding it. This distinction allowed Grierson to subsume 'the relative objectivity of the documentary, in relation to fiction cinema' into a broader documentary theory which was 'primarily an aesthetic of symbolic expression'. Thus, Aitken convincingly argues, 'Grierson's first definition of the documentary film was primarily formalist, with actuality footage having a relatively low priority' (ibid., pp. 7, 12 and 101).

The problem is that this sophistication surfaces neither in the definition itself nor in the practices it justifies. While I am convinced by Aitken that Grierson was making sense (at least to himself) when he coined the phrase, it is clear that, as Aitken himself reports (p. 70), even Grierson knew he was not making much sense to others: 'Although he recognised that film interpreted reality, and was not mimesis, he did not believe that the average spectator should share that recognition and believed that a convincing illusion of reality was essential in order to make the narrative as powerful as possible.'

This then leaves Grierson in exactly the position in which previous critics had placed him. 'I cannot say clearly what I am seeking in this cinema of the actual,' he wrote in 1929 (Grierson, 1981, p. 30). The lack of clarity meant that Grierson gave no guidance to his followers as to what the 'creative treatment of actuality' meant but rather allowed them to contradict him and each other in their attempts to explain the phrase. The result is that it remains, *pace* Aitken, as contradictory as it ever was for the average spectator (which includes all those without the benefit of Grierson's education).

Philosophy, then, will not save the sense of the definition; nor, obviously, will it suffice to treat the expression as an utterance *de novo* from Grierson, as if it had no history and no context outside film. This is, for instance, what Barsam tries to do (1973, pp. 1ff.).

These problems were not unnoticed by the Griersonians themselves. The terms used to explain the work became a source of difficulty, if not of embarrassment. Alberto Cavalcanti, one of Grierson's team in the 1930s, expressed what many of them came to feel: 'I hate the word "documentary". I think it smells of dust and boredom' (Sussex, 1975, p. 52). Grierson's American opposite number, Pare Lorentz, claimed (1975, p. 170) that the word gave him a headache. One of the camerapersons on Lorentz's first film, Leo Hurwitz, agreed with Cavalcanti: 'I got to hate the word documentary.' In the United States, claims Hurwitz, 'Documentary was a dirty word for a long while' (Hurwitz, 1934, p. 12). (It still is – see p. 58.)

Some tried to remove the difficulties by self-deprecating references such as the one with which Grierson himself begins his 1932–4 manifesto: 'Documentary is a clumsy description but let it stand' (Grierson, 1979a,

p. 35). So effective is this ploy that Basil Wright, another colleague of Grierson's at this time, repeats it, virtually verbatim, in an interview thirty-seven years later: 'A clumsy description, and he [Grierson] admitted it was no good. But let it stand' (Levin, 1971, p. 55).[6]

It is hard to see how making pleas for other (equally problematic) terms, such as 'non-fiction' or 'factual' film, reduces the confusion (Baddeley, 1963, p. 9).

Nor does it help to assume that the Griersonians used the terms 'documentary' and 'actuality' as specific and idiosyncratic derivations from the French. Grierson must have known that French critics distinguished by the term *documentaire* serious expedition films from travelogues, although he referenced French usage as meaning simply travelogue at the outset of the 1932–4 manifesto (Aitken, 1990, p. 80; Grierson, 1979a, p. 35).[7] It is not unreasonable, therefore, to suppose that Grierson also understood that all non-fiction films, including *documentaires*, were initially termed *actualités*. *Actualités* originally meant nothing more than the conversational topics of the hour. In French the term, being applied to the cinema, moved from meaning 'factual film' in general to obtain its current more limited sense of 'newsreel'.

It is possible, then, to suggest a reading of the Griersonian definition of documentary which assumes it to be a species of Franglais – that is to say, the creative treatment of newsreels. Ivor Montagu tried this assumption (1966, p. 281): 'Presumably Grierson is referring ... to actuality in the sense that raw material which the documentary film worker composes is the cinematographic record of visual aspects of reality.' According to this reading, all Grierson might have meant by the 'creative treatment of actuality' was that the documentary goes beyond the 'purely journalistic skills' of the newsreel in that it treats the same sort of material 'creatively'. This is not, in itself, an impossibility, although it does require a sophisticated understanding of the balance between manipulation and evidence which is not elsewhere indicated. As Montagu well understood, it is to strain credulity to suggest this is really how the Griersonians wanted the term 'actuality' read (Grierson, 1979a, p. 35).

'Actuality', for them, was not a self-conscious translation from the French. It was what it has been for all English speakers since it first appeared in the language in 1675, a synonym for 'reality'. Nor was it a word with the added sense of 'realism in description'. This meaning was acquired from 1850 on but it is not in the forefront of the Griersonians' usage.

For instance, Paul Rotha, another of Grierson's colleagues and the other major writer in the movement, pointed out that newsreel and documentary 'both go to actuality for their raw material' (Rotha, 1966, p. 88). (Note that in this context, where newsreels are being specifically discussed, Rotha still avoided the potential Franglais sense of 'actuality'). Writing in 1974, Basil Wright stated that the Lumières 'showed *actuality*' (Wright, 1976, p. 6). 'Actual' is 'real' and 'actuality' is 'reality' – and habitually so. These attempts to vary, avoid or gloss the everyday meanings of the words involved fail. There is no Franglais interpretation that will allow us simply to recover Grierson's sense and avoid the confusions his idealist philosophy brings in train.

The problem is, of course, that Grierson, secure in this philosophy and somewhat elitist about the intellectual capacities of his fellows, never really

13

addressed himself to the fundamental issues raised by his use of the term 'documentary' and the definition he gave it; nor did any of his followers.

Of course, avoiding the deeper issues did allow Grierson to adopt a strategy which permitted the films to be made and documentary to be established as a discrete film form. The short-term advantages were tremendous but, in the long term, the flawed foundations Grierson laid have proved to be ever more threatening to the structure he built. For neither in the late 1920s nor thereafter did Grierson in his extensive polemical writings confront the underlying problems involved in recognising and reproducing 'documentary value' on the screen. The funding agencies would not sit still for idealist reflections on the nature of reality and the realist image. Grierson was not inclined to bring them to this debate. The audiences, such as they were, were equally unconcerned. The critical reception of the works was at that time, almost exclusively, laudatory. Why would he or the documentary film movement worry?

Thus, all the basic common-usage contradictions inherent in Grierson's original formulation must stand – in a 'documentary', what is the nature of the 'actuality' or reality left after 'creative treatment'? Montagu (1966, p. 281) put the problem like this: 'In a sense every work is the creative treatment of actuality. Actuality is the raw material that, as experience, must pass through the consciousness of the creative artist (or group) to become transformed by labour and in accordance with technical and aesthetic laws into the art product.'

Grierson's own followers would seem to be aware of these problems. Why else would Forsyth Hardy, his editor and biographer, omit the 'creative treatment of actuality' phrase from the abridged edition of Grierson's writings on documentary? As late as 1966, it is there (Grierson, 1966, p. 13). For the reissue of 1979, it is not (Grierson, 1979a, p. 11).[8]

However, when questions are being raised, by scholars such as Bill Nichols (1991, p. 7), as to whether or not 'separation between an image and what it refers to continues to be a difference that makes a difference', I do not think we have the luxury of simply pretending these initial difficulties were never in play. The foundational issues raised by these terms can no longer be avoided.

So: 'creative', 'treatment', 'actuality' – on what cultural maps can such terms be found?

PART TWO

CREATIVE: DOCUMENTARY AS ART

4

Photography as Art

The term 'creative', in the context of the documentary film, relates to a broader debate about the creative nature of photography.

The possibility of manipulating the photographic apparatus was crucial to all the eventually successful efforts made to turn first photography and then cinematography into a plastic art. It is here in this possibility that Rudolph Arnheim (1957 [1933], p. 35), for instance, located his opening plea for film as art:

> As distinguished from the tools of the sculptor and the painter, which by themselves produce nothing resembling nature, the camera starts to turn and a likeness of the real world results mechanically. There is serious danger that the film maker will rest content with such shapeless reproduction. In order that the film artist may create a work of art it is important that he consciously stress the peculiarities of his medium.

This is done specifically by the manipulation of camera, lighting, lens, and so on.

This opposition between mechanical reproduction and artistic selectivity is a constant theme in this debate. Walter Benjamin quoted (1969, p. 228) 'ultrareactionary authors' such as Franz Werfel commenting on 'the sterile copying of the exterior world which ... had obstructed the elevation of the film to the realm of art'. These pleas persisted. 'It is wrong to make art too life like,' claimed Manvell in 1946. He went on, again, to talk of camera placement, lens choice, shot selection and lighting, much as Arnheim had done more than a decade earlier (Manvell, 1946, pp. 21ff.).

The argument repeats, in essence, what Benjamin called the 'devious and confused' nineteenth-century row about the artistic value of photography. At the outset, in 1839, the painter Delaroche claimed: 'From today painting is dead' (Freund, 1982, p. 81). In 1865, one defender of photography cried, 'One cannot but acknowledge that there are arts which are on their way out and that it is photography which has given them the death-blow!' (Scharf, 1974, p. 46).

Baudelaire was unenthusiastic about the technology but he too thought that photography was painting's 'mortal enemy' (Sontag, 1977, p. 144). It was 'an invention resulting from the mediocrity of modern artists and a refuge for all unsuccessful painters' (Freund, 1982, p. 79). Ingres lamented: 'Now they want to confuse art with industry' (Freund, 1982, p. 77). In fact the whole thrust – the supervening social necessity (Winston, 1986, pp. 21ff.) – which led to the development of photography was for a more readily available system of portraiture, as the Pre-Raphaelite Ford Maddox Brown understood: 'Photography has taken the place of portraiture, but a revival must ere long take place. Photography is but the assistant (saving the artist and sitter time) of portrait painting, which can never exist but by the effort and will of genius' (Scharf, 1974, p. 75). But the revival of jobbing portraitists and miniaturists never came. The debate about art and photography swirled on for decade after decade. It lingers yet because, as Roland Barthes put it (1981, p. 30), 'Photography has been, and is still, tormented by the ghost of Painting.'

Benjamin (1969, p. 227) saw the argument, for all its uselessness, as an important response to the changed circumstances of 'the work of art in the age of mechanical reproduction'. 'Earlier much futile thought had been devoted to the question of whether photography is an art. The primary question – whether the very invention of photography had not transformed the entire nature of art – was not raised.'

André Bazin, though, was to accept Benjamin's point: 'Photography is clearly the most important event in the history of plastic arts.' Its most significant effect, Bazin claimed, was to free painting from a 'resemblance complex' (Bazin, 1968, pp. 16 and 13). Bazin also took Benjamin's additional point as to how cinematography exacerbated the issues raised for traditional concepts of art by photography. Benjamin had noted: 'Soon film theoreticians asked the same ill-considered questions with regard to film. But the difficulties which photography caused traditional aesthetics were mere child's play as compared to those raised by the film' (Benjamin, 1969, p. 227).

Although these theoretical concerns were not consciously cited by the film-makers, this tension, between 'film as art' and 'film as mechanical reproduction' was to be echoed in the world of documentary.

5

The Documentarist as Explorer/Artist

Dominant opinion throughout the heyday of the Griersonian documentary had the fiction film-maker becoming an artist by struggling against and overcoming the 'shapeless reproduction' produced mechanically by the camera. We have seen that for Grierson, the idealist philosopher, taking 'actuality' as a starting-point was not incompatible with seeking a place as such an artist. The very same elements Arnheim and others used to distinguish film artists from non-artistic users of the cinematographic apparatus Grierson also claimed as the special marks of the documentarist vis-à-vis the newsreel and other non-fiction film producers. The practical result was that Grierson was not interested in 'shapeless reproduction' either. Wearing his film critic hat, he once wrote of Sternberg, 'When a director dies, he becomes a photographer!' (Grierson, 1981, p. 58).

From the beginning documentarists have rewarded themselves, for their success in the struggle against 'shapeless reproduction', with the title 'artists'. When Frances Flaherty noted (in 1914) her hope that Robert's films would 'gain recognition for R as an explorer, *as an artist* and interpreter of Eskimo people' (Ruby, 1980, p. 68; my italics), she was doing nothing untoward. Flaherty claimed, she wrote in another place (1960, p. 10), that 'All art is a kind of exploring. To discover and reveal is the way every artist sets about his business.'

Flaherty was very much the practical model, the template, for Grierson's 'creative' documentary director. Flaherty was also responsible for the idea of 'treatment' in that it was he who first fully explored the use of narrative as a means of structuring 'actuality'. This, his one undeniable contribution to the history of the cinema, is discussed further in Part Three (see p. 100).

More obliquely, and far less positively, Flaherty marked the realist documentary in other ways. He deeply influenced both its politics and ethics.

The stars and settings of Flaherty's earliest films were found in the North West Territories of the Dominion of Canada, and the Samoan Protectorate of the Dominion of New Zealand. Flaherty's immediate and direct successors were equally drawn to far corners of the globe. Merriam Cooper and Ernest Schoedsack, for instance, documented the epic journey of the Baktyari people from their winter grazing to their summer camps towards Isfahan in Iran in the 1925 feature *Grass*. Cooper and Schoedsack went on to make *Chang* (1927) in Thailand and, obviously distilling all they had learned of tribal peoples, eventually directed *King Kong* (1933). There were more of the same breed (Barnouw, 1974, pp. 50ff.; Rotha, 1973, p. 16).

Flaherty's was to be largely an imperial film-making career. It was to be almost entirely spent in the far-flung corners of empire or domestic backwaters, in the pay of governments or exploitative commercial interests. The mystery is how untainted by this is his reputation – as if the cinema were too puny, its pantheon too insecure, to support the vicissitudes suffered by other imperial artists – Kipling, say. Flaherty's explorer stance, although remarked on, is deemed to be without import. It is not even defended (as is Riefenstahl's fascism); it is ignored. No mistake must be made about this imperialism, though, for Flaherty was not a man to rise above his time.

His career as a prospector, in the years before the First World War, was encouraged by Sir William Mackenzie – in Flaherty's words, 'the Cecil Rhodes of Canada'. Flaherty was a child of the last age of imperial expansion, and beneath the veneer of sympathy and understanding for the peoples he filmed there is nothing but the strong whiff of paternalism and prejudice. Nanook's clowning with the phonograph record, where Allakariallak (who played him) is supposed to be comically astonished at the device, stands as a good example of Flaherty's biases. The truth is that, far from being as naive as the sequence suggests, the Inuit were actually technologically sophisticated enough to maintain Flaherty's equipment (Wollheim, 1980, p. 12). Flaherty, however, was never one to allow the truth to obscure a racial stereotype. For the BBC in 1949 Flaherty recalled:

The white man has a way of expression. His face reveals so much to a native. He can read your face like a book, while his face remains impassive.

'How old would you think it would be?' I asked him [an Inuit, Nero]. 'Oh', he says, 'maybe a t'ousand years'. 'How would you know it's a thousand years old?' 'Oh', he says, 'I see it when I am a small boy'. A thousand years doesn't mean anything to an Eskimo. (Rotha, 1983, p. 13)

What it might have meant to the Inuit in his own tongue in terms of his own cultural referents casts no shadow over Flaherty's understanding of this all too typical incident.

After his marriage, the filming trips became family outings in a particularly imperial mould, replete with nannies and large rented houses – even a palace on one occasion (Rotha, 1983, pp. 52, 111, and 116; Flaherty, 1937, p. 25). Harry Watt recalled that his year on the Aran Islands off Eire, where Flaherty filmed *Man of Aran* in 1932–3, was 'the easiest time of my life'. 'The extraordinary thing was that Flaherty always lived like a king in these primitive places' (Sussex, 1975, p. 31).

Flaherty, who was thirty-two when America entered the First World War, and therefore not an impressionable soul when these expeditions began, was encouraged by all this in a certain view of himself: 'When making *Moana*, he had cultivated the idea that the islanders on Savaii should regard him as the Big White Chief. Only if they revered him and respected him could he get them to do what he wanted' (Rotha, 1983, p. 169). It is not that the man failed to exhibit late-twentieth-century sensitivities towards native peoples (though, if he had, it would have been, to use

Gandhi's term, 'nice'); rather, it is that he allowed his own lordly view of himself totally to condition whatever project was at hand.

Thus the Native American symbiosis with the land becomes, in *Nanook*, an adversarial and exploitative relationship, just like Flaherty's. The personal relationships of the Inuit also echo Flaherty's. The lives of Nanook and Nyla, his wife, played by Alice (?) Nuvalinga, 'are shown as low temperature versions of bourgeois domesticity' (Wollheim, 1980, p. 14) – even to the extent of Flaherty's never quite explaining what the other woman, Cunayou, is doing in the film. (She is the second wife.) These recastings, as much as any direct faking or 'reconstruction', are what is ideologically significant in Flaherty's *œuvre*. The major ideological thrust of his films lies in the universalisation of capitalist relations to other cultures. That is the essence of their imperialism.

As to ethics, Flaherty put the film above everything. The film, the 'aggie' as Allakariallak called it, 'come first' (Ruby, 1980, p. 66). Of the Aran people, who acted in *Man of Aran* [1934], he said, 'I should have been shot for what I asked these superb people to do for the film, for the enormous risks I exposed them to, and all for the sake of a keg of porter and five pounds apiece' (Rotha, 1983, p. 116). What he asked them to do was nothing less than risk their lives. Maggie Dirrane, who plays the mother in the film, is at one moment steadied in the waves by having her hair grabbed. A boatload of fishermen is put at considerable risk in the climactic storm sequence. Some argue – Harry Watt for instance in an interview filmed for George Stoney's *How the Myth Was Made* (1978) – that the danger was more apparent than real, the clever result of the manipulation of depth occasioned by the use of very long lenses. However, the film *Man of Aran* patently reveals otherwise. The danger was real.[1]

Flaherty has a sort of basic unrepentance about him. Allakariallak was dead within months of the film's release. Flaherty's reaction to the death was 'remarkably impersonal' (Wollheim, 1980, p. 13). Some suggest, although this has been disputed, that the painful tattooing of Ta'avale, who played Moana, was not an authentic part of contemporary Samoan life, the ceremony having fallen into desuetude.[2] What has not been questioned is the fact that it took six weeks to do the tattooing and a further two weeks for Ta'avale to recover (Rotha, 1983, p. 69). Then there was the elephant which nearly stepped on a baby during the filming of *Elephant Boy*. Flaherty wrote to his producer Korda from India, 'Please do not mention the incident of the baby to the press. I have already been accused of trying to drown a boatload of wild Irishmen on Aran!' (ibid., p. 174).

All this is possible because, as Mrs Flaherty desired, Robert had indeed become an artist. Within the Flaherty myth, his film-making methods have been compared to those of artistic Inuit carvers. Rotha explains how the Inuit, according to Edmund Carpenter, see the piece of ivory as hiding the sculpture within so that the form is not created but released. Rotha comments (ibid., p. 49): 'We believe that these two Eskimo qualities – the acute power of observation and the letting of material shape its own meaning – form an integral part of Flaherty's art as film maker.'

The artistic right of documentarists encompasses not only a freedom to exploit the subject but, as Flaherty's career also illustrates, a licence to exploit producers as well. Flaherty is seen as a heroic defender of the individual artist against the seamy barons of commerce – 'Hollywood is like sailing over a sewer in a glass-bottomed boat,' he once said (ibid., p. 5).

21

Much of this – the attitude to the people filmed, the relationship to the sponsor or producer, the implicit support for the existing order – was to be carried forward by Grierson and his colleagues. And so too was the self-image of the documentarist as artist.

There is no question but that Grierson thought of himself and his colleagues as artists. Often, though, there is a certain manly reticence about how this vision is expressed. Basil Wright, for instance, stated: 'I regard the film as an art. I don't pretend that any film I am going to make is a work of art – though I always hope something of the sort will turn up' (Levin, 1971, p. 46). What hopefully will turn up is something recognisable as art within a received (that is, nineteenth-century) vision of artistic enterprise. In documentary film practice this vision of art is measured by Arnheim-style considerations of selectivity, which distance the form from other types of non-fictional filming.

Without such selectivity, the director becomes a mere photographer and the documentary film diminishes into the mechanical 'shapeless reproduction' of the newsreels and other non-fiction films. Conversely, if one can rise above these dangers, according to Grierson (1979a, p. 36), 'one begins to wander into the world of documentary proper, into the only world in which documentaries can hope to achieve *the ordinary virtues of an art*' (my italics). But what then are the ordinary virtues of an art for Grierson?

> The word *Art*, which had commonly meant 'skill', became specialized during the course of the eighteenth century, first to 'painting', and then to the imaginative arts generally. *Artist* similarly, from the general sense of a skilled person, in either the 'liberal' or 'useful' arts, had become specialised in the same direction, and had distinguished itself from *artisan* (formerly equivalent with artist, but later becoming what we still call, in the opposite specialized sense, a 'skilled worker'), and of course from *craftsman*. The emphasis on skill, in the word, was gradually replaced by an emphasis on sensibility. (Williams, 1983, pp. 43f.)

Williams argued that far from being an expression of universal truth what we think of as art is not only culturally specific but also grounded in a corpus of ideas and attitudes traceable to the taste-making elite (particularly in London and Paris) around the turn of the 19th century. In the first half of the 19th century, the vision of the artist as a person apart becomes central. It suffuses the response art offered to that main thrust of early-nineteenth-century society, which we can conveniently sum up in another word coined at this time (by Carlyle), 'industrialism'.

Utilitarianism, the philosophical underpinning of industrialism, was producing a distortion of human life. As Dickens makes the utilitarian villain in *Hard Times* say:

> You are to be in all things regulated and governed ... by fact. ... You must discard the word Fancy altogether. You have nothing to do with it. You are not to have, in any object of use or ornament, what would be a contradiction in fact. You don't walk on flowers in fact; you cannot be allowed to walk on flowers in carpets. ... You never meet with quadrupeds going up and down walls; you must not have quadrupeds represented on walls. ... This is the new discovery. This is fact. This is taste.

'Men', Matthew Arnold wrote, 'are grown mechanical in head and heart, as well as in hand. ... Their whole efforts, attachments, opinions, turn on mechanism, and are of a mechanical character.'

The dominant Victorian bourgeoisie legitimated all those activities and artefacts, largely stolen from the court and the great house and abhorrent to the utilitarian, as 'art', or, rather, 'the arts'. In this way the time-honoured proposition that humankind cannot live by bread alone was obeyed, at least by the economically privileged.

Beyond this, such activities and artefacts by and with which the proletariat similarly sought to escape from the desolation of Coketown were relegated into a nether land of artisanship. These were to be recuperated as 'folk art' only towards the end of the century, when the rural 'folk' who had produced them were long since gone to the industrial slum. 'Folk art' then joined the 'crafts' which, in a residual confusion, had remained yoked to art because artistic practice was seen as a species of craft and some types of craft production were still treated as being in some sense art.

The central point, however, was that in the proletarian slum the activities and artefacts which performed the function of 'high art' (what the arts had now become in contradistinction to the 'folk' variety) were still beyond the pale to society's taste makers – dismissed as 'popular' or (even worse) 'mass art'.

Thus, instead of an Arnoldian view of culture as being 'a pursuit of our total perfection by means of getting to know, on all matters which most concern us, the best that has been thought and said in the world', we have in Williams (1986, p. 115) a rather more limited vision of art clearly inflected by class and time.

It is only comparatively recently that the cinema, no longer the front-runner mass medium, could be generally reclaimed from the 'morass' of mass art. Among its worst sins *as art* was that it was 'mechanical' and mass-produced; but now film could be safely placed, at least on occasion, with the other 'high' arts, as these were so classed by the *haute bourgeoisie*. Instead of film-makers being relegated to the ranks of 'artisans', where the widespread popularity of their works constantly threatens to place them, some could become 'artists'. Thanks to the valiant efforts of the Sarrises and the Kaels, and others of Arnheim's heirs writing for the quality press, all film-makers could now aspire to this title.

It is an irony pointed up in Williams's analysis that the inflated nineteenth-century rhetoric of 'art' and 'artists' is in some sense a recompense for a loss of clearly defined social function. Williams states (1983, p. 36): 'At a time when the artist is being described as just one more producer of a commodity for the market, he is describing himself as a specially endowed person, the guiding light of common life.' It is only a utilitarian (or materialist/consumerist) society which needs so fervidly to justify this commoditisation by having its artists become, potentially, 'a clerisy' or, actually, 'bohemians' (a word first used in English in this sense in 1848).

6

The Griersonian Artist

Those professing the arts were relieved of normal morality not only in the daily conduct of their lives but also, more significantly, in the conduct of their work.

'Does a man die at your feet, your business is not to help him, but to note the colour of his lips; does a woman embrace her destruction before you, your business is not to save her, but to watch how she bends her arms.' Thus Ruskin advised the young artist whose job it is, not to aid the dying nor protect the fallen, but only to observe. This unchristian injunction carried, in the age of 'art for art's sake', but the barest hint of irony. It is justified because the concept of art claimed it, in Blake's terms, as 'the seat of imaginative truth' and 'the imitation of a universal reality'; in short, 'the best that has been thought and said in the world'. The purpose and effect of this art for those who consumed it was ameliorative.

According to William Morris, 'It is the province of art to set the true ideal of a full and reasonable life before him, a life to which the perception and creation of beauty, the enjoyment of real pleasure that is, shall be felt as necessary to man as his daily bread, and that no man, and no set of men, shall be deprived of this.' So important was this function of art to society – in Morris's phrase, 'the one certain solace of labour' – that the artist, in producing these super-truths, was absolved from more prosaic concerns (Williams, 1983, p. 149).

Flaherty is the bridge whereby all the prerogatives of the nineteenth-century realist artist become the common property of the twentieth-century documentary film-maker. Thanks to Flaherty, a documentarist operates untrammelled by responsibilities even when her or his institutional position suggests otherwise. For the Griersonian documentarist, claiming the title 'artist' – as opposed, for example, to 'publicist', 'educator', or 'propagandist' – was therefore crucial.

The film documentarist is selective and thus creative, creative and thus artistic, and artistic and thus, to a certain extent, absolved from the everyday norms of moral and ethical behaviour. The duty of care towards others becomes attenuated, as Flaherty's potent example taught. This is not to say that documentarists were to be as cavalier as Flaherty about putting people into physical danger. They did not do that, at least not often. But they were largely blinded as to the consequences of documentary filming – to issues of privacy, false light and any consideration of the general impact that appearing in a film might have for an ordinary person, a non-professional participant. Ethics in general were not on the agenda and, in part, late-Victorian rhetoric about artistic privilege was responsible for the omission.

24

The concept of the artistic was at work everywhere in documentary production, starting with 'the way in which the camera is used'. Newsreel cinematographers are dismissed exactly because 'they make no effort to approach their subjects from a creative or even dramatic point of view, no attempt to govern the selection of images by methods other than those of plain description' (Rotha, 1966, p. 77). That documentary cameramen – as they all were – behaved differently constituted a source of admiration. 'No man of cameras ... can pan so curiously, or so bewilderingly anticipate a fine gesture', as can Flaherty, in Grierson's opinion (Grierson, 1979a, p. 34). Of Wright, he said, 'As with good painters, there is character in his line and attitude in his composition' (ibid., p. 43). Such observers become, as it were, 'poets of the camera'. Grierson can send Wright off to film one of the most persistently and perniciously exploited of all groups of non-European workers, the tea-pickers of Sri Lanka, with the following valedictory (at least as Wright remembered it): 'Right, you're a poet' (Orbanz, 1977, p. 133).

Post-production also afforded equal opportunities for creativity:

> The belief that nothing photographed, or recorded on to celluloid, has meaning until it comes to the cutting bench; that the primary task of film creation lies in the physical and mental stimuli which can be produced by the factor of editing. The way in which the camera is used, its many movements and angles of vision in relation to the object being photographed, the speed at which it reproduces actions and the very appearance of persons and things before it, are governed by the many ways in which editing is fulfilled. (Rotha, 1966, p. 79)

Within the legitimation provided by the realist aesthetic, Grierson and his followers can locate these arenas of creativity – cinematography and editing (and later sound) – as the specific sites of both the mechanical reproduction of what Grierson called 'the living article' *and* imaginative work. Critics could find these various aspects of film-making creatively in one documentarist so that a straightforward analogue of the traditional solo artist could be constructed. For example Rotha and Wright are both respectively discussed by a contemporary avant-garde critic in these terms: 'a film directed, mounted and photographed by one man, an artist'; 'one of the few men in England making real films which he writes, directs, AND EDITS' (Dusinberre, 1980, p. 43).

The result is to move documentary altogether away from the established modes of factual communication in science, economics, politics, etc. – the 'discourses of sobriety' that are or ought to be, in Nichols's view (1991, p. 3), documentary's 'kin'. As Grierson pointed out (1979a, p. 37), 'The choice of the documentary medium is as gravely distinct a choice as the choice of poetry instead of fiction.' It is a painterly tradition that allows for 'poetry' rather than, say, 'essay' or 'belles-lettres', which might at first sight seem more apposite alternatives to fiction in such an analogy.

7

Documentary Film and Realist Painting

For the Griersonians and their followers, nineteenth-century art was a critical source of rhetoric. Grierson could claim the documentary film as a species of artistic enterprise with serious implications for social betterment because that was how art in general, according to Linda Nochlin (1966, pp. 49ff.), was deemed to function by many nineteenth-century theorists.

Within the general development of art and art theory in the 19th century, one strand was to be of extreme significance for Grierson's documentary project. The French realist school, its practice and its theory, had a profound, if unacknowledged, effect on his rhetorical positions and the general reception of the documentary film. Grierson echoed the realists in his claims about everything from working methods (the flight from the studio) to subject matter (the working class); from purpose (public education and social agitation) to justification (the artist as a political actor).

When Grierson wrote in 1937 (1979a, p. 77) 'The thought of making work an honoured theme, and a workman, of whatever kind, an honourable figure, is still liable to the charge of subversion', he but echoed the critic Champfleury, who had coined the term 'realism' in 1851, and who wrote in 1856 that 'M. Courbet is seditious for having represented in good faith bourgeois, peasants, village women in natural size' (Nochlin, 1966, p. 39).

The theorist and artist Thomas Couture, Manet's master, proclaimed on the eve of the revolutions of 1848: 'These are the new subjects. Our workmen have not been represented; they remain yet to be put upon canvas' (Nochlin, 1966, p. 7).

Compare this with Grierson (1979a, p. 77): 'The workers' portraits in *Industrial Britain* were cheered in the West End of London. The strange fact was that the West End had never seen workmen's portraits before – certainly not on the screen.' Or Harry Watt:

[The films] were revolutionary because they were putting on the screen for the first time in British films – and very nearly in world films – a workingman's face and a workingman's hands and the way the worker lived and worked. It's very hard with television nowadays and everything, to realize how revolutionary this was, that British films, as such, were photographed plays, that any working class people in British films were the comics. (Sussex, 1975, p. 76)

There is now some doubt as to how true this was. In fact, about two out of every five British features had working-class characters and one out of

26

three was set in a working-class environment in the decade 1929–39 (Jones 1987, p. 23). The point here, however, is not whether Watt was overstating the case for the documentary film movement but that the documentarists shared an older realist rhetoric, a rhetoric which Rotha (1966, p. 113) could state thus: 'Documentary must be the voice of the people speaking from the homes and factories and fields of the people.'

When Grierson (1979a, p. 41) claimed 'Realist documentary, with its streets and cities and slums and markets and exchanges and factories, has given itself the job of making poetry where no poet has gone before it, and where no ends, sufficient for the purposes of art, are easily observed' he again overstated the case. Such locales and themes were central to the realist school which Courbet represents. Courbet said, in replying to a critic who accused him of dragging art through the gutter: 'Yes. ... Art must be dragged in the gutter' (Clark, 1982a, p. 69).

'We began to wonder', wrote the Goncourts in 1864, 'whether ... in a country without caste or legal aristocracy the sufferings of the poor and humble could touch our interest, our pity, our emotions as sharply as the sufferings of the rich and mighty' (Nochlin, 1971, p. 34).

The painter Millet mused in the early 1860s: 'Why should the activity of the potato or bean planter be less interesting or less noble than any other activity? Let it be understood that nothing is noble or low except the manner of understanding or representing things, not the things themselves' (Nochlin, 1966, p. 58). This was no small matter. As Berger points out (1980, pp. 69 and 77), Millet's 'life's work was to introduce a new subject into an old tradition, to force a language to speak of what it had ignored. The language was that of oil painting; the subject was the peasant as individual *subject*. ... There was no formula for representing the close, harsh, patient physicality of a peasant's labour *on*, instead of *in front of*, the land.'

Nochlin suggests it was exactly these social concerns – these new subjects and the implications of choosing them – which distinguishes the verisimilitude of this group of painters and writers from previous schools of what may be termed naturalists. Thus the critic G. H. Lewis, writing in 1858, mixed a request for verisimilitude in the representation of drapery which could have been addressed to a seventeenth-century Dutch master, a Caravaggio or a Velásquez with other demands that could only be answered by a Courbet or indeed a Rotha: 'Either give us true peasants, or leave them untouched; either paint no drapery at all, or paint it with the utmost fidelity; either keep your people silent, or make them speak the idiom of their class' (Nochlin, 1971, p. 35).

Nineteenth-century realism was claimed for the radical interest. Courbet was proclaimed 'the first of the socialist painters' by Proudhon: 'Velásquez was a courtier of the court; Courbet is a Velásquez of the people' (Nochlin, 1966, p. 48). Thus,

The passion which fills Courbet and his supporters is ... fundamentally political: their self-assurance comes from the conviction that they are the pioneers of truth and the forerunners of the future. Champfleury asserts that naturalism is nothing more than the artistic trend corresponding to democracy, and the Goncourts simply identify bohemianism with socialism in literature. (Hauser, 1983, p. 62)

For the sake of the socialist cause, Théophile Gautier was even ready, in the heady spring of 1848, to abandon the concept of the individual artist: 'We should like to see organized great camps and armies of painters ... No doubt individualism would suffer, and a few would lose their little originality, their mastery of details; but the great works of art are almost all collective' (Clark, 1982, p. 31).

There is therefore a considerable continuity when Grierson (1979a, p. 189) pins his colours thus firmly to the same mast: 'It is true that we hoped that individual artists would have every opportunity within the framework of public service; but the other half of our socialized or public conception of art was that we could only secure this larger hope by tying our effort to the organized forces of social growth under whatever form they came.' (In the event, the 'socialized conception' lost out to the individual artist, but the thought was there, however tenuously.)

For Grierson (ibid., p. 13), 'The documentary idea demands no more than that the affairs of our time shall be brought to the screen in a fashion which strikes the imagination and makes observation a little richer than it was.' For Proudhon, true painting functioned in much the same way: 'To reproduce realities once again is nothing: one must make people think; one must touch them, illuminate their consciousness' (Nochlin, 1966, p. 51).

In another place Proudhon cried: 'Let the magistrate, the soldier, the merchant, the peasant, let all orders of society, seeing themselves both in the idealism of their dignity and in their lowness, learn through glory and shame, to rectify their ideas, to correct their customs, and to perfect their institutions.' (ibid., p. 45).

Grierson's emphasis on 'the affairs of our time' or Rotha's insistence that 'above all, documentary must reflect the problems and realities of the present' echo the injunction of the realists, 'Il faut être de son temps' (Rotha, 1966, p. 116; Hauser 1983, p. 65). When Grierson (1979a, p. 37) called for a cinema dependent on 'the living scene and the living story', he was repeating Courbet's instruction: 'Faire d'art vivant' (Hauser, 1983, p. 65).[3]

Despite this, Grierson often claimed that his was an 'anti-aesthetic' position. He wrote (1979a, p. 112): 'Documentary was from the beginning ... an anti-aesthetic movement.' Yet this does not affect the case I have been making for the connections and continuities between the realist painters and their twentieth-century documentarist heirs. Griersonian 'anti-aestheticism', upon closer examination, turns out to be little but a reiteration of realist pleas for the artist to be *engagé*:

> The artist, with the exception of a few writers and architects, still refuses to accept his real position in society, preferring instead to keep up this pretence of evasion. ... Your art-for-art's-saker, and there are plenty of them, will exclaim that the true artist is deserting art if you suggest that it should serve a definite purpose in the social sphere. (Rotha, 1966, p. 67)

Grierson often followed this line, not really addressing aesthetic issues at all but rather attacking some sense of artistic self-indulgence and irrelevance. By 1935, he was claiming that 'the relationship between the artists and the themes of the community, so far from binding the artist, has opened new horizons for it' (Grierson 1979a, p. 64). By 1942, Grierson, the latter-day Courbet, said, 'We have all, I suppose, sacrificed some personal capacity in "art" and the pleasant vanity that goes with it' (ibid., p. 112). But, thanks to French realism, he had not done any such thing.

8

The Politics of Realism

Realist, or naturalist, aesthetics, as enunciated in mid-nineteenth-century France, were inexorably intertwined with progressive social concerns. As Williams points out (1989, p. 113), 'Naturalism, in fact, has close historical associations with socialism. As a movement and as a method it was concerned to show that people are inseparable from their real social and physical environments.'

It is, however, the case that by the 1930s the intimate connection of realism/ naturalism as a mode of representation in the arts and radicalism in politics had long been attenuated. This allowed Grierson to avoid confronting the contradictions implicitly inscribed in his political heritage by Flaherty and Courbet. He was helped in this by the fact that, in general, the echoes and implications of the realism's politics were often remembered as nothing but a source of confusion. For instance, a critic, R. D. Field, could state (1938, p. 127) in a series of lectures on the realist school in the late 1930s: 'I am ... bewildered ... by my inability to determine whether to treat it [realism] as a particular style of representation, as a state of mind, or as a social attitude.'

Essential here is the unexpected (for an art historian of that period) intrusion of political considerations ('social attitude') into more usual formalist concerns ('style of representation'). That these should be yoked together is, primarily, Proudhon's legacy; and the clue to the bewilderment registered by Field lies in the general disparagement of Proudhon's ideas and his battered twentieth-century reputation.

Proudhon was deeply concerned with the social function of art and wrote extensively on this topic. He was also very close to Courbet (Nochlin, 1966, pp. 49ff.). Yet within a generation the relation between the political theorist and the artist was a source of disorientation: 'Somehow ... the association of Proudhon's sometimes complicated and sometimes naive theories with realism was either laughed away ... or gingerly set aside' (Rubin, 1980, p. 81).

Despite these unfortunate results of Proudhon's advocacy, the power of the 'social attitude' in the realist project could not be avoided nor totally forgotten. For more perspicacious critics in the 1930s – Max Raphael, for instance – the Proudhonian legacy remained the key to understanding contemporary left-wing artistic rhetoric:

> Any visitor to Paris familiar with Marxist criticism will be surprised to discover to what an extent Proudhon's ideas still influence French 'Communist' politicians, intellectuals, and even artists. But a little

reflection will reveal that there is nothing surprising in this. Most artists are of petty-bourgeois origin, and their Communism serves to provide them with emotional support, rather than with weapons useful in their practical activities. In point of fact, they are Proudhonians, although – or perhaps because – they have never read Proudhon. (Raphael, 1979, p. 3)

In London, the discussions were perhaps as likely to be about socialism as about communism, but Raphael's point remains. By Grierson's heyday, on both sides of the channel the politically engaged were likely to be as unaware of the political legacy of nineteenth-century French painting as were the politically naive; yet for both the legacy was still significant.

Although, obviously, as Colls and Dodd have argued (1985, p. 22), on occasions Grierson's rhetoric reflected early twentieth-century collectivist thinking, nevertheless the importance of the overlapping rhetoric of Proudhon and the realist movement should not be underestimated. After all, it was they, not Fabians like Sidney Webb, who shared Grierson's concern about modes of representation. Proudhon, like Grierson, saw realism as having a role 'in the inevitable flow of social development' (Rubin, 1980, p. 98). Most importantly, Proudhonists, like Griersonians, were, despite the rhetoric, able to make their peace with the existing order.

That this was the case allows us to deal with the most salient difference between the Griersonians and the French realists. Grierson and his team pursued their creativity and sought the 'ordinary virtues of an art' as civil servants or the employees of great corporations. (As such they were following Flaherty.) The French, on the other hand, were on their own, distanced from, and indeed often in apparent opposition to, both state and business. Nevertheless, Grierson is a child of the nineteenth-century realists in every particular, despite this.

Courbet might be credited with the reputation of being an anticlerical firebrand and his career described as 'one long scandal after another'; but that means less than it might (Foucart, 1977, p. 13). The fact is that Courbet, and Proudhon for that matter, remained uncommitted and did not fight on the barricades in 1848. Here, in a letter to his parents written by Courbet at the height of the June days, is the source of Grierson's political stance as radical rhetorician and creative government servant:

It is the most distressing spectacle you could possible imagine. ... I am not fighting, for two reasons: first, because I do not believe in war with rifles and cannon, it is not consistent with my principles. ... The second reason is that I have no weapons and cannot be tempted. So you have nothing to fear on my account. (Clark, 1982a, p. 49)

Courbet and Proudhon more or less sat out this, the most important revolutionary event of their lives. (Proudhon was dead and Courbet ill by the time of the Commune.[4]) Similarly in the 1930s, a decade of political extremes, the Griersonians were also to sit outside the mainstream of conflict. It is this realist/Proudhonist heritage that distinguishes Grierson's politics from common middle-class, middle-of-the-road reformism. His actions were those of a reformist but, thanks to realist aesthetics as much as politics, his rhetoric seldom was.

31

Grierson was a socialist at Glasgow University after the First World War, committed enough, according to his biographer, to push for the dissolution of the university's Fabian Society in favour of a more actively engaged New University Labour Club. As a graduate at Durham, he did social work in the worst of Newcastle's slums. As a film critic, he wrote for a succession of socialist journals, well into the 1930s (Hardy, 1979, pp. 23, 29 and 60). On occasion, his analyses of mainstream cinema could sound Marxist (Macpherson, 1980, p. 146).

This must be put in context, however. The year before Grierson went to Glasgow, the Clyde Workers Soviet Committee was calling for armed revolution (Mackie, 1964, p. 351). The local communist party changed its name to the Anti-Parliamentary Communist Federation (Newton, 1969, p. 15). Grierson's socialism must be seen against the extremely radical background of the 'Red Clyde'. In an era when such things were not too hard to come by, Grierson's left-wing credentials lacked substance. Contrary to myth, for instance, he did not attend the celebratory reception given in honour of John Maclean's release from prison in 1918 (Aitken, 1990, p. 31). (Maclean had been appointed the first Bolshevik consul in Scotland and had been imprisoned for sedition shortly thereafter. A storm of protest brought about his release.)

Grierson the Proudonist (as it were) would all his life claim such myths. For instance, he would acknowledge, in his 1952 preface to Rotha's *Documentary Film*, Keir Hardie, Bob Smilie and John Wheatley as his 'masters', despite there being little or no evidence of their influence unless one counts the condescending and romanticised vision of the working class presented in the films. (This reference is, typically, less than it seems for Grierson goes on to add Walter Elliot to this list of left-wing political influences. A bastion of the Scottish establishment, Elliot was a Conservative MP who served as Minister of Health between 1936 and 1940. He had also been chair of the Empire Marketing Board Film Committee, of which more below (Tallents, 1968, p. 20).)

When Tom Nairn argues (1977, p. 19) that, in English civil society, the intelligentsia has 'played an unusually central and political role in promoting social integration', it seems to me that he could find few careers as apt for his thesis as Grierson's. Despite the rhetoric, Grierson ultimately supported the existing order in everything he did. Nairn suggests that this sort of reversal of the intelligentsia's characteristic distant and critical position vis-à-vis the rest of society is specific and central to the British 'intellectual stratum'.

It was very easy to treat the group around Grierson as upper-middle-class dilettantes. To modern eyes the films they made, virtually all of them stilted and condescending, tend to reinforce the unfortunate impression that, as a group, they were nothing but poseurs.

Yet I do not want to question the sincerity, at one level, of their impulse to 'give the workingman ... a dignity' on the screen or indeed to help the working class in other ways. There is no reason to doubt that 'to start with we were left wing to a man. Not many of us were communists, but we were all socialists' (Sussex, 1975, pp. 76ff.). The point is that their socialism was as Raphael describes – an emotional support. It is therefore not too apparent on the screen. As articulated in the movies they made, their position exactly accords with Nairn's analysis (1977, p. 21): 'The world view of this social group [the intelligentsia] is a conservative liberalism, and in terms of socio-political strategy this entailed the preservation of rule from above by constant adaptation and concession below.'

Nairn shows us how to make sense of Grierson's political stance. Grierson claimed to have been offered parliamentary constituencies, which his biographer was unable to prove. The anecdote is nevertheless presented as significant since it indicates 'a disinclination to make an explicit party commitment – a disinclination which was to be present throughout his life' (Hardy, 1979, p. 29).

Rotha, one of the most politically active of the group, acknowledges the Griersonians' disengagement, which he curiously describes in *Documentary Film* (1966, p. 34) as a 'refusal to be henchmen or mercenaries'. (Yet a few pages on (p. 43) he is quoting Mayherhold as a motto for his book: 'Art cannot be non-political.' Basil Wright (1976, p. 109), whose politics took a distinct second seat to his 'art', boasts that 'the documentarists did not fall into the trap of identifying or being identified with any political party or policy. That their "moderate" attitude was decried as pusillanimous by some is, to my mind, irrelevant.'

It is in this pusillanimity that they were the true heirs of Proudhon and Courbet and the perfect exempla of the British intellectual class. It is far from being irrelevant both to their work and, more importantly, to their legacy. That is why I do not think one can excuse the politics of the documentary film movement simply by explaining its opportunism as an inevitable, common and insignificant consequence of being somewhere in the supposedly neutral and supposedly neutered centre ground.

Grierson's first major job was an attempt to 'sell' the British Empire, by establishing a film production programme at the Empire Marketing Board (EMB). The Empire was becoming at that time an object of derision to much progressive opinion. Only some engaged in the Fabian search for 'national efficiency' continued to embrace imperialism as a species of necessary reform of 'backward' societies. Grierson tapped into this Fabian strand as a way of containing the hostility. 'Our original command of peoples was', he would claim in 1933, 'slowly becoming a co-operative effort in the tilling of soil, the reaping of harvest, and the organisation of a world economy' (Grierson, 1979a, p. 48). (In fact, this seems to have been something of an established formulation. Leo Amery, who was Dominions Secretary at the time, used similar phrases about the EMB in his autobiography: 'We wanted to sell the idea of the Empire as a co-operative venture between living persons interested in each other's work, and in each other's welfare' (Aitken, 1990, p. 94).)

Grierson's rhetoric is overstated when he claims (1979a, p. 48): 'Its [the EMB's] principal effect in six years (1928–1933) was to change the connotation of the word "Empire".' But how can this be true? During this very period the Empire was transformed into the Commonwealth in a series of momentous constitutional moves from the Imperial Conference of 1926 to the enactment of the Statute of Westminster II in 1931. In effect, the word 'Empire' was being given up as a bad job, from the public relations point of view at least, exactly at the time when Grierson claims the EMB was making it more publicly acceptable. The EMB, designed to achieve a continued imperial preference in consumption but by persuasion rather than by tariff, was itself killed off in 1933 (Hardy, 1979, p. 71; Aitken, 1990, p. 91; Dickinson and Street, 1985, p. 27).

This is not to deny the continued importance of the Empire/Commonwealth to Britain, especially in time of economic depression. In 1932, for instance, protectionist legislation once more encouraged imperial trade. Exports to the Empire rose from 22 to 47 per cent while imports from non-imperial sources fell from 80 to 61 per cent (Thurlow, 1987, p. 160). For Scotland in general and for the Clyde in particular, the imperial connection had been of critical importance throughout Grierson's life. There is no reason to suppose, for all that the PR aspects of the move from Empire to Commonwealth palpably did not play out very well on the stage of history, that Grierson would not have appreciated the EMB's continued economic significance.

More than that, for Nairn, the Empire was critical to the existence of the English state, which, he suggests (1977, p. 10), would otherwise have collapsed under the weight of its outmoded pre-modern political structure. By this reckoning, there could be few tasks more important for an intellectual like Grierson than working to support this structure.

Grierson's new-found interest in the cinema, the result of his studies in America in the mid-1920s and his growing sense of what he might himself do with that medium, also meshed particularly well with the imperial. At the time he went to the EMB, the documentary as Grierson had experienced it was an imperial form *par excellence*; for documentary meant, primarily, Flaherty.

Between the Flaherty documentary and imperial publicity there was thus a fine fit. As we have seen, political radicalism, thanks to the realist tradition, was not in the way of this. So it is far from being an accident that the documentary film in the service of the selling of the Empire (albeit unfortunately at exactly the moment of its formal disappearance) was Grierson's initial supposedly radical 'social purpose' in the cinema.

9

Running Away from Social Meaning

However imperfectly, it was understood that film, officially funded and produced, could have a political role to play in promoting social integration within the liberal reformist state. There was thus no fundamental difficulty with the basic idea of government sponsorship of film. Even those who suggest that this was Grierson's own invention acknowledge that he was ably abetted by his patron, Sir Stephen Tallents of EMB (Reeves, 1985, p. 4, fn. 8). That the EMB already had a film office before Grierson appeared is glossed over (see, for example Hardy, 1979, p. 45; Rotha, 1973, p. 21).

In fact, considerable government sponsorship of film production had taken place during the First World War and even a little before. For instance, Reeves (1985, pp. 261ff.) lists some 190 titles made between 1914 and 1918 and Hiley (1985, pp. 166ff.) describes a full-length recruiting film released in January 1914. Although the production structure was rapidly dismantled at war's end, nevertheless there was precedent for the Tallents initiative a decade later (Tallents, 1968, p. 16). The Federation of British Industries, convinced that 'trade did follow the film', had also, in 1924, sponsored a series of productions (Dickinson and Street, 1985, p. 18). Film had already apparently demonstrated its worth as a propaganda tool and, as the pre-Griersonian EMB acknowledgement of cinema shows, was an established area for government activity.

Extending film's potential from imperial propaganda tool to instrument of domestic social engineering required nothing more than the provision of an aesthetic theory. This is exactly what in the late 1920s Grierson conjured out of his American experience, his training in idealist philosophy, and the remains of the realist tradition. As Grierson followed Tallents from the EMB to the General Post Office, the domestic film production agenda which emerged turned out to be as supportive of the status quo as Flaherty-style efforts in imperial exotica or the wartime propaganda output. Political 'disinclination' was critical to this result. It enabled Grierson to focus the general social concern of his time into a programme of state-supported film-making.

Realism's political potential might have been exhausted, as Max Raphael attested; yet it still had the aura of radicalism, a lingering tinge, that ensured it could be presented to funders as socially engaged and thus more useful than were other aesthetics for the sort of social engineering they had in mind. Claiming the Griersonian documentary as a 'realist' enterprise was critical for its success.

At the same time, realism had become sufficiently distanced from its socialist roots not to alarm those same funders. It is the frame of political action (or inaction) determined by the leading realists of 1848 which allowed Grierson to announce the creative intentions of the documentary film-maker as, vaguely, radical. Working within the tradition established for them some eighty years previously, Grierson and his school could take government and industrial money for the making of liberal films selling the existing order and its capacity for gradual social amelioration.

Thus this official support does not betoken political partisanship. Rather, it was statist and capable of implying either a conservative or reformist project. The governments involved in the Griersonian enterprise were, with the one exception of the Labour administration between 1929 and 1931, Conservative. Film, after its successful exploitation in the First World War, was seen as a potentially viable propaganda tool by the Tories. As early as 1925, the party was using the medium in its election campaigns. The films were produced by military propaganda staff. By the early 1930s the Conservative and Unionist Film Association had ten large cinema vans and a film library and was reportedly so well financed that it was equipped with sound before the industry (Jones, 1987, p. 19; Macpherson, 1980, p. 143). According to T. J. Hollins (1981, p. 362), 'The principle was not dissimilar to that employed during the early 1920s by the Russian Bolsheviks with their cinema trains and cinema vans, although there is no evidence that the Conservative Party took the idea from this example.'

Labour, unable to fund or even articulate a coherent film policy, was not as active. Between the party, the unions, the TUC and the co-operative movement, little was done. Left film-making was to be the province of 'independents' (Jones 1987, pp. 137ff.; Macpherson, 1980, pp. 150ff.). (See p. 76.)

The Conservatives were alive to the possibilities of film as an instrument of government as well. Moreover, such were conditions during the great depression that even on the right in Britain the need for measures of state intervention in many fields was accepted. (Indeed, the generation of young Conservatives whose political philosophy was formed at this time were exactly those post-war leaders who agreed to the welfare state and thereby established that social consensus which was the object of attack in the 1980s by their successors in office.)

In such circumstances, the documentary film movement fitted perfectly into the essential broad function of the British intelligentsia of the time. So well did the Griersonians work to promote 'social integration within civil society' that Grierson could have been justly proud, if he so chose, of the part (however marginal) played by his documentary films in propagandising social integration along these lines. Only once in his writing did he come close to doing this when he stated that there was a 'whole movement of social understanding' that the films he produced helped to create without which 'history would have found another and bloodier solution' for Britain (Grierson, 1979, p. 114). But this remark is exceptional. Most of the time he claimed the myth of opposition and, as the true heir of Courbet, he positioned the films as radical and critical.

The radical ideology was donned in the pub and the editorial offices of the little magazines. It was doffed for Whitehall and the corporate sponsors. Given the climate of the times, this did not adversely affect Grierson's leftist credentials. These remained impeccable. For instance, in a rare reference to film in the pages of *Scrutiny*, Grierson is described by William Empson (1935, p. 335) as 'The Englishman [*sic*] who seems to me nearest to a proletarian artist'. The line between proletarian and artist was fudged with only a few, like the founders of Mass Observation, seeing that although 'there is a general wish among writers to be UNLIKE the intellectual, LIKE the masses', very few were of the masses themselves (M.-L. Jennings, 1982, p. 18).

Amid such confusions, Grierson's 'sixth sense, that of showmanship' (Lee, 1984, p. 1), could flourish. The essence of this showmanship was Grierson's own charm. His charismatic personality was most effectively reinforced by his writing. The man was a first-rate journalist, a writer with a most distinctive and seductive personal style.

Drifters, Grierson's first film (for the EMB), was first seen publicly on 10 November 1929 at a meeting of the (London) Film Society. The main attraction at that screening was the UK première of *Battleship Potemkin*, interest in which was augmented by Eisenstein's being in London at the time. *Potemkin* had long been banned by the British authorities and this harassment of the film was to continue unabated into the thirties. *Potemkin*'s status as a martyred revolutionary text infected the reputation of *Drifters*. This infection helped radicalise the nascent documentary movement's (and Grierson's) reputation, despite the fact that the London Film Society, at 25 shillings membership, was a safely middle-class enterprise. (Indeed, only because it was so safe was it permitted to screen the film.)

That Grierson might not be all he seemed was spotted at the time by a few critics like Arthur Calder Marshall and David Schrire. The latter wrote in 1935: 'Remember the contempt Grierson had for the actual marketing of the fish, the great regret he appeared to express that the fish, the fruits of the glorious adventure, was bought and sold for money. ... Grierson dealt with actual industry or occupation but ran away from its social meaning' (Rotha, 1973, p. 30). I believe that *running away from social meaning* is what the Griersonian documentary, and therefore the entire tradition, does best. It sums up, in one succinct phrase, the real price paid by the film-makers' political pusillanimity.

Despite Grierson's philosophical understanding of *Drifters* as 'symbolic expression' rather than 'naturalistic verisimilitude', he nevertheless acknowledged (1979a, p. 22) the absence of industrial context in the film as a problem: 'As the catch was being boxed and barrelled I thought I would like to say that what was really being boxed and barrelled was the labour of men.' But what he actually said instead, in the intertitles, was: 'And the sound of the sea and the people of the sea are lost in the chatter and clatter of a market for the world' and, after some shots of bidding and more of boxing, we get 'So to the ends of the earth goes the harvest of the sea.'

It was to be the case that the films made by his school were seldom able to resist – into the present – flimflam of this sort. Stuart Hood calls it 'a turgid style of rhetoric' (1983, p. 107). (Grierson's collected journalism avoids the worst of this, it must be said.)

The documentary film movement's flight from social meaning is exemplified for me by a graphic in *Children at School* (1938). A portentous voice, that of H. Wilson Harris, the editor of the *Spectator*, announces, 'This is how the system works.' The structure of English education is then illustrated by craning up a caption which contains the following information decorated with suitable emblemata: 'Nursery 2–5', 'Infant 5–7', 'Junior 7–11', 'Senior 11–15/Secondary 11–18', 'Technical School/University'. There is no further comment. So much for the educational system, that crucial mechanism for determining both social integration and the maintenance of class divisions.

The bathos of this image is not untypical. The 'movement' usually thus concentrates on surfaces, even while managing to run from the social meaning of those surfaces. Given the aesthetic preferences of these filmmakers, camera and editing style always tended to mannered composition and baroque image flow. This meant a tendency to seek the picturesque topic, but the search for the picturesque is to be found in even the least 'aesthetic' subjects.

Smoke damage in *The Smoke Menace* (1937) looks as if it has been photographed by a prizewinner in a local photographic club competition, despite Rotha's claim (1966, p. 196) that the film 'showed small care for the visual importance of the medium'. The slums are nearly always photographed in elegant compositions and became, in consequence, settings as exotic and strange as the North West Territories or Samoa. The compositional opposition of dale and northern slum, in films like *Today We Live* (1936), was especially seductive.

So even in films about what Rotha called 'the social thing' (Morris, 1982, p. 12), such as his own *Shipyard* (1935), as romantic a camera style as Flaherty's is employed. For example, on the soundtrack of *The Face of Britain* (1935), inspired by the journeys Rotha took to Barrow-in-Furness to film *Shipyard*, he has the liberal journalist A. J. Cummings explaining: 'A new kind of work arose and disfigured the face of the land.' Yet this comes over a dramatic low-angle shot of the statue of a heroic worker. There are scudding clouds and wind noise over blast-furnaces and in general the camerawork, by George Pucknall and Frank Bundy, constantly undercuts the commentary's talk of 'terrible degradation'.

Industry became a site of high-contrast drama between light and shade, not a place of hazard and alienation. High tech, 1930s-style, was the close-up abstractions of electronic tubes or the rhythmic splendour of some machine or other – *Aero-Engine* (1932) would be a case in point. The dehumanising quality of industrial life was never captured.

Take *Industrial Britain* (1931), the key early film. Forced to confront British industry, Flaherty and Grierson filmed potters and glassblowers. (In fact *The English Potter* (1935) and *The Glassmakers of England* (1935) were produced by Grierson's sister Marion out of Flaherty's footage.) *Industrial Britain* actually concludes by arguing that modern production methods do not in fact mean an end of craft. That a terrible West End newsreel voice (Donald Calthrop) ventured this hypothesis did not help it much.[5] (The only possible explanation of the film's absurd vision is that Flaherty understood how antiquated were the industries he was filming – but this is unlikely. It is perhaps more significant, as Annette Kuhn suggests (1980, p. 27), to note how such images of craft mirrored the artisanal way in which Grierson was constructing his own film-making enterprise, even down to having Flaherty play the role of master craftsman.

Industrial Britain vividly demonstrated how to run from the social meaning of British industry – concentrate on individuals and thereby avoid the alienating and repetitive realities of the world of work. Tallents thought

Flaherty had been imported for this job to destroy 'the belief that the industrial life of Britain and her grey city atmosphere could never be portrayed on the screen' (Rotha, 1973, p. 52). Flaherty and Grierson showed that industry and atmosphere could be filmed. All that was needed was to make them pretty and personal. Indeed, this aestheticising was, like dramatisation, a further essential mark of difference between documentary, as Grierson was seeking to define it, and other forms of non-fiction film, such as newsreels.

It is not, then, insignificant that fishermen and sailors received so much attention from the movement. Certainly Tallents had been amenable to Grierson's suggestion that he make a film about herring drifters because funding would have to come from the Treasury, where the financial secretary was Arthur Samuel (later Lord Mancroft), author of *The Herring: Its Effect on the History of Britain*. This fact alone does not, however, explain *Granton Trawler* (1933), *On the Fishing Banks of Skye* (1935), *North Sea* (1938) and the rest. (Watching *The Savings of Bill Blewitt* at the National Film and Television School some years ago, Stuart Hood was so exasperated by the theme of shipwreck as to query ironically what effect the documentary film movement's destruction of shipping must have had on the country's attempts at economic recovery.)

The running from social meaning was not just a matter of prettifying aesthetics at home. Abroad, Flaherty's romanticism ran riot. Thus Wright could make a film for the Empire Tea Marketing Expansion Board (*The Song of Ceylon*, 1935) which, obviously given this sponsor, 'totally avoids the question of colonial labour and the economic exploitation of the colonies' (Hood, 1983, p. 102). Such images of tea harvesting as are in the film were either taken from material already held by the board or by Wright during the one morning when he actually went to a tea paddy and observed people at work. Significantly, these are the worst shots in the film, not least because Wright, as he once explained at the NFTS, developed a headache while taking them.

Wright, it should not be forgotten, was after all 'a poet'.

10

Poor, Suffering Characters:
Victims and Problem Moments

Running from social meaning was not just a question of aesthetics. As the decade advanced and the depression worsened, the Griersonians discovered how to focus and structure their films so that no meaningful analysis would be required whatever the subject matter, however searing the social problem. The clue to this was to put a further spin on the coverage of individuals. This transformed the ways in which the movement characterised the working class. In essence the worker now became a social victim and the films became what might be called 'victim documentaries'. The victim documentary is the Griersonians' most potent legacy. Social victims are the realist documentary's staple subject into the present.

The image of the worker as victim was latent from the beginning. It had been part of the painterly tradition in the work of artists such as Courbet, who moved from the indecorous majesty of the peasants in *The Burial at Ornans* to the *misère* of the figures in *The Stone Breakers* or *Beggar's Alms*; or Millet, who made back-breaking labour in paintings like *The Sower* or *The Gleaners* a major realist theme.

The Griersonian version of this image of heroically suffering humanity need not be developed as long as the screen was silent and the full economic implications of the 1929 crash were not felt. With sound – with all the class connotations of voice and accent in Britain – and with deepening economic depression, the latent image did then develop; and, just as it had in the previous century, it turned out to be the image of the worker as social victim. In the major films of 1935, the Griersonians, once more following their nineteenth-century painterly predecessors, shifted their focus from the heroic to the heroic victim, a move which allowed for the poetry of poverty and the exoticism of the underclass to be displayed washed over with 'social purpose'.

This turn was accomplished between 1931 and 1935. In *Industrial Britain* (1931), Flaherty largely reduced modern industry to a series of individuals in close-up, some of whom were even named by Calthrop. The issue was how to combine this romanticised concern with the individual with a simulacrum of social analysis. In *Shipyard*, *Workers and Jobs*, and *Housing Problems*, one can see how the model of *Industrial Britain* was adapted by the 'serious-minded chaps' who (in Edgar Anstey's words) 'wanted to lay on what the problems were for Britain so that we should see and learn and do something about it' (Sussex, 1975, p. 76).

Shipyard was a typical Griersonian project about the building of a ship. The movement was to make a number of films for the shipping industry, some as publicity materials to help sell luxury cruises – for instance,

Northern Summer, made for the Orient Line. Such films are seldom cited within the movement's catalogue because they are commercials, not documentaries; but the distinction is not immediately apparent on the screen. *Northern Summer* involved documentarists. Alex Shaw was an established movement figure and responsible for the production. The film was shot by 'the greatest character of them all', George Noble, a freelance (as were all the cinematographers during the initial phase) (Sussex, 1975, p. 36). And the sponsor of this commercial was, even while it was being filmed, commissioning Paul Rotha to make another film.

Rotha was looking for industrial support when the Orient Line, or more specifically Sir Stephen Tallents's brother Tommy, Orient's publicity manager, asked him to document the building of a new luxury liner (Marris, 1980, p. 8). The film was also paid for in part by the shipbuilders, Vickers.

Shipyard is a fine film. Indeed, it is arguable that of all the movement's directors Rotha was always the most talented by the standards they themselves would accept. His determination to produce more socially relevant films than the run of GPO work, however thwarted by his sponsors, was also apparent. It remains startling to hear a Lancastrian speaking the commentary on *Shipyard*. Another local voice, supposedly a worker in the yard, says: 'Queer to think that women will walk here dressed in silk dresses. ... Don't suppose they'll think of the bloke that hit the blinking rivet.' Rotha's commentary includes 'Every mouth being fed, everybody being clothed by the work of the men in the yard'. Yet even this degree of tangential social comment was not acceptable. The sponsors objected and the film was distributed, re-edited, with what Rotha calls 'a newsreel commentator' (Orbanz, 1977, p. 29).

Paradoxically, the sponsored censorship of the soundtrack confirms that Rotha had otherwise created a visual track which contained nothing objectionable, nothing that could not be revoiced. This is because he still romantically made riveting and other shipyard tasks the site of skill and heroic labour. Rotha, although one of the most political of the movement's directors, was nevertheless in the grip of the painterly. The bulk of 'Job 697' (launched as the *Orion*) looms picturesquely over Barrow. *Shipyard* visually romanticises the nature of the work and the skills of the worker, just as *Industrial Britain* does.

Rotha, however, claimed a broader social relevance for *Shipyard*. To Elizabeth Sussex (1975, p. 57) he recalled 'that this was perhaps the first of the British documentary films with what I call a social implication'. Some years later, to Paul Marris (1980, p. 9), Rotha suggested that this social implication was quite specific, making *Shipyard* 'perhaps the first film which dealt with unemployment in this country'.

This interpretation of the film turns on the last sequence, the launch. The sequence was confused because it was shot in bad weather and also because the launch itself was done by a royal personage, then in Australia, using a radio link. The crucial point that Rotha remembered was 'the despair of those men watching her [the *Orion*] slide away, hands in their pockets, and then turning off to the Employment Exchange' (Rotha, 1973, pp. 101–2).

There is certainly a shot of a group of men, hands in pockets. They are cross-cut with the top-hatted 'Establishment' or 'Nabobs' (as Rotha calls them) walking hurriedly into the lens, the workers being the last image of the film. The object of their gaze must be the ship but the despair that Rotha recalled could just as easily be boredom. They certainly do not turn away. There are no employment exchanges in sight. Most important, Rotha's desire to place the job in its social context, his clear understanding that its completion was 'a tragedy', is nowhere any more explicitly inscribed in the film than in this ambiguous final shot; and, perhaps, in the equally tangential use of references to the passing months, which Rotha uses to structure the film.

All this is not to question Rotha's memory and sincerity but rather to query his effectiveness. Sponsorship meant self-censorship, and self-censorship had not prevented the sponsors from remaking the work any-way; but the sponsors were uneasy for nothing. The film, even in the form Rotha wanted, does not do what Rotha remembered it as having done. On the contrary, it runs away from examining unemployment – and in that lies its importance.

This film is nothing less than the model whereby the social irrelevance of *Industrial Britain* could be extended to encompass negative aspects of contemporary life. It was the critical and needed demonstration that the Griersonian documentary, whatever its subject matter, need not ever involve serious analysis. Rotha's idle workers, like Grierson/Flaherty's busy ones, were aestheticised, their actual social relationships sufficiently fudged for them to be acceptable within the depoliticised discourse Grierson had established for the documentary.

Rotha was thus right to claim the presence of these idle men as signifi-cant, but not for the reason he suggested. Rather they showed how a move from the celebratory, a move increasingly necessary given the general eco-nomic situation, might be accomplished. Not only could Britain's grey atmosphere be put on the screen without offence, but Britain's social problems could be put there too, and, in the putting, be rendered grey.

The other film Rotha was working on at this time, *Face of Britain*, con-tained, *inter alia*, the first material on the slums of the industrial heartland. This film revealed another technique, a way of structuring material, which was to be of particular value to the documentary film movement. Let us call this the 'problem moment' structure.

The Face of Britain begins, as does *Industrial Britain*, with an evocation of a lost land: 'The face of Britain was beautiful'; 'Thus as men first made it, the framework of Britain was a pattern of hedges'; and so on. Then come the slums in the sequence titled 'The Smoke Age' and, as I have previously indicated, very pretty slums they are, too. Finally comes 'The New Age' of electricity and with it a restoration of the lost beauties of the land. The last images involve cycling and exercise and a man, a woman and a dog on a hillside. 'So electricity is born to bring back the sun to Britain,' says Cummings in the commentary. The Central Electricity Board was the sponsor.

The slums are thus sandwiched between a wonderful past and a beauti-ful future. The slums are but a moment, a 'problem moment', in the unfolding history of the nation, a moment that will pass – thanks to the electricity generating industry. This 'problem moment' structure allows for a social ill to be covered (permitting a radical reading of the final film) while at the same time denying that the ill has real causes and effects (per-mitting conservative funding for the film). In some sense it is the precur-sor of the concept of balance in television documentary output. 'Balance' and the 'problem moment' structure both work to cripple the possibility of meaningful social analysis and comment within a realist text.

In that same year, 1935, Elton was making *Workers and Jobs*, one of the earliest Griersonian films to use synchronous location sound. It was about the employment exchanges run by the Ministry of Labour, who paid for the production. 'There are at least fifty thousand different kinds of work,' announces an extremely plummy-voiced commentator. How many posts are available in each type (or in general) are questions the film does not address. We learn nothing of why the men are unemployed in the first instance, how long they have been looking and with what costs, what time it takes to get them placed. Those are, of course, all matters beyond the control of the employment exchange and not, therefore, covered in the film. Instead, employment is simply a question of logistics requiring the matching of the unemployed to work and that is easily accomplished by an enlightened bureaucracy.

Just as the camera in *Industrial Britain* and *The Face of Britain* showed how to prettify the factory and the slum, so in *Workers and Jobs* the microphone was demonstrated as a tool which could prettify social relations. Stilted performances now became another mark of the Griersonian documentary. It was a mark which, like all others, had considerable ideological import. The overall impression of the British presented in these films is of a people almost completely without emotion. In *Workers and Jobs*, one official says in a slightly tetchy monotone, 'Stand back, give me a chance.' This is the nearest the film comes to showing social tension.

On the basis of this performance style (that is, this mode of representing behaviour) a romanticised picture of workplace interaction could be created, as in the deferential but non-subservient way in which the supervisor in *Night Mail* (1936) is treated; or, in *North Sea*, where the earthy reality of fisherfolk talk becomes: 'Don't forget the code.' 'Oh! That rubbish! Shut yer blather.' This stilted camaraderie was to become an important trope in the wartime propaganda output – a way for a class-ridden and historically divided society to be portrayed as 'one nation'.

Elton also worked with Anstey on the crucial *Housing Problems* for the gas industry. The victim documentary *par excellence*, this too employed synchronous sound and the 'problem moment' structure. For me, it is the movement's most important template, summing up the solutions discovered in 1935.

Housing Problems was sponsored by the Gas Council, the publicity arm of the British Commercial Gas Association. In it cockney slum dwellers address the camera directly to explicate the living conditions the film depicts. It is another example of the 'problem moment' film. Just as Rotha sandwiched the slums between a better past and a glorious future, so Anstey revealed that all these interviewees were just temporarily in the conditions they describe. Even as they were being filmed, new housing was being prepared for them. The suffering would have an end to it. 'Enlightened' (that is to say socialist) local councils and the gas industry, also (in Anstey's words) 'liberal' and 'non-conformist', were working hard to make slums a thing of the past – just as the electricity industry was doing (Sussex, 1975, p. 62). All that was needed were plans, and *Housing Problems* lays out plans aplenty.[6]

In Housing Problems, in addition to deploying the 'problem moment' structure, Anstey also brought the documentary subject as social victim into clearer focus than had yet been done. He has described it thus: 'Nobody had thought of the idea which we had of letting slum dwellers simply talk for themselves, make their own film ... we felt that the camera must remain sort of four feet above the ground and dead on, because it wasn't our film' (Sussex, 1975, p. 62).

It should be noted that this is overstated because others had indeed thought of letting slum dwellers talk for themselves, albeit not on film. The 'invisible' history of the BBC radio documentary, now being brilliantly recovered by Paddy Scannell, reveals, for example, that by 1934, a year before *Housing Problems*, Felix Greene was allowing ordinary people to speak at the microphone about their experiences of such things as unemployment. Under first Hilda Matheson and then Charles Siepmann, Talks Department, which was responsible for radio documentaries (or 'features' as they were then called), produced programmes on unemployment, industrial relations and 'the condition of England'. Of course, this list also included the slums, in programmes such as *Other People's Houses*. It is clear that the entire range of documentary film subjects was heard on the radio and was heard earlier. Scannell's researches suggest that further study of this forgotten tradition might do much to put Griersonian claims into a fuller context (Scannell, 1986, pp. 1 and 7ff.).

Nor, in another sense, can Anstey's claim of non-intervention ('it wasn't our film') be taken too seriously, since the interviewees were chosen and coached by the team and the results edited without consultation. Although Rotha thought that *Housing Problems* suffered through lack of direction, it obviously was directed (Sussex, 1975, p. 62).

Yet none of this detracts from the film's fundamental importance. The use of interviews proved to be a crucial development for subsequent realist documentary work. Moreover, letting people do their own talking did indeed require a new way of thinking about the function of documentary directors, casting them as enabling agents – if only to a limited extent. This attentuated attempt to rethink the relationship of the film-maker to a film's participants is critical to the current debate about documentary's future.

Because Elton and Anstey eschewed the usual proprietary attitude, the people in *Housing Problems* are all named, allowed the dignity of their best clothes and the luxury of their own words, albeit somewhat stiltedly expressed for the gentlemen of the production unit. Ruby Grierson, John's other sister, played a critical role in setting up these interviews (ibid., p. 64). It is clear that her ability to elicit extended responses was essential to this project. (Such an ability remains a key talent for the documentarist. It is interesting that in television practice it should be split off into a research function, feminised and then downgraded.) There is no reason to suppose that the people in the film were, as Paul Swann suggests (1989, p. 88), alienated by the filming, although, of course, they were not exactly enthused by their living conditions.

In his attitude toward his subjects, Anstey had moved considerably from his initial belief, in the silent period, that unless the working man was heroic 'he couldn't be a working man, almost'; but not as far as he thought since the working class in *Housing Problems* are still battling monumentally and indeed heroically against the ravages of poverty (Sussex, 1975, p. 19). The heroism has simply expanded to include suffering and thereby the heroic worker has been transformed. Rotha saw his shipbuilders as playing a role in a tragedy; Anstey thought of the interviewees in *Housing Problems* as 'poor, suffering characters' (ibid., p. 63). Unlike the shipyard workers, these slum dwellers are unambiguously inscribed as social victims. This is the first time they appear in the Griersonian mainstream. Given that the victim was to become a staple of the realist documentary, especially on television, the significance of *Housing Problems* cannot be overstated.

Such radical tinges as exist in these texts, the calls for urban renewal and even for a more equitable society in general, are nothing more than the examples of Nairn's 'constant adaptation'. Social problems can be solved, the films as a body suggest, if society is given over to the enlightened managers of industry and the experts in government. Even the hardest-hitting commentaries pulled their punches. For instance, in *Enough to Eat* (1937) Julian Huxley, the film's narrator, says: 'No complete solution is possible without considerable economic changes either by providing the lowest-paid members of the community with increased purchasing power or with cheap or free milk and other protective foods', but he concludes that this is a 'difficult long-term matter', and leaves it at that.

This film offers advice to working women about nutritional practices. Housewives from the 'lowest spending group', one of whom is named, are seen being interviewed by medical officials about their eating habits. The film corrects any impression of ignorance these remarks might create by having an expert tell us that working-class women might not know the difference between 'a vitamin and a bus ticket but ... nevertheless do well if they have enough money'. Gas unquestionably ameliorated living conditions but suggesting it as a solution to urban degradation in isolation takes the sting out of potent social studies, such as the one by Sir John Boyd Orr which clearly linked class to nutrition and health and inspired *Enough to Eat*. *Enough To Eat*, it should be said, represents the closest the movement comes to direct social analysis.

Anstey's strongest work, apart from *Enough to Eat*, appears in the American *March of Time* series. He covered a bitter strike in the Welsh coalfields. He juxtaposed a miners' choir begging in London with the thought that 'vast fortunes' had been 'piled up for the mine operators', and that royalties had gone 'to those who owned the coal-bearing land'. The 'lurcher-loving collier' (which is how Auden's commentary describes him in the romantic *Coalface* (1935)) becomes a victim forced to work 'dangerously for a few shillings a day'. In conclusion, he says of his striker victims that 'a once mighty British industry can no longer support them. Time marches on.' (Given that the reel was hardly leftist, offering, for instance, sympathetic reports on the French far right and hostile attacks against New Deal agencies, getting this report into it was no mean feat (Macpherson, 1980, pp. 120ff.).)

Harry Watt was also to do exposés for *March of Time* on the scandal of church tithes and the riches of football pools promoters. For the gas industry, Wright, the most poetic of the pioneers, made *Children at School*, which contains, apart from the graphic mentioned above, an interview with a working-class mother ostensibly talking to a headmistress about her child, who has fits and sleepwalks. Another 'problem moment' film, it also has an un-gas-heated school with primitive sanitation, frozen ink in the inkwells and arctic cloakrooms – but the final thought is that out-of-date schools can be pulled down and replaced.

Like all these texts, it was not particularly effective, or indeed effective at all in the long term, as Wright himself admitted to Sussex (1975, pp. 99ff.) many years later:

> You know this film was made in 1937. The other thing is that this film shows up the appalling conditions in the schools in Britain in 1937 which are identical with the ones which came out on television the night before last: overcrowded classes, schoolrooms falling down, and so on. It's the same story. That is really terrible, isn't it?

A serious ethical question is hereby raised, since the tradition of the victim inevitably requires that some measure or other of personal misery and distress be, if not exploited, then at least exposed. The justification for such exposure is the public's right to know as a species of public good. Yet if no, or little, social effect can be demonstrated, how can that justification stand? This means that just as 'terrible' (or at least regrettable) as the failure of the 'problem moment' films to effect social amelioration is the placing of social victims in the power of the 'creative' documentarist.

Grierson's social responsibility rhetoric was largely negated by the artistic privileges implicitly and explicitly claimed by this 'creative' person. This did not do the victims much good and created a considerable, if seldom acknowledged, moral dilemma for the film-maker. Paul Rotha writes (1973, p. 104):

> A monstrous, giant, smouldering slagheap towering over a shabby street of slum houses, hovels fallen into ruin with one lavatory for fifty persons. But inhabited. Rent for a house was 25 shillings per week. All the property belonged to the company that owned the mine. Few men were in work. I watched the rent collectors at their disgusting job; wringing a few shillings from women some of whose men were bloodying hands and shoulders in the earth hundreds of feet below where we stood, or standing on the street corners. From some petty cash I had with me, I paid the rent for some families and bought beer in the pub for some of the miners. It gave me pleasure that the profits of Gaumont-British should be so used. How I justified it in my accounts when I got back to London is neither remembered nor important.

Rotha went to the village of East Shotton in Durham because J. B. Priestley had reported on it in a series of newspaper articles which became the book *English Journey*.

This is not only a rare mention of the people documentarists film outside the immediate context of that filming; it is in fact one of the few references of any kind to a film-maker's relationship to such people that I can find. It is possible that, in reality, these directors were caring but simply never mentioned it. What is certain is that they indeed seldom if ever mentioned it. For instance, even Joris Ivens, the most overtly political and socially concerned of them all, details in his memoir (1974, pp. 193ff.) only one non-unidimensional relationship with his subjects in four decades of regular film-making activity.

When faced with real people caught up in real difficulties, the Griersonian social activist and public educator tended to be replaced by a dispassionate and distant journalist. The creative artist became a reporter.

The artistic legitimations implied by the use of the word 'creative' in the definition gave way to other legitimations, in fact those evoked by the word 'actuality'. What these other legitimations involve is the subject of Part Four of this book. It suffices to note here that by implicitly adopting these 'actuality' legitimations Grierson and his colleagues, already clothed in artistic rights, totally avoided addressing any ethical questions of exploitation. The move to the victim documentary occasioned no moral debate at all.

Shipyard, Workers and Jobs and *Housing Problems*, then, expand the range of the Griersonian documentary to include iconography of the slums and idle workers, and to embrace unemployment and poor living conditions as subjects. This expansion, though, offered no violence to the previous romantic vision of the individual. The use of the victim motif precludes social analysis and allows Flaherty's individualism to work in this expanded arena of direct social comment. The victim documentary seeks to substitute empathy and sympathy for analysis and anger. The 'problem moment' structure removes any need for action, or even reaction, on the part of the audience.

Serious-Minded Chaps: Politics and Poetics

The reading I have just given of the movement in Great Britain in the 1930s suggests a trajectory for the entire Griersonian *œuvre* from the gropings of the EMB period through to the establishment of a series of filmmaking strategies, all in place by 1935, which allowed the realist documentary to go forward to the present. This is at odds with most accounts, which see Grierson and his school subject to widely different influences, contradictory pressures and outright schism.

These supposedly oppositional influences came to be variously encoded as 'Flaherty v. the Russians' or 'aesthetic v. anti-aesthetic' or 'the poetic view v. social purpose' or 'personal expression v. public education'. In essence, each formulation suggests that, on the one hand, there was a documentary form essentially poetic and personal in nature and, on the other, a very different form, political and engaged. However, I see this, in its various guises, as nothing more than an attempt to preserve a residual radicalism for some of the films by sacrificing others as being without it. I do not think this can be done.

At the outset of the enterprise, it was supposedly possible to contrast the legacy of Flaherty's romanticism with the practices of the Russians. The Soviet silent cinema was claimed as an alternative source of filmic practice, inspiration and, above all, social engagement. Yet serious questions can be asked about how extensive these putative communistic influences were.

This is not to deny a formalist influence by the Soviet silent cinema on the early Griersonian films. One of Grierson's odd jobs during his years in the United States was the preparation of the American titles for *Potemkin*, which enabled him to come to know the film 'foot by foot and cut by cut' (Aitken, 1990, pp. 75 and 77). The result of this careful study of Soviet work can be seen in a number of stylistic elements – extreme camera angles, swift cutting and bold intertitles. Therefore, a not inconsiderable degree of influence on filmic practice can be demonstrated in *Drifters* and (decreasingly) the other films made during the silent period.

However, some claim that the Soviet influence went beyond these surface techniques to inspiration and social engagement, actually affecting content. As Anstey recalled, 'There wasn't any serious attempt at characterisation of the kind you find in Flaherty because we regarded this as a bit romantic. We were all pretty serious-minded chaps then, you know, and we believed, like the Russians, that you should use individuals in your film in a not exactly dehumanised way but a sort of symbolic way' (Sussex, 1975, p. 18).

This, though, is a minority view among the film-makers themselves. For most the influence of the Russians was more specific and more limited. For example, Rotha said, 'I remember seeing Pudovkin films and so on, and I was tremendously influenced technically by them, not in terms necessarily of subject matter' (Marris, 1980, p. 6).

In the same vein, of his *Cargo from Jamaica* Wright has said (Sussex, 1975, p. 34): 'Of course, this was all very influenced by the Russians – not merely by Eisenstein but by Vertov. I was trying to get a tremendous amount of dynamic clashing in the cutting without breaking up the actual movement, which was getting the stuff off the quayside and into the boats.' The 'stuff' was bananas; despite the dialectic of the editing, there is no comment on the broader significance of this cargo from Jamaica.

The point is summed up by Stuart Hood (Orbanz, 1977, p. 146): 'Politically the realist movement did not go beyond that broadly based anti-fascism which characterised the era of the popular front and the illusions that accompanied it; this was the time of naive fellow-travellers, who discussed Russian revolutionary films ... above all in terms of technique – of *montage* – not of political content.' So, despite the osmosis of the *Potemkin/Drifters* première and all the camera angles and cutting techniques, there was little of communism on the screen.

However, there is another possibility – that the sway of the Russians did in fact go deeper but was, unexpectedly, *not* political. Such an argument can be mounted on the basis of Victor Turin's documentary *Turksib*, thereby ignoring or downplaying the influence of the classic revolutionary fiction films of Eisenstein and Pudovkin. *Turksib* was released in October 1929, too late to have had much effect on *Drifters*; but despite this, it was acknowledged – by Tallents, for example (1968, p. 19) – as an important model. Turin was at the first GPO screening of the film. Tallents reported that one sequence in the film – of gathering waters, from trickle to mighty river – was closely studied. Grierson, as with *Potemkin*, recut the film for distribution (Rotha, 1966, p. 95).

Turksib is a straightforward piece, a film made by Vostock-Kino specifically for the Asiatic Soviet republics that were as yet without film industries of their own. It tells the story of the building of a branch of the Trans-Siberian Railroad down into Turkistan. It not only shows the effort of the construction but also explains the effect the railroad will have on the economy of the USSR; Turkistan cotton goods and cloth from Kazakstan wool will replace materials being imported from Egypt and America. 'Unpretty', Jay Leyda labelled the film (1960, p. 260), but, as it has camels against the skyline, abstract patterns of railway coaches and rails and the like aplenty, this seems a little unfair.

Aitken is correct to suggest (1990, p. 87): 'The influence of *Turksib* on Grierson has been underrated, just as the influence of *Potemkin* has been overrated.' He believes that this is because Turin demonstrated on the screen how Grierson's theoretic vision of a bridge between epic cinema and documentary might be constructed in practice. I would want to suggest that more potent than this was Turin's demonstration of how to deal, or rather *not* deal, with politics in the documentary.

Turin needed to keep just as low a political profile with his paymasters in the USSR as Grierson did in the UK. *Turksib* was therefore important to the Griersonians, pretty or not, exactly because it showed how a filmmaker could be *unpolitical*, even in a highly charged political situation with an overtly political topic. In *Turksib* direct references to the communists who are building the railroad (and sponsoring the film), and why they are doing so, are absolutely at a minimum. In the German-language version, for instance, there is just one shot, of a commissar leading a study group, which directly references the political system. For the rest, it is exotic types on camels juxtaposed with planes, trucks and trains.

That Turin could make an effective documentary with so little of the overtly propagandistic in it under such close political supervision was a more important example for the Griersonians than the other overtly revolutionary fictional Soviet films. Certainly this would explain the high regard in which the movement held *Turksib*. Aitken (1990, p. 87) quotes Grierson as believing *Turksib* was 'the most influential model of the time for documentary men outside Russia' and 'the single job which takes us into the future'. Rotha (1966, pp. 94f.) echoed this opinion: 'Turin's *Turksib* alone defined the line of Soviet approach to pure documentary. ... *Turksib* marked the beginning of a new documentary method and has probably had more influence on later developments than any other picture.'

And why? In *Turksib* Flaherty's primitives, Nanook and Moana, are made subject to economic development. *Turksib*, a film as imperialist as any of Flaherty's, is the bridge which carries the documentary towards the modern industrial world. It does so without overt politics by taking an oblique approach to the structuring of its message of support for the social integration of the new Soviet empire. Grierson stated: '*Turksib* is an affair of economics, which is the only sort of affair worth one's time and patience' (Aitken, 1990, p. 87). But, in fact, the economics are simpleminded and sanitised. With its happy Asiatics, heroic Russian surveyors and exhortations to get the job done by 1931, *Turksib* runs from the social and political meaning of the railroad.

If *Turksib* is the model, the Soviet example itself need not involve 'politics'. With the slow coming of sound, which took longer to arrive in the documentary field than it did in the commercial cinema, Soviet editing and intertitling died away. Only elements of the camera style remained.

This is why the main authority for the movement is not really *Drifters* with its Soviet fiction film influences. The Griersonian enterprise was never to escape from its imperial beginnings – Flaherty's *Industrial Britain*, augmented by the depoliticised *Turksib* – especially after these had been recast as social engineering for domestic subjects and audiences. Yet, in preserving the radical tinge of realism and in claiming that the superficial use of Soviet techniques was something more ideologically substantial, it became convenient to deny Flaherty, aesthetics, and personal expression.

The result of this can be seen in Elizabeth Sussex's different cut at the *œuvre* to create another version of two sub-schools. Here both *Drifters* and *Industrial Britain* – that is to say, the Russians and Flaherty – are, in her formulation, cast aside as public education texts so that films made during and after 1934–6 can better be received as such. Sussex puts it thus (1975, p. 79): 'Although this shift in emphasis from aesthetic to social purpose had been developing gradually in the early thirties, it was only after *Night Mail* that it began to have an obvious effect on the careers of all Grierson's closest adherents.'

Sussex is supported in her interpretation by the film-makers themselves. In 1936 Elton claimed that in *Housing Problems* the audience was transported into the skin of the subject. On this basis, he went on, 'The modern realist film has given up the loving caress of the industrial process and statuesque treatment of workers for a racy intimacy with men and women which we hope will blow away the romantic cobwebs of an earlier vision' (Macpherson, 1980, p. 154). This interpretation of the significance of the work done in the mid-years of the decade was to condition the movement's memory. For instance, twenty years on, Wright (1956, p. 322) saw it in this way too: 'The meaning of the word "documentary" split in two. On the one hand, it refers to the new methods of approach to public information and enlightenment through film. On the other, it still retains its original reference to the work of the individual artist who seeks to use film for "the creative interpretation [*sic*] of reality".'

Grierson (1979a, p. 112) was also happy to acknowledge a split, but in a typically obfuscating fashion: 'Documentary was from the beginning – when we first separated our public purpose theories from those of Flaherty – an anti-aesthetic movement.'

In response to this strategic claim of the movement dividing, and Sussex's acceptance of the reality of such a divide, one must remember that social purpose does not date from Grierson's 1936 pronouncement, 'I look upon cinema as a pulpit, and use it as a propagandist' (Rotha, 1966, p. 42). Earlier, it had suffused his manifesto of 1932–4 (Grierson, 1979a, p. 39). Before that, the 1926–7 discussions about the rationale for the EMB Film Unit and the funding of *Drifters* also had public education as their main point (Tallents, 1968, p. 17). Public education and social purpose were not in opposition to personal expression. On the contrary, the combination was just what distinguished documentary: 'My separate claim for the documentary is simply that in its use of the living article, there is *also* an opportunity to perform creative work' (Grierson, 1979a, p. 37).

Sussex is, therefore, in my view, reading too much into developments that were implicit from the outset and required no major change of direction in the mid-1930s. This is why I argue that the persistent influence was Flaherty's – 'The Spell of Flaherty', as Sussex calls it (1975, pp. 23ff.).

Grierson might claim that what he called 'our local fisherman *et al.*' are *transformed* into 'our answer to Flaherty', but in fact Grierson's approach to his participants and Flaherty's approach are all but indistinguishable from each other (Rotha, 1973, p. 48).

Grierson (1979a, p. 64) was to become dismissive of what he described as Flaherty's emphasis on 'man against the sky' in favour of films 'of industrial and social function, where man is more likely to be in the bowels of the earth'. Yet, in Grierson's hands, this is a distinction without a difference because he and his followers never quite came to grips with the bowels of the earth. Even in *Coalface*, to be literalist, the miner functions neither industrially nor socially but as the excuse for Auden's words 'O lurcher-loving collier, black as night' – 'man against the coal seam', you might call it. (The soundtrack does make reference to accident and danger but implies that these are without cause, a natural consequence of mining. The passage is spoken over close-up images of men's hands working with machinery, not over footage of the results of these frequent occurrences. Pneumonoconiosis is not mentioned.)

There are real and obvious advantages in making this distinction for the sake of the movement's public relations effort, but there is no real change, it seems to me, in the direction of the work; no meaningful *ideological* divide. The development that certainly took place was organic and can be accounted for by the coming of sound and the tenor of the times, that is the deepening depression. The sponsors' need for social-purpose films does not alter; it is just that the worsening social situation required that they become ever more overt in commissioning films propagandising social integration. After all, there was less and less of 'Industrial Britain' to celebrate.

One cannot justify a split or division more easily if one deals with it in terms of personnel, either. Such a reading of the 'the poetic v. social purpose' recasts the putative schism in terms of people rather than films. It places the more active leftists (Anstey and Rotha, for example) against the less (Grierson and Wright, for example.) However, Rotha left EMB in 1931 after a very brief sojourn with the master and that event is read into the history as a matter of personalities rather than principle. At best, political difference was '*behind* the personality clash' (Marris, 1980, p. 3 – my italics). Anstey and Elton, who were responsible for the 1935 sound films which demonstrated the supposedly new rising concern with social purpose, initially made these films for Grierson. He loaned them to various industrial sponsors and their first independent venture, Associated Realist Film Producers (ARFP), involved, among others, the independent Rotha, the GPO staffer Wright, and Grierson as a consultant. Departures were as much (or more) a question of seizing funding opportunities as of ideological divisions.

Finally, in 1937, Grierson himself left the GPO. Hardy suggests that a tincture of anti-red hysteria played a role in this because the sponsors, or rather the Conservative Research Council, saw communism in the work and alerted the Treasury. Ernest Tristram Crutchley, Tallents's successor as chief PRO for the GPO, wrote in his diary in the summer of 1936: 'For Communism read realism and a certain healthy liberalism and there might be something in it. But I am convinced we can't have the Treasury butting in' (Hardy, 1979, p. 88). This conflict can be grist to the view that Grierson's 'ideology contravened ... many basic tenets of dominant Conservatism' (Aitken, 1990, p. 193).

However, Swann persuasively shows that the reason for the Treasury's hostility to the Film Unit was not grounded in ideological objections but was a response to Grierson's and Tallents's constant manoeuvrings around its authority. Told to limit the size of the unit, Grierson finished up with thirty-seven people on the payroll. Told not to work for outside bodies, Grierson promptly lent personnel out for such work (Swann, 1989, pp. 59ff.). Finally, to defeat Treasury restrictions, half the unit was working for a species of holding company – Associated Talking Pictures (Kuhn 1980, p. 30). Grierson also grossly inflated audience figures for the government committee which audited his budget – to its knowledge (see p. 63).

These incidents will not support a picture of an heroic radical Grierson battling right-ring bureaucrats (cf. Flaherty v. Hollywood). As Nicholas Pronay points out in a very important demythologising article (1989, p. 235):

By 1936 ... his [Grierson's] civil service seniors came to regard him as unreliable, and, above all, someone who broke the cardinal rule of never misleading fellow civil servants. Cooking figures, loading arguments, bringing discreet pressure by leaks to the press were perfectly all right by civil service conventions – provided it was aimed at the politicians. But to do that to your fellow civil servants broke the rules of the club.[7]

It was not politics – Politics – but office politics that cut short his civil service career.

Here, though, I part company with Swann, who sees on the screen the results of Grierson's removal in 1937. In effect, Swann constructs a sort of reverse of the supposed earlier divide suggested by Sussex. Despite his insights into Grierson's civil service career, Swann (1989, p. 85) nevertheless recasts him not as the rightist but as the radical. The leftist *bona fides* of some (Cavalcanti and Watt by this formulation) are sacrificed to preserve the radicalism of others (Grierson; or if not of Grierson himself, then certainly of the Grierson-produced films): 'Cavalcanti led the Post Office Film Unit away from theoretical discussions about public education and "art" towards films which relied heavily upon some of the narrative techniques of the commercial film industry. In essence, this was exactly the type of influence which Grierson had tried to exclude from the documentary film.'

In this analysis, the pivotal film (like *Industrial Britain* in the 'Flaherty v. the Russians' reading, or *Housing Problems* and others in the 'the poetic v. social purpose' formulation) is *The Saving of Bill Blewitt*. This was made in 1936 (released in 1937) by Harry Watt as Grierson was leaving. It is a film that, despite its non-actors and real locations, borders on social fantasy. It asks us to believe that a Cornish fisherman at the height of the depression could save enough from his work as a tin-miner to replace his lost smack. (It also carried the stilted quality of performance to a new level of embarrassment.) Swann (1989, p. 86) nevertheless sees it as the founding text of a new subgenre, 'the story-documentary', which rejected 'the earlier Griersonian tradition of didacticism in favor of a much more humanistic approach'.

Again, some within the movement support this view. Pat Jackson, who entered the unit straight from school in 1934, suggested that 'the early school of documentary was divorced from people. It showed people in a problem, but you never got to know them, and you never felt they were talking to each other. You never heard how they felt and thought and spoke to each other, relaxed. You were looking from a high point of view at them' (Sussex, 1975, p. 76).

But the last films of the decade are not necessarily closer to people than the early ones. There are few viewpoints as 'high' as that of the Humphrey Jennings of *Spare Time* (1939). As Grierson once said to a visitor, 'Let's go down and see Humphrey being nice to the common people' (Vaughan, 1983, p. 38). (The visitor was Denis Forman.) *Spare Time*, bravely perhaps, 'refuses to ennoble' (Nowell-Smith, 1986, p. 326); but the result is that it contains what are easily the movement's most alienated and alienating images of the working class in the pre-war period. And lest this charge of elitism seem *ad hominem*, let me point out that the sequence in *Spare Time* of which this is most true, the children's kazoo band, was suggested as a possible element in an early memo before Jennings took over the project. Whoever thought of it, the final result on screen vividly confirms the initial idea that 'This recreation is rather pathetic' (Vaughan, 1983, p. 43).

Just as I see little evidence on the screen of increased humanism, neither do I detect this putative move towards greater fictionalisation. Cavalcanti's regime did not, in my view, bring in train more acting or a more transparent Hollywood editing style. Subjects were always coached and directed during the earlier period. Non-actors had been asked to perform scripts for the previous several years. This was nothing but an element in 'the creative *dramatisation* of actuality' – as Rotha, significantly, in one place (1966, p. 105 – my italics) misquotes Grierson's definition. That Cavalcanti might have encouraged the 'narrative or dramatic' or 'story' documentary means that he was simply continuing Grierson's agenda in a situation where the group's collective assurance about working with synch sound was growing (Low, 1979a, p. 121; Swann, 1989, p. 86). In other words, here again there was development but no schism. Drama was not only already present in Grierson, it is the ontological mark of the Griersonian documentary, the essence of what is meant by 'treatment' (see p. 97).

As to increased obedience to Hollywood's spatial and temporal continuity rules, at the outset Grierson had faked the cabin in *Drifters* (and the swimming fish) and Rotha actually used two different but similar hulls in *Shipyard* to help continuity and speed the filming.[8] The movement's use of Soviet montage did not stretch to symbolic experimentations; on the contrary, even when at their most 'Soviet' the Griersonians adhered to Hollywood norms. Like Flaherty before him, Grierson did not seek out an alternative documentary-specific code to represent time and space. Both were content with the legacy of Hollywood, not least because dramatisation was seen as being essential to the form. With the coming of sound (1935, in effect), this obedience to dominant feature-film practice simply continued. So, for instance, the *Night Mail* sequences, whether shot in a studio or in Crewe, were every bit as much a drama documentary as *Blewitt* or *North Sea* and the earlier film's editing is as transparent as the later one's. Synch conditions this development, not an ideological refocusing.

Swann holds Cavalcanti responsible for these trends, with Harry Watt as his lieutenant. And, despite what I have just indicated, some agree. Elizabeth Sussex (1975, p. 51) quotes John Taylor: 'That was the beginning of the division ... it was a great mistake to hire Cavalcanti, really, because he didn't understand what documentary was supposed to be doing' – a pretty harsh judgment on the maker of *Rien que les heures*. It is arguable that Cavalcanti knew exactly what a documentary – or, better, film in general – was supposed to be doing *in the context of the General Post Office*.

Take *Pett and Pott* (1934), Cavalcanti's first contribution to the movement. 'Cavalcanti's most obvious contribution was the fantasy and the lightly surrealistic touches by which he stylised the English middle class' (Monegal, 1955, pp. 346ff.). Although I would scarcely describe the surrealist touches as 'light', *Pett and Pott* is not the disaster, the experiment with sound and nothing more, Grierson positioned it as being. Cavalcanti himself said: 'It's not quite a film.' Grierson 'told everybody what a wonderful film it was and made sure nobody ever saw it' (Sussex, 1975,

p. 51). In fact it is no cruder than the other films of its year. *Pett and Pott* is an overdrawn parable about the accidents which befall a middle-class family which dares to do without a home telephone. The film's sin, I would suggest, is that, of all the major productions, it is the one which most directly reveals the effects of sponsorship. It is a commercial for the telephone.

Cavalcanti had learned sound in the French commercial studios, a period seen as hack work, despite *En rade*. He swapped 'the extreme poverty of his commercial experience in France' for the pay of the GPO (Monegal, 1955, p. 346). *Pett and Pott* reveals that he knew who his pay-masters were. That *Bill Blewitt* is a commercial for the Post Office Savings system, and that senior GPO officials begin to appear in the unit's films towards the decade's end, signals nothing more than a sense that the sponsor's understanding of what the unit ought to be doing was also growing.[9]

The most significant putative new characteristics of 'the story documen-tary' antedate the suggested point of the split. This conjectured new drift to fictionalisation therefore revisits other formulations of schism with the same result. If 'Flaherty v. the Russians' suggests that the movement had an apolitical side which lost out to engagement, this reading does the opposite, suggesting politically engaged qualities in the previous output which disappear under Cavalcanti. In both instances, though, the false assumption is that at any point there was an engaged cinema. Grierson's 'didacticism' (that is, politics) was never abandoned for the simple reason that it was not there in the first place.

This explains why Grierson pleaded guilty to the charge of killing off the 'poetic' film. Sussex (1975, p. 79) quotes him:

> We worked together and produced a kind of film that gave great promise of very high development of the poetic documentary. But for some reason or another, there has been no great development of that in recent times. I think it's partly because we ourselves got caught up in social propaganda. We ourselves got caught up in the problems of hous-ing and health, the question of pollution (we were on to that long ago). We got on to the social problems of the world, and we ourselves devi-ated from the poetic line.

However, the social problems he and his fellows put on the screen tended to become 'poetic' in the putting. 'Poetry' conditioned even the most sup-posedly engaged of social-purpose films, like *The Face of Britain* or *The Smoke Menace*. The tradition of prettifying continued in the wartime work of Jennings and was transported into British television practice by Dennis Mitchell. Conversely, mainstream (that is, integrative) social propaganda was always part of even the most 'poetic' of films – for example, the fish market sequences at the end of *Drifters*, the closely observed attitudes to work in *Night Mail*, the 'business' of commerce in *Song of Ceylon*. After all, Flaherty had himself been forced to confront *Industrial Britain*.

In effect, then, there were no significant ideological divisions. The Griersonians worked in a universe which did indeed opportunistically combine Flaherty and the Soviets, personal artistic expression and the veneer of social engagements, dramatics (and whimsy) as well as social realism. The most the Soviets did for them, apart for encouraging the use of low camera angles, was to reinforce the radical tinge of their realist heritage. A certain legitimacy was added to Grierson's efforts by the oppositional flavour imparted by the Russian connection – rather as Shakespeare heightens the patriotic effect of *Henry V* with a scene on the eve of Agincourt between the King and some common soldiers, one of whom believes Henry 'could wish himself in Thames up to the neck ... so we were quit here' (IV. i. 116). The character turns out all right in the end, though; and so does Grierson.

12

He Never Used the Word Revolution

The point is that Grierson never meaningfully 'got on to the social problems of the world'. That was not the name of his game. Indeed, the enterprise had as little to do with a real political analysis of social problems as it could. How could that be otherwise, given the funding sources? Joris Ivens (1969, p. 216) put it like this when commenting on *Housing Problems*: 'If the British films could have been sponsored directly by social organisations fighting the bad housing conditions, instead of by a gas company, they would have closed in on such dramatic reality as rent strikes and protest movements.'

It is because of the sponsor (rather than because of any personal political failing) that Grierson, at the outset, could not say what he thought he would like to say about the labour of men in *Drifters*. It is because of the sponsor that, for instance, *Coalface* is silent on the fact 'that the miners had been starved back to work after the General Strike', or that the employment exchanges are implied rather than shown in *Shipyard* (Hood, 1983, p. 107). It is sponsorship more than personal political opportunism or self-delusion that leaves others to film the hunger marches (see p. 77). It is sponsorship that conditions and creates the movement's fundamentally roseate picture of Britain in the 1930s. Finally it is the sponsorship of state propagandists which required, during the war, Grierson's sort of 'Greek academy' of young men to drop their pretensions, both poetic and radical, and shape up to the reality of their real 'public education' function.

In general, any critics who drew attention to the implications of funding on content were dismissed by the Griersonians as living in an ivory tower (Hardy, 1979, p. 80). Grierson claimed that 'throwing up the government relation' was 'suicidal' and not 'realistic, either socially or aesthetically' (1979a, p. 190).

At the outset, *Drifters* attracted only 'the occasional voice of dissent' along these lines (Rotha, 1973, p. 29). Such voices, and most subsequent dissenters, were largely dismissed; the 'proletarian' Grierson, created in the founding movement of his film-making career, was to overcome all nay-saying for the next half-century.

For instance, W. H. Auden, who worked for Grierson on two films, reviewed the first edition of Rotha's *Documentary Film* in *The Listener*. He denied that film was a good medium for factual information, claimed that the film-makers worked too quickly to understand their subjects, and charged that directors were all too middle-class to relate to workers. Auden's final point was that sponsoring organisations were unlikely 'ever to pay for an exact picture of the human life within their enormous buildings' (Carpenter, 1981, p. 189). For his pains, he was ticked off in the pages of *World Film News*: 'As Auden's apprenticeship matures he may feel less despondent.' Carpenter, Auden's biographer, believes that Grierson was personally responsible for this paternalistic castigation.[10]

The Griersonians did not adopt the readily available if dubious strategy of claiming that sponsorship exploited the contradictions supposed to exist within the system. Instead, they ignored the problem. The nearest the film-makers came to confronting the truth of their situation was, as Stuart Legg put it, to talk of the 'art of sponsorship' (Sussex, 1975, p. 82). This was the critical tactical position that allowed the Griersonians to function, but a price was exacted for it. Arthur Calder Marshall summed it up: 'Mr Grierson is not paid to tell the truth but to make more people use the parcel post. Mr Grierson may like to talk about social education, surpliced in self-importance and social benignity. Other people may like hearing him. But even if it sounds like a sermon, a sales talk is a sales talk' (Hardy, 1979, p. 80).

Sponsorship was always simply a question of survival. It was pointless to question it, even for those of the movement who saw themselves as being more politically engaged than was Grierson. Legg thought: 'The whole problem of the purpose of sponsored documentary, the relationship between the film maker and the sponsor, is at the root of everything we've done for the last forty years. I think in the GPO one wasn't terribly conscious of it. Grierson looked after all that' (Sussex, 1975, p. 82).

In seeking to make a living without Grierson, Paul Rotha demonstrated how little a documentarist could afford to examine the implications of sponsorship. He analysed his options after parting from Grierson in 1931 to set up his own business as follows: 'I thought, "Well, Grierson's got government sponsorship through the EMB and later the GPO, where else is there sponsorship?" and I said to myself "Well, obviously industry"' (Marris, 1980, p. 10).

Rotha (1973, pp. 32 and 114), and many others, went further, converting the necessity for sponsorship into a positive advantage by seeing it as an escape from the tyranny of the commercial box office. As many sponsors were drawn from the most 'progressive' sector of the establishment, this argument was not entirely specious.

But, not surprisingly, the meaning created in the films flows directly from Grierson's approach to the vexed issue of sponsorship and therefore of politics, too. Were the films what received critical opinion holds them to be – that is, a high spot in world cinema creativity ('this country's most important contribution to cinema as a whole') – perhaps one would be more accepting of his tactics; but, in the event, the films produced were, in their time, at best palliatives and at worst repressive (Rotha, 1966, p. 96).

Basil Wright could not, therefore, have been more incorrect when he said that the charge of pusillanimity was irrelevant because political trimming was only the price paid to get the money to make the films. The money exacted its price and the films are, largely, flawed almost beyond interest as a result. In the light of history they are, almost without exception, mediocre exactly because their analyses of social issues are naive or, rather, non-existent.

Grierson's own vision of the work, written in November 1938, inadvertently confirms this failure:

58

In many of the documentary films, the country is shown tearing down slums and building anew, or facing up to unemployment and reorganising economically: in general in passing from the negative to the positive. It is in this, precisely, that most of us have felt that the strength of democratic Britain is made manifest. (Grierson, 1979a, p. 85)

Dai Vaughan, with his usual insight, points out (1983, p. 30) that 'one has only to read a smattering of Grierson's statements to realise that they were not meant to make sense. They were meant to make things happen.' So here is Grierson making liberal reformist social integration happen, for what else can this vision of the strength of democratic Britain imply?

In the final analysis it did not matter to the Griersonians that the films, for all the public relations cavorting that went on around them, were not what they were claimed to be – documents of serious social purpose designed to have a tangible educational (or propaganda) effect on audiences. Despite the rhetoric, the public effect of documentaries was largely insignificant. Lord Tyrrell, President of the British Board of Film Censors, could say in 1937, 'We may take pride that there is not a single film showing in London today which deals with any of the burning questions of the day' (Dickinson and Street, 1985, p. 8). This was the year of *Enough To Eat* and *Today We Live* (Rotha's production, directed by Ralph Bond and Ruby Grierson, about community self-help in the depressed South Wales coalfield and the Cotswolds).

But this failure to register did not matter to the film-makers because the entire enterprise was actually not about reception at all, much less education. It was about something else – it was about film. It was about getting films made, being film-makers – nothing more.

There are no passages more tendentious in all of Grierson's writings than the following (1979a, pp. 78 and 113):

The British documentary group began not so much in affection for film *per se* as in affection for national education.

The documentary idea was not basically a film idea at all, and the film treatment only inspired an incidental aspect of it. The medium happened to be the most convenient and most exciting available to us. The idea itself, on the other hand, was a new idea for public education.

It would be foolish indeed to take with anything other than a grain of salt the notion that Grierson decided even-handedly between film and, say, mimeographed newsletters, only to reach the cool conclusion that film was, after all, better for his purposes. The Griersonians never wavered in their allegiance to film rather than 'public education'. When asked in the 1970s: 'Was all this enthusiasm for film *per se*, or was it for causes and social goals, or was it a mixture?', Basil Wright replied unequivocally: 'It was for film. Grierson had to put the brakes on us. What he was getting was people who wanted to use film for purposes of aesthetic experiment, avant garde and whatnot. And he said, "Okay, I'll let you do this within a discipline. The discipline is that you are spending public money and you are working towards a sociological purpose"' (Beveridge, 1978, p. 69).

Despite the fact that they were all 'left-wing to a man', Grierson still used his anti-aesthetic rhetoric to keep the youthful Elton and the other young graduates he had hired in line. They were, he said, 'Too damned arty and post-war to get their noses into public issues' (Low, 1979a, p. 56). Grierson was fond of reminding his people that, whatever the chatter in the pub, 'First of all we were civil servants and were responsible for spending public money'. 'You must get interested in social betterment,' Wright remembered him saying (Levin, 1971, p. 37).

Yet he did not really mean this. It was nothing more than rhetoric for the sponsors' ears; for Grierson, too, was only concerned with film. Wright goes on to recall that Grierson 'never used the word revolution'.[11]

The rhetoric of social betterment and public education both unconsciously echoed 1848 and consciously aped the Russians. Any potential contradictions involved were more than justified because the rhetoric oiled the wheels of sponsorship by making the obsession with film seem reasonable. The logic is clear. Government and commercial sponsorship could not be bought on the basis of cinephilia. On the other hand, public education requirements, to be met in a realist mode almost drained of radicalism, could be moulded into a far more effective sales pitch.

It is equally clear that if the medium available had not been film few if any of the Griersonians would have been in the public education business. As Rotha, for instance, ran through the various subtypes of non-fiction film in a 1935 survey he found no space for films of public education – they were simply propaganda. 'Educationals', in his list, 'fall short of documentary requirements' altogether. Grierson, in effect, brilliantly squared the circle for the entire tradition – right-wing money, left-wing kudos and films of dubious social worth in the middle.

It has proved to be a most seductive model.

To Command, and Cumulatively Command, the Mind of a Generation

The model, has been far more seductive to film-makers than to audiences, however.

In *Busman's Honeymoon*, Dorothy L. Sayers has Lord Peter Wimsey and his friend Sir Impey Biggs kill a few hours by turning into a news cinema and seeing 'a Mickey Mouse and an educational film about the iron and steel industry'. The year is 1937.

In 1954, Lindsay Anderson (p. 181), in an appreciation of Humphrey Jennings, wrote: 'Jennings's films are all documentaries, all made firmly within the framework of the British documentary movement. This fact ought not to strike a chill.'

Nearly a quarter of a century later, Gus Macdonald, speaking for more than himself, said, 'I must therefore confess to reaching adulthood almost untouched by the British documentary' (Macdonald, 1978, p. 15). He was giving the address on the occasion of the inauguration, at Stirling University, of the John Grierson Archive.

A decade or so after that I caught a presenter on American cable television introducing *Australia Live*, an extravaganza celebrating the bicentennial of the European settlement of that continent, with the words 'It's not a documentary, let me assure you'. By this time, at least as far as American network television executives were concerned, 'the word "documentary" is a pejorative. ... It sounds too much like a long trek through TV-land, a dry approach to a dull subject' (Diamond, 1991, p. 30). Grierson's self-deprecating references to the 'clumsiness' of the term have come home to roost.

Grierson's stated purpose, as a film-maker, was 'to command, and cumulatively command, the mind of a generation' (Grierson, 1979a, p. 48). Yet his legacy is an audiovisual form that most of the time nobody – certainly nobody who is not middle-class – wants to watch; and it is arguable that they never did. Any consideration of the realist documentary must confront the reality of its reception.

As originally planned, the Griersonian documentary was to take its place in the cinema – 'creativity' demanded nothing less. 'The EMB Film Unit, when first set up, intended that documentary films should mainly be distributed theatrically, as any other shorts' (Arts Council, 1947, p. 57). By 1932, it was claimed that there had been 1,873 bookings involving 4,380 films screenings (Aitken, 1990, p. 2). However, this was not to continue (if indeed it had occurred), for two reasons.

The first is advanced by the Griersonians themselves and has some merit. The failure of the documentary to secure a regularly scheduled place in the cinema programme is laid, by this account, at the door of the exhibitors. Certainly they were hostile to governmental production, unwilling to pay rentals for these productions and assertive about their unpopularity. More than that, they had imported from the United States a marketing ploy which adversely affected all short forms, including the commercial production of travelogues, nature studies and the like – the double feature.

Between 1929 and 1935, exactly the years during which Grierson was trying to establish the documentary in the UK, these various factors combined to reduce the registered footage of short films licensed for the-atrical screening from 170,000 to 68,000 feet (Arts Council, 1947, p. 58). Since the short subjects that survived were often 'packaged' with the features by distributors, even the 15 shillings or so which was the average rental paid for a documentary between the wars was money which often did not need to be spent.

While there is certainly an element of truth in all this, it is equally true that, from the exhibitors' point of view, these films were still nevertheless cheap, very cheap. They had been paid for by others who justified the pro-duction costs involved by public relations considerations. From the spon-sors' point of view, the money had been spent to secure attention. Any returns were a bonus. Further, in a period when British production was protected by quotas, the documentaries counted as British films. Even if only 6 per cent of screen time was occupied by shorts in 1934; even if this fell to 4.21 per cent the following year; even if by 1939, the figure was only 2.25 per cent, still this time was not taken up by documentaries (Swann, 1989, p. 72).

It is the second factor which explains why this was so – there was no public demand. The exhibitors were more or less right about that.

In the silent period a few feature-length documentaries had been suc-cessfully screened theatrically. *Nanook*, Grierson claimed (1979a, p. 60), was a hit in Paris and was still playing twelve years after its opening. *Moana* was going strong after eight years. Of *Nanook*, *Grass* and *Chang*, an early film historian, Benjamin Hampton, could write (1931, p. 422) that 'each attracted large audiences'. There was no general audience hostility to the documentary idea at the outset.

Yet the Griersonian version of the form, specifically after the spin of 'public education' had been put on the films, was unable to establish itself in the cinemas between 1927 and the coming of the double feature. Most EMB films were simply unpopular (Dickinson and Street, 1985, p. 28). The ones that were not, such as *Drifters*, were the exceptions. Before the double feature was put in place, the documentary had already been largely vanquished by cartoons and newsreels. These last might have been laugh-able as sources of information but were, until the war at least, nevertheless popular (Richards and Sheridan, 1987, p. 409). *March of Time* was mas-sively so; it 'swept the country' (Arts Council, 1947, p. 26).

There were glimmers of success for the British documentary. *Drifters* almost recouped its production costs of £2,948. (Since the EMB's feature *One Family*, its earliest effort, managed only £334 of receipts against a production cost of £15,740, it is easy to see why Grierson's plan for an alternative documentary approach prevailed with the government's bureaucrats (Swann, 1989, pp. 33ff.). Also distributed widely was Paul Rotha's first film, *Contact* (1933), a paean to Imperial Airways sponsored by Shell. On the basis of these limited successes, the initial GPO plan was for the unit to produce six theatrical titles a year, but the public response did not sustain this rate. After two years, by 1936, only one film was commercially released – *Night Mail*. Nearly all the films continued to bask in critical acclaim, yet, frustratingly, such support could not be converted into a regular mass audience.

Grierson was not above looking for topics which could achieve a breakthrough with the public. For instance, *BBC: The Voice of Britain* (1935) was conceived of as a sort of documentary entertainment film with variety artists (and Adrian Boult) filmed during studio performances. There is a whole sequence of chorines in costume sitting around rehearsals and performing under the watchful, if not leering, eyes of various production chaps. The commentary states they are so dressed (or undressed) 'to get in the mood'. Despite these ploys, the film fared no better with audiences.

(This one did not quite carry the right message to the critics either. Graham Greene (1980, p. 10) wrote: 'The superb complacency of the BBC was never more delightfully parodied than in the title of an official film made by Mr John Grierson and the GPO film unit: *The Voice of Britain*. ... I doubt if the BBC realise the devastating nature of Mr Grierson's amusing and sometimes beautiful film.' This from a friend who usually, as in this instance, bought into both the 'art' and the ideological complicity of Grierson's efforts. But the sponsor could not have been pleased.)

Overall, the public was less enthusiastic than were the critics. '*Night Mail* and *North Sea* did better than most [in the cinemas], but this was because they were less pedagogic than many documentaries. Attempts to portray industrial life – for example *Housing Problems*, *Coalface* and *Industrial Britain* – could seem patronising to the working class' (Dickinson and Street, 1985, p. 66).

'Why do we spend our pocket money and our leisure hours at the cinema?' a correspondent to *Film Pictorial* asked in 1933. 'To see our ordinary everyday lives portrayed on the screen over and over again? Emphatically not!' (Jones, 1987, p. 23).

Thus it was that at the moment of greatest public education and propaganda need, the outbreak of war, Grierson's people were virtually ignored. In planning the film activities of the nascent Ministry of Information (MoI) in 1939, it was the newsreel producers not the documentarists who were enlisted by the civil servants. And why not? All political considerations, real (the reactionary quality of the newsreels) and supposed (the radical stance of the documentarists) aside, it was the newsreels which had been delivering the audience (Aldgate and Richards, 1986, pp. 5ff.).[12]

That the Griersonians were failures as mass communicators would not have mattered had they stuck to being film artists. But they had not. In addition, they had set themselves up in business as public educators. It was wonderful PR for Grierson to claim the cinema as a pulpit but what was to be done when the church refused to fill?

The failure to create a form with mass appeal elicited a multifaceted blitz from Grierson. Invoked were pleas for the imposition of the documentary on the public, arguments about the unimportance of the mass audience experience, plans for massive non-theatrical exhibition and claims for the superiority of the audience experience delivered by such exhibition. He even on occasion in the later 1930s simply denied that the theatrical audience was not there: 'In the seven or eight years following *Drifters* we put together some two hundred films of the documentary type and at the end of that time it was no longer so difficult to get into the theatres' (Grierson, 1979a, p. 77). But it was.

The quota system had not helped documentary production. Grierson on occasion suggested that the quota be extended specifically to guarantee screen time for documentary: 'I would urge that the leavening of the average programme with a single short item of more serious intention either socially or culturally would have the effect of improving the relationship between cinemas and the public' (Dickinson and Street, 1985, p. 65). Given that, in 1934 for instance, Britain's, 4,305 cinemas sold 963 million tickets – that is, 42 tickets for every human in the country or 18½ million a week – it is hard to see what improvements, except moral, Grierson might have in mind (ibid., p. 1). The suggestion was not adopted.

The best possible construction to be put on Grierson's change of position as to the importance of the movie experience was summarised by Harry Watt (1972, p. 47):

> Grierson became convinced that the enormous non cinema-going audience was the one to go after, and that a non-theatrical circuit with an assured public was better than our sporadic and fleeting showings in news-reel cinemas. Cavalcanti and I together with Humphrey Jennings ... and some others disagreed. We felt we had to make the cinemas.

I would not want to read this as evidence of schism, but rather, once again, of a development arising organically from changing circumstances. Grierson was developing a tactic in the light of events while the others simply wished to stick to the original plan, even though it was not working very well. In either case, there is no suggestion that the films themselves should adopt novel strategies or significant new directions.

There were difficulties with Grierson's new tactic. Suddenly to deny the efficacy of cinema as a mass persuader required repudiating everything that had attracted Grierson's attention to it in the first place. For one thing, sponsorship was threatened because that turned on the selling of the cinema as an effective tool for moulding mass opinion. There was also some considerable question as to the reality of the size of the 'enormous non cinema-going' audience. But the cinemagoing audience was refusing to watch and the government was demurring at thrusting documentaries down its throat.

So, behind a smokescreen of anti-box-office rhetoric, the new direction was taken. By 1949, the whole initial thrust of the movement towards the cinema had been recast as an ugly illusion, a silly curse and a rotten and limiting circumstance:

> The illusion rears again its ugly head that the odd spot among the theatre millions is worth more in public information than the persistent influence of the community groups that in every known way lead the opinion of the community. What disturbs me, however, is the limiting and rotting effect of a theatre distribution policy for documentary as a whole; and it was ever so from the beginning. ... We ought, I think, to make our minds up now that because of the special laws of the popular theatre and because exhibitors do not largely share our special hopes of

documentary, much of what we do and want to do has no relation whatever to theatrical distribution. ... In fact the biggest and silliest curse that has come over us is the thought that the success of documentary as an idea means any difference to its prospect in the theatre. (Grierson, 1979a, pp. 198ff.)

With considerable economy as to truth, he went on to claim that the 'audience of our original documentary persuasion' was non-theatrical. It was not.

Grierson began suggesting alternatives to the cinema in 1933: 'If it [documentary] fails for the theatres it may, by manipulation, be accommodated non-theatrically in one of half-a-dozen ways' (Grierson, 1979a, p. 50). Two years later he was talking of 'the new critical audience of the film circles, the film societies and the specialised theatres': 'As I see it, the future of the cinema may not be in the cinema at all. ... It may creep in quietly by way of the YMCAs, the church halls and other citadels of suburban improvement. This is the future for the art of the cinema, for in the commercial cinema there is not a future worth serving' (Grierson, 1979a, p. 69).

Grierson could not hope to command the mind of a generation in these citadels of suburban improvement, but he could still argue with his paymasters that he could *cumulatively* command it, bit by bit:

The commercials [i.e. mainstream producers] are interested only in the first results of their films, that is to say, in the amount of money a film takes in a twelvemonth. The long range propagandists [i.e. Grierson's sponsors] are not. Quick takings are a guarantee of immediate public interest and are therefore important, but the persistence of a film's effect over a period of years is more important still. To command, and cumulatively command, the mind of a generation is more important than by novelty or sensation to knock a Saturday night audience cold; and the 'hang-over' effect of a film is everything. (ibid., p. 48)

Just as the documentary film-maker was, the Griersonians claimed, a uniquely independent film-maker, so too the documentary audience was differentiated from the mass of cinemagoers. The documentary audience grew little by little but remembered more and more – 'the hang-over effect'. There is no need to debate the reality of this supposed effect (memory?) and how, for instance, it might differ from the effect left in the collective mind of the knocked-cold audience by, say, *Gone with the Wind* or *Snow White*. Let us just note that this new audience was smaller than the mass one attracted to the cinemas. It became a mass only slowly, in aggregate.

The question is, did it in fact become a mass *even* in aggregate?

Certainly there is evidence of the beginnings (at least) of an alternative distribution and exhibition system. Projectors were available outside of cinemas. The EMB had established a non-theatrical distribution system on a small scale in conjunction with its theatrical plans. Some 73 organisations and 294 schools had booked films in 1932 (Aitken, 1990, p. 2). As we have seen, others, such as the Conservative Party, had also been exploring the possibilities of non-theatrical exhibition. By 1935 the GPO had experimented with film vans along Tory lines. Manufacturers of

16mm projectors offered machines to sponsors for road shows. When war broke out, 76 other mobile units were planned by the Films Division of the MoI; by war's end there were 144 in operation (Manvell, 1974, p. 76; Arts Council, 1947, pp. 59 and 161). During the war, the Conservative vans were hired to the National Savings Campaign.

There were also projectors in a number of educational, civic and private organisations, and they were available for hire. Some schools were equipped with them, although by 1939 only 1,700 were in place and only 400 of those were capable of playing sound films (in that year in England there were some 30,000 teaching establishments) (Arts Council, 1947, p. 21). The left were actively using them. For instance, between 1931 and 1934, the Royal Arsenal Co-operative Society screened *The General Line* to 40,000 around London (Hogenkamp, 1986, p. 75).

The documentary film movement's films were gathered into libraries and distribution was established. But, if there is evidence of non-theatrical exhibition possibilities, it does not follow that there was an audience of any size or significance using those venues. So this brings us to the second aspect of the question – how many people did this system reach? While there are no firm data, there is a plethora of claims and assertions.

Grierson's initial claim was for a non-theatrical audience of 4 million a year (Pronay, 1989, p. 235). By 1938, the GPO was estimating 3½ million (Swann, 1989, pp. 76, 103 and 16). In the year till August 1942, an audience of 12 million was suggested (Forman, H., 1982, p. 224). For 1943/4 this rose to 18½ million, the maximum level claimed during the war (Swann, 1989, p. 169). For 1944/5, the number was 16 million (Arts Council, 1947, pp. 15 and 151).[13]

It would seem that maximal assumptions were governing these estimates. For instance, the 12 million people of 1941/2 were reached in three ways – 4½ million via loans from the Central Film Library; 1 million at special screenings in cinemas during off hours; 6½ million by the mobile units.

Of these three elements only that of the audience claimed by the Central Film Library system seems inherently probable. 130,212 'dispatches' (films) were sent to over 8,000 organisations; 45,000 screenings at these venues yields about 4½ million at an average of 100 per show (Arts Council, 1947, p. 15). Slightly less likely but still possible is the special screening figure. There were about 1,600 off-hours screenings in cinemas. An attendance of 650 per screening, again a not impossible number, would yield a total of 1 million people.

The figure for the largest audience, the 6½ million who were supposed to have gone to mobile screenings, is somewhat less credible. There were somewhere between 76 and 144 mobile units. To reach 6½ million, each unit had to play before 90,000 to 45,000 people a year, 234 to 123 a day. Given that the estimated average audience was less than this, around 100, the number claimed is too high.

Other figures calculated on the different basis of the total number of screenings in various venues over a single week reinforce the suggestion that these overall annual figures are more than just a little too high. For instance, in one week in November 1942, there were 1,224 film shows, a third in factories, a third to women's groups and villages and a third to more specialised audiences (Home Guard, Civil Defence, and the like). In March 1943 there were 1,298 such screenings (Forman, H., 1982, p. 229; Swann, 1989, p. 170). An average audience of 100 means an annualised maximum of less than 1½ million. And this result still requires accepting 100 people as the average audience. In some circumstances, specialised showings to farmers for instance, we are told that an audience of 20 was considered good (Forman, H., 1982, p. 231).

It would seem prudent to treat all these estimates with caution. Pronay (1989, p. 235) holds that Grierson's initial claim of 4 million was inflated tenfold. It was the provision of this misleading figure, easily seen as over-inflated at the time, to the Government's Select Committee on Estimates which contributed to his downfall as a civil servant. The head of the Central Film Library, William Farr, believed that in 1942/3, only 1 million saw loan films in that year, only 750,000 attended special shows and the mobile units reached only 2¼ million viewers – a total of 4 million (Swann, 1989, p. 169). This is one-third of the official estimate.

Swann suggests that the numbers could not have risen markedly in the last years of the war; and in the pre-war period they were clearly considerably less. It would seem that dividing all claims by anything from three to ten is reasonable.

However, whether the non-theatrical audience was actually measured in thousands or some millions is beside the point. For one fact is incontrovertible – it was minuscule when compared with the theatrical audience. The maximum annualised wartime audience claimed, 18½ million, was the number of tickets sold in one week by the cinemas in 1934. By 1944, weekly ticket sales were over 25 million (Arts Council, 1947, p. 198). Even by the most optimistic estimate, non-theatrical exhibition delivered 2 per cent of the cinema audience. The actual figure, certainly before the war, was likely to have been closer to 0.2 per cent.

This is not to deny that the non-theatrical experience might have been satisfying in ways different from the experience of the picture palace – the 'hang-over effect'. Audiences might have a particular identification with the content of the film. The possibility of audience discussion after the screening could also contribute to 'hang-over effect'. (George Stoney tells how he used the official US government films made by Pare Lorentz with rural audiences in this way decades after they were made.)

These are the sorts of factors leading to Grierson's suggestion that the films could deeply influence particular groups – 'middle opinion', in Aitken's phrase (1990, p. 182). Gus Macdonald (1978, pp. 21ff.), while acknowledging Grierson's failure to reach a mass audience, argued that 'in getting to the intellectuals and the socially involved, whether in churches, co-op halls, union branches, or schools, the documentaries may have helped encourage the confidence which brought about such a sweeping social change in the decade that followed.' To believe this, though, requires that those particular elements of identification and involvement be attached to the Griersonian output. There are, however, a number of reasons for doubting that this happened.

First, these putative millions watching the documentary film movement's films in the UK were neither so targeted nor led to debate. Second, the special groups did not necessarily want special programming. For instance, Helen Forman reported that during the war the Women's Institutes complained so bitterly about 'special women's films' that the MoI promised not to make any more pictures about cooking.

Third, there was the question of quality. I believe a serious commitment to alternative distribution would have required that 16mm be actively explored as an origination as well as a distribution medium as soon as the push of alternative venues began. Given the ambitions of the movement, this in turn could have led to a large enough market for the gauge to justify effective technical research and development. 'Public education' could have constituted a supervening necessity which would have moved the existing sub-35mm technology into the mainstream of production. Magnetic sound, for instance, languished everywhere except in Nazi Germany (Lafferty, 1983, *passim*). For the mainstream industry, secure behind the economic barrier 35mm represented, to ignore the smaller standard made sense: 16mm theoretically threatened the oligarchic exhibition situation. What is more curious is that the documentarists, having set their face against the industry and despite the existence of 16mm projectors in the alternative exhibition structures they were trying to create, also ignored it as a production standard. Grierson regarded the stock as amateur and avoided it.

The result was that 16mm, languishing as an underused amateur stock, was barely adequate for these exhibition purposes when the war started. So bad was the quality that Helen Forman reported a constant battle with the producers to make 35mm films with uncluttered soundtracks and clearly designed, bold and simple graphics so that they could be reduced to 16mm and still be visible and audible.

There also have to be serious questions about the physical quality of these screenings. Can the following description be dismissed as unlikely or exceptional?

'Lights please', shouted a voice over the babble of laughter and children's voices. 'Listen children', said the man operating the movie projector, 'for the second time I must remind you that this is a free show given by the Ministry of Information. If you cannot keep quiet you will have to leave'. ... The hall was ice cold, and the chairs were hard. The projector squeaked and rattled. (Forman, H., 1982, p. 229)

Helen Forman acknowledged that this might not be too untypical but pointed out that despite conditions of this sort the films were booked and booked increasingly. However, there was a war on. The films were free and, for instance, in the factories there was nothing much else to do during breaks. At best, the case for greater attention or influence – the 'hang-over effect' – must remain unproved, especially for the pre-war documentary.

What is undeniable in all this is that the audience for the documentary was small and the form, as Grierson developed it, failed to find a niche in the popular cinema. Almost from the beginning the Griersonian documentary was in a ghetto. Grierson pretended he wanted and liked being there, but it was a ghetto all the same. Because the sponsors demanded education, Grierson in effect sacrificed any populist advantage his artistic heritage might have conferred. Instead, the films twisted and turned on the horns of the dilemmas where sponsorship had skewered them, to little purpose, while the film-makers' artistic pretensions further alienated the mass audience. So Grierson did not command the mind of his generation, cumulatively or otherwise. He did not even attract its attention.

That too has turned out to be an enduring part of his heritage.

14

Running Away from Social Meaning in America

This critical reading of Grierson's project is not merely *ad hominem*. On the contrary, I want to argue that running from social meaning is an inevitable structural flaw in any film which creatively treats actuality in the name of public information, education, social purpose, or what you will – whoever makes it. That is why wherever and whenever such work has been undertaken it has almost always reproduced on the screen the facile attention to surface detail, and little else, which characterises the Griersonian *œuvre*.

Take the American example. Although the British work precedes the American by a number of years, there is no evidence that Grierson's activities (or, come to that, Turin's) were known or exerted any influence in the United States until the 1930s were well advanced – if then. The parallels, both behind and on the screen, between British and American documentary are, therefore, significant evidence for the above hypothesis.

At first sight, American antipathy to state media intervention, enshrined in the First Amendment's press protection clause, might seem to offer a very infertile climate for the application of Grierson's model of government-sponsored film-making. In fact, it did not. Social engineering in Britain needed to be pioneered as 'public education'. In the United States, on the other hand, the Department of Agriculture, at least, had long had 'public education' within its remit.

Part of the department's mission, as a draft of the enabling statute of 1862 makes clear, was 'to acquire and diffuse among the people of the United States useful information on subjects connected with agriculture in the most general and comprehensive sense of that word' (MacCann, 1973, p. 53). The department began making films in 1908 and was to continue with them as part of its educational extension services. By 1935, its production schedule was large enough to justify building a sound stage in Washington. Other agencies were more intermittent in their film work but by 1940 at least seventeen had dabbled in film. As Richard MacCann, the historian of US government sponsored film making, put it (1973, p. 44): 'Quantatively the record is surprising.'

Just as one film critic, Grierson, is widely credited with the paternity of the official documentary in the UK, so another film critic, Pare Lorentz, played the same father-figure role in the USA. However, just as government film in the UK does not start with Grierson's first effort, *Drifters*, so too (as the above indicates) it does not begin in the USA in 1936 with Lorentz's first documentary, *The Plow That Broke The Plains*. Nevertheless, Lorentz's five contributions to official US film-making have been distinguished from all other such activity. He too, unlike the faceless film workers in other government departments but very much like Grierson, turns into an artist. The received history of US documentary in the later 1930s becomes the story of Pare Lorentz.

However, Lorentz was even less effective than Grierson. He lacked Grierson's public relations skills and did little or nothing to protect his exposed Washington base. Because of the Department of Agriculture's prior claims and the closeness of his operation to controversial presidential policies, Lorentz's position was anyway more fragile than was Grierson's in Whitehall. At least until he squandered it, Grierson did have the consensual support of Conservative organs of government within the context of a liberal, if not a radical (Proudhonist?) milieu. It was the bureaucrats who were hostile.

Lorentz, on the contrary, was always embroiled in partisan politics. He failed to insert himself into the Department of Agriculture's film-making activities as effectively as Grierson had moved in on the publicity operations of the EMB and the GPO (Snyder, 1968, p. 89). Even at the height of the New Deal, the sort of federal agency that the Roosevelt administration spawned remained contentious. So in establishing his own operation in 1938, the United States Film Service, Lorentz achieved nothing permanent. The Film Service was even more fragile than the agencies under Agriculture's wing, since it was created by a flurry of presidential orders without congressional approval. This lack, and the constant use of relief monies to pay film production and distribution costs, caused the Senate to scuttle the service, and Lorentz, in 1940 (Snyder, 1968, pp. 149ff.). In contrast, the span in the UK from EMB to GPO to the Crown Film Unit (Ministry of Information) to the Central Office of Information (COI) runs from 1926 to the early 1950s and, fitfully, beyond.

Lorentz was widely identified as 'an enthusiastic New Deal Democrat' but, Jack Ellis suggests, one with a strong populist streak, which can – in US terms – embrace a conservative bent on many social issues (Snyder 1968, p. 31; Ellis, 1989, p. 101). Certainly, Lorentz was no radical. He would 'get socking mad if you tag him as a "leftist" or with any other cultist label, artistic or political. He insists', he told a magazine in 1939, 'he's a realist' (White, 1939, p. 9). Lorentz had little sympathy for radical film work. He found, for instance, that Eisenstein was 'blunt, exaggerated and naive in his story-telling. The workers are always right, the employers are always wrong' (Lorentz, 1975, p. 119).

At the same time, of course, he respected Eisenstein's techniques – as did Grierson. Reviewing *Thunder over Mexico* (1933), an edited version of Eisenstein's Mexican footage, Lorentz wrote (1975, p. 119): 'You can call this "montage in hieroglyphics", or whatever you like. I call it moviemaking.' Lorentz, as this quotation indicates, lacked Grierson's taste for theory and theorising but the work they produced was ideologically identical. Lorentz, too, ran from social meaning, positing bureaucratic solutions to deep-rooted social problems.

Take, for instance, the first two efforts, *The Plow* and *The River* (1937). They have similar structures, both being historical analyses leading to specific social solutions. In *The Plow*, the closing Beltville sequence illustrates a New Deal plan to resettle the rural dispossessed on smallholdings situated at the edge of the industrial cities. In *The River*, the solution to erosion and flood is deemed to lie with the work of the Tennessee Valley Authority, the epitome of Rooseveltian agencies.

So irrelevant is the Beltville sequence considered that prints of *The Plow* exist with it simply omitted. Received opinion considers this no loss. The sequence is 'a long string of Okies turning into a government camp somewhere in California', so puny a response to the dust bowl as to be 'Republican in its mockery' (MacCann, 1973, p. 66).

The TVA finale to *The River* elicits the same response: 'Unfortunately, the last one-third of the film (approximately ten minutes) does not have the imagination of the first two-thirds, as Lorentz was obligated to show what the government was doing to solve the problem' (Barsam, 1973a, p. 106). The solutions are 'tacked on', 'commercials' for the New Deal plan being proposed in each film (Ellis, 1989, p. 86). In this way, the overt political purpose of the films, what the sponsor actually paid for, is relegated to a position of secondary importance and the works are claimed for the realm of art. This mode of reception is identical to the response elicited by the Griersonian canon, and, I may as well add, Riefenstahl.

I agree that in Lorentz's case the closing sequences of these first two films are certainly bathetic; but I do not see them as being 'tacked on'. The films do not abruptly adopt a facile tone in offering these solutions; rather the turgid shallowness of these final sequences is the inevitable result of the facile romanticism that precedes them. In fact, these films are further perfect examples of the 'problem moment' structure.

Lorentz's political position was thus not limited to an overt final 'message'; the message was implied throughout. It was expressed primarily through Lorentz's own major personal contribution to the works, the scripts. Linguistically, it is specifically located within these scripts in the curiously passive or collective voice he adopted.

In *The Plow* the commentary poetically distances economic forces from real people; indeed, often it seems as if people are scarcely present at all: 'The cattle rolled into the old buffalo range'; 'Land syndicates sprung up over night'; 'Wheat will win the war'. The images reinforce this curiously unpopulated analysis. Tanks are cross-cut with tractors. The Great Crash is tickertape cross-cut with an African-American jazz drummer. (Not for Lorentz the standard radical iconography of tickertape, top hat, and cigar.) So we come to the heart of the film: 'Uncomplaining, they fought the worst drought in history'; and 'The sun and the wind wrote the most tragic chapter in American agriculture'. It is no wonder, I would argue, that they finished up uncomplaining in a Beltville.

The same impersonal forces roll through *The River*: 'There was lumber in the North ... The Railroads killed the Steamboats'; 'The water comes down hill spring and fall'; 'The old river has taken its toll from the valley'; 'Poor land makes poor people'.

When the destructive force is not inanimate it becomes a collective, and often guilty, 'we': 'We rolled a million bales'; 'We fought a war'; 'But we left the old south impoverished and stricken'. (It was inevitable that Lorentz, although a self-conscious West Virginian, should take an aggressively neutralist view of the Civil War (Lorentz, 1975, p. 223).) 'We mined the soil'; 'We cut the top off the Alleghenies and sent it down the River'; 'We left the mountains and the hills slashed and burned'; 'We planted and ploughed with no regard for the future'.

71

But the 'we' is not always guilty. In fact it is not actually any accusable group, as can be seen in the contrast between it and those do-gooders, 'the entire nation' or 'the Congress'. Thus, in contrast to what 'we' have done, 'In 1937, the entire nation sent help to the stricken people of the valley – Congress appropriated millions ... to rehabilitate the flood victims.' This eagerness to create blameless sequences of causes and effects eventually transforms the 'we' into a potentially positive force: 'We have the power to take the valley apart.' This 'we' then is glossed to 'you': 'You cannot plan for water unless you plan for land ... but you cannot plan for water and land unless you plan for people.' Which is what the TVA does. Q.E.D.

I am not disputing that this was effective writing, arguably one of the finest commentaries in the annals of the realist documentary, in both a literary sense and in the way in which it echoes and reflects the film's images. I am simply saying the obligation to the TVA and the government conditions the entire film, not only the last sequence. The pattern is the same as in the British films of the same period (or *Turksib*) – the social problem is but a moment in the history of the nation. Already plans are in train to correct it. Real causes and how effective those plans might be are beyond the remit of the film.

Proposing solutions in the inevitably 'can-do' style of the 'problem moment' film chimes particularly well with the American way. Perhaps this is why Lorentz was so adept at 'problem moment' structure. For instance, in 1939, called in to advise on *The City*, he suggested exactly this pattern: steel-town slums and New York congestion are but a problem moment in the history of a nation on its way from idyllic eighteen-century New England villages to equally arcadian contemporary garden cities.

As for distribution, Lorentz's experience again matches Grierson's. Hollywood was hostile to the government in its guise as competitor and refused to distribute *The Plow*. *The River*, somewhat curiously, was a different matter. Best Documentary at the Venice Film Festival in 1938, it was chosen by Walt Disney, although he was as opposed as any to government film-making, to fill the bill with *Snow White and the Seven Dwarfs* (Snyder, 1968, p. 79). Apparently, he simply admired the film's formal qualities, much as Lorentz admired Soviet work. So *The River*'s national release is the exception that proves the rule. No later Lorentz production was to be seen as widely.

If Hollywood (except for Disney – once – and Walter Wanger) distrusted Lorentz, so too did progressive opinion. His opportunism was called into question from the first, even as he was making *The Plow*. The realist project was as residually radical in America as it was in Britain. Lorentz, in turning to the only experienced cinematographers available to help him with *The Plow*, was forced to hire people whose commitment to a radical agenda was far greater than his own. He assembled the politically engaged team of Ralph Steiner, Paul Strand and Leo Hurwitz. All three of them were connected with the New York left film organization, Nykino. They started in Montana and worked down the country. By the time they got to Texas, the three men were, as *Variety* put it, 'on strike'. Lorentz complained in the 1939 interview that the film-makers wanted *The Plow* 'to be all about human greed and how lousy our social system was. And he couldn't see what this had to do with dust storms' (White, 1939, p. 9).

Lorentz did not make the same mistake again. For *The River* he hired a younger man, Willard Van Dyke. According to Van Dyke's own account, Lorentz considered him not nearly as experienced as Steiner but he did have the advantage that his 'ideas weren't so set either'. Nevertheless, Van Dyke was also in the Nykino circle and Lorentz was still worried enough to grill him one night about his New York leftist connections (Van Dyke, 1965, p. 45).[14]

Lorentz did not ape Grierson. Indeed, he insisted that 'he had never heard this term [documentary] until he was told he had made one' (White, 1939, p. 8). That is why the broad significance of this comparison between them turns on this ignorance, the crucial point being that the only way official films can be made is officially. Social problems were presented as passing phenomena, actively being corrected by the officials paying for the film. Serious social analysis was impossible. Like Courbet in 1848, the US and UK government documentarists of the 1930s preferred to be fence sitters as much as possible. Grierson and Turin ran away from social meaning. Lorentz had so much dust in his eyes that he could not see it either.

15

Staatspolitisch Besonders Wertvoll

Let us add consideration of another of the canonised documentarists. By introducing Riefenstahl, I most emphatically do not intend to suggest that the British and American documentarists were, like her, fascist. I simply want to reiterate the more limited point about how official films, officially funded and produced, run from social meaning. All that Grierson proposed as distinguishing marks separating the documentary from other non-fiction films can be seen in Riefenstahl's documentary work – a concern for public education and the creative treatment of reality, including manipulative editing of actuality material and reconstruction.

The Nazis articulated a comprehensive arts policy which favoured a particular version of realism to the exclusion of other styles – not for Nazi realists the aggressive concentration of socialist realism on the modern. Instead Nazi realism favoured genre painting which revisited the subjects of the French 19th century with images now intended to evoke not outrage but sentimentality. Painters were directed to portray 'men who follow the old callings close to nature', and to avoid 'the grim uniformity of the slums, urban desolation, and dives' (Hinz, 1979, p. 77). What was the cutting edge of social comment in the 1840s had become a romanticised lost world of rural verities; and what had replaced it, the alienation of the city, was *verboten*.

In general, the cumulative result of such controls was art 'that did not reveal alienation but disguised it' (Hinz, 1979, p. 53). 'It [the art of the Third Reich] was evasive, in that it made no reference whatever to what we regard as the salient features of the regime, and it was corroborative, in that it went along with what people most wanted to be told. As to the true nature of the times, it tells us nothing. As to the true nature of art, it tells us even less' (ibid., p. 75). At this level, then, a realistic documentary project, and indeed other non-fiction forms such as the newsreel, would fit perfectly within a range of state-supported artistic and media activities.

Riefenstahl has been embarrassed by the title on the release print of *Triumph of the Will* which claimed that the producer of the film was the party's own film section. She remembers private arrangements with Hitler and cites the independent nature of her Olympic film production company, set up a few years later, to prove the independence of this earlier work. But the reality is that film-making independence under National Socialism was impossible. Through the *Reichskammer* registration system, the arts, including the film industry, had been purged of Jewish and other 'alien' elements. Goebbels, who was – significantly, given Grierson's rhetoric – Reich minister for public education (*Volksaufklärung*) as well as propaganda, had also instituted, by a law of 1934, a positive vetting system for scripts (Welch, 1983, pp. 18ff.). He did not then want (or need) individual artists to be members of the party. In fact he preferred that they maintained a simulacrum of independence, which was all they had after *Reichskammer* registration and vetting, because this would serve the regime's propaganda aims more effectively.

Riefenstahl's claims as to her independence of the party/state – for example, '*Triumph of the Will* was never made from the party, never' (Hitchens, 1973, p. 101) – are thus fraudulent. She was, in effect, as much a civil servant as Grierson and Lorentz. The only difference is that she cannot be accused of political fence-sitting.

Triumph of the Will was not only produced 'by order of the Führer', it was made under the eyes of Herbert Seehofer (credited as the party propaganda consultant), classified as *Staatspolitisch besonders wertvoll* (politically especially valuable) and awarded the National Film Prize for 1935.[15] Moreover, the film has, despite its mind-numbing repetitiveness and interminable length, a careful and coherent structure which articulates a quite clear social/public-education purpose in an approved Griersonian manner.

This purpose was not, as many critics have suggested, solely to demonstrate that 'Hitler has come from the sky to kindle ancient Nuremberg with the prime Teutonic fire, to liberate the energy and spirit of the German people', and other such Nazi-inspired gibberish (Kelman, 1973, p. 163). Rather it was to present an image of a united party to both members and the general public at a point where the reality was quite other.

The importance of the Sixth Annual Party Congress and, therefore, of *Triumph of the Will* lay in the account both the event and the film offered of the aftermath of the Röhm putsch. The SA, the brownshirted street-fighting wing of the Nazis, was seeking to redefine its role now that the party was in power. Somewhat to Hitler's embarrassment, SA leader Röhm was still aggressively proposing a populist socialist agenda. He had also equipped the more than two million Brownshirts with machine-guns, declaring that 'The SA is and will be the arbiters of Germany's fate'. Pressured by Hindenburg, the rest of the German establishment, including the army, and the French, Hitler wiped out Röhm and his staff at Bad Wiesse immediately before the congress in the so-called 'night of the long knives' (Orlow, 1973, pp. 107 and 115).

The largely naive, complicit and laudatory reception which the film enjoys depends, crucially, on the synch being ignored. Even acute readings, such as Steve Neale's (1979, p. 85), tend to ground their arguments as to the film's ideological complicity only in the visual track. Indeed, as with the *Plow* prints which lack the Beltville sequence, there is a widely circulated version of *Triumph* which cuts the speeches out almost entirely. Yet, as with the Beltville shots, these are integral to the film. Virtually every synch word is directed towards the SA problem and the renegotiation of the Nazi Party's populist stance in the aftermath of the putsch. Placating the SA was the main object of the Sixth *Reichsparteitag*. That is why Hitler wore his Brownshirt SA uniform nearly all the time. It is also why Riefenstahl's selection from the speeches overwhelmingly included statements which praised the German working man even while they pointed out that the populist revolution was to be put on hold.

Speakers lauded the 'special youth' (the SA was dominated by twenty-year-olds as well as schoolteachers and minor civil servants) who were 'tempestuously charging forward'. These elements will 'one day be called upon to continue the efforts begun in stormy years of the 1918 Munich revolution'. 'One day' the populist revolution then attempted will be resumed – but not now! For now the message was that 'no revolution could last for ever without leading to total anarchy' (Taylor, 1979, pp. 179ff.). Yet this was still the 'Nazi-Sozi' Party, as it was originally nicknamed. The party was not abandoning the workers: 'One thought alone must dominate all our work: to make the German worker an upstanding proud citizen enjoying equal rights with the rest of the nation' (Winston, 1981, p. 106).

There were more direct references to the SA purge – for instance at the ceremony for the (party) fallen. This parade centred on the very flag that was stained with blood during the Munich putsch twelve years earlier. A contemporary American diarist described the scene in the Luitpold Stadium, where no less than 97,000 SA men were assembled, thus: 'Hitler faced his SA stormtroopers today for the first time since the bloody purge. There was considerable tension in the stadium and I noticed that Hitler's own bodyguard was drawn up in front of him separating him from the mass of Brownshirts' (Burdon, 1940, pp. 20ff.). Hitler did not rise to the occasion:

> 'Men of the SA and the SS. A few months ago, a black shadow spread over the movement. Neither the SA, nor any other institution of the party, has anything to do with this shadow. ... And if anyone sins against the spirit of the SA, this will not break the SA but only those who dare to sin against them. Only a lunatic or a deliberate liar could think that I, or anybody, would ever dissolve what we ourselves have built up over many long years.'

The eyewitness reports that the SA seemed unimpressed. Even as Hitler spoke, thousands of lower-level SA cadres were being dismissed from the party and some arrested. Between two and four hundred had already been killed.

Lutze, Röhm's successor and one of the least effective of Nazi speakers, introduced this speech of Hitler's by affirming that the SA is 'the same as we always were'. In another sequence, Lutze says: 'Comrades, many of you who are here tonight know me from those first years of our movement when I marched with you in your rank and file as an SA man. I am as much of an SA man now as I was then. We SA men know only one thing: fidelity to and fighting for the Führer.'

In the last speech of the film, Hitler returns to the task: 'In the past our adversaries, through suppression and persecution, have cleaned the party from time to time of the rubbish that began to appear. Today we must do the mustering out and discarding of what has proven to be bad.'

Triumph has the containment of the SA as its specific social purpose, as clear in its own way as the pitch for the Gas Council in *Housing Problems* or for the TVA in *The River*.

Not surprisingly, Riefenstahl, unlike Grierson and Lorentz, has been eager to deny her service to the state. For instance, understanding full well the import of those readings of the film, such as mine, which demonstrate her political engagement, she claims she knew nothing of the Röhm putsch because she was out of Germany over the summer of 1934 – as if radio and newspapers were yet to be invented:

I was at this time in Spain. ... I have not one moment thought of Röhm. ... Even Hitler has spoken only a very few words about this. ... Look, in the whole film as Hitler is speaking to the SA he mentions in one moment the Röhm affair. ... Hitler mentions this because it was coming out from this and so he mentions this. But I have not thought to make this ... it is only separate. (Hitchens, 1973, p. 101)[16]

I told Hitler that I don't know what is SA and what is SS. (Infield, 1976, p. 74)

The point here is not Riefenstahl's personal duplicity nor the extent to which she was, or was not, a covert, or an overt, Nazi. It is rather that, as the cases of Grierson and Lorentz (and Turin) also demonstrate, any realist documentary project pushes a film-maker towards the politics of social integration. These will take their colour from the state and can therefore be as easily fascist as liberal reformist or communist.

It can be argued that Nazi film policy was not only more overtly directed at social integration but was also more sophisticated about how to achieve it than were the film policies of the reformist states. Goebbels said in 1933: 'We are not satisfied with having 52 per cent of the nation as supporters while terrorizing the other 48 per cent. We want the people as the people, not only passively but actively' (Taylor, 1979, p. 158). He saw the media as crucial in this persuasive effort but thought they should be used obliquely. 'We National Socialists do not place any particular value on our SA marching across the stage or screen. ... The National Socialist government has never asked that SA films should be made. On the contrary – it sees the danger in a surplus of them' (ibid., p. 163).

This broad policy was confirmed by the comparative failure of *Triumph*. Goebbels was hostile to the project, a fact Riefenstahl was to use to good effect in her de-Nazification proceedings after the war. His reasons were exactly that the film seemed too much devoted to celebrating the *Führerprinzip* and too overtly concerned with the Röhm problem. The Führer, though, was of a different mind; hence the National Film Prize in 1935. But the general release showed that Goebbels was right after all. *Triumph* was not widely used in Germany at the time, being crass and boring and too obviously about Hitler's SA difficulties.

Riefenstahl claims that one of her demands of Hitler was that she should never be asked to do a film for the government again. Yet why would Goebbels want another? She had proved his point. International cinephiles, with a taste for fascist aesthetics, might award the film prizes at the time and continued critical acclaim. However, its real usefulness was (and is) as a species of awful warning, a mine of shots to illustrate the perils of fascism.

Goebbels, therefore, prevailed and the creative treatment of actuality in the name of social engineering took second place to newsreels, which became the main form in Nazi non-fiction cinema. The newsreel companies were left with a carefully preserved veneer of independence to increase their legitimacy – just as individual artists were encouraged to remain 'independent' of the party. UFA was purchased by the Nazis anonymously. It was not until November 1940 that these pretences were dropped and the *Deutsche Wochenschau* became the sole reel (Goethe Institute, 1984, pp. 4ff.; Taylor, 1979, p. 162; Welch, 1983, p. 195).

This does not mean that in Germany actuality material in both its news-reel and documentary forms was more popular than in other developed countries. On the contrary, the newsreels became so unpopular that by spring 1941 audiences had to be locked into the cinemas to make them watch (Welch, 1983, p. 200). As for documentary efforts, the antisemitic *Der ewige Jude*, *The Eternal/Wandering Jew* (1940), a compilation of Nazi 'facts' about the Jews, was a failure, unlike *Jud Süss*, a comparatively lavish costume melodrama about a supposed Jewish takeover of the state of Württemberg in 1733. This offered entertaining 'proof' of both the Jewish menace and the time-honoured German solution of judicial murder and expulsion. With audiences, the fiction worked apparently where the documentary did not (Welch, 1983, pp. 284ff.).

The pertinence of *Triumph* and its successors to my thesis is obvious. It is not the case that, as received opinion has it, Riefenstahl's 'film is true to the reality of Nuremburg' (Barsam, 1973, p. 34). Leaving aside the naivety of such truth claims, I would want to make a more fundamental point. *Triumph* is an official film which does nothing more or less than run from social meaning – even within its own limited terms. By this I mean not just that it obviously ignores the reality of the regime in line with the dominant thrust of the depoliticised aesthetics of the Nazis; *Triumph* more particularly runs from the actual political reality of the Sixth Annual Nazi Congress and, instead, works to support the big lie about the SA situation. In doing this, it reveals itself as a true Griersonian text, an 'official' film obsessed with surface and dedicated to social integration – in this case, the social integration of both the Brownshirts and the nation into the Führer's plan.

16

To Win New Comrades for the Cause

The argument that realist documentary avoids social meaning can be further bolstered by consideration of radical film production during this same period. Here the point is not similarity to Grierson's work, as with *Turksib* or the Lorentz or Riefenstahl *œuvre*, but contrast.

In the UK, the Griersonians, as we have seen, luxuriated in their ability to avoid taking sides in a decade when taking sides was to be, for many, of primary importance. 'The social situation is critical,' cried LeftFilmFront (1937, p. 1). 'Everywhere there are poignant scenes in the breakdown of capitalism and stirring aspects of the birth of a new order ready to be documented to win new comrades for the cause' – but not by the Griersonians. Despite the left rhetoric, their 'blunt ideals', to paraphrase MacNeice, never found such 'whetstones', their spirit never found its 'frontier' in such an agenda.

To the left of them were film-makers of the sort LeftFilmFront addressed. These were grouped in struggling 'independent' production entities, such as the British and American Workers Film and Photo Leagues (WFPL/FPL).[17] These radicals wanted no gap between their own political positions and what they put on the screen; and their work highlights the essential limitations of the Griersonian documentary to make good on its radical intentions, explicit and implicit.

A staple of this radical output was coverage of left political activities, needed in view of the predilection of the commercial newsreel companies to avoid the serious matters of the day – a predilection reinforced in some countries, the UK for example, by the censorship apparatus (Pronay, 1982, pp. 103ff.). Newsreels were, with or without formal censorship, 'a quite distinctly tainted source of news ... with a tolerance for "reconstruction" and a taste for trivialisation', although they were popular with audiences despite (or perhaps because of) all this (Winston, 1993, p. 183; Richards and Sheridan, 1987, pp. 392 and 409).

What effect the usual newsreel editorial approaches had in the UK on the coverage of one big story of the decade, the advance of fascism in Europe, has been well documented (Lewis, 1977; Aldgate, 1979). The results were equally lamentable with the other major story, the Depression. As we have seen, the documentary film movement avoided the Depression as well.

For all the documentarists' talk of putting the image of the British worker into their films, it is overstating the case to assert that, as a result, the 'working man in Britain saw and recognized himself on the screen' (Hardy in Grierson, 1979, p. 12). What he (or, come to that, she) saw was

a figure virtually without passion and anger, without unredressed griev-
ance, almost without culture and institutions, and above all a worker without politics. It could not have been a much more recognisable character
than the comic servants showing up in some of the feature film output.
The cumulative documentary movement image of the working class and
the lack of any such coherent image making in the newsreels were both
sins committed in the name of social integration. It was merely that the
one was of commission, the other omission.

The newsreels' sin of omission was well understood at the time. 'This,
then, is the newsreel,' wrote one left critic in 1929. 'Its object is not to
present news, but to breed a race of society gossipers, sport-maniacs, lick-
spittles and jingoes' (Macpherson, 1980, p. 133). The deepening economic and political crisis had no effect on this agenda. Formal research
analysis confirms this impression. Nearly half of all British newsreels were
taken up with news of royalty and sport in the summer of 1936, for
instance. In the USA it was fashion, disasters and sport (Aldgate, 1979,
pp. 77ff.). By the time of the war, the British were ignoring their newsreels
as a serious source of information; after it had started, a third were complaining spontaneously about them to pollsters (Lewis, 1977, p. 69;
Aldgate, 1979, p. 62).

Hence news coverage of the working class and left oppositional politics
was a first task for the 'independents'. Prominent among such political
activities were marches and rallies. In the UK, a 1922 hunger march from
Glasgow to London inaugurated a form of protest which was to become
common. Ten years later, the National Unemployed Workers Union
marched 3,000 people to London from all over the country. The last great
demonstration was the Jarrow Crusade of 1936. In 1932 and 1934, the
newsreel companies were asked by the London Commissioner of Police
not to cover the marchers (Hogenkamp, 1986, p. 111). Some of these
demonstrations were filmed by left-wing film-makers. Coverage of other
rallies survives too, such as May Day parades and anti-fascist counter-
demonstrations.

Strikes were also filmed. *Revolt of the Fishermen*, a Workers Film and
Photo League production, tells of a fishermen's strike during Easter of
1935. Instead of 'the chatter and clatter' of the titles in the market
sequence in *Drifters*, here the titles are direct, prosaic and emphatic, for
example 'Less than 30s a week' and 'Not covered by unemployment or
work comp'. These are realities overlooked by the Griersonians in the films
they made about this industry (Hogenkamp, 1986, p. 174, n. 62). *Tenants
In Revolt* (1939), about rent strikes in the East End of London, covers the
sort of activities Joris Ivens was referencing when he complained that
Housing Problems fell 'into the error of exotic dirt' because it ignored such
dramatic events (Hogenkamp, 1986, p. 208; Ivens, 1969, p. 88, n. 216).

In America, the response on the part of radicalised film people to media
misfeasance was much as it was in the UK. A direct impetus in the founding of the New York Workers Film and Photo League, for instance, was
the mainstream press's failure to cover a major demonstration of the
unemployed in New York in 1930 and the suppression of the newsreel
coverage of this event at the behest of the city's police chief (Campbell,
1985, p. 125). Initially, the 1937 police murder of ten striking steel-
workers in Chicago captured on film by a Paramount newsreel camera
operator was similarly suppressed (Rosenweig, 1980, p. 11).

The independents knew that something different could be done on the screen. They looked to *The March of Time*. This was not, strictly speaking, a newsreel, for all that it was awarded a special 1937 Oscar for 'having revolutionised' that form. As Raymond Fielding points out, it had done no such thing. It was twice as long as the average reel; it embraced rather than eschewed controversy; and it dealt with few topics per issue (and after May 1938 reduced itself further to covering only one story in each edition). None of this was copied commercially, not least because, unlike the newsreels which were issued bi-weekly, it came out monthly (Fielding, 1972, pp. 231ff.; Fielding, 1978, *passim*). For the political 'independents', though, these same factors – controversy, periodicity – made it something of a model, a model all the more potent because certain opinion on the left saw *The March of Time*, at least on occasion, as 'going fascist' (Macpherson, 1980, p. 121).

The New York circle of film-makers tried to produce a reply, specifically, to *March of Time*, to be called *The World Today*. They managed to complete only two editions (Alexander, 1981, pp. 125ff.). But long-form newsreels about foreign affairs, sometimes with documentary embellishments such as poetic commentary, were a more successful enterprise for the New York group.

For instance, a newsreel cameraman took them the first footage out of Yenan, Soviet China. It became *China Strikes Back*. Such was the dimension of this scoop that the film actually achieved a measure of commercial release (Campbell, 1978, pp. 291ff.). But in the US, even without theatrical distribution, effective fund-raising films, themselves funded by friends and supporters, were made on Spain, Czechoslovakia and Poland.

This pattern can be seen in the UK, too. Ivor Montagu and Norman McLaren went to Madrid with two 16mm cameras late in November 1936. Within the month they had premièred in London the results, *Fall of Madrid*, one of the most successful of British 'independent' films (Hogenkamp, 1986, p. 155).

The UK and US left were not alone in efforts of this kind. In Germany in 1927, the socialists attempted to produce a regular *People's Weekly Newsreel* as well as filming specific topics such as a children's camp or workers' welfare homes (Murray, 1990, p. 102). In Holland, with Joris Ivens offering guidance, newsreel production was undertaken from 1930 on, while in Japan, under extreme censorship conditions, the reels were made initially on 9.5mm stock (Hogenkamp, 1984, pp. 55ff.). Although the Censorship Law of 1919 in France specifically forbade the censorship of newsreels, nevertheless this was regularly ignored and coverage was suppressed (Buchsbaum, 1988, pp. 24 and 28ff.). However, there was no response *on film* until the events leading to the founding of the Popular Front in 1935 were covered by the left's own film-makers (Buchsbaum, 1988, pp. 56ff.; Hogenkamp, 1984, pp. 64ff.).

Since coverage of public demonstrations was, when permitted, a part of commercial newsreel output too, it must be noted that the images of public protest in particular (and the films in general) produced by the 'independents' tended to differ from the mainstream in a number of regards.

First, these films' makers were part of the events they were documenting, people within the political movement. This meant a committed editorial voice, expressed in intertitles which owed more to the Soviets than to commercial practice. In the British WFPL's *Newsreel No. 1* (1934), for instance, a story of the opening of a new co-op store is followed by the titles 'Whilst' and 'Capitalism Destroys' to introduce footage of the Hendon Air Pageant. 'Workers made these machines to destroy workers and their CHILDREN', proclaims a title.

Moreover, because they were insiders, the League camera operators took a point of view literally different from that of the commercial newsreels. In the FPL's *March Against Starvation* (subtitled, 'Story of the National Protest of 1936'), there are behind-the-scenes shots of the demonstration being planned and run. The New York FPL reel *Bonus March, 1932* covers the same elements. Sometimes, as with footage taken by the Detroit WFPL of a 1932 strike in which four people were killed by the police, there are shots of a panicking crowd taken by a panicking camera operator. As Jim Hoberman has pointed out, 'Commercial Newsreels were shot from a comfortable distance with telephoto lenses but FPL cameramen ... were in the midst of the action' (Rosenweig, 1980, p. 7). 'As a matter of fact', wrote one of these cinematographers about one such demonstration, 'we "shot" the March not as "disinterested" news-gatherers but as actual participants in the March itself' (Campbell, 1985, p. 129). This applies to the UK reels as well.

Second, the films were not limited by the event being covered. The event is but a peg on which to hang other material, as in the *March Against Starvation*. This in fact becomes nothing less than an 'independent' version of *Enough to Eat* (cf. *The Fishermen's Revolt* v. *Drifters*). The Boyd report is extensively cited in this film as it is in the Griersonian *Enough to Eat*, but with a difference. In the place of impotent references to poverty as a 'difficult long-term matter', there is, for instance, a title, 'Four and a Half Million People Spend Less Than 4/- A Week On Food', followed by a shot of what 4 shillings would buy in 1936. The actual images of the marchers, animated maps of their routes and the final rally in Hyde Park on 8 November are much augmented by other material suggested by the event and the film-makers' general political stance. In *Le Mur des fédérés* the French socialists, in much the same way, augmented coverage of a demonstration in 1935 with images of the Commune and photographs of nineteenth-century socialist leaders (Buchsbaum, 1988, p. 59).

As a result of these techniques, the line between newsreel and documentary becomes very blurred, especially with the films on foreign wars. Joris Ivens was in New York at the time Montagu was going to Madrid. Ivens persuaded John Dos Passos, Lillian Hellman, Ernest Hemingway, Archibald MacLeish, Clifford Odets, Dorothy Parker and Herman Shumlin to back him. The few thousand dollars raised were used to shoot, with Hemingway in attendance as scriptwriter, *The Spanish Earth* (1937) (Ivens, 1969, pp. 103ff.; Alexander, 1981, p. 150). These same backers raised funds for Ivens to make *The 400 Million* (1938) on the Sino-Japanese War (Ivens, 1983a, pp. 17f.; Alexander, 1981, p. 190).

This leads to a third point. In a practical sense, 'independence' describes nothing more or less than a certain type of private sponsorship. This, though, is no small matter. I have been trying to demonstrate the apparently by no means obvious point that the official sponsor closely called the realists' tune in various countries. Alternative sponsors were (and are) necessary if different tunes are to be called; if, indeed, the flight from social meaning, which is an inevitable consequence of official support, is to be avoided.

Because of their funding, the war documentaries of the 1930s are particularly vivid in demonstrating how such private sponsorship could allow for a more structured analysis of situations than was usual in the mainstream documentary world. For instance, *The Spanish Earth*, although it was being made to raise money for ambulances, centrally addresses the issue of agricultural productivity and, by implication, land ownership. To feed besieged Madrid the farmers collectively work to build a new irrigation system. The filmic device connecting this activity to the battle is an enlisted village son returning on leave to witness the work.[18]

Despite appeals to 'art' and other arguments by some critics and historians, there is, in fact, an almost total isomorphism between the political attitude of the sponsor – whether official, commercial or private – and the political stance of the final film. Sponsors, by and large, got what they paid for. As we have seen, the British gas industry, say, and social reform went sufficiently hand in hand to allow the Griersonians to make just those films – *Housing Problems*, *Enough to Eat* – which seem to come closest to a left political analysis. But the limits of such analysis are those of the Gas Council, not the documentarists.

The same can be seen in the USA, despite the confusions caused because the radical film-makers were also working for Lorentz in the official documentary movement. When officially sponsored, they were, as we have seen with *Plow*, as inhibited as were their British counterparts. When they were working as 'independents', they were independent. For example, they even turned down support from the American Civil Liberties Union when it came with suggestions about content (Campbell, 1978, p. 221). But the far more usual pattern was that the film-makers had to live with the editorial problems of sponsorship.

For instance, Willard Van Dyke, for the American Institute of Planners, could only ask questions in *The City*. Over the slums, the commentary says, 'Who built this place? What put us here? We're asking. Just asking.' And answer came there none. The following year, 1940, in *Valley Town*, which Van Dyke made for the Sloan Foundation to address the issue of job displacement through mechanisation, he got a little closer to cause, essentially because the Commission was just that much more open-minded. 'Why are we finished?' asks a voice. 'Because the strip mill can make the steel cheaper,' comes the answer. In a curious Brechtian song sequence, by Mark Blitzstein, the unemployed worker's wife seems to come close to referencing a workers' paradise: 'Far away, there's a place / with work and joy and cheer / far away, oh far away from here.' However, we are also informed: 'We can't blame the machines. They do what they're told to do. They benefit a great many people in a great many towns.' This in effect turns the film, once again, into a plea for social integration. The Sloan Foundation permitted Van Dyke slightly more freedom than did the American Institute of Planners but it did not allow him to confront basic issues.

The obviousness of this point about the effect of sponsorship can also be shown with Ivens himself. When he was funded by industry or government, he could no more escape paying the price of that embrace than anybody else. For instance, he made *Power and the Land* (1940) for Lorentz's US Film Service and the Rural Electrification Administration (REA) of the US Department of Agriculture. Stephen Vincent Benet's commentary is more interested in stereotyping rural life than in exposing social problems. The commentary says of the farm family at dinner: 'They may not say much but they have the word "home" in their hearts.' Elsewhere we are told that their land supports five 'healthy Americans' and 'that's something for land to do'.

The REA was concerned throughout that this was not going to be the Lorentz film they thought they had commissioned, but rather a piece by a radical Dutch director. Lorentz kept a close eye on Ivens (Snyder, 1968, p. 129). In such circumstances, Ivens quickly realised that 'I could not include the drama of the conflict between farmers and private utilities' (Ivens, 1969, p. 190). Only in the constant references to collective action – 'A farm is the oldest co-operative there is' – and to the power companies' need for profit can a tincture of Ivens's politics be seen.

The distinction here, however, is not between official and private. Sponsors, whether official or private, who were dedicated to the status quo or reformism got films so dedicated. It is just that the chances of a sponsor wanting change or revolution were greater if the sponsor was not official; but not always.

Paul Strand found like-minded sponsors in officials of a radical Mexican government, who were impressed with his work as an art photographer, and together they produced in *Redes/The Wave* (1936) an 'official' film with, as it were, uncompromisingly 'independent' politics. *The Wave* is about the plight of a Mexican fishing village. In its use of fisherfolk as actors, it is not a little like *The Savings of Bill Blewitt* – in effect an early 'docudrama'. It is also, again somewhat like *Blewitt*, not comfortable with synch. In general a tentative soundtrack slows the movie down enormously, as do the occasional cues on camera and other equally basic editing problems. Not even Strand's exquisite shots entirely overcome these deficiencies.

The importance of *The Wave* in this context is that Strand makes the economics of fishing, which is ignored in the British films about the industry, his whole point. In *The Wave* it is not the poeticised sale of the catch but the brutal murder of a strike leader, protesting at the price of the catch, which provides the climax. Strand's sponsor lets him report what Grierson's sponsor (according to Grierson) did not want to hear. Strand's fisherman says, 'Your brain gets wet and your heart gets dry.' Grierson's says, 'Shut yer blather.'

As final examples of this third point about sponsorship and independence, let us consider the rare situation where the film-maker and the sponsor are, in effect, one and the same. *A propos de Nice* (1930) and *Las Hurdes: Land Without Bread* (1933) can be placed in such a category.

Vigo's sponsor was his father-in-law, who put up enough money for a camera and film without any interest in the result. Vigo saw the skull beneath the skin in Nice, a city, he thought, 'dedicated to death' (Gomes, 1971, p. 56). He produced a vision of contrasts, rich foreigners and poor natives, public gaiety which generates nothing but refuse, life that kicks against death and the fires of hell (or industry). *A propos de Nice* is bitter enough and highly textured enough to avoid the simplicities of agitprop, not least because of the iconography of Catholicism with which it plays.

Buñuel made *Land Without Bread* with funds won in a lottery (Matthews, 1971, p. 106). Thus beholden only to fate, he produced a parody of a travelogue, complete with graphics as a species of the 'Voice of God' and a narrative voice that is 'insolent' in its 'indifference' to the images (Rubinstein, 1983, p. 8). *Land Without Bread* is so 'independent' as to call into question the implicit truth claims of the realist cinema in general – to call them into question and to mock their pretension.

It is hard to see who would sponsor either of these films since nothing they touch is presented as being untainted – accurate reflections of 'a low, dishonest decade'. As a critic (Mellin, 1978, p. 251) has said of *Land Without Bread*, Buñuel is denouncing, as a crime, 'the human condition itself'. Paymasters for such messages are hard to find.

In general these 'independent' film-makers were different from their counterparts inside the documentary film movement (or themselves when working officially). They were much more part of what they were filming, seeking controversy, topicality and commitment. They were much more willing to exploit the medium by melding newsreel and documentary and other experiments. (Griersonian experimentation, some work on sound aside, was otherwise limited to the most overt advertising projects which are only connected to the documentary at all because the GPO produced them.) Above all, the independents were eager to discover and reveal social meaning – because of the nature of the sponsorship and support they obtained. The existence of these independents demonstrates that it was possible to make films, even in Britain, without embracing the political confusions of the documentary film movement and official sponsorship.

This does not mean that, as a rule, all these films therefore penetrated beneath the surface of their subjects and avoided the other pitfalls of the mainstream. In fact, political engagement created its own difficulties. It would be comforting to be able to hold the independents up straightforwardly against the Griersonians, but that is not quite possible.

First there was the vexed issue of 'technical' or 'professional' standards. Consider *Construction* (UK, 1935), one of the few films actually to be made by members of the working class themselves, as a prime example of this problem. *Construction* is a simple parable, as it were, of how an instant strike instantly reinstates a worker who had been dismissed for trying to organise the union. On the one hand, no better example of the specifically different point of view in these films can be found. *Construction* was 'made', as the opening title tells us, 'by the men on the job'. Not only that, it was apparently largely shot in secret without the permission or knowledge of their bosses. As a result, it gives a remarkable sense of surreptitious filming on an actual work site.

Yet all this is at some cost. It is unconvincing as both agitprop and film. Like many 'independent' films it in no way replicates normative production standards. It departs from norms of composition, narrative structure and image quality. 'Some of the shots are blurred,' Hogenkamp reports (1979, pp. 262ff.). Indeed they are; and yet more curious is the narrative structure which becomes particularly opaque at the climax. Although this level of narrative confusion was uncommon, *Construction* is by no means unique within the independent archive in flouting filmic norms. On occasion every mainstream 'standard' was traduced.

In *Workers Newsreel No. 2* (1934), for instance, coverage of the counter-demonstration to a London fascist rally is augmented with coverage of an anti-fascist sports rally in Paris. This footage 'is in poor over-duped condition, but was significantly included to reinforce the message that only an International United Front could defeat Fascism' (Wegg-Prosser, 1977, p. 246). Such willingness to allow ideological concerns to override the established 'standards of technical quality' would, of course, not have been permitted either in the commercial newsreels or by Grierson. The results could be easily dismissed as 'amateur'.

'New developments had taken place in left-wing *amateur* film production' is how the standard history of the British cinema describes this entire effort in the UK (Low, 1979b, p. 178 – my italics). Even sympathetic critics, then and now, remarked on the 'rudimentary', 'naive' or 'amateur' quality of the work as a whole. Indeed, overall, the films exhibit what some see as nothing but an 'amateur aesthetic' with 'no coherent point of view, no coherent strategy of address in the sequencing of the images' (Neale and Nash, 1977, p. 79).

I want to stress that this is not necessarily a disaster, if these are aesthetic *choices*, rather than accidents. It is possible to justify such an aesthetic strategy on political grounds. 'Standards' are not ideologically neutral and the norms of production, reinforced by audience expectation, have always created barriers to entry for film-makers which work to limit the range of cinematic expression. Breaking those norms can therefore be positioned as a deliberate blow against hegemonic practice. For instance, it can be argued that *A propos de Nice* and *Land Without Bread* depart from the norms exactly to critique them.

Joris Ivens also understood the need to escape from accepted aesthetics. He had first discovered this while making *Misère au Borinage* in 1933. *Borinage* was filmed in the same Flemish coalfield where Vincent Van Gogh had lost his faith half a century earlier. The film deals with labour organisation and protest in the aftermath of a bitter strike and, although sponsored by a cine-club, was far from 'poetic' in style – not by accident, as Ivens pointed out in his autobiography (1969, p. 87f.):

> Critics have said that the absence of 'interesting' photography in *Borinage* can be explained by the poor and primitive equipment that was used. This is not the explanation. The style of *Borinage* was chosen deliberately and was determined by the decency and unrelieved plight of the people around us. We felt it would be insulting to people in such extreme hardship to use any style of photography that would prevent the direct honest communication of their pain to the spectator. ... During the filming of *Borinage* we sometimes had to destroy a certain unwelcome superficial beauty that would occur when we did not want it. When the clean-cut shadow of the barracks window fell on the dirty rags and dishes of a table the pleasant effect of the shadow actually destroyed the effect of dirtiness we wanted, so we broke the edges of the shadow.

The result is a picture of poverty – unexotic dirt – of some brutality and satiric edge. For instance, a doctor literally walks over a sea of children to get to a sick, and filthy, baby. The bed in the barracks where these families live is turned into a table during the day. But not to worry – there's a 'Museum of Hygiene' nearby.

The application of this studied overall unpicturesque approach – an 'accusatory' or 'confrontational aesthetics' – was also employed in the Ivens war films made later in the decade (Delmar, 1979, p. 29; Waugh, 1982, p. 32). (Conversely, the film he made for Lorentz, *Power and the Land*, is very pretty – birds circling the farm at dusk, horses in the mist, and so on. On behalf of the American government, Ivens luxuriated in the 'superficial beauty' of St Clairsville, Ohio, without any hint of accusation or confrontation.)

Unfortunately, few film-makers were as much in command or as conscious of these issues as Ivens. The 'independents' as a whole made no coherent attempt to tackle general audience hostility to 'accusatory' or 'confrontational aesthetics' or any other departures from the norm. They were abetted in this failure by committed audiences who, at least on occasion, received the films with enthusiasm whatever the techniques and aesthetics. New comrades might not be easily won for the cause with such works but this was ignored. There was no attempt to raise awareness of the ideological implications of film-making norms, even among the committed during the 1930s.

Ralph Bond, a leading pioneer of the workers' film movement, was still not quite making this connection in the 1970s when he wrote (1979, p. 255) that these films 'were received with enormous enthusiasm *despite their technical limitations*' (my italics); this from a film-maker aware enough to be worried by the need to obey normative standards, coded as an 'apeing of Hollywood', as early as 1929. Discovering alternative technically viable, and above all affordable, modes of practice proved very difficult for him and for others.

There was a specific and ongoing failure to see how the marketing of 16mm as an 'amateur' stock struck at the production and reception capabilities of the 'independents' (16mm was introduced by Kodak in 1923 specifically to open up the home movie-making market). Again, some saw the importance of addressing the issues raised by amateurism and 16mm. Irene Nicholson, for example, writing in January 1936 in the only newsletter the WFPL managed to produce, said: 'Sub-standard is the only way out. But it must be taken seriously, built up into an organised working form, not left as a hobby' (Wegg-Prosser, 1977, p. 246). But most did not see it this way and a few of these were actively opposed to 16mm. 'Amateur' was a term of abuse.

So Bond, despite his worry about copying Hollywood, could write of an amateur group in 1929: 'Everybody recognises the difficult conditions under which the British amateurs have to work today. But these difficulties cannot always be used as an excuse for careless work. Carelessness is impermissible in amateur production' (Macpherson, 1980, p. 199). It is hard to see what 'carelessness' might mean, unless it also referenced mainstream norms in some fashion.

A certain confusion confounded the search, in so far as there was one, for non-Hollywood film-making models. For instance, 'hard study', albeit of Pudovkin as well as Rotha, is recommended for amateurs by some in left film-making circles while such an interest, even in the Soviets, is decried by others, such as Huntley Carter writing in *The Plebs* in 1931, as merely talk 'about technique, "montage" and *cinema mind* ... obscuring the socialism in films and loudly despising all films that need no technical tricks to make their socialist message clear' (Macpherson, 1980, p. 140). This confusion was then compounded by 16mm's amateur aura.

Yet, whatever the specific loss of status involved in using 16mm, there was – at least in Britain – one inestimable advantage to using that gauge. Since it was amateur, it was not subject to censorship. Major agitprop productions appeared in 16mm, such as *The Road to Hell*, a 40-minute silent made by the Socialist Film Council at a cost of £66 and released in 1933. Of the 93 titles in the UK 'independent' archive listed by Hogenkamp (1986, pp. 215ff.) the single largest category is 16mm silent (49 titles). There are 7 16mm sound titles, 5 films on 9.5mm. This is against 19 titles on 35mm, 9 with sound. (The balance are lost, their formats uncertain.)

In the USA, the amateur problem never really arose since the left film-makers were dominated by professional still photographers, including major talents such as Paul Strand. These were people who could sustain their political commitment by a few days commercial work a month (Alexander, 1981, p. 109). As a result, the American WFPL newsreels are markedly more in line with mainstream standards than are the British ones. These practised camera operators, as we have seen, constituted the only available pool of technicians for Lorentz. Thus the American Film and Photo League, although aware of 16mm as a production possibility and already distributing films in 16mm sound by 1933, nevertheless tended to work with 35mm silent cameras (Alexander, 1981, pp. 37, 50 and 229, n. 9). This allowed for occasional theatrical screenings (Campbell, 1985, p. 127). Shooting on 35mm continued in radical film-making circles after the demise of the League (Alexander, 1981, plates 6, 19, 20ff. and 174).

The failure to create a coherent analysis to justify or explain the gap between the independents' technical standards and those of the main-stream reflects a second and more potent failure of analysis. The left film-makers seemed not to understand how problematic the entire realist enterprise was. They were as committed to an uncomplicated vision of camera truth as were the Griersonians. Bond argued in 1935 that: 'We can take our cameras out into the streets, and at the expense of little more than film, patience and an infinite capacity for taking trouble, photograph our material as it actually exists' (Macpherson, 1980, p. 150).

As a result, 'Montagu and Bond did not see themselves as political film makers engaged in a struggle in ideology' any more than the Griersonians saw themselves as active proponents of social integration (Ryan, 1980, p. 59). Both parties were merely, according to their own thinking, engaged in recording material as it actually existed. In consequence, for Montagu and Bond, their sort of film-making remained somehow apart from the political struggle. (This was despite the fact that, paradoxically, they themselves understood that film-making was itself a species of work, as their pioneering efforts in forming the professional film union attests (Avis, 1983, p. 10; Bond, 1980, p. 10).)

This naivety about the realist image became divisive in the USA. For some in the League, their very mastery of the basics of newsreel coverage bred a discontent, a desire to go further into the area of dramatic 'recon-struction'. This was seen as a crucial next step 'to widen the scope of the document, to add to the document the recreated events necessary to it but resistant to the documentary camera' (Hurwitz, 1934, pp. 14f.). There were extensive precedents for such dramatic techniques. The reconstruc-tion of everyday, iterative, activities was (and is) commonplace. What had been straightforward instructions to his cast for Flaherty on *Nanook* had become, of necessity with synch, full-scale dramatic direction for Watt on *Blewitt*; but such directorial intervention was still regarded as a totally acceptable documentary (and indeed newsreel) production technique.

In both the silent and sound periods, the 'independents' were as ready to tell people to do things for the camera as were their mainstream rivals. Ivens, for example, had routinely reconstructed events from the very beginning of his career – the windows closing against the shower in *Rain* (1929), for instance. But what some in New York now wanted to explore was rather more interventionist than this. Again, though, Ivens had shown the way.

In *Borinage* he had not hesitated to use reconstruction on a new scale, to film a specific episode that had taken place in the past (Ivens, 1983b, pp. 81ff.). When the coal owners blacklisted the miners' leaders, police were sent to seize their families' goods and chattels. The strikers developed a technique of passive resistance to this which Ivens and Storck wanted in the film. But the strike was over, so the film-makers reconstructed one incident using the actual house and same people, except for the two gendarmes, who were miners dressed in uniforms obtained from an opera company in Brussels. The event consisted of these two parties staring each other down in the main room of the house, until the 'policemen' slunk away. As a sequence, it worked because the demands made of the 'actors' were in the nature of the case minimal (Ivens, 1969, pp. 89f.).

This was the sort of thing some in the New York group wanted to emulate. Others believed, as a banner put it, that 'THE CAMERA IS A WEAPON IN THE CLASS STRUGGLE' but could only be so if 'real' images were presented (Campbell, 1978, p. 60). They thought reconstruction meant a 'synthetic' dilution of the revolutionary power of the camera to 'capture reality' and a split occurred. The group, led by Steiner and Hurwitz, who wanted to move towards fiction broke away (Hurwitz, 1975, p. 10).

In addition to a lack of an aesthetic strategy and an uncomplicated vision of the power of the camera to capture 'reality', there was also a third confusion, that of purpose. Were the films to build solidarity or 'to win new comrades for the cause'? This difference, which can be seen as revisiting the 'standards' problem but this time from the point of view of audiences rather than film-makers, profoundly affects the film-making strategies deployed, but it was never clearly articulated.

For some, especially in the British Labour Party and the British unions, films targeted at the committed were coded as propaganda while films to persuade 'new comrades' had to be 'entertaining'; and, it was felt, 'propaganda is always an unwelcome stranger in the home of entertainment' (Jones, 1987, p. 156). The position was 'films first and propaganda second'; that is, professional production norms had to be met so that the public would be engaged and the support for 'the cause' would increase. 'Film propaganda had to be conducted via the commercial cinema' or else run the danger of merely 'preaching to the converted' (Bond, 1979, p. 255). (It is also not accidental that the *engagé* professionals to do this work had just been organised into a union which saw 'amateur' production of any kind as a threat (Macpherson, 1980, p. 151).)

But obeying mainstream norms was fraught. In the UK and the USA, 'standards' worked, as they always do, to limit production because of the expense involved. So although the group around Hurwitz began to use fictional techniques, for instance, in *People of the Cumberland* (1937) to show the murder of a union organiser, making a feature took years of effort. It was not until 1942 that Hurwitz and Strand finally produced, in *Native Land*, the sort of full-length film with extended fictional elements Hurwitz and Steiner had began to argue for eight years earlier.

In *Native Land* there are reconstructions of actual events, as well as a totally fictional sequence about a union *agent provocateur* which dominates the movie. Although the dramatic sections are now assured – with, for instance, a fine if somewhat curiously stylised agitprop performance from Howard Da Silva as the management spy – it is the conventional documentary elements which survive best. (For example, over shots of the city, Paul Robeson, the narrator, says, 'It was Thursday morning in a thousand places. Friday morning ... or Monday morning. American day. ...') Either way, the effort was so great that it was not to be repeated; and the film still failed to find a large general audience.

The possibility of the left obeying mainstream fictional production norms was greatest where a coherent exhibition structure, unpersecuted by political censors, was institutionally connected with a film-making arm.

This was not the case in Britain and America, where either the distribution and production were done by different radical groups with little overlap, or the censors prevented effective box office receipts being achieved, or both. The main problem in the UK was that the commercial exhibition of Soviet films was prohibited, so that they were seen only in more limited venues, yielding insufficient revenues to sustain production. Even the London Film Society, which was seen as middle-class because of its high membership fee, only charged 25 shillings, a significant sum in terms of discretionary spending but not enough to create the sort of cash flows feature production required.[19]

Further party and private funding was not forthcoming in sufficient quantity to permit a feature production programme either. In such a situation the position of the British Labour Party and the TUC in arguing for feature production was, in effect, disempowering. Bond pointed out the naivety of believing that the industrial and censorship structures in place at the time would ever have permitted such production.

On the other hand, in Germany, during the last years of Weimar, and in France, during the Popular Front period, the conditions were different. Distribution and production were integrated and the strategy was to put 'films first' by making features. In Germany, the socialists, the communists and even the equivalent of the FPL (*Volksfilmverband* – VFV) made features, some of which were well received at the box office. The communists funded their efforts from the proceeds of distributing Soviet work. *Potemkin* was something of a box office success in Germany and allowed for no less than three feature films to be made (Murray, 1990, pp. 121ff.). Later, there were direct co-productions between the USSR and the film organisation of the German Communist Party (KPD). The German socialists funded two films from their own resources (Murray, 1990, p. 98f.).

In France, feature production had the support of the parties, if only during the Popular Front period. This phase starts with *La Vie est à nous*, a 62-minute 1936 campaign film which integrates newsreel elements and speeches by leaders into a fictional narrative. It concludes with Renoir's feature film *La Marseillaise*, which was released in 1938 after the Popular Front government had fallen (Buchsbaum, 1988, pp. 83ff.).

But feature production was not necessarily the answer. The propaganda in these films took such a second place to mainstream demands that, on occasion, it became invisible. For instance, although written by Béla Balázs and possibly intended as parody, *One + One = Three* played like a social comedy. Indeed, the only interesting thing about it, apparently, was that it was produced by Prometheus, the film arm of the KPD (Murray, 1990, p. 127).

Similar points can be made, albeit not so dismissively, about *La Marseillaise*. One can agree with Bazin's note that 'Renoir puts heroic acts into concrete perspective, in psychological relief. He demythologizes history by restoring it to man' (Bazin, 1973, p. 66). But what about politics? On the one hand Bazin might have been correct in regretting the 'tremendous didactic naïveté' of *La Vie est à nous*, but on the other hand in *La Marseillaise* the didacticism is ineffectual. The only villains are foreign and the most sympathetic character in the film turns out to be the King (played by Renoir's brother) (Buchsbaum, 1988, pp. 258ff.).

One can only wonder how 'the left-wing labour mystery film' Dashiel Hammett was plotting with Ralph Steiner would have tackled these problems (Alexander, 1981, p. 184).

The one chance was that the approach taken in some of these films might create a new and popular genre which would combine the propaganda needs of 'the cause' with the otherwise apparently disempowering requirements of 'entertainment'. There is a mixture of documentary, docudrama and dramatic elements in *Native Land* and *La Vie est à nous* which could perhaps have become the mark of such an *engagé* feature if circumstances had permitted a sufficiency of such productions for a genre to emerge. As it was, the French followed the Germans into the realm of the purely fictional and the Americans exhausted themselves, as it were, getting one full-length film made.

So, finally and perforce, the 'independents' finished up preaching to the converted or not preaching at all. And even here there was a measure of confusion. I agree with Bond that preaching to the converted was a far from contemptible activity. As Bond claimed (1979, p. 255), the converted 'needed stimulation and encouragement to fortify their faith' – especially in the face of uniformly hostile media. But again this task was not as clearly articulated as it might have been. Although the films, features apart, were not in any sense 'popular', yet neither was it acknowledged that they were destined for specialised audiences. For all that they failed to reach large numbers of uncommitted people or give those people expected production values, the rhetoric was all about winning converts.

This is not to say, however, that the work was without audience. Grierson's activities are often justified on the dual grounds that he got the films made and he reached large audiences. While I do not dispute that he did the former (obviously), I have here simply suggested that so did the 'independents'. As to audiences, I have disputed how large Grierson's were. I would like to add to that argument a parallel corrective about the audience for the 'independents', which is usually dismissed as too small to be of any significance at all. This is somewhat too harsh.

The films did fortify the faithful. There are reasons for believing that, in terms of Grierson's idea about 'hang-over effect', these independent films were more successful than his. Bond argued in 1931 that the radical subject matter could be 'sufficient compensation for the lack of plush seats, mural decorations, super organs, and beautifully attired usherettes' (Hogenkamp, 1986, p. 77). Films were a regular feature of the British radical meeting. Between 1927 and 1939 Trevor Ryan (1983, p. 122) estimates that at least one radical film a month was made in the UK.

Although he estimates the average audience at no more than 50, it is possible that as many as 100,000 saw these movies in 1935–6 and 200,000 in 1938 (Ryan, 1983, pp. 124f.). There was, on occasion, an even more direct test of the 'hang-over effect': money was collected for the cause. Montague's *Fall of Madrid* is credited with raising no less that £6,000 for Spanish Aid in collections of £10–40 per screening (Hogenkamp, 1986, pp. 155ff.).

Because they worked in 35mm, the Americans had occasional theatrical screenings, although nothing that would resemble a release, except for *China Strikes Back* (Campbell, 1978, p. 62). Campbell (1978, pp. 219ff.) shows that Frontier Films, the collective where Hurwitz, Steiner and Strand finished up, had receipts of over $115,000 between 1937 and 1942. This was a not inconsiderable sum when a documentary could be made for around $5,000, although not enough to sustain the collective and its production plans.

While one cannot claim that the films won many (or any) new comrades for the cause, they nevertheless did reach at least some of the faithful, and that regularly.

In conclusion, then, the 'independents' were unable to create an alternative aesthetic strategy to the mainstream, were naive about the nature of the realist image and were confused about their targeted audience. As Trevor Ryan points out (1980, p. 57), these factors will not allow their approach to be held up as a totally successful alternative to that of the documentary film movement:

> The presentation of the 'real' on film was thought to be self-evident and supposedly unproblematic to the audience; it was assumed that the audience was also a unity, possessing a unified political consciousness, at one with the subject on the screen. The implications of these assumptions for 'independent' film practice were considerable ... virtually exclusive reliance on 'realist' techniques of cinematography; concentration on representing 'workers in struggle' – presupposing that the significance of this experience was readily apparent to workers in other spheres, thus overlooking the ideological and political fragmentations which characterised that audience.

Ryan is thus right (ibid., p. 51) to warn against simplifying and mythologising the film-making efforts of the left during this decade and thereby creating a counter-history to the received account but one equally flawed.

However, for the purposes of my argument, I do not need the 'independents' to be entirely successful. Their strengths and shortcomings are not of importance in this context. What is significant is that there were film-makers who managed to produce material, however marginal, arising from, rather than at odds with, their announced political and personal positions. And they had an audience, however small. Their very existence, therefore, gives the lie to Griersonian claims that any pusillanimous political behaviour was both unavoidable and necessary. Bond, Montagu, Ivens, the New York group, Buñuel, Vigo and others involved in *engagé* film-making around the world prove that it was not.

17

A Curious Comment

The Griersonians were, of course, aware of these efforts and tended to be condescending about them. Grierson dismissed the work of the foreign avant-garde as the products of 'family fortune and youthful enthusiasm'. The film-makers, some of them at least, lacked 'principle' because they could not withstand 'commercial temptation' and went on to make features. The avant-garde', he wrote in 1935, 'made its dash for liberty by exploiting its friends' (Grierson, 1979a, p. 62). In the same piece (p. 63) he contrasts this with his own funding situation:

> The EMB dived into what it called 'Documentary' giving a freedom to its directors never before recorded in cinema. Indeed, it is a curious comment on our art that the *only* [my italics] freedom given to directors since has also been by propagandist groups: by Shell, the BBC, the Ministry of Labour, the Ceylon Government, the Gas Light and Coke Co., and by certain shipping, creosoting and radio firms in Europe.

The last two firms mentioned were Dutch, sponsors of Ivens's films *Creosote* and *Philips-Radio*, both made in 1931. Not surprisingly, Ivens (1969, p. 67) took a different view of the 'freedom' he achieved in these works: '*Philips-Radio* and *Creosote* mark a turning point in my career. I could have continued the commercial success and the technical facility which I had achieved with them. I could probably have become a successful advertising film maker. But this artistic suicide was prevented by a fortunate decision.' The decision was to visit the USSR. Ivens returned to make *Borinage*, a film which required that 'the approach used in *Philips-Radio* had to be dumped overboard' (Ivens, 1969, p. 87).

Grierson (1979a, p. 48) sought to square the circle by claiming, as a 'curious comment' or a 'principal point of interest', that, although there were 'necessary propaganda limits' involved, there was also this 'unique measure of freedom'. I have argued above that, on the basis of the films themselves, this freedom was largely illusory.

Be that as it may, Grierson clearly needed to attack the avant-garde and especially its funding sources as a way of justifying his own practice. It is then indeed a curious, if not spurious, comment he made on this practice. Had Grierson's fudging of the sponsorship issue – a fudging which has continued to feed the cognitive dissonance of realist documentarists down into this present television age – been less effective, it would not still be necessary to point out, as I have been doing, how closely the final film always reflected the sponsors' politics.

Much avant-garde work was aesthetically appealing to the Griersonians. It was, after all, 'art'. Hence the attack was limited to the 'principles' of its makers. When the Griersonians turned to the overtly political output, they saw no 'art' and were unreservedly hostile to the effort. For instance, *The Road to Hell* was lambasted by Grierson for its 'silly sensationalism'. 'It is propaganda for the worst type of defeatism,' wrote Basil Wright in *Cinema Quarterly* (Hogenkamp, 1976, p. 71). 'I have seen them both', said Rotha of this film and *What the Newsreels Do Not Show*, 'and declare them amateur and immature. ... It reminds me of what was once called the fashionable habit of slumming. In other words, they stink' (Hogenkamp, 1986, p. 93).

Other critics at the time thought differently, though, praising *What the Newsreel Does Not Show* for its 'propagandist effectiveness'. The *Daily Herald* reported that 'much cheering' greeted these two films at the Labour Party Conference in 1933 (Jones, 1987, pp. 142f.).

Conversely, Grierson defended *March of Time* and its European producer de Rochemont against attacks from these same 'amateur and immature' quarters. 'Pay no attention to the charge that Richard de Rochemont is fascist. I give you my word that he is not' (Macpherson, 1980, p. 121). (De Rochemont was employing Grierson as a consultant at the time, and others were filming British stories for him. Anstey was so successful at this that he was shipped to New York for a period to work as the reel's foreign editor (Fielding, 1978, p. 93).)

The Griersonians were as patronising to the left film-makers as they were dismissive of their work. Grierson, in 1970, remembered the nature of his relationship to Bond: 'Why, once when Ralph Bond was out of work, we hired him privately to sharpen up our reading of Marx' (Rotha, 1973, p. 42). Rotha used Bond as one of two directors on *Today We Live* – although he claimed he had to step in, taking over the direction (Marris, 1982, p. 22). It is hard, therefore, to agree with Aitken when he states (1990, p. 181) that 'far from being distanced from these leftist film mak-ing organisations, some of which were directly associated with the Communist Party, the documentary movement maintained strong links with them, and frequently offered them material support.' What support?[20]

Forty years on, when a German film crew visited Rotha and Bond, there was still an instantly apparent rhetorical difference between them. Rotha told the Germans: 'I'm an old socialist and like my independence. I don't like working for capitalists' (Wildenhahn, 1977, p. 11). Bond, on the other hand, 'hardly talks about his films, hardly about the good old days, hardly mentions former colleagues – he speaks about politics the whole time' (Orbanz, 1977, p. 122). Bond was not a Proudhonist and for this firmness of purpose he paid the price of marginalisation from the documentary movement (Cole, 1989, pp. 22f.). The Griersonians perhaps paid some-thing more.

At the time, Spain was one touchstone. As we have seen, *The Defence of Madrid* was shot by Norman McLaren. Doubt can be cast on Forsyth Hardy's vivid account of how Grierson assigned McLaren to this task, because the conversation is dated to the summer of 1937, while the film was shot the previous November and premièred in December 1936 (Hardy, 1979, p. 83; Hogenkamp, 1986, pp. 155ff.). It seems likelier that McLaren, a committed radical, delayed his arrival at the GPO until he had worked on this picture. (It is also clear that McLaren was hired by Grierson because of his 'art' rather than his politics.)

The documentary film movement was as remiss in covering Spain as it was in noting civil tension in the UK. Only one film was produced by the Griersonian mainstream – *Modern Orphans of the Storm*. It is perhaps significant that this deals with the plight of children during the war, a serious problem but scarcely a politically controversial one. It was sponsored by the National Joint Committee for Spanish Relief. 'It all sounds very alarming,' someone remarks in a synch scene of a meeting of the committee, inadvertently summing up the tone of the film. At the conclusion of this sequence, as stilted as any in the movement's archive, the Duchess of Atholl is asked, 'Well, Duchess, what's the verdict?' The verdict has to be Bert Hogenkamp's (1986, pp. 166f.): '*Modern Orphans of the Storm* was the only film on Spain made by one of the established documentary units (i.e. Realist, a film unit led by Basil Wright); a failure which clearly calls in question the documentary movement's progressive character.'

Another touchstone was the film union, the ACT, which was founded in 1933. Grierson never joined. When Bond tried to get him involved, he claimed to be a member of the Transport and General Workers Union (Bond, 1980, p. 10). For all that Bond remembered Grierson with affection and that Grierson finished up with an honorary ACTT membership in 1968, the fact is that the GPO constituted a production area resistant to unionisation in a time when such resistance was an overt mark of hostility to the left.

Those on the left at the time saw the GPO as (in Ivor Montagu's words) 'a very exploited field. People were paying and accepting salaries under the Union rates because they were keen to work on this at any cost. ... But the trouble was that the documentary people began to feel they were superior in some way because they were working for art. ... because they were taking less wages, so it must be art' (Lovell, Wollen and Rhodie, 1972, p. 91). The 'regrettable conditions and low wages' of the GPO film unit were a byword in the industry (Vaughan, 1983, pp. 58f.).[21]

As we have seen, on occasion, Grierson could turn in a brilliant 'Marxist analysis of the film industry under capitalism' (Macpherson, 1980, p. 146). He and others sat on the editorial boards of journals such as *Cinema Quarterly* mixing promiscuously with those more coherent in their political actions. Nevertheless, in more direct political fora, from those which led to the founding of the film technicians' union to those which sent film-makers to Spain, the Griersonians were conspicuous by their absence.

To see the rapprochement in old age between Bond and Montagu, on the one hand, and the surviving Griersonians on the other as an indicator that these absences were not serious is, I would argue, to misunderstand the temper of the times (Hogenkamp, 1989, p. 21, n. 5). To see Bond and Montagu and the Griersonians 'as engaged in the same struggle' (Aitken, 1990, p. 182) is to misread, in the roseate glow of memory, the heritage of the Popular Front. I think Grierson's 'struggle' was for social integration and was thus, ideologically, more of a piece with the newsreel producers' efforts.[22]

It is the bitterness of the Depression and the struggle against fascism that conditions my view of the Griersonian *œuvre*. It is the Depression and fascism which allow us to discern in the stand of those to Grierson's left a species of rebuke to his stance. Aneurin Bevan, who was the South Wales miners' spokesperson during the General Strike and Labour MP from 1929, gives in a famous 1948 speech some flavour of the times I want remembered when the Grierson record is considered: 'No amount of cajolery, and no attempts at ethical or social seduction, can eradicate from my heart a deep and burning hatred for the Tory Party that inflicted those bitter experiences on me. So far as I am concerned they are lower than vermin. They condemned millions of first-class people to semi-starvation' (*The Times*, 7 May 1948).

It can be claimed that Bevan, too, was concerned with social integration. Nevertheless, there was something of a line here and Grierson was firmly on the other side of it in the sense that Grierson's role was the making of films sustaining the order of things which Bevan was denouncing.[23]

That, ultimately, is where 'creativity' led. By claiming the privileges of the artist, Grierson allowed the realist documentary to avoid serious engagement. Let me repeat Ruskin's advice to the artist: 'Does a man die at your feet, your business is not to help him, but to note the colour of his lips; does a woman embrace her destruction before you, your business is not to save her, but to watch how she bends her arms.'

Not only was this – impotent observation – in effect what Grierson and his followers did in the 1930s; it is also the virtually inescapable legacy of the realist documentary down to the present.

PART THREE

TREATMENT: DOCUMENTARY AS DRAMA

18

Life as Narrativised

Grierson wanted the term 'documentary' reserved as an exclusive description of a particular form of factual cinema, set aside from and above newsreels, travelogues and educationals, and the like. What really was to make the documentary different, beyond a certain quality of observation, was its need for 'very different powers and ambitions at the stage of organising'. These 'powers and ambitions' came into play via the second term in the Griersonian definition – 'treatment'.

'Treatment' was used as a synonym for 'dramatisation'. 'The creative dramatisation of actuality' was one of the first 'demands of the documentary method', as Rotha put it (1966, p. 105). 'Treatment' or dramatisation (also sometimes referenced as 'interpretation') reflects the documentarists' desire and willingness to use actuality material to create a dramatic narrative.

Nearly forty years after the event, in recalling his initial visit to Chicago in 1924 and the birth of his 'theory of documentary film', Grierson said:

> What fascinated me as a European was the way the Hearst press and its imitators on every level of journalism had turned into a *'story'* what we in Europe called a *'report'*. They had in fact made the *story* – that is to say, a dramatic form – the basis of their means of communication. This seemed to me a highly logical way of approaching the problem of mass communication. What was most significant was that the story line was a peculiarly American story line. ... The active verb had become a hallmark of every worthwhile story. Something had to *do* something to something else. Some*one* had to do something to someone else. ... All I did in my theory of documentary film was to transfer that concept to film making, and declare that in the actual world of our observation there was always a dramatic form to be found. (Beveridge, 1978, p. 29)

Grierson knew that the 'actual world of our observation' could be filmed and structured to be dramatic along such lines. Dramatically structured actuality was exactly what he had seen, perspicaciously, in Flaherty's work. It was the very thing which distinguished the Flaherty films from previous efforts in factual film-making.

I think Flaherty's reputation is overblown but, curiously, his apologists – such as Richard Barsam (1988, pp. 20ff.) – never seem to make as much as they might of his one real and indisputable contribution to the development of the cinema. In what seems to have been a flash of genius, while reshooting his Inuit footage (the first rushes having been lost in a fire),

Flaherty understood the need to make a drama arise from the life being observed (or better, being constructed through the process of observation). This was very different from imposing a drama from without, as Curtis had done in *In the Land of the Head-Hunters*.

The echoes between *Head-Hunters* and *Nanook* are strong – the use of native peoples in directed sequences and the painstaking recreation of their past culture. There is even the death of a great sea creature, a whale, in *Head-Hunters* which compares with the deaths of the seal and the walrus in *Nanook*. Without a consideration of *Head-Hunters*, Flaherty's achievement in *Nanook* cannot be readily understood (Lyman, 1982, p. 114).

Curtis's story was an inauthentic white man's melodramatic vision of native American life. It was not grounded in Kwakiutl culture. To satisfy his backers and public taste, Curtis had head-hunting, magic, a damnable villain and an unwilling bride. The result is a film of historic ethnographic interest only because of the costumes and the dance kinesics which Curtis carefully re-created for the film. Paradoxically, it tells us nothing of the Kwakiutl beyond that – even if we allow that it presents a picture of Kwakiutl life in the time of the actors' immediate ancestors.

Flaherty, by contrast, filmed the supposedly everyday life of a single Inuit family, albeit once again set a generation in the past; but he imposed no external melodrama on them.

The first two reels of the film are a series of 'postcards', vignettes and two longer sequences. The 'postcards' are portraits of Nanook and Nyla or one or two shots of such things as 'The Mysterious Barren Lands' (as the intertitle has it); building a moss fire; walking to the river; the children being fed by the fur trader; Nanook clowning with the gramophone, and so on.

The vignettes consist of from three to eleven shots. For instance, there are the three shots used to cover the arrival of Nanook's kayak at the shore; the three shots showing how a kayak is covered with skin; the shots showing fur pelts at the trading post; or the eleven shots which show the large, open four-oared omiack boat being launched, crossing a body of water and landing by the post.

There are also two full-scale sequences. In the first, which lasts for 5 minutes 20 seconds, Nanook goes fishing among the ice floes. There are 33 shots including 6 intertitles. In the second sequence, Nanook and his comrades hunt walrus. This lasts for 5 minutes and has 40 shots including 7 intertitles.[1]

The 'postcards' and vignettes together establish the environment of the film. There are the beginnings of a narrative in the way Flaherty deployed some of these proto-sequences. For instance, Nanook's arrival in his kayak establishes the fur trader's post which is the location for a number of other events – for example, the trading, the feeding of Nanook's children and Nanook's clowning. There is, though, little sense of temporal continuity and certainly no causal relationship between these elements. In other words, there is a chronology if only because all films in the act of projection are necessarily chronological; but there is no causality (Bordwell, 1985, pp. 80f.; Branigan, 1992, pp. 11f; Chatman, 1990, p. 9).

Three sorts of material are being used in these first two reels. First, there are the portrait shots, a form which was to disappear from the professional cinema. In these a subject is simply caught in close-up doing nothing but look at the lens. Then there are specific events – the arrival of the kayak, the feeding of the children and Nanook's clowning with the gramophone – all of which culminate in a portrait-style acknowledgement of the camera. But the bulk of these 'postcards' and vignettes are, to use a term of Gérard Genette (1980, pp. 113ff.), iterative: that is, they represent a narrative instance or an event or activity which can be read as a typical instance of that event or activity.

In a realist text, the iterative is a crucial element contributing to the reader's sense of the text's reality. We see Nanook light a moss fire, for example, but that stands for his regular fire-lighting activity. Of course, in film 'the concrete expression of the unique texture of every moment' (Stam *et al.*, 1992, p. 122) makes the idea of the iterative difficult; but nevertheless, such shots are too brief to be seen as singular and specific. Moreover, their iterative effect is sometimes reinforced by the generalised titles, for example 'This is the way Nanook uses moss for fuel'.

The two longer sequences, on the other hand, are straightforward narratives with a clear hermeneutic, as Barthes uses the term. Barthes (1990, p. 17) defines the hermeneutic code in narrative as 'a variety of chance events which can either formulate a question or delay its answer'. Will Nanook succeed in his hunt for food? In each of these two sequences, Nanook leaves by sea. We witness his arrival at a hunting site and his preparations. He then kills the prey and makes a start on the return journey. The answer each time is 'Yes! he succeeds'.

But these sequences are not integrated into the iterative material which surrounds or precedes them in any way. Overall, the first two reels of the film are a more or less random selection of scenes of Inuit life, some more specific than others, featuring Nanook and his family.

What happens some 23 minutes in, after the title 'Winter Comes', is very different. Bill Nichols has said (1986, p. 114): 'Documentary operates in the crease between life as lived and life as narrativised.' And it is 'life as narrativised' that we now witness in *Nanook* for the first time.

At first sight, it might seem that Flaherty is simply continuing with his previous film-making strategy. We see Nanook and his family begin a journey by land. He traps a fox, builds an igloo, hunts a seal, loses control of his dogs, gets caught in a blizzard and, finally, finds a disused igloo. But there is a difference between these sequences and the earlier *mélange* and it is considerable.

First, all these events are quite firmly part of one journey. There is a strong temporal sense governing the progress of this journey with at least two days and nights being very carefully delineated. Even the iterative vignettes of life in and around the igloo – for example, Nanook plays with his son, teaching him to shoot with bow and arrow – are integrated into this narrative.

Moreover, and in absolute contrast to the first part of the film, these sequences depend on each other causally. It is to hunt that the family makes the journey. They cannot feed on the fox so they need to hunt seal. The seal meat causes the dogs to fight, which delays Nanook's search for shelter. The blizzard then endangers them and they have to race for safety in a disused igloo.

This diagesis can be read as an example of Tzvetan Todorov's notion of 'transformation' as a main principle of narrative (Todorov, 1981, pp. 41ff.). The equilibrium of the family's life at the post, where food and shelter are provided, is broken by winter coming and the need to make a journey.[2] Nanook then repairs the disruption by providing food and shelter once again.

Or Barthes's analytic system can be used. His concept of the hermeneutic is as easily applied to the last 50-odd minutes of *Nanook* as it is to the two earlier sequences. Questions, raised in part by the visuals but more directly by the intertitles, create a series of textual enigmas to engage the spectator's interest. Within the large question of the family's overall chance for survival, as the film progresses, more specific questions are posed. Will the family eat? Will the dogfight mean a fatal delay? Will they find shelter? As is not the case with the fishing and hunting sequences, such questions now extend across a number of discrete episodes. There is even a closure when, after their race against the blizzard, the family settle down, fed, in safety for the night.

Nanook also exhibits that 'logic in human behavior' which Barthes (1990, p. 18) makes into the proairetic code of narrative. From the series of events he chose thus to string together in these reels Flaherty constructs a perfect melodramatic climax brought on by Nanook's successive activities in hunting the seal and feeding his dogs as a storm blows up. These become 'a series of actions, natural, logical, linear' (Barthes, 1990, p. 158).

Further, we can note that a third system of narrative analysis also 'works' for *Nanook*. William Guynn's conclusion (1990, pp. 50f.) is that Christian Metz's syntagmatic system, developed for the fiction film, can be readily applied to *Nanook*.

This demonstration of how to construct out of (supposedly) observed material a text which exhibits all the characteristics of a fictional drama is Flaherty's major contribution to the cinema. And it must not be underestimated. For he put it together, at the 'stage of organising', out of various discrete elements which he had filmed at different times and in a different order, perhaps even for different story purposes.

First, he used intertitles. The climax of the film has the dogs fighting over the seal meat, which delays the family's search for shelter as a storm blows up. It is the intertitles which tell us why the dogfight matters, how this imperils Nanook and his party. Using the intertitles in this way to 'clarify the action' had been a technique of the American fictional cinema since at least 1905 (Musser, 1990, p. 410). Here these titles are the source of the suspense.

Along the storyline told in these intertitles Flaherty then hangs the sequences as he needs them, not in any way as they occurred. Most notoriously, he uses the retiring to sleep and awakening actions of Nanook and the family he has filmed in a false (one-sided) igloo in two different places. Half of the sequence – getting up – starts the final 'day' of the film. The other half of the sequence – going to bed – comes right at the end of that day (and the film) and is, according to the intertitles, supposedly set in a quite different 'abandoned' igloo. (In the same way, in the earlier fishing sequence, Nanook leaves his kayak, and skips across the ice floes only to find himself next to a kayak – apparently the one he has left, but now mysteriously with his fishing gear on board.)

The point here most emphatically is not to complain that we cannot trust Flaherty; neither, even more emphatically, is it to complain about his failures of continuity. It is rather to point up how he dramatised his material in the cutting room and on the titling bench. Flaherty's genius, and I do not use the word lightly, lay in building his story of this journey to the abandoned igloo out of bits which by no means necessarily went together in this particular way.

Understanding not just how to manipulate his 'everyday' material, but also what dramatic necessity imposed on that manipulation, is the essence of Flaherty's contribution. He was obeying the generally understood requirements of structuring a multi-reel fiction film at this time. As the subheadings for a chapter in an early screenwriting manual put it: 'Sequence and Consequence; Logical Cause and Complete Solution; Sustained Climax; All Expectations Fulfilled' (Bowser, 1990, p. 257). That is exactly what happens in *Nanook* after 'Winter Comes'.

This, then, is 'treatment'. Grierson's understanding of the need for dramatisation, though, immediately takes us far from a vision of documentary cinema as being in stark opposition to a cinema of fiction. Indeed, for Grierson, it is exactly the fictionalising quality of narrative – 'dramatic form' – that is the distinguishing mark of documentary.

Grierson was at pains to distinguish documentary from other sorts of non-fiction film. This was a task of more than just taxonomic moment. If what marked the documentary as special was unclear, that would confuse the funding agencies enormously. He needed to separate what he was proposing quite carefully from what had gone before. As he saw it, the problem was acute:

Where the camera shot on the spot (whether it shot newsreel items or magazine items or discursive 'interests' or dramatised 'interests' or educational films or scientific films proper or *Changs* or *Rangos*) in that fact was documentary. This array of species is, of course, quite unmanageable in criticism and we shall have to do something about it. (Grierson, 1979a, p. 35)

What he did about it was to class 'interests', which included the subspecies travelogues (*documentaires*), as 'lecture films'. Although these might 'describe and even expose', most significantly they do not 'dramatise; they do not even dramatise an episode'. Likewise, anthropological and other scientific films of record, including 'nature films', were seen as purely 'utilitarian observation cinema' – 'how beautiful they have been', but how untreated. Newsreels, 'actualities', were dismissed as exhibiting 'purely journalistic skills' – 'just a speedy snip-snap' (Grierson, 1979a, pp. 35f. and 73f.).

These 'lower forms' of non-fiction cinema all claimed the real, as did documentary, but they did not dramatise. Fiction dramatised but did not claim the real. Ergo documentary was unique in dramatising the real.

However, because it shared dramatic narrative, documentary thus slipped, almost without friction, into the fiction cinema as a species of genre. Grierson's taxonomic triumph was to make his particular species of non-fiction film, *the* non-fiction genre while at the same allowing the films to use the significant fictionalising technique of dramatisation.[3]

19

Chrono-Logic

Modern theory treats genre as something more than type or category. 'Genre notions are ... potentially interesting ... for the exploration of the psychological and sociological interplay between film-maker, film and audience' (Tudor, 1973, p. 141). 'In fact, genres construct the proper spectator for their own consumption' (Andrew, 1984, p. 110). The claim on truth necessary for the documentary exactly depends on spectators 'constructed' by the genre to have that prior faith in it. According to this view, documentary's 'truth' is a function of the viewers' interaction with the text rather than any formal quality of the text itself. As Robert Fairthorne put it sixty years ago, '"Actuality" is not a fundamental property, but a relation between film and audience of precisely the same order as slow motion which demands previous knowledge of natural motion to give its peculiar effect' (Macpherson, 1980, p. 171).

With such a belief-system in place (primarily because of photography – see p. 126), the development of the documentary then critically depended on the discovery of dramatic formulations to turn the everyday into drama. Flaherty used the model of the journey to accomplish this. Charles Musser suggests (1990, p. 21) that a journey to China was the Ur-documentary subject in a sequenced late-seventeenth-century illustrated lantern-slide lecture. This should not surprise. Journeys and narratives go together: '*To depart/to travel/to arrive/to stay*: the journey is saturated. To end, to fill, to join, to unify – one might say that is the basic requirement of the *readerly*' (where the readerly is glossed as 'what can be read ... a classic text') (Barthes, 1990, pp. 105 and 4).

The despised but popular travelogue was in essence based on filming journeys; but the journey also figures in many diverse 'higher' documentaries – from the epic march of the Bakhtiari in *Grass*, through the voyage of the fishermen in *Drifters* to Buñuel's alienated and ironic wanderings across the *Land Without Bread* and beyond.

Journey films solved actuality's big narrative problem – closure. How should such films finish? Obviously, a journey film ends with the end of the journey. Another quite simple solution was to construct the film to run apparently for the duration of a period of time with a well defined culturally determined closing – a day, most commonly.

This became documentary's preferred way of capturing the urban experience on film. Shots (often taken over a period of months or even years) were organised into thematic clusters and those clusters into a chronological progression. The chaos of the modern world was thereby shaped into a day in the life of a city – 'an event-oriented, vaguely chronological approach' (Uricchio, 1987, pp. 15f.). As in *Berlin: Symphony of a City* (1927), the trajectory of the film is from the early morning through the working day to the entertainments of the evening. Even Dziga Vertov, who stridently opposed the idea of fiction film on ideological grounds and claimed he was escaping from narrative, made a city documentary, *The Man with the Movie Camera*, which still puts 'Waking' before 'The Day and Work Begin', which is itself before 'The Day's Work'. The film's 'day' concludes with 'Work Stops, Leisure Begins', although it must be admitted that many of these last activities also take place during daylight (Petric, 1987, p. 73). Vertov proves the rule. For most documentarists, the diurnal was as seductive an organising principle as the journey.

Take the wartime work of Humphrey Jennings, according to Lindsay Anderson (and *pace* Grierson's view of Wright): 'the only real poet the British Cinema has yet produced' (Anderson, 1954, p. 181).[4] There is a denseness about the ways in which Jennings, and his editor Stewart McAllister, wove images together, an associative intuitiveness, which is apparently capable of confusing some into believing that films such as *Listen to Britain* (1941) exhibit a 'non-narrative style' or an 'absence of narrative editing' (Lovell and Hillier, 1972, p. 89; Sorenssen, 1986, p. 57).

Yet, for one thing, shots within the sequences of this film are classically edited. There are matched cuts on the couple sitting out the dance in the dance-hall sequence; on the soldiers singing in the night train; and on Dame Myra Hess in the famous sequence in which the Queen is discovered among her subjects listening to a lunch-time concert in a makeshift performance space at the National Gallery. 'Absence' is a little strong.

And, for another thing, it is also a little strong when the overall structure of the film is considered. Sorenssen, for instance, does note, following Dai Vaughan's observation, that the film 'is organised around a 24 hour time cycle' (Vaughan, 1983, p. 89; Sorenssen, 1986, p. 57). But somehow the implication of this is resisted.

The chronological element was not something added at 'the stage of organising' in the cutting room. The film was conceived around time, as the treatment reveals: 'It is half past nine – the children are already at school ... and at 10.30 the BBC comes "Calling All Workers". ... At half past twelve, the clatter of typing in the Ministries and offices in London lessens' (Jennings, M.-L., 1982, p. 30). Moreover, this was a response to the brief, which was to make a film about the lunch-time concert series in the National Gallery which was considered by itself to be 'too dreary' (Vaughan, 1983, p. 85). The time-cycle was the key to dramatisation.

This is extremely important:

As has been clearly established in recent narratology, what makes Narrative unique among the text-types is its 'chrono-logic', its doubly temporal logic. Narrative entails movement through time not only 'externally' (the duration of the presentation of the novel, film, play) but also 'internally' (the duration of the sequence of events that constitutes the plot). (Chatman, 1990, p. 9)

The 'internal chrono-logic' of *Listen to Britain* arises from its strongly inscribed diurnal pattern, in this case from afternoon to afternoon. The pattern compensates for the film's admittedly weakened proairetic.

And this is often the case. The diurnal is not simply another major way documentarists have to dramatise actuality; it also works to reintroduce the narrative logics of the proairetic code in films, such as this, where single characters give way to a changing series of individuals who collectively represent the mass. Guynn argues (1990, pp. 76f.):

> The documentary text rarely exhibits [the] functional economy characteristic of the fiction film. ... Motivation, the causal alibi that seems to emerge effortlessly from the narrative telling, is precisely what is lacking at certain jointures of the text; the segmental units do not call each other into being in an inexorable logic of time. Rather segments tend towards closure, the short circuiting of their narrative potential.

He suggests that these gaps are normally filled by spoken commentary (or, one can add, previously by intertitles). But more than that they are also filled exactly by an 'inexorable logic of time'; to wit, the diurnal pattern. It is because of this, as Guynn notes (ibid., p. 7), that Jennings here 'takes pride' in avoiding commentary or 'any sort of mediating language of this kind'.

Designed in part for US and Commonwealth consumption, *Listen to Britain* poses big hermeneutical questions about the state of Britain's morale in the Blitz, including the issue of how well the very fabric of the country is surviving. (London is 'not being left in ruins', wrote Jennings in his treatment (Jennings, M.-L., 1982, p. 30).) Each shot and each sequence is evidence for the viewer of how such questions are to be answered. The propaganda importance of offering positive answers to these enigmas is clear. And this element of narrative is expressed in, as well as being considerably bolstered and strengthened by, the use of time.

In Jennings, the poet/painter's imagination struggled with the inevitable chronological prison of the cinema. For instance, in the summer of 1940 he was planning a short film in which the theme of men leaving for war would be told through the family images found on the walls of a remote rural home: 'On the walls are portraits, photographs, watercolours of men – predominantly men – engineers and soldiers going back to the days of Robert Stephenson and the Crimea – little framed fragments of regimental colours – photographs of railway bridges – men in uniform and men as children' (Jennings, M.-L., 1982, p. 26).

But Jennings knew that this needed to be made to work as drama; so, deftly, he suggested that these images be cutaways seen in the after-dinner calm of a day, the children asleep and the adults listening on the radio to Haydn's 'Midi' symphony *while* he crosscuts 'the bombers going out from a neighbouring airfield'. The film and the music climax as 'The bombers are already over the white coast line'.

In the film he actually realised that year, *London Can Take It* (made with McAllister and Watt), there was not only a diurnal pattern, from evening to morning, but the added structure of an American journalistic report, written by Quentin Reynolds for *Colliers Weekly*, as the soundtrack. Building these sound-picture complexities against a temporal logic became the Jennings hallmark most perfectly seen in *Diary for Timothy* (1945).

The visual complexity of his mature style is held together in this film by a perfectly simple chrono-logic. *Diary* takes the events of the last winter of the war – essentially the Arnhem raid and the Battle of the Bulge – and weaves them around the first weeks in the life of the eponymous baby. The film's commentary, by E. M. Forster and arguably the most elegant yet written for a British documentary, is less Timothy's diary than a chronology of avuncular conversation and observation:

It's the middle of October now ... and the war certainly won't be over by Christmas. And the weather doesn't suit us. ...

And suppose you went up to London. London in November looks a nice quiet place, but you'll find things are chancy here too. ...

In those days before Christmas the news was bad and the weather was foul. Death and darkness, death and fog, death across those few miles of water for our own people and for others, for enslaved and broken people – the noise of battle getting louder, and death came by telegram to many of us on Christmas Eve. ...

Jennings's strategies well illustrate the strength of the prison of narrative into which the Griersonian demand for 'treatment' locks the realist documentary. His is the most poetic, impressionist *œuvre* and yet it is usually strongly time-based. All the significant war films but one (see p. 109) are structured in this way and his two 1943 films (*The Silent Village* and *Fires Were Started*) were actually scripted fictions which maintained their documentary connection only because they used non-actors going through actions supposedly historically determined.

In all this, the use of time and the drift to fully fledged fictional work, Jennings was following the lead of the other Griersonians. Because of the need for 'treatment', it is no surprise that Grierson's pre-war insistence on films of social moment did not mark the abandonment of chronology either. On the contrary, the 'problem moment' structure has an implicit narrative trajectory which comes from the time element explicitly involved – there was an idyllic past; there is a current problem; there will be an idyllic future.

What is true of the overall structure of the classic realist documentary is, of course, equally true of the structure of sequences within it. Flaherty showed how to bring shots taken at different times and places together to make up mini-narratives. This became a staple in the documentarists' narrativising repertoire. Even newsreel-style material could thereby be given new documentary shape. Consider Riefenstahl's *Triumph of the Will* as an extreme example of the deployment of fictionalising techniques at this level.

The overall effect of *Triumph*'s opening sequence (at least on some critics) is, as we have seen, that Hitler makes a godlike descent to meet his faithful followers, a little mini-narrative introduction to the greater story of the party conference. A plane descends through heavy cloud and at the same time casts a sharp-edged shadow on the ground below, where columns are seen marching – a meteorological situation not often encountered. All normative readings of narrative suggest that the shadowed columns are marching to meet the plane. They never get there. Not only that, the crowd supposedly at the airport is shown standing on walls and in front of trees; but there are no walls or trees at the airfield, as is revealed in the widest of the establishing shots of the plane. The plane itself appears to have quite different markings on either side of its tail. Yet this sequence is almost never questioned as evidence of this particular event exactly because, I want to argue, the narrative trajectory of descent and arrival is so powerful.

Other sequences are similarly created out of disparate material. For instance, Hitler drives into Nuremberg in a Mercedes with a windscreen which in successive shots is first up and then laid flat on the bonnet. His hair is untidy and combed in different close-up shots within the same sequence. During the drive from the airport, he enters a tunnel of quite different proportions from the one he exits from, and so on. Nevertheless, so powerful is the frame of the journey that these continuity slips, Riefenstahl correctly assumed, would go unnoticed; and they did.

That Riefenstahl can do this with the material is a measure not of her editing skill, for one can see her doing it quite plainly, but of the limited variety of coverage she had.[5] Bits from any one scene can, more or less, fit into any other scene, save only that night and day, interior and exterior are not cross-cut. That a certain rhythm is achieved is because most of the events, as she records them, all took place at about the same pace – a medium march or a 20 m.p.h. car ride.

Something more is going on here than the simple juxtaposition of shots taken at different times. Normative editing rules (that is to say, Hollywood spatial and temporal continuity conventions) are a species of contract between film-maker and audience as to the nature and quality of 'the reality' on offer. The matched cut is, in a multi-camera shoot at least, a sort of guarantee on the contract implied by the editing. Yet, despite the forty-nine (or so) cameras there are a scant half-dozen matched cuts in this entire film (and most of those are false – in the blanket-tossing sequence). Instead, Riefenstahl uses the cutaway-to-cutaway style of the city films such as *Berlin*, a style invented not so that the normative rules of narrative editing might be suspended but rather that they might be bypassed when the footage was non-repetitive 'actuality'.

The cutaway-to-cutaway technique destroys the possibility of the viewers' reading off the relationship of any shot to any other shot to the point where 'the concrete "reality" of Nuremberg becomes tenuous' (Kelman, 1973, p. 162). Of course, at ninety feet a minute, on portable cameras, long takes were then difficult. But Riefenstahl deployed her accumulation of cutaways with such disregard for the maintenance of continuity of time and place that she reached an extreme. In the final march past, such are the changes among the leaders standing before the Mercedes which Hitler is using as a reviewing stand that one has no idea *from the film* how many parades there actually were. So disoriented is the editing that it calls into question material the veracity of which is assured to us by other sources, other witnesses.

Needless to say, Riefenstahl uses these micro-editing techniques to create overall an edited representation of the event for the purposes of telling the story of the conference. The sequences are assembled according to perceived dramatic needs, not, as they might have easily been, according to the actual order in which they occurred. Riefenstahl builds a straightforward structure involving a day of arrival and a second day with various meetings and rallies culminating with a rousing close for the inner group of party leaders and a final march past of the banners. That this is not the order in which these events occurred proves nothing more than that Riefenstahl was obedient to the need for 'treatment'. Riefenstahl's reordering of the chronology is done in the service of the powerful hermeneutic which she established for the film, the enigma of the Brownshirts and Hitler's response to them in the aftermath of the Röhm putsch.

Some scholars, accepting as true a 1935 claim of Riefenstahl's, believe that the events were specially arranged for the camera (Kracauer, 1973, p. 301). Apart from the special camera mount built into the stadium superstructure, I am not persuaded that Riefenstahl was given control above and beyond what a director of a multi-camera shoot might expect; nor that her intervention was markedly greater than that of other documentarists of the day. If only because of the size of the event, it was probably less.

On the other hand, Riefenstahl's later non-interventionist counter-claim is even more absurd: 'Not a single scene is staged. Everything is genuine ... pure history.' 'I [Riefenstahl] state precisely: it is film *vérité*. It reflects the truth that was then, in 1934, history' (Delahaye, 1965). Yet her rearrangement of material to make coherent sequences out of disparate footage matches anything in Flaherty. For her implicit authority for these manipulations at all levels is Flaherty, as theorised by Grierson. As with Nanook's winter excursion, so with Hitler's trip to Nuremburg. The point is not the mendacity or otherwise of the final film; it is simply that the material has been 'treated'; it has been dramatised.

For a final argument for the overwhelming dominance of recognisable narrative structures in the realist documentary, let us turn to the exceptions that prove this rule. It could be objected to the above that, Flahertian melodramatics apart, these 'simple' narrative shapes – journeys, days – are in fact too simple to be recognised as such. In fact, they are nothing more than a sort of automatic consequence of film's fundamental temporality (its 'external chrono-logic') and nothing more. I would rebut this on the basis of Flaherty's own *The Land* (1942). This has elements of both journey and time but nevertheless does not produce a coherent narrative. It stands, then, as a demonstration that narrative structure in the documentary is by no means an automatic result of simply assembling sequences.

Flaherty, despite *Nanook*, seems never to have understood how films are made and never really created any alternative to the normative practices of which he remained in ignorance. Had Flaherty offered a coherent alternative to the normative rules of continuity and narrative, his cavalier disdain of them would have been more than acceptable and his place as an important innovator, the man who not only created narrativisation but also freed it from Hollywood editing, would be assured. But the groans with which he routinely accompanied screenings of rushes and the months of toil in the cutting rooms speak to the opposite, to attempts at making the material work in an accepted sense.

It was as if *Nanook* with its central discovery of how to mould a narrative out of footage and, crucially, titles, was a fluke. Flaherty never wrote a script, he did not cover scenes, he could not maintain continuity and he never learned to direct dialogue.

He had shot some marvellous backgrounds. We ran some 17,000 ft of them and, of course, the absence of story was noticeable.

Flaherty sent us a shot of a man throwing a ball at a pile of ninepins, but he ain't sent us a reverse angle.

Not once did the 'actors' use exactly the same words or sentence-formation. (Rotha, 1983, pp. 176, 229 and 250)

Without a hunt, Flaherty seemed lost. For months he searched the caves of Samoa, looking for a great sea creature. On Aran, he made of the peaceful basking shark a prototype Jaws. In his last major project, *Louisiana Story* (1948) (a tribute to the beneficence of offshore oil, paid for by Esso), there is of course the alligator. There might be some deep psychological significance in this search for krakens but it is just as likely that Flaherty, having found in the seal hunt the clue to *Nanook*'s climax, simply did not know how to find a climax in anything else. It is not for nothing that he said: 'A film is the longest distance between two points' (Rotha, 1983, p. 5). For him, with silent footage ratios of 35:1 the norm, this was simply the truth.

So powerful was Flaherty's personality, and so profound the effect he had on most of those who came into contact with him, that any attempts to re-evaluate his work seem to provoke anguish and rage among them. Remarks like those above are met with accusations of betrayal and claims that envy and self-aggrandisement are motivating the critical voices. Richard Leacock, who was Flaherty's cameraman on *Louisiana Story*, is one of those who are disturbed by contemporary attempts to reassess Flaherty. Yet his defence of the master is somewhat opaque:

At first it was just Bob that I concentrated on. Was he stupid? How could a man of his stature and experience not know how to film a sequence?... Bob just huffed and puffed and looked and looked and tried this and that and looked some more. But then I *knew* he wasn't stupid, so I tried to understand that what most people regarded in him as a lack of discipline was, in fact, the supreme discipline. (Leacock, 1973, p. 39)

But how can *we* understand this 'discipline'? Such arguments really do not begin to explain films like *The Land*.

The Land was conceived by Lorentz's US Film Service but was made, after Congress had destroyed that agency, by the Agricultural Adjustment Administration. The film was to be about the intricacies of New Deal agriculture policy but, by the evidence on the screen, 20,000 miles of travel over two years were not sufficient for Flaherty remotely to grasp what these were. His editor, Helen Van Dongen, wrote: 'My consternation at finding 75,000 ft of apparently unorganised material changed to horror when I learned that there was no story outline or synopsis in the accepted sense' (Rotha, 1983, p. 199).

The Land is as if *Nanook* had never been. In its incoherence it seems almost to come from the cinema's founding moments, its sequences barely more connected than the shots in the Lumière reel of 1895. No less than 37 times in 43 minutes, the film simply fades to black, its forward impetus exhausted.

It starts *in medias res* in Pennsylvania's rich countryside. 'It takes good land to raise a house like this,' says Flaherty himself on the soundtrack over a shot of a well-founded farmstead around which the farmer and his wife and child stroll. But they stroll to no purpose. They are not observed doing anything. 'Trouble has crept in,' says Flaherty, and the film fades to black, leaving the family still wandering about. Next sequence, we are still in Pennsylvania and still in trouble. Over a farmers' meeting, Flaherty says the trouble is country-wide, 'Problems that no longer can any one man solve'. And, again, we fade to black.

Soon we are not even given the continuities of these two opening scenes. The script is reduced to an itinerary. 'We found this in Tennessee'; 'It is here in the old Cotton South'; 'We came upon an old Negro'; 'A thousand miles west'; 'We came to a town that cotton farmers founded not so long ago. Go Forth, they called it. Go Forth, Texas'; 'We came to this family moving out'. On and on the movie trudges, each fragment fading to black, sometimes heralding a change of location, sometimes only to fade up in the same place. Flaherty, on the soundtrack, paraphrases what this chance succession of rural strangers told him – from corn to cotton, to cotton to corn, to erosion, to squalor to squalor to plenty, until at last we are back with the Pennsylvania farmers and, finally, a great row of midwestern combine harvesters advancing across the prairie. 'The great fact is the land, the land itself, and the people, and the spirit of the people.' The end.

The Land vividly demonstrates the centrality of 'treatment' by showing how far from any concept of a fully formed film a series of almost random shots and mini-sequences, even if they are on a consistent theme, is. It does not offer a sustained chronology, much less any causal connections between its sequences. Such a quantity of fades to black would short-circuit the narrative potential of the sequences, had the sequences any narrative potential to short-circuit.

The fades are an act of desperation, a final attempt to throw viewers a diagetic life-raft; but it does not work. Returning to Pennsylvania, but not quite at the starting-point location and not quite for the final shot, symbolises this failure. This seems to me nothing so much as a half-hearted and incomplete gesture on Flaherty's part to the narrativising norms which he had himself established.

Beyond this, there is little or no evidence of the presence of a hermeneutic. The film poses no questions because one cannot discover what it is about.

This is not the end of the matter, however. Although *The Land* shows what happens if causality and chronology are insufficiently inscribed, there is still the possibility that such insufficient inscription could nevertheless sustain a documentary. And within the Jennings *œuvre* there is a film for which such a case could possibly be made.

In *Words for Battle* (1941), Jennings 'sets' seven texts, spoken by Laurence Olivier, against film images, in the fashion of a composer setting words to music for a song. Jennings's films are all concerned with sound at a level of sophistication not much previously attempted and music analogies and stimuli constantly occurred to him, as in the example of the Haydn 'Midi' project or in *Listen to Britain*, which, significantly, for a time bore the working title *The Tin Hat Concerto*.

The concept of 'echoing' or 'punning' the soundtrack against the image is most fully deployed in *Words for Battle*. For instance, Lincoln's 'And that government of the people by the people and for the people ...' is over a shot of the House of Commons. The sentence continues '... shall not perish from the earth'. This is heard over a wider shot of the Palace of Westminster from Parliament Square while in the foreground a tank is revealed passing a bus and the Lincoln statue which stands on the west side of the square. (Since tanks were not immediately needed to patrol Westminster, the shot was specially set up for the film (Vaughan, 1983, p. 76).) As Geoffrey Nowell-Smith points out (1986, p. 329), 'The effect here is no mere illustration of Lincoln's famous (too famous) words, but the generation, through montage, of a cluster of ideas around democracy and armed defence; and it all happens in a moment, both chilling and exhilarating, which no amount of verbal explanation can re-create.'

My point is not to examine these semiotics but to see to what extent it can be claimed that Jennings and McAllister here abandoned causality and chrono-logic (or at least reduced them to a bare minimum) while still producing an effective film.

The roster of writers quoted is chronological (by order of their births) from Camden to Churchill, with only Lincoln out of place. Hillier hints at a movement in the film from an introduction which gives a general description of Britain (Camden) as a land which prizes liberty and toler-ance (Milton) to more specific references to the war; children first – being evacuated against Blake; next, adult activities – against Browning; and then death and destruction in the form of blitz damage and a funeral against Kipling (Lovell and Hillier, 1972, p. 84). This last, 'When the English began to hate', cues the defiance of Churchill's 'We shall never surrender' speech while Lincoln's Gettysburg address in some fashion returns us to the Milton. All this suggests that the sequences are secured in their places by something more than the birth date of the author who wrote the words and that they could not be easily rearranged.

But this logic is not bolstered by any sort of further chronology or other pattern in the visual track. For instance, a sunset occurs in the middle of the film because the poem being quoted (Browning's 'Home Thoughts, from the Sea') makes reference to it, not because we are in the middle of a dusk-to-dusk structure of the sort Jennings elsewhere favoured.

Words for Battle represents the end of a rather short road. It followed a similar effort, *The First Days* (1939), which Jennings co-directed with Harry Watt and Pat Jackson. This has neither 'chrono-logic' nor the sus-tained word/image density of *Words for Battle*, and therefore, as Watt said, 'There was no shape. It wasn't a good film' (Sussex, 1975, p. 117). *Words for Battle*, although more successful than this, nevertheless did not become a model, not even for Jennings himself.

Instead, as we have seen, Jennings and McAllister turned to chronologi-cal structures and *Words for Battle*, with its extremely tenuous chronology, remains an exception. Despite this, for some, the film is a piece of 'extra-ordinary bravura' whose 'effect is irresistible', largely, I would argue, because of the words (and Olivier's delivery of them) (Nowell-Smith, 1986, p. 330; Lovell and Hillier, 1972, p. 85). Essentially, though, reduc-ing the organising potential of time this much was too dangerous a strat-egy. It turned out to be easier to create a safety net in the form of a chronology. *Words for Battle*, in so far as it was a non-narrative, represents an effective form but one that has never much been exploited. As Dai Vaughan observes (1983, p. 75), the film 'works better in the head than on the screen'.

112

20

Non-Narrative:
Works Better in the Head than on the Screen

'Treatment', according to Guynn (1990, p. 70), means that 'we cannot say that documentary demands a separate semiotics, because we are faced with the simple fact that documentaries are full of narratives and that in telling their stories these texts quite "naturally" call on signifying structures that the fiction film created for its own uses'.

While it seems obvious that documentaries tell stories, not least because that is what the documentarists said they were doing, this was often hidden. Of *Nanook*, *Grass* and *Chang*, an early historian could write, 'None of these pictures told a story in accordance with the accepted patterns of the studios' (Hampton, 1931, p. 422). Time did not bring greater insight.

Instead a trope has developed which tends to assume that the documentary does indeed demand separate formal structures. Documentary difference in this regard is almost tacitly accepted. It is assumed that documentaries are non-narrative, and, therefore (in some quarters) not even 'real' films: 'Remove "drama", and there is no fiction, no diagesis, and therefore no film. Or only a documentary, a *"film exposé"*' – that is to say, 'mechanical reproduction' (Metz, 1974, pp. 94 and 194). In such a climate, it is no wonder that documentary is deemed to lack all narrative requirements – even, for instance, closure (Andrew, 1984, p. 45). 'Endings are not supposed to be "neat" in the genre of the documentary' (Branigan, 1992, p. 98).[6]

This position on documentary difference is also supported by scholars directly interested in the form. Take, for instance, the discussion of documentary in the most intelligent of introductory film textbooks. In *Film Art*, David Bordwell and Kirstin Thompson describe four types of 'non-narrative', two of which, 'categorical film' and 'rhetorical film', are species of documentary.

They offer (1990, pp. 89f.) a hypothetical example to explain what they mean by the 'categorical' documentary:

Suppose we are setting out to make a film about our local grocery store and are considering different ways of organising its form. ... Categorical films, as the name suggests, divide a subject into parts, or categories. In our hypothetical film, the grocery store would be our overall subject. We could go through the store and film each portion, to show what sort of things the store contains. We might show the meat section, the produce section, the checkout counters, and other categories within the store.

What strikes me as being awry here is that this procedure does not suggest a film. It suggests rushes.

Bordwell and Thompson offer some examples of categorical film – for instance, travelogues. But travelogues are almost always journeys, implicitly or explicitly, and the journey is, as we have seen, an archetypical narrative form. The significance of the 'and so we say farewell' cliché is not discussed.

Bordwell and Thompson (1990, p. 91) also offer nature films as another example of the categorical, specifically describing how a study of the butterfly might be organised. Such a film 'might use scientific groupings, showing one type of butterfly and giving information about its habits, then showing another with more information, and so on'. But again, these are rushes; and the dramatic structure often deployed in such films is being ignored. If I were making a butterfly film, I would likely subordinate all information to the great natural drama of the larva's progress through chrysalis to insect. This is one way to turn the Bordwell-Thompson rushes – an inchoate catalogue of categories – into a film.

The actual film Bordwell and Thompson analyse, although without question a documentary, unfortunately makes no better argument for the existence of a categorical form. They take the second part of the American version of Riefenstahl's film of the 1936 Berlin Olympic Games as their case-study.

It is not without significance that an argument for a non-narrative documentary should be based upon the second part of a work, very much an afterthought made up of leftovers – that is, minor sports such as yachting and cross-country horse-riding.

Riefenstahl, faced with the task of making the first Olympic feature film, knew full well how to tell the 'story' of an Olympiad. These were the games at which the business of the torch was introduced. Riefenstahl effectively uses this as a shaping device – from lighting the torch in Greece, which she uses at the start, through to the climactic marathon and closing ceremony featuring the Olympic flame, with which she finishes the film. This framing and ordering, in effect, narrativises the coverage of the sporting events. But all this happens in *Olympia: Part One* (1938).

In consequence, for *Olympia: Part Two* (1938), she has neither beginning nor ending, having already used both. Nevertheless, the first sequence of *Part Two* is shot in morning mists with images of insects and animals. Moreover, the nude males in this sequence echo the start of *Part One* with its nude female 'Greek temple-dancers'. This sense of beginning is then reinforced when the second sequence explores the Olympic village, with shots of the athletes practising, exercising and being massaged, icons of preparation.

There is also a clear ending constructed from diving footage. (The documentary status of many of these shots is ambiguous.) The diving progresses as the day moves via heavily filtered skies to dusk. Eventually, the divers are silhouettes against the sky. The sky above the diving pool then becomes the night sky above the stadium, the first shot in the final sequence. This echoes the closing ceremony of *Part One* (Olympic flame and bell, flags, the stadium at night), omitting only the people performing with flags. Nevertheless, the day is done. The games are done. The film is done.

I would agree that, within these trajectories in both parts, events are not ordered temporally nor do they relate causally. On the other hand, in *Part*

One, the pole-vault sequence goes on into the night and thereby inscribes a new day into the film. Also, this sequence, and some other field events such as the javelin and the high jump, are mini-narratives suspensefully cut as we wait to discover who finally wins. But, again, there is less of this in *Part Two*.

Seymour Chatman cites (1990, p. 20) the Bordwell-Thompson analysis of *Olympia: Part Two* as evidence that 'films, at least documentaries, can also be predominantly descriptive, though subservient moments may follow a narrative line'. It is perhaps not insignificant that Chatman, in reprinting the Bordwell-Thompson list of the 'segments' in *Part Two*, omits 'epilogue in the stadium'. My point is that it is only 'subservient' moments in *Olympia: Part Two* which follow a narrative line because the film, as an afterthought, *is so flawed*.

It is rather like *The Land*, a flawed work which says nothing about documentary exceptionalism; or rather it would be, were it not, from the point of view of formal structuring, not really that exceptional. Without question it does have narrative 'moments' – a beginning and an end, the beginning being in the morning and the end at night.

Beyond that, I would claim that *Olympia: Part Two* can also rely on any audience's understanding of the overall form of the Olympic Games to make up for the lack of causality between its sequences. In any event, it is far more like a story than the hypothetical film-making exercise in the grocery store which Bordwell and Thompson suggest for the categorical.

They propose another non-narrative formal system. The rhetorical documentary 'presents an argument and lays out evidence to support it'. Back to the grocery store:

> We might state the idea that a locally owned store gives better service than does a chain store. For this version we might film the owner of the store giving the customers personal help; we might interview him or her about the services that the store tries to provide; we might interview customers about their opinions on the store. … Overall, we would organize our film to give our audiences reasons to believe that this locally owned store is a better place to shop. (Bordwell and Thompson, 1990, p. 90)

But this, crucially, is *not* organised as a film. It is, once again, a description of rushes.

This is not to question that documentaries do attempt to persuade the viewer by argument and that in so doing elements within the film will be arranged to support an argument. Indeed, the film Bordwell and Thompson cite as a model of the rhetorical documentary is a very good example of this – *The River*. However, their idea of the rhetorical is drawn from Bordwell's gloss as to how Soviet silent fictional cinema 'rhetoricised' (that is, politicised) the *fabula* (story) (Bordwell, 1985, pp. 235f.). So, focused on this, the Bordwell-Thompson analysis of *The River* fails to pinpoint that Lorentz's argument is expressed in a film which has the form of both a voyage and a history.

The River not only progresses down the Mississippi river system from source to delta but also moves in time from the earliest European agriculture in the valley to the present (that is, 1937), with such markers as the Civil War, the years of bad flooding and the start of the Tennessee Valley Authority, clearly indicated.

These time references are very significant, as Bordwell and Thompson well understand. When introducing their list of the various hypothetical ways available in which to film the grocery store, they say (1990, p. 89): 'We could use narrative form by, say, showing *a typical day in the store*. But there are other, non-narrative ways of constructing such a film' (my italics). Chatman points out (1990, p. 9): 'Non-Narrative text types do not have an internal time sequence.' In other words, non-narrative forms depend on the absence of time markers and, conversely, time markers must (at a minimum) offer a presumption of narrative.

Although clearly *The River* does have an internal 'chrono-logic', the question remains: are its sequences causally related? I would make both a particular and a general response to this. In particular, the sequences of *The River* causally relate the flooding of the valley to tree felling on the mountains and its poverty to the overplanting of cotton. The film uses an unexceptional historical causality in these cases both to advance its argument and at the same time to tell its narrative story.

I would also accept, for the more general defence of this position on the inevitability of narrative forms in the Griersonian documentary, Chatman's gloss (1990, p. 9) on narrative causality itself:

In traditional narratives, the internal or story logic entails the additional principle of causality (event *a* causes *b*, *b* causes *c*, and so on) or, more weakly, what might be called 'contingency' (*a* does not directly cause *b*, nor does *b* cause *c*, but they all work together to evoke a certain situation or state of affairs *x*).

This definition more than covers *The River*'s causality. (In fact, even *Olympia: Part Two* would fall within the embrace of Chatman's concept of 'contingency'.) But, nevertheless, Chatman sees *The River*'s as a non-fictional argument like Lincoln's Gettysburg Address. At best such narrative structure as it has is 'in the service' of the film's 'argumentative logic' (Chatman, pp. 10f.). But how can this be so?

The film's argument depends on the last sequence and, as we have seen, that is commonly received as being so slightly integrated as to be an unnecessary addition, the Rooseveltean 'pitch' required by the sponsor. Why? Because, although clearly inscribed via a time marker as a culmination of the history of the river, the sequence comes *after* the journey to the delta is completed. *The River* is certainly a fine example of one text type at another's service, but in exactly the reverse way. The argument serves the narrative.

Bordwell and Thompson see Lorentz's claim in the first section of the script, that 'This is the story of a river', as mendacious: 'Such a statement disguises the rhetorical purpose of the film, implying that the film will be ... presented in narrative form' (Bordwell and Thompson, 1990, p. 102). But it is so presented and, therefore, *The River* will not serve the Bordwell-Thompson case for a rhetorical non-narrative any better than *Olympia: Part Two* does for the concept of the categorical.

Alan Rosenthal also suggests (1990, p. 64) a non-narrative documentary form in his documentary production manual – a structure which he terms 'intellectual'. However, Rosenthal's examples of this 'intellectual' structure – one an episode of James Burke's series *Connections* (1978), and the other his own scenario for a proposed film about car accidents – work no better than do Bordwell and Thompson's since both are really chronological.

Burke's seeming associative method in the *Connections* episode leaps from plastic to credit cards to credit to funding medieval armies to feeding armies and canning food to refrigeration and vacuum flasks to V2s. But Burke's producers were too astute to let him really leap around in both time and space and thereby almost inevitably lose his audience. In fact, after the plastics tease, this is virtually a straight historical chronology – from medieval warfare through Napoleon to Von Braun – with a very pronounced causal relationship between the sequences (Rosenthal, 1990, pp. 61f.). As Rosenthal points out (ibid., p. 51), this series 'was really *history* of technology' (my italics). There is no reason to exclude this episode by suggesting it has an 'intellectual' rather than a chronological structure.

The scenario for Rosenthal's own proposed film on car accidents progresses from a present-day accident through roads, drivers and car design to the safer car of the future – virtually a 'problem moment' structure (ibid., pp. 62f.).

I have chosen the Bordwell-Thompson textbook and the Rosenthal manual rather than other more elevated work exactly to illustrate how pervasive the assumption of documentary difference is; but I am no happier with other accounts in the literature of documentary narrative exceptionalism.

For instance, although Edward Branigan acknowledges (1992, p. 202) that 'many documentary films ... make use of narrative principles to some degree', he still thereby assumes that some, at least, eschew such principles. He offers no examples of these within the classic (that is, the Griersonian) documentary. Nevertheless, he argues that such documentaries cannot have, among other things, 'subjective flashbacks and even point of view shots'.

I will admit that the former are rare, but not impossible, especially in oral history films. There the archive of a well filmed event can be used to illustrate interviews with subjects recalling the event. A close-up of the interviewee, followed by the archive footage, would constitute a subjective flashback.[7] And for all the ambiguity of its meaning, what are the shots at the end of *Shipyard* if not point-of-view? The viewers' maxims (Glasgow Media Group, 1980, p. 243) governing the reading of the relationship between a shot in which a person is seen to be looking at something unseen and the adjacent shot exist as much in the documentary as in fiction.

Branigan (1992, p. 285) makes Dai Vaughan his authority for claiming that 'the traditional notion of the documentary is subverted by the use of such subjective devices'. But Vaughan was concerned with the question of authenticity in two non-Griersonian documentaries where something akin to tricks are being played. He does not address the possibility of subjectivity in the Griersonian documentary at all (Vaughan, 1979, pp. 183 and 185).[8]

Formalist claims for documentary exceptionalism have a *post hoc ergo propter hoc* feel: since documentary is recognisably different in broad terms from fiction, then it ought to differ formally, including being different in its narrative strategies. This then allows for these 'automatic' (as it were) readings of this difference – seeing no closures where there are closures; seeing no temporal schemas where there are temporal schemas; even seeing no drama, only 'exposés'; and so on.

For working documentarists, and those teaching documentary production, obeying narrative norms is usually the most challenging task to be faced. The real work of 'the stage of organising' is, in my experience, almost entirely taken up with making one's materials conform as closely as possible to a 'chrono-logical' and dramatic narrative.

Documentarists do not, in my view, look for closures on the basis of what they have demonstrated – a QED. In my experience, a documentary moves through the following stages, which necessarily include what might be called a QED stage, though this does not necessarily mark the finish:

1   Research to produce an essay (e.g. funding document)
2   An essay to produce a QED closure
3   Analysis of essay to produce a list of sequences to be filmed
4   A reordering of the sequences (in the cutting room) to produce a narrative story, normally with obvious temporal markers

QED is thus subordinate to story structure.

In a script I wrote for Rosenthal on the Holocaust for an American public television documentary series, I traced the development of punitive Nazi race laws and regulations from 1933 to 1941 in one sequence in order to have a background against which the actual course of events could unfold in the next. Rosenthal quite properly pointed out that no mainstream television documentary could hope to cite regulations enforced in 1941 *before* getting to *Reichskristallnacht* in 1938 and not assume that its audience would be confused. I restructured the script (and therefore the film), unscrambling the dates.

I am not here arguing that non-narrative documentaries cannot be made. But *Words for Battle* is as close as any example I know of a film that eschews almost all traces of temporality and causality and still 'works'. But there can be no argument that, far from epitomising the typical documentary structure, its form is most uncommon.

Nor am I suggesting that documentaries are identical to fiction because they are narratives. Rather, I join those who hold that the narrative seems to express a fundamental impulse to tell stories – a characteristic of *mulier narrans* (Fisher, 1985, pp. 74ff.). Some believe that 'a narrative voice pervades virtually every genre and medium of human discourse, ranging from novels and television dramas to sermons, political campaign orations, advertisements, journalistic reports, historical treatises, and everyday conversations' (Lucaites and Condit, 1985, p. 90).

For instance, Paul Atkinson has readily demonstrated (1990, pp. 175ff.) that strong parallels exist between ethnographic writing and fiction. It has even been suggested, by Bruno Latour (1987, p. 53), that narratives can be detected in scientific papers devoted to the hardest of sciences:

Science texts look boring and drab from the most superficial point of view. If the reader recomposes the challenge they take up, they are as thrilling as story telling. 'What is going to happen to the hero [the scientist writing the paper]? Is he going to resist this new ordeal [refuting objections to the data]? No, it is too much even for the best. Yet, it did win? How incredible.'

If narrative is unavoidable, it cannot subvert truth claims *because it is not limited to fiction*. Atkinson (1990, p. 175) makes this point in connection with ethnography: the 'conventions of textuality' – whereby field notes which have been 'written down' get 'written up' for publication – do not of themselves undermine sociology's 'scientific' status.

Bill Nichols is therefore correct to castigate (1991, p. 107) those who use the fictionalising requirements of narrative to make a case against documentary's truth claims. For such an argument to have force requires the existence of a mode of discourse that does not tell stories. If such a mode does not exist, and I incline to believe that it doesn't, then clearly documentary's narrativising propensity is beside the point as regards its truth claim. Narrative is unavoidable and therefore the truth claim has to be, and is, located elsewhere. (See p. 123.)

I rather take the position described by Guynn (1990, p. 154):[9]

> We are thus led to the conclusion that what distinguishes documentary from the fiction film is not the simple presence or absence of narrative. Narrative is never absent in documentary films, even if its presence is more or less marked. Nor can we ascribe a particular mode of narration to documentary, given the heterogeneity of [its] texts. ... Certain documentaries closely resemble the fiction film in that they deploy its basic signifying structures at many textual levels; others mark out their distance by adopting these structures episodically or by restricting them to certain textual functions.

The bottom line is: 'Narrative is never absent in documentary films.' That is why Bordwell and Thompson in the grocery store are caught amidst rushes only halfway to a movie. Non-narrative, in reality, always 'works better in the head than on the screen'.

21

Sincere and Justifiable Reconstruction

There was another aspect to 'treatment'. It could, did, and needed to, occur during the filming. Narrative required 'coverage' (that is, multiple shots from different viewpoints to facilitate cutting); and coverage required, at a minimum, repeated or repetitive actions so that the fictional editing norms could be obeyed.

The Griersonians seemingly never tired of discussing, especially post-1945, the techniques of intervention or 'reconstruction', as this aspect of treatment came to be called. Reconstruction of events which had actually taken place was distinguished from reconstruction of events which had never taken place. The latter were dismissed as unacceptable – fiction. It followed that reconstruction of events which had not necessarily taken place but could have, because they were typical or were syntheses of different actual events, was acceptable also. It was documentary, but only just. The issue of reconstruction came to be virtually the only issue in 'documentary theory'.

Initially, the line between fakery and reconstruction had been extremely blurred. Prizefights were restaged and billed as 'reconstructions' before the turn of the century. This was also done with news coverage. Vitagraph added a 'Battle of Santiago Bay', shot on a tabletop with cut-out models of the boats, to its coverage of San Juan Hill (1898). The Boxer Rebellion was restaged on a Philadelphia roof (1900). Méliès shot the coronation of Edward VII in what was called an authentic 'reconstitution' (1903). Students at a military school in New York played both sides in the re-enactment of a battle in the Russo-Japanese war (1904) (Barnouw, 1974, pp. 24ff.; Musser, 1990, pp. 200ff. and 287). Vitagraph persisted with such practices. In 1909, it re-enacted a ship collision which took place on Long Island Sound, the first time a general radio call for help was sent.

Nanook of the North was thus in a well established tradition in offering its 'most inexact picture of the Eskimo's life', consisting to a large extent of reconstructions (Rotha, 1983, p. 42).

Grierson also used a high degree of intervention and reconstruction from the very beginning. According to his producer, for *Drifters* Grierson had a sculptor design 'an excellent set to represent [the trawler's] cabin, which had been erected somewhere near the port' (Tallents, 1968, p. 27). 'Asked to reproduce their everyday life under these artificial conditions, the fishermen responded magnificently. They never twitched an eyelid. They turned in for the night, got up to haul, cooked, conversed at their meals and swore at the cook as though they were on the high seas fifty miles away' (Hardy, 1979, p. 51). 'A shoal of small roach was assembled in a tank at the Plymouth Marine Biological Station, with fierce looking dogfish mouching around at the right moment, to provide under-water close-ups of the life of the herring shoals. Both roach and dogfish did their parts admirably' (Tallents, 1968, p. 27).

Usually such things were so commonplace as to be unworthy of comment. They were simply part of how a documentary film was made. Grierson does not mention any of this in his contemporary account (1979a, pp. 19ff.) of the difficulties of the film's production.

Intervention might become necessary even in the most lavish of documentary film-making circumstances. For instance, I have already pointed out how Riefenstahl augmented Hitler's arrival at the airport in *Triumph of the Will* with material clearly taken in other locations. But the sequence as a whole has an even more distinctly reconstructed air about it than this alone would suggest.

Riefenstahl is forced to use an out-of-focus shot of the Führer. It begins with two out-of-focus Lufthansa stewards running for the door of the plane; Hitler steps out and the camera does not focus up until Goebbels steps out after him. It is not until five shots after this first appearance that we see Hitler in focus. On the evidence of the film, it seems as if Riefenstahl, wrong-footed at the time of the actual arrival, eked out what she had not only by using other material but also by restaging the landing without Hitler but with a small crowd of extras (six files of about thirty people before a curiously deserted plane).

Albert Speer recalled that Riefenstahl was required to reshoot speeches by Hess and three others in Berlin. There are two shots of Hess and they do not mesh together; in one the serried ranks of men behind him suggest that the lectern was facing Hitler, in the other the background is a ('cookie') light pattern on the wall with a flagpole. The lectern seems to be facing the hall. This speech of Hess's has the worst synch, apart from the music, in the film.[10]

Synch was a major problem. Shooting synch in everyday situations was virtually impossible. In *Night Mail*, real mail-sorters sort mail in a faked rail coach in a studio because the technology would not allow the scene to be shot *in situ*. Harry Watt recalls:

> We couldn't afford what they have in feature films – that is, a rocker set, a set which can be rocked and moved. The studio was tiny. So all we could do was to move by hand, out of picture, certain things like balls of string hanging down, make them sway regularly to give the impression of the train moving, and get the chaps to sway a little bit. With the sound of the train, it gave absolute verisimilitude of the train moving along. (Sussex, 1975, p. 68)

By the late 1940s, the strain of adapting a studio-based technology to the supposedly very different work of documentary filming necessitated regular reconstruction to the point where it was clear that Grierson's 'actual world of our observation' could no longer stand even as a merely rhetorical basis for documentary work. In 1948 a definition stated that documentary film is

> all methods of recording on celluloid any aspect of reality interpreted either by factual shooting *or by sincere and justifiable reconstruction*, so as

to appeal either to reason or emotion, for the purpose of stimulating the desire for, and the widening of human knowledge and understanding, and of truthfully posing problems and their solutions in the spheres of economics, culture and human relations. (Barsam, 1973a, p. 1 – my italics)

That is to say, documentary film had indeed become 'quite unmanageable in criticism' and largely indistinguishable from the more 'realistic' fictional styles then in vogue, of which neo-realism is but the greatest and most fruitful.

In some people's opinion this was the result of the coming of synch sound. Rotha, for instance, felt (1966, p. 195) that 'natural, direct-recorded speech ... is the direct development of the documentary film into the fiction film field'. The worry about this blurring proved to be well founded. Documentarists learned how to direct action and, during and after the Second World War, became increasingly involved in mainstream fiction. For instance, Watt metamorphosed into a feature director while Grierson's last role in the British film industry was to head a feature pro-duction operation, Group Three (1950–3). The thin line between recon-structional synch sound documentaries and regular movies was crossed both stylistically and by the people involved – but not just in one direc-tion. Ian Dalrymple, a producer for Korda, took over the GPO in August 1940, by which time it had been renamed the Crown Film Unit (Sussex, 1975, pp. 125ff.). Figures as theatrical as Noel Coward made films deeply influenced by the Griersonian realist image (Aldgate and Richards, 1986, p. 207). Documentary subjects were remade as features (Sussex, 1975, p. 141).[11]

What had happened, in effect, was that since synch documentaries used the same technology and the same working methods and had the same dramatic objectives as fiction, there was confusion. At the same time, it was increasingly claimed in the years after the Second World War that these inevitable reconstructions, which by now had become something of an ethical problem, were the result of the technological limitations of the apparatus. The answer, more and more documentarists thought, was spe-cial cinematographic apparatus which would allow them to shoot synch in almost any conditions. As the 1950s progressed the necessary equipment to do this became available piece by piece.

The intellectual ground was also shifting. I am not saying that the docu-mentarists in Britain and America were aware of the critical advances in film theory under way in France and associated with André Bazin. The 1950s were over before that began to happen. But Bazin's vision of the cinema was to offer a theoretical framework in which creativity could be downgraded and treatment supposedly ignored in favour of a passionate attachment to actuality.

Following the Surrealists (Sontag, 1977, p. 88, fn.), and in stark con-trast to Arnheim, Bazin luxuriated in the camera's capacity for mechanical reproduction, claiming that an 'advantage' was thereby derived from the absence of man. In photography, he wrote, 'nature does more than imitate art: she imitates the artist'. This allowed for a new aesthetic for the cinema, one based on the 'integral realism' mechanically produced by the apparatus (Bazin, 1967, pp. 15 and 21).

In the long term the significance of the Bazinian view of the apparatus for the documentary project cannot be overstated. It contributed to an aesthetic climate in which these new machines of documentary production could flourish – machines that would supposedly allow for actuality to be filmed for the first time without intervention or reconstruction.

PART FOUR

ACTUALITY: DOCUMENTARY AS SCIENCE

22

Photography as Science

By invoking the term 'actuality' in his definition, Grierson added a third major strand to the documentary film's legitimations. Beyond art, beyond drama, the documentary is also evidential, scientific. The philosopher Grierson may have understood that actuality footage was of 'low priority', but using such a term suggests otherwise (Aitken, 1990, p. 101). The very word 'documentary' depends on the actuality concept in the definition. 'Document', to quote the *OED* once more, is 'something written, inscribed, etc., *which furnishes evidence or information*' (my italics). The 'etc.' embraces photography. This was crucial, especially since Grierson allowed creativity and treatment, both of which worked against any truth claim.

Contemporary positioning of photography as an art does not detract from the camera's status as a scientific instrument. There are two main reasons for this: first, the long history of pictorial representation as a mode of scientific evidence, a history which conditions, in part, the research agenda that produces the modern camera; and second (to be dealt with in the next chapter), the tendency of modern science to produce data via instruments of inscription whose operations are analogous to the camera.

On 3 July 1839 François Arago, the Radical representative for the East Pyrenees, rose in the Chamber of Deputies to persuade the French government to purchase Daguerre's patents for the world. In his arguments he stressed the scientific uses of the apparatus – for instance, to make accurate copies of hieroglyphics and, more generally, for physicists and meteorologists. In short, the camera was to join, as Arago listed them, 'the thermometer, barometer, hygrometer', and the telescope and microscope as nothing so much as the latest of scientific instruments (Eder, 1972, pp. 238f.).

This was the period of 'the professionalisation of precision', when considerable attention was being paid to scientific instrumentation in general. Improved measuring rods, chemical balances and specialised telescopes were at the forefront of advancing knowledge. Self-recording instruments (and the camera is nothing but one such) were also prized as limiting the possibility of observer error (Swijtink, 1987, pp. 263ff.). Arago was able to mount his political argument because the entire enterprise of modern science, an observational and an experimental (and therefore observational) enterprise, had already produced the instruments he mentioned and more, thus creating a class into which the camera could be inserted.

Although used primarily as an artist's aid, the prototype photographic device, the *camera obscura portabilis*, was already part of this scientific culture and had been from the outset. For instance, as early as 1620 the astronomer Kepler had decided that the *camera obscura* removed the artistic element from image making. He had used his, which he normally pointed toward the heavens, to make a traced image of a field near his house. When a visitor expressed astonishment that he was such an artist, Kepler replied, 'Non tanquam pictor' (I'm not so much a painter') 'sed tanquam mathematicus' ('but rather a mathematician, a scientist') (Alpers, 1983, pp. 49f.).

Thus, Arago was able to point out that, although photography would certainly affect some sorts of artistic production, these were of a kind that had long gone on in the service of science. Hence his offering the example of the laborious business of hand-copying Egyptian hieroglyphs as a specific case of what photography might best replace.

Images in the service of science are, Elizabeth Eisenstein argues (1983, p. 26), a result of the spread of the press in Europe. With print, maps, tables, architectural and other patterns, botanical, geographical and anatomical images acquired a new scientific – that is, an evidential – force: 'Fruitful forms of collaboration brought together astronomers and engravers, physicians and painters.'

The use of images for scientific purposes can also be found in a distinct painterly tradition uncovered by Peter Galassi. He suggests that the impulse behind works from Dürer's *The Great Piece of Turf* (1504) to de Valenciennes's studies, in the 1780s, of atmospheric conditions is essentially observational in a scientific sense (Galassi, 1981, p. 25, fig. 17 and p. 27, figs 21–22 and plate 1).

Even as late as the early 19th century, when art and science were assuming their modern oppositional guises, the observational impulse continued to lead some artists to cleave to a certain scientism (Williams, 1976, pp. 233f.). In 1834, Turner rushed to make sketches, which were to be the basis of a future painting, of the burning Houses of Parliament. On another occasion he was sketching on board a steamboat in a snowstorm. On being told that a friend's mother liked the painting that resulted, he said: 'I did not paint it to be understood, but I wished to show what such a scene was like: I got the sailors to lash me to the mast to observe it; I was lashed for four hours, and I did not expect to escape, but I felt bound to record it if I did. But no one had any business to like the picture' (Berger, 1980, pp. 146f.).

In 1836, Constable could still suggest that 'painting is a science, and should be pursued as an inquiry into the laws of nature. Why, then, should not landscape painting be considered as a branch of natural philosophy of which pictures are but the experiments?' (Galassi, 1981, p. 25). Clearly this is an enunciation of the tradition that grows out of Dürer's clump of grass to include all the great naturalist-illustrators up to the present.

Galassi argues that photography, which required no technological or scientific breakthroughs to be 'invented' in the 1830s, lacked an aesthetic basis until then. This basis he locates in the development of a new scientific observational thrust to art which, in Galassi's opinion, brings the various elements together to create photography; although, it can be noted, rhetoric such as Constable's represents at the same historical moment a recovery, or memory, of the Renaissance observational impulse – a tradition Galassi himself outlines. Nevertheless, one would want to add Galassi's insight to more generally understood factors influencing the development of photography, such as the needs of the middle class for personal and decorative images in the years following the French and Industrial Revolutions (Tagg, 1988, p. 37; Freund, 1982, pp. 35 and 57).

The social pressure to create specific images of individuals resulted in a succession of fashionable techniques from the silhouette through the physionotrace to photography. Despite Arago's rhetoric, it was the portraitists and the miniaturists who were most affected by the introduction of photography, and noisiest in expressing their distaste for the development.

It is, of course, possible to read Arago's speech, which gave barely a nod towards photography as a substitute for such painting, as nothing more than a ploy to placate an outraged army of painters. His insistence on science does make this sort of political sense, but it also makes just as much cultural sense – that is, as a plea for science. The 'political' solution was that the portraitists figured prominently among the first users of Daguerre's techniques.

The *carte de visite* democratised the aristocratic miniature. Before photography, it would take the likeness on a coin to trigger the capture of a Louis at Varennes. After photography, the Paris police would use photographs of Communards at the barricades as a basis for arrest. Photography was to become an indispensable and widely used criminological tool in the last third of the century (Freund, 1982, p. 88; Tagg, 1988, pp. 74ff.; Sekula, 1986, p. 5).[1]

If the democratisation of the individual likeness was of primary importance, the provision of other images was a not-too-distant second as an element in the supervening social necessity that engenders photography (Winston, 1986, pp. 21f.). This demand for images, arising as did the need for likenesses among the increasingly culturally dominant bourgeoisie, occasioned a series of technological responses beginning with lithography and continuing with and beyond photography to modern printing and image-reproducing techniques of all kinds. The idea of the photographic reproduction of artworks occurs to an entrepreneur as early as 1860 (Freund, 1982, p. 96). By the late 1880s, the entire Louvre collection could be ordered in photographic form from a catalogue. It is possible to see in this use of photography for artistic reproduction a final affirmation of its scientific heritage. The photograph's scientific ability to produce an image mechanically is the earnest of its accuracy as a copy of the original art.

Arago wanted the camera to take the place of all artistic endeavours in the service of science and his wish has been largely granted. Indeed, by the 1870s, cameras were producing knowledge of physical phenomena, such as motion, that could not be gained in any other way. (Muybridge's first Palo Alto horse sequences were published in the *Scientific American* of 8 August 1878 (Hass, 1976, p. 116).) Yet the old painterly tradition was vibrant enough to persist. Modern scientific artwork can still most readily be seen in natural science texts, the *fons et origo* of the enterprise. Many contemporary versions of these works eschew photography in favour of traditional art. The first Audubon *Field Guide* to use photographs of birds rather than paintings and drawings was not issued until 1977. Paradoxically, it is the contemporary heirs of Audubon who most vividly remind us of one of the camera's primary purposes.

23

Science as Inscription

In photography's founding moment in 1839, the climax of six months of enthusiasm and fear (on the part of the artistic community), Arago, by stressing science, helped condition the public reception of the new technique. By so doing, he officially (as it were) confirmed for the public that the photographic camera, as a scientific instrument rather than an artist's aid, never lies.

Or, rather, the camera lies no more than does the thermometer, the microscope, the hygrometer and so on. Considerable cultural force, the entire thrust of modern science, had already been vested in such a proposition by this time. The instruments cited by Arago were in the service of observation, which was, and remains, critical to modern science.

The modern analytic method emerged in the work of Fernel, a French doctor of the first half of the 16th century. *De Magnete*, the earliest treatise entirely based on the observation of physical phenomena, was published in 1600 by William Gilbert, the Queen's physician and the coiner of the term 'electricity'. This empiricism was propagandised by Francis Bacon:

> Man is the helper and interpreter of Nature. He can only act and understand in so far as by working upon her or observing her he has come to perceive her order (Hill, 1974, p. 36).

> Now my direction for the interpretation of nature embraces two generic divisions: the one how to educe and form axioms from experience; the other how to deduce and derive new experiments from axioms (Gregory, 1981, p. 237).

With Bacon, observation and experiment become the bases of judgments about the external world. This reflects the modern belief, only now coming under attack, that, as Galileo put it, 'The conclusions of natural science are true and necessary, and the judgement of man has nothing to do with them' (Ravetz, 1973, p. 18).

Elizabeth Eisenstein (1983, pp. 191ff.) cautions us not to read too clean a break with the immediate past here. Observation, as a method, dates back to the Greeks. Conversely, for Bacon and his contemporaries the 'Great Book of Nature', itself a medieval conceit, was still to be found more in ancient texts, now newly printed, than in the proto-laboratory. This was in part because books themselves became more reliable as data. Eisenstein argues (p. 199) not that observation was unknown prior to the printing press but that the dissemination of observations was particularly prone to scribal degradation. In the scrolls, 'words drifted apart from pictures, and labels became detached from things'. Print fixed that.

The dominance of empiricism was to be the defining mark of the modern post-Baconian world. Observation alone became paramount in the life sciences and astronomy, while in physics and chemistry it became the prick to theory and thence to 'theory-laden' experimentation (Hill, 1974, pp. 178, 127 and 247ff.; Ravetz, 1973, pp. 123f.). *'Fiat experimentum'*.

The resultant observation of experiments was, for Bacon, 'the most radical and fundamental towards natural philosophy; such natural philosophy as shall not vanish in the fume of subtle, sublime or delectable speculation, but such as shall be operative to ... the benefit of man's life; for ... it will give a more true and real illumination concerning causes and axioms than is hitherto attained' (Boas, M., 1970, p. 236).

The 'true and real illumination' of experimentation was, over the next few centuries, to effect a major epistemological shift in which 'evidence' in the form of experimental data became paramount. 'The defining characteristic', according to Carl Hempel (1983, p. 10), 'of an empirical statement is its capability of being tested by a confrontation with experimental findings.'

The centrality of experimental observations in the modern world brought the sorts of devices Arago was to list more and more generally into play. Eventually much of the 'Book of Nature' was to be read in the gauges, meters and physiographs of the modern laboratory. 'Nothing', wrote Arago's contemporary, Sir Humphrey Davy, 'tends so much to the advancement of knowledge as the application of a new instrument. The native intellectual powers of men in different times, are not so much the causes of the different success of their labours, as the peculiar nature of the means of artificial resources in their possession' (Swijtink, 1987, p. 265).

Moreover, the instrument had become the guarantor of scientific truth, ensuring that conclusions are, just as Galileo asserted they should be, safely removed from human judgment. 'Instruments of observation and measurement make scientific knowledge independent of the testimony of judicious and honest witnesses. ... Such direct read-out systems say, as it were, out loud what they "observe", and the observer literally reads the Book of Nature' (ibid., pp. 266 and 268).

The result is the strong claim, which remained uncontested almost into the present, that 'Scientific data do not belong to the consciousness of the perceiving subject, we believe, because different observers will obtain the same data' (ibid., p. 268).

Yet, at the same time, Bacon's vision of empiricism leading to a 'more true and real illumination' of the natural world was somewhat thwarted. The sum of observations as they steadily began to accumulate did not add up in ways that would replace the old certainties of faith, as Bacon had hoped they would. Science began to undermine religious certitudes but produced something less certain in their place. This was because of 'the dullness, incompetency, and deceptions of the senses', and the inadequacies of instruments such as the microscope as correctives, all of which Bacon fully understood (Gregory, 1981, p. 236). These deficiencies were to erode the ancient distinction between knowledge and opinion, eventually causing more complex patterns of belief to arise.

Scientific data came to occupy a sort of middle ground, fudging the knowledge/opinion dichotomy. Scientific knowledge was then further divided between the greater certainties of logic and mathematics and the lesser certainties of experience and observation (Shapiro, 1983, p. 29). Within years of Bacon's death came the suggestion that these new lesser certainties could perhaps be bolstered, as it were, by an appeal to mathematics. This appeal, if successful, would give experience and observation the same sort of claims on truth as mathematics. It was grounded in probability.

The mathematical concept of probability emerges in the middle years of the 17th century and by 1668 Leibnitz was suggesting that probability theory could function as a logic, moving observational results to the plane of mathematical demonstrations – a plane where assent was compelled rather than vouched for 'morally'. Thus began what Thomas Kuhn calls 'the mathematisation of Baconian physical science' (Cohen, B., 1987, p. 41).

By the early 19th century science was ready to abandon the residual Newtonian certainties of cause and effect in favour of a less well determined, more probabilistic (and statistical) *Umwelt*. The trajectory that accomplishes this movement occurs from around 1800 to about 1930 and has been considered so momentous as to merit the term 'revolution'. Whether or not that is appropriate is debated; but, without question, a major paradigm shift can be discerned (Cohen B., 1987, p. 40). 'In 1800 the world was deemed governed by stern necessity and universal laws. Shortly after 1930 it became virtually certain that at bottom our world is run at best by laws of chance' (Hacking, 1987, p. 45).

The rise of probabilistics in science, like the status of the camera as a scientific apparatus, is of first importance to the concept of 'actuality' as it was generally understood in Grierson's day.[2] It is not so much the mathematisation of the physical sciences but rather the closely related rise of statistics which that mathematisation involved that is significant here. For the realist documentary, the social science effects of the new probabilistic paradigm are what matters.

> It is customary to designate various sociological generalisations, as for example 'Gresham's Law', as scientific 'laws'. These are in fact typical probabilities confirmed by observations to the effect that under certain conditions an expected course of social action will occur, which is understandable in terms of the typical motives and typical subjective intentions of the actors. (Weber, 1971, p. 99)

The paradigm shift to this Weberian probabilistic universe was phased.

As Ian Hacking periodises it, first came an 'avalanche of printed numbers'. These were produced not only by the professionalisation of measurement in the pure sciences, mentioned above, but also in the 'moral' (that is to say, social) sphere. Censuses, marriage and suicide rates, natality and mortality tables all proliferated at a level of accuracy never before seen. These statistics revealed, for the first empirical social scientists, the paradox that individual differences masked profound regularities when considered across a mass of data. That these regularities encompassed seemingly random individual acts such as marriage, suicide or crimes astonished early researchers.

The search for such regularities became dominant and has remained so. The Belgian astronomer and meteorologist, Adolphe Quetelet, was a major pioneer of such insights. For instance, he used the *Compte général de l'administration de la justice en France* to generate the first statistically based study of crime, his 1831 *Research on the Propensity for Crime at Different Ages*. In another project, he set about measuring the chests of whole Highland regiments to determine an average for such soldiery. On the bases of these 'social mechanics', Quetelet coined one of the defining terms of the modern world, 'l'homme moyen' (Quetelet, 1984, pp. 4 and 6ff.). Quetelet's example, and the work of other statistically minded scientists and social researchers, generated something akin to a faith in 'the regularity of numbers' between 1835 and 1875 (Hacking, 1987, pp. 52f.).[3]

What this faith portended was summed up by Sir John Herschel in 1835:

> Men began to hear with surprise, not unmingled with some vague hope of ultimate benefit, that not only births, deaths, and marriages, but the decisions of tribunals, the results of popular elections, the influence of punishments in checking crime – the probable limits of error in numerical results in every department of physical inquiry ... might come to be surveyed with that lynx-eyed scrutiny of a dispassionate analysis which, if not at once leading to the discovery of positive truth, would at least secure the detection and proscription of many mischievous and besetting fallacies. (Cohen, B., 1987, p. 38)

Although this did not quite come to pass, enough of it occurred for Mark Twain, born in the year Herschel wrote these words, to be more than witty when he railed against 'lies, damned lies and statistics'. He was speaking for an older, more obviously causal and less probabilistic world.

Against this background of numbers, social investigation became transformed. For instance, John Clay, prison chaplain at Preston Gaol in the 1830s, found his impressionistic annual reports (required by the reforming Gaol Act of 1823) taken up by the Manchester Statistical Society (Clay, 1969, p. 125). In this context the first-person accounts Clay solicited from the prisoners were elevated to the level of data rather than literature. Thus the concept of the average man, that most potent creation of the 'avalanche of numbers', legitimated new forms of social investigation, such as those of Henry Mayhew.

The *Morning Chronicle* articles of 1849–50 on the London poor for which Mayhew is best remembered are replete with statistical information, much available from official sources and much more (on average wages, for instance) created by Mayhew himself. His methods involved calling mass meetings of workers to determine pay levels and terms of trade (Thompson, 1972, pp. 24 and 29). Even the essentially impressionistic portraits of individuals and their first-person biographical accounts, the literary element that has kept his reports in print, were worked up from formulaic interviews, some conducted by other interviewers trained and closely supervised by Mayhew (Yeo, 1972, pp. 63ff.). These are the elements that elevate the work from the higher journalism into the realm of social science.

Robert Colls and Philip Dodd point out the continuity of the line from Mayhew to Grierson via such works as Sims's *How the Poor Live* (1887) or Reynold's *A Poor Man's House* 1907. As they say (1985, p. 22), 'The titles and subjects ... might be those of documentary film'.

The wide reception of these sorts of reports, investigations, studies and books has meant that the statistical frame came to be implied; for, in general, the numbers, as it were, could now be taken as read. 'Causal explanation depends on being able to determine that there is a probability, which in the rare ideal case can be numerically stated, but is *always in some sense calculable*, that a given observable event (overt or subjective) will be followed or accompanied by another event' (Weber, 1971, p. 98 – my italics). It is this implied statistical frame, grounded in probability, that allows much social science to maintain its 'scientific' claims, despite such things as the strong formal parallels between fiction and ethnographic writing, for example.

Implicit probabilistics allow for any particular account of an event or person, if presented as being of social significance, to be received as evidence of whole classes of such events or persons. Probability leads to synecdoche and synecdoche thus becomes critical for documentary film 'actuality'. Grierson's entire push for 'public education' comes in a decade where 'never before, it may be assumed, have statistics been so greatly in demand' (Muggeridge, 1971, p. 259). Grierson endowed the documentary with, exactly, Mayhew-style social significance, thus bringing the form within this realm of probabilistics and statistics. One fishing smack is the herring industry. One train is the night mail system.

This is why realist documentaries ever since have existed in free fall between the general and the particular. Documentary titles often in themselves reinforce this synecdoche: *An American Family, Symphony of a City, Man of Aran, The Plow that Broke the Plains.* Films are never called *Events observed during a facilities visit to a military establishment by me and my crew when we happened to have the camera switched on.* On the screen, every last Inuit, industrial worker, and deep-sea fisherman comes to stand both for themselves and for a class of persons of their type. The actual image is of one particular person; the rhetoric of the title and the genre is of a tribe. Parts need to stand for whole classes if a claim of social relevance is to be sustained.

The 1966 *CBS Reports* 'Sixteen in Webster Groves', directed by Arthur Barron, is the exception that supports this contention. Barron, with a doctorate in sociology from Columbia, gave his filmed study of an upper-class St Louis suburb the underpinnings of a full-scale research survey. The instrument to do this was designed by the University of Chicago's National Opinion Research Center. At a cost of $12,500 the survey documented, in approved probabilistic ways, the value system of all the sixteen-year olds in the community. This Mayhew-like exercise has seldom been repeated by documentarists. Perhaps the reception of the film explains why.

The overt sociological ambitions of 'Sixteen in Webster Groves' caused a backlash – including 'a howl of rage' from the community itself (Rosenthal, 1971, p. 139). The designer of the research instrument felt: 'There was an awful lot of Fellini in the show, which was artistic rather than sociological' (Hammond, 1981, p. 54). Barron was accused of selecting a narrow group of conservative parents and, despite all his efforts, still distorting the image of the community (Rosenthal, 1971, pp. 134f.). Alan Rosenthal comments (ibid., p. 132) that 'for a programme that purports to be based on serious scientific research, the resultant picture seems to provide a mere surface description rather than any serious sociological analysis'.

My point is that no 'serious sociological analysis' can ever be provided by the Griersonian documentary because of the flight from social meaning implicit in the form. It has therefore proved better for documentarists to trade upon *implied* sociology. If a film takes the otherwise neglected road and puts back this normally assumed sociological apparatus, its failure to deliver on that promise becomes too glaring. 'Sixteen in Webster Groves' is a proof of that contention.[4]

Synecdoche grounded in probabilistics explains how, for instance (and obviously only in part), Humphrey Jennings came to be a realist film-maker. Probabilistics, in this received sense, made coherent his interest on the one hand in surrealism – he was an organiser of the International Surrealist Exhibition in London in 1936 – and, on the other hand, his role as a founder of Mass Observation, a prototype sociological survey organisation, which led to his work as a documentarist. Probability is the bridge; because, while measuring one Highlander's chest is an unexceptional activity, measuring the chests of whole Highland regiments has to be a somewhat 'surreal', as were it, caper. Seeking to know what each and every Briton does in various situations (as Mass Observation set out to do) is in like case. Mass Observation's initial survey agenda reads almost like a surrealist poem:

> ....
> Shouts and gestures of
> motorists
> The aspidistra cult
> Anthropology of football pools
> Bathroom behaviour
> Beards, armpits, eyebrows. ...
> (Jennings, M.-L., 1982, p. 17)

Surveying such phenomena was, as one of Jennings's colleagues Tom Harrisson put it, 'a kind of social super-realism' (Hodgkinson, 1975, p. 32). In a general sense, this surrealism/super-realism of the average becomes a bridge for all Griersonian documentarists between the creative and the actual, a way in which the 'poetic', as they saw it, could neverthe-less function within the scientism of 'actuality'. Thus in Jennings's notes for *Diary for Timothy* we see these Mass Observation classes of person individualised for the camera but not losing their claim on the more general at the same time:

> the airman, peering through the perspex windscreen
> the engine driver leaning out of his cab
> the farmer looking over the years accounts
> the actor holding up Yorick's skull: 'I knew him, Horatio ... a fellow of
>   infinite jest ...'
> The miner combing the coal dust out of his hair.
> (Jennings, M.-L., 1982, p. 39)

It is, then, both in these probabilistic ways and because the camera is a scientific instrument that the documentary remains very close to the enter-prise of modern science. Indeed, it is so close that the modern scientific inquiry can appear to be identical to documentary investigation. This is because, as I was noting above, science depends on modes of representation if the 'Book of Nature' is to be read. And these modes are analogous to the audiovisual processes of the documentary film.

Consider Bruno Latour's 'obstinate dissenter', a somewhat deviant person of our own time, who refuses to believe a result reported in a scientific paper.

In Latour's exposition (1987, pp. 64ff.), this person eventually penetrates the laboratory of the professor who has produced the result being questioned. The dissenter wants to go behind the text to the actual experiment. '"You doubt what I wrote?", says the professor. "Let me show you."' The obstinate dissenter is led to an array in which a physiograph has been mounted. Out of the device comes a paper on which is an image just like the ones the dissenter saw reproduced in the original paper.

The obstinate dissenter realises that, as Latour puts it, 'We are at the junction of two worlds: a paper world that we have just left, and one of instruments we are just entering. A hybrid is produced at the interface: a raw image, to be used later in an article, that is emerging from an instrument.' Latour describes this hybrid as a 'fragile film that is in between text and laboratory'.

At the heart of the array is a glass chamber in which is suspended the ileum of a guinea-pig. When the professor injects substances into the chamber, the ileum responds and the needles of the physiograph dance. Latour writes: 'This perturbation, invisible in the chamber, is visible on paper; the chemical, no matter what it is, is given shape on paper.' That is the shape to which the professor points to stifle the obstinate dissenter's doubts about his results.

Latour equates *scientific instrument* with *inscription device*. For Latour, the work of science is to create set-ups, arrays, which produce inscriptions which can be used in texts, scientific papers. 'What is behind a scientific text?' he asks (p. 71). 'Inscriptions. How are those inscriptions obtained? By setting up instruments.' And what happens when we are confronted with an instrument? Latour says, 'we are attending an "audio-visual" spectacle. There is a visual set of inscriptions produced by the instrument and a verbal commentary uttered by the scientist.'

I would like to suggest that we have reached a place not unlike that occupied by the viewer of a documentary film.

There is, then, a powerful argument, grounded in centuries of modern scientific inquiry, for seeing the camera as no more and no less than a device for representing the world of natural phenomena, a device like any other Latourian 'instrument'. At this level of history and culture, there is no difference between the camera and, say, the thermometer. Like the thermometer, the camera is culturally positioned to 'say ... out loud' what has been observed. Indeed, as a self-recording inscription device, it is positioned, as it were, to shout.

Arago wanted us to believe in the photograph as evidence, as truth; and we have. Within a couple of decades, the philosopher Charles Peirce was categorising the photograph as a perfect exemplum of his concept of the indexical relationship of sign (the photograph) to signified (the object(s) photographed) because one 'really affects' the other (Peirce, 1965, p. 143). Photographs, he thought, were produced, by a 'physical connection'; that is, they were 'physically forced to correspond point by point to nature' – as if the camera was indeed a species of hygrometer (ibid., p. 159; Ormiston, 1977, fig. 2).[5]

Such naivety persisted into this century. In the 1940s, James Agee could still claim (1966 [1941], p. 211), without fear of much contradiction, that cameras 'like scientific instruments and unlike any other leverage of art' are 'incapable of recording anything but truth, absolute truth'. Bazin suggested (1967, p. 12, n.) that light moulded the phographic image as a face moulds a death mask. As the *Encyclopédie française* puts it: 'The photographic plate does not interpret. It records. Its precision and fidelity cannot be questioned' (Bourdieu, 1990, p. 73). However false this might be to some current thinking, Agee, Bazin and the *Encyclopédie* without question accurately sum up the nature of photographic authority as it was still popularly understood in Grierson's day: 'A camera or a recording apparatus, it was argued, had no possibility of falsifying the objects or sounds they reproduced; therefore ... truthfulness was assured' (Muggeridge, 1971, p. 254).

Malcolm Muggeridge goes on: 'Such an attitude of mind presupposes that life's outward appearance exhausts its whole nature.' But such cynicism and sophistication was exceptional until well into the 1950s, if not beyond. Photographs, for most people, even at their least powerful, 'furnish evidence' (Sontag, 1977, p. 5). 'A good photograph is, above all, a good document' (Hambourg, 1984, p. 29).

Documentary's scientific connection is the most potent legitimation for its evidential pretensions. 'Actuality' came with the territory, as it were – so much so that the truth claims of the Griersonian documentary were able to survive the artistic claims of the film-makers and the narrativising mediations of their practice exactly because of the inherent scientific status of photography. To this day, documentarists cannot readily avoid the scientific because that context is built in to the cinematographic apparatus.

So, when documentary film-makers liken their work to data collection or 'voyages of discovery' (Atkins, 1974, p. 233), they implicitly position their audiences as Latourian obstinate dissenters who have penetrated the lab of their film-making experiments.[6] Watching 'actuality' on the screen is like watching the needles dance on the physiograph: the apparatus becomes transparent; the documentary becomes scientific inscription – evidence.

24

Evidence in the Law

The cultural concept of evidence also, obviously, involves the law. The positioning of legal evidence within our culture serves, by analogy and extension, further to legitimate and bolster the reception of the documentary camera's output as evidence of 'actuality'.

Despite this, though, there is a considerable difference between the evidence in science and in the law. In science, evidence bolstered by probabilistics has been held, almost without question until recently, to be congruent with truth. In law, the gap between evidence and truth was, and remains, wide. For the better part of a thousand years it was a chasm and, in the common law tradition at least, it has never been bridged by scientific concepts of probability.

At the outset of the common law so unprovable were facts that judgment could only be reached by appeals to the Almighty (*judicium Dei*) in the form of ordeals or, later, battles (judicial duels). Compurgation, where third parties came forward to swear that a party to or in an action was honest, was also used.[7] With this system of procedure, as Maitland pointed out (1965, p. 115), 'in the courts before the Conquest, the proof comes after the judgement' – that is, the court decided only who bore the burden of proof and what ordeal or compurgation should be used to determine it. Even an eyewitness offered only contestable opinion, an opinion which he or she might be required to prove true by battle.

It was not that the concept of evidence, as it is now understood, was alien. There was of course 'the violent presumption' of guilt occasioned by the perpetrator having been caught red-handed or in possession, although even one taken by the hue and cry was not to be denied ordeal, in theory at least (Ireland, 1942, pp. 245f.).

There was also the possibility of 'light presumptions' of guilt, including more circumstantial data. In the 9th century, for instance, a rustler was apprehended in part because, 'as he fled, a bramble scratched him all over his face; and when he wished to deny the charge, this was brought as evidence against him' (Harding, 1973, p. 128).

Above all, there was the law's ever-growing appetite for documentation. The main thrust of much legal procedure was to become the proving of fact by written documents. However, in the early period, even documents required witnesses to attest to their authenticity – which again, vexatiously, occasioned the need for judgment as to the credibility of the witnesses.

In Roman systems, the difficulty of establishing truth was in part resolved by a mechanistic approach to evaluating evidence, especially after the Lateran Council condemned trial by ordeal in 1215. Elaborate values were given to different sorts of evidence and the differing social status of witnesses. These were totted up by the judge, who was then bound to find according to the result of this sum. These procedures are referred to as 'rational modes of proof'.

'Rational' in this context, though, still does not mean modern rationality. Although obviously a step closer to current notions than was believing in ordeals, giving the nobleman (for instance) more 'points' than the peasant woman simply because the one was who he was and the other who she was scarcely seems rational to the modern mind. (Yet the propensity of modern British courts until very recently to believe the police in all circumstances is clearly in this tradition.) Even worse, under the Roman system 'full proof' in criminal cases required confession, which led to the regular and widespread use of torture (Shapiro, 1983, 173f.).

Unless the party were caught in the act, courts found converting evidence to proof, still no easy matter, extremely problematic. In England, where the Roman Canonist approach with its inevitable concomitant of torture was eschewed, the jury slowly rose to pre-eminence as the determiner of fact. Juries were first empanelled exactly because they already knew the circumstances of the case and so needed little evidence. As they became more distanced from any particular set of circumstances which they might be required to consider, their capacity to try the facts became more attenuated and so evidence became more significant. Still, all they heard under oath was treated as being equally valid. Even eyewitnesses were as yet not cross-examined and the distinction between eyewitnesses (*de visu*) and hearsay witnesses (*auditu*) was not clearly drawn (Bigelow, 1880, pp. 250ff., 308 and 336).

The result was that some in court simply disbelieved as a matter of principle everything they were told and relied, as being the best evidence available, on the demeanour of the parties before them (Harding, 1973, p. 49; Green, 1988, p. 359). Rhetoric continued, therefore, to play a critical role in the matter of proof, as it had done in ancient times (Twining, 1985, p. 11). In consequence, the concept of evidence, the relative value of its various forms, and systems by which all these could be weighed and evaluated were imperfectly understood.

This was still the situation in Bacon's time, despite the decline of ordeal and battle, the emergence of the jury and the beginnings of modern cross-examination (Potter, 1932 p. 256). In 1616, for example, nine women were condemned as witches at the Leicester assizes on the uncorroborated testimony of one child (Cockburn, 1972, p. 120). Moreover, a hedge of extraordinary technicalities coalesced around common law legal procedure so that, as scientifically-minded seventeenth-century judges sought to import new scientific insights into the nature of evidence, they were nevertheless thwarted.

Slowly, however, the rationalist implications of the rise of modern science – that events occur and it is possible to have knowledge of them albeit incompletely – began to impinge even on these extremely conservative legal practices (Twining, 1985, pp. 13f.). The Baconian approach had influenced lawyers, despite themselves as it were, in a number of ways. Barbara Shapiro points out (1983, p. 168) that the rise of casebook and systematic court reports, as a legal equivalent of experimental data collection, begins only after Bacon. More important, both judges and philosophers begin to talk about weighing evidence in probabilistic ways, although in England this approach continued to smack of despised continental procedures. Despite this rising awareness, it was not until the middle of the 18th century that evidence became sufficiently distinct as a legal topic to warrant a textbook, and even longer before reforms in the actual conduct of trials were undertaken (Shapiro, 1983, p. 181).

Jeremy Bentham was the first to propose radical reform, in the name of a 'natural' (that is to say, rationalist) system, rather than just offer philosophical speculation (à la Locke and others) as to what such a system should encompass. By Bentham's time, the well-established philosophical position was that each piece of evidence should be subject to rationalist testings, namely: Is the witness confident of the truth of the testimony? Is the testimony likely as conforming to general experience? Is the witness credible? Is the testimony contested by other testimony? (Twining, 1985, pp. 48 and 55). Yet it was only in 1808 that Bentham began to convert this into an agenda for action by demonstrating how this could be worked in practice.

These Benthamite reforms were eventually to vanquish 'Judge & Co.' and install the modern trial and with it the modern cross-examination. Now, instead of the truth being sought, rather tests for a 'balance of probability' in civil cases or degrees of commonsense certainty ('beyond reasonable doubt') in criminal ones are used to evaluate the weight of evidence. It thus took the better part of a millennium to get from grasping hot pokers, dunkings, torture and the like to 'Where were you on the night of ...?'

Yet, despite Bentham's talk that such new procedures could be made to constitute *a thermometer* of persuasion, the sort of 'calculus of probability' which was becoming so important in science remained alien to the law. Bentham himself, perhaps because he saw the mathematics of probability as being applicable only to closed classes of events such as dice rolls, denied that it could be of use in weighing evidence (Twining, 1985, pp. 56ff.). Others, following Leibnitz, were not so unwilling. The mathematician George Boole, in the 1850s, 'had no hesitation in applying the mathematical theory to the probability that a person accused in a criminal court is guilty'. Yet, even if a prejudice against continental practice is laid aside, most have felt that in reality the calculation cannot be done because legal data are limited and the human situations involved are so complex (Cohen, J., 1977, p. 52). And that view has prevailed among common lawyers.[8]

The legal concept of evidence is important to the idea of documentary 'actuality' in two ways. Although documentary's truth claim depends, I have been arguing, on the fact that, because of the camera, scientific evidence is what is on the screen, scientific evidence itself is influenced by the concept of evidence in the law. After all, the law, as it were, came first. Bacon, let us not forget, was a lawyer, and so was Leibnitz, at least by training. So the law provides the general cultural concept of evidence into which science and documentary's truth claims in general both fit.

Also, the law is the source of a critical documentary technique – the interview. The filmed interview is causally related to Benthamite legal reforms because, almost as soon as the new 'natural' legal interrogatory was in place in the courts, it was borrowed for journalism and, as we have seen, for social science, and then borrowed again for radio and the cinema.

Newspapers had from their very beginnings reported in their own words accounts of events witnessed by others. One such appears to be a story on the death of Blackbeard the pirate published in 1719. From the early 19th century on, occasional question-and-answer pieces began to appear in the English-speaking press, significantly in connection with crime stories. These took the form of reported courtroom conversations. By the 1830s they were a popular feature:

Mag. 'You are charged with being drunk in Catherine Street'.

'I was not drunk', exclaims [the prisoner] indignantly, 'but I allow that sleep overtook me when I was woke up by this fellow of a watchman'.

Watch: 'He was rolling about like a tar barrel, Sir'. (Nilsson, 1971, p. 712)

That this style should emerge as part of court reporting was obviously no accident.

The next stage was for the journalist himself to talk with the witnesses, using '"the interview method" from the court, putting himself into the position of the magistrate' and printing the answers as a first-person account. This innovation is usually credited to James Gordon Bennett, who interviewed a key witness in a New York murder case in 1836 (Nilsson, 1971, pp. 713 and 708).[9] Within thirty years, the 'interview method' was beginning to be used in a modern way for eliciting general information:

HG: What is the position of your Church with respect to Slavery?

BY: We consider it of Divine institution, and not to be abolished until the curse pronounced on Ham shall have been removed from his descendants.

HG is Horace Greeley obeying his own dictum ('Go west, young man; go west!') by interviewing BY, Brigham Young, head of the Church of Jesus Christ of Latter-Day Saints, in Salt Lake City on 20 August 1859 (Turnbull, 1936, pp. 275f.).

This procedure of Greeley's differed from the sociological interrogatories of Mayhew in a number of regards. It stands alone, not being designed, as was Mayhew's, to flesh out a probabilistic statistical picture. It is also not formulaic but tailored to the particular ebb and flow of the interrogation. Mayhew was a journalist and his survey appeared in a newspaper, but his 'dogged preoccupation with employment and poverty' also made him different from Greeley and other journalists (Yeo, 1972, p. 66). Greeley, as a journalist, was not 'dogged' about anything. Journalism, investigative reporting aside, was to eschew dogged preoccupation in favour of instant sensation most of the time. But journalism, even sensationalist journalism, was willing to borrow an evidence-gathering technique from the courts, just as social science was.

Newspaper interviews were to become common practice in the 1870s, the word itself with this specific journalistic connotation being dated to 1869. The rise of the interview, though, was controversial. It was described as 'the most perfect contrivance yet devised to make journalism an offence, a thing of ill savour in all decent nostrils' (Mott, 1962, p. 386). Some worried about the degree of collusion which could be present: 'The "interview" [*sic*] as at present managed is generally the joint product of some humbug of a hack politician and another humbug of a reporter' (ibid.).[10]

Despite the interview's basic artificiality and unnaturalness as a mode of discourse, it becomes, after *Housing Problems*, a staple of the Griersonian documentary. It is even to be found, as we shall shortly see, in modern direct cinema films (where the film-makers ostensibly eschew interviews but do not mind filming people interviewing each other).

This heavy reliance on legalistic modes of evidence does not mean that filming is, without further corroboration, an actual legal record. That this is the case, however, is nothing more than an acknowledgment of the general overall difficulty the law has had over the centuries, in contrast to science, in establishing evidential procedures. The result is that the camera produces a record, on the legalistic model, of the events filmed – even down to legal-style interrogatories, interviews. The legal tradition casts the documentarist as witness to the original scene (and, even more overtly, the interviewee as witness to data unfilmed or unfilmable).

But science casts the documentary film *audience* as jurors of the film as evidence. Documentary mimesis is grounded in assumptions about the nature of evidence that come from using the camera as a scientific instrument. The law thus interposes itself to offer a cultural context in which this audience as jury can operate; but the camera's scientific status is the bedrock upon which documentary's truth claim must rest or collapse.

25

Technologising the Documentary Agenda

The power of this legal framework released the first generation of realist documentarists from the need explicitly to exploit the scientific connection – that is to say, the cultural strength of the idea of photographic evidence. Narrative requirements, which imprisoned the Griersonians in the Hollywood norms of spatial and temporal continuity, anyway inhibited them from so doing. The more they sought to avoid 'shapeless reproduction', the further they removed themselves from evidence, observation and science. Yet this did not prevent science from being crucial to their enterprise.

Since documentaries used the same technology and the same working methods and had the same dramatic objectives as fiction, the resultant confusion could only be unscrambled by referencing science implicitly in terms of the purposes of the film-makers and the responses of audiences ('public education'). The implicit cultural positioning of the apparatus was central to this effort, but it had a cost.

In the long run (that is, by the late 1940s), science was ceasing to be the documentarists' willing servant, silent and unseen. Instead, it was becoming a demanding boss. Specifically, conventional documentary techniques requiring intervention and mediation were more and more seen as unfortunate or bad practices, in conflict with truth claims inherent in the camera. Reconstruction, increasingly commonplace since the coming of sound, was becoming particularly suspect. If what distinguished the documentary was that it offered evidence of the real world, how could such manipulations be justified? More and more it was held that they could not.

Documentary found itself in this difficulty because Arago's claim for the apparatus was too strong at the outset. For post-war documentarists, the suggestion that the machine could obtain its evidence with any ease was particularly overstated. In fact, the cinematographic apparatus, as it had developed in the film studio, did not allow for representations of the real world to be made in real time with any facility at all. To record with it required massive interventions, especially if sound was being taken and especially in anything less than bright sunlight. This was a problem, and an ever more vexed one, for these film-makers. This new generation increasingly thought that, as the camera was too unwieldy and too intrusive, the documentary's truth claim could be sustained only if it could be redesigned.

Technological solutions, in the form of a sound camera small enough and sensitive enough to light to be carried into any situation unobtrusively, had not immediately occurred to their predecessors, the documentary pioneers. First, for Grierson, Lorentz and their immediate followers, the implicit scientific foundations were still uncracked. Second, downsizing the studio gear was not as attractive an option as it was to become. As I have pointed out, in the 1930s, small – sub-standard, 16mm or less – meant the amateur or, perhaps worse, the politically active. The technology was suspect for more than just its supposed deficiencies in quality.

Anyway, this first generation of realist film-makers tended to avoid confronting technological developments. Not only did they virtually ignore 16mm; they had also attempted to sidestep synchronous sound:

> Generally speaking ... synchronised sound and speech obtained simultaneously do not play a large part in documentary production.... There is a practical point that we might well remember in this connection – the greater difficulties attending the portability of sound equipment when compared with the compactness of the modern automatic camera. Sound trucks are essentially large and cumbersome objects. They attract attention, disturb the natural characteristics of the material being shot and upset the intimacy which the documentarist tries to create between himself and his subject. Mobile sound ... is most useful for the gathering of natural wildtracks, in which case it is used separately from the picture camera. (Rotha, 1966, p. 165)

Sound was seen by the Griersonians as the site of experimentation exactly because it was non-synchronous. The authority of Pudovkin, Eisenstein and Alexandrov was cited for 'asynchronism', and Cavalcanti joined the GPO unit specifically to experiment with sound (Sussex, 1975, p. 12). Synch sound limited the artistic possibilities which Cavalcanti was exploring. In one sense it moved documentary back towards shapeless reproduction. On the other hand, as Cavalcanti's developing interests in the late 1930s reveal, it also forced what were regarded as too overtly fictional techniques on the material.

Finally, the introduction of a number of small, or rather smaller, umblimped cameras (the American Eyemo and the German Arriflex, for instance) allowed for hand-holding, which was becoming acceptable in certain circumstances, initially war coverage. But synch sound, with its microphones, booms and enormous optical recorders requiring two people to carry them, 'restricted' this possibility (Van Dyke, 1946, p. 406). In the opinion of Richard Leacock's partner-to-be, Robert Drew, such a sound machine, 'when you finally put it down ... became the centre of the universe' (Allen and Gomery, 1985, p. 221). Nevertheless, the development of more appropriate sound apparatus was no more on the documentarists' agenda than was the refinement of 16mm. The existence of a lighter-weight magnetic alternative sound system was, needless to say, ignored in the 1930s – as it had been by the feature film industry (Lafferty, 1983, *passim*).

None of this affected the next generation. They were not inhibited by memories of the circumstances surrounding the introduction of sound in the late 1920s and they had also benefited from the 'professionalisation' of 16mm during the war. Especially in North America, they were therefore ready to work with the gauge and push for improvements (Allen and Gomery, 1985, p. 221). For these film-makers, the problems of documentary production, specifically reconstruction, could be solved by technology. It was hypothesised that less obtrusive gear was an essential prerequisite to the task of documentary film-making. In the 1950s the technological came to dominate the debate. A major shift was getting under way. All ethical issues, questions of purpose and authenticity, and problems of sponsorship were about to become swamped by technological considerations. It would take a further quarter-century for this flood to abate.

Richard Leacock is the emblematic figure in this shift. His willingness to deal with the machines, to see them as objects requiring the creative attention of film-makers, is the crucial mark of difference from the older generation. But, as we have seen, his career starts in the bosom of the pioneers working with Flaherty:

Already when we were working on *Louisiana Story* [1946–8], I saw that when we were using small cameras, we had tremendous flexibility, we could do anything we wanted, and get a wonderful sense of cinema. The moment we had to shoot dialogue, lip-synch – everything had to be locked down, the whole nature of the film changed. The whole thing seemed to stop. We had heavy disk recorders, and the camera that, instead of weighing six pounds, weighed 200 pounds, a sort of monster. As a result of this, the whole nature of what we were doing changed. We could no longer watch things as they developed, we had to impose ourselves to such an extent upon everything that happened before us, that everything sort of died. (Bachmann, 1961, p. 19)

This sense of the studio technology as a dead weight was exacerbated because a few film-makers at this time began to essay a move away from the safe, and increasingly suffocating, sponsored world that had spawned documentary. *On the Bowery* (1956), for instance, was an improvised docudrama shot with 35mm studio equipment on New York's Skid Row. 'Some of the filming was secret, involving a hidden camera with an ingenious reflex-finder arrangement, hidden in a bundle' (Sufrin, 1955, p. 139). The idea of more portable cinematography, as Leacock fully understood, was in the air (Levin, 1971, p. 202).

In 1954, Leacock himself had shot a television documentary for Willard Van Dyke. The film, *Toby and the Tall Corn*, dealt with one of the last travelling tent shows in America. Leacock used a standard NC Mitchell 35mm camera, which was essentially designed for the studio, but he also had one of the then new ½-inch Ampex magnetic tape recorders, based on German patents, to go with it. With the new gear, Leacock endeavoured to go 'behind the scenes' with camera and tape recorder (Jaffe, 1965, pp. 42f.). He did just this in sequences showing Toby in his dressing room and wandering round town chatting with the townsfolk. ... When Van Dyke saw the footage he called it "a breath of fresh air for the documentary'.

It is a measure of how attitudes were changing to note that a decade earlier Van Dyke had argued, as documentarists did at that period, that documentary film-makers 'are free from the restrictions of the microphone and the sound stage' because they employ 'principles which are closely allied to the techniques of the silent film' (Van Dyke, 1946, p. 406).

Patricia Jaffe suggests that *Toby* be considered as an important beginning for direct cinema. Leacock had an appetite to be liberated from the tripod *and* shoot sound, for he had been nurturing the 'idea of photographing events as they occurred' for years (Jaffe, 1965, p. 44). Yet hand-held synch had never been shot and was therefore not sought after – except by him and a few others.

To develop the equipment necessary for this change involved struggle, not least because of the marginal economic importance of the documentary industry and the willingness of other non-fictional film-makers – the scorned travelogue producers, for instance – to use feature-film equipment. The 'supervening necessity' which worked to aid the documentarists was to be found elsewhere, in the economically (and ideologically) far-from-marginal world of television news. This had established itself in the mid-1950s as a staple of the new medium's output, encouraged by the Federal Communications Commission's rules about local origination and the public's acceptance of the form. A synch news camera, the optical-sound Auricon, was developed for this new market.

Television news thus provided the documentarist for the first time with a small sound camera, but it was scarcely portable. Even when Walter Bach, the Auricon's designer, substituted a magnetic sound head for the original optical system, the camera, renamed the Filmagnetic, was still sold as a standard news-gathering tripod-mounted machine (Bach *et al.*, 1956, pp. 603f.; advertisement in *Journal of the SMPTE*, 1955, p. 705). However, the Auricon camera body, it was realised, could be recast in lighter metal and its weight significantly reduced; and elaborate corset-like camera body mounts could be designed to bring the eyepiece more appropriately to the eye. The results might not have been ergonomic or particularly unobtrusive, but they worked. The camera could be carried while recording sound.

Enter Robert Drew, a sometime picture editor at *Life* looking to become a documentary film-maker, who had contacted Leacock after seeing *Toby* on TV. By 1957 the two were together and Drew was gathering around him at Time-Life Broadcast a small group. The modified Filmagnetic was the chosen instrument of the revolution in documentary technique which they were planning.

This was not the end of the matter, though. What the revolutionaries needed was a camera which would fit around an operator's head and shoulder, something that had never been built. It was necessary to design it from scratch but nobody in North America was quite ready to do that for them.

This was first done in France by André Coutant under pressure not from documentarists or TV news people but from social scientists eager to obtain a tool for ethnographic purposes. Coutant brilliantly adapted a small cinematographic telemetry device, which he had developed for the French missile programme, into a camera ergonomically designed to rest on the shoulder (Rouch, 1985, p. 34). The prototype was ready in 1958 and the camera itself was introduced commercially in the early 1960s as the Eclair NPR.

Unlike Bach, Coutant made no attempt to build a sound system into the Eclair. The camera required a separate audio recorder to be run in synch with it – a double (as opposed to single) system. Broadcasters and others had pushed for a battery-driven recorder that could match the quality of studio machines. The Perfectone was the first to be widely sold but the industry adopted the rival Nagra because it was lighter and its designer, Kudelski, eventually manufactured a model especially for the 16mm film market – the Nagra IIIB, introduced in the USA in 1962.

Rifle microphones, which cut down wind noise, and the apparatus needed in the cutting room (16mm double-system flat-bed editing machines, etc.) had all been developed prior to this. It only remained to break the umbilical cord that tied the recorder to the camera. This was done in the mid-1960s by mounting in the camera a transmitting crystal which sent the guiding synchronising pulse to a receiver on the tape recorder. The 16mm synch sound outfit was in place.[11]

Although from the last years of the 1950s on it is clear that the documentarists were having some effect on these technological developments, the 'official', as it were, American technical literature makes no mention of their contribution. These developments had taken place largely in Canada, France, Germany and (even more obscurely from Hollywood's viewpoint) New York. As far as the industry was concerned 16mm had become essentially a province of TV news. Technologically speaking, it was focused on meeting the challenge of TV with large-screen formats and the like.

As a result, the earliest account of a documentary production using the new equipment I have found in the trade journals is of a Wolper film, *The Fabian Story*, shot on an Eclair and a Nagra by Villis Lapenieks in 1964 (Bronson, 1964, pp. 582f.). The film slotted into a series devoted to *Teen Age Idols*.

Hollywood might not have been paying attention but Wolf Koenig and Roman Kroiter at the National Film Board of Canada (NFBC) had made *Lonely Boy* on the same topic (about singer Paul Anka) three years earlier with hand-held 16mm synch among the fans and in the dressing-room. In fact, there had been considerable interest in the Filmagnetic at the NFBC, because they had been experimenting with hand-held synch for some years before that. For instance, the cinematographer Michel Brault had made *Les Raquetteurs* (*Snow Shoes*) in 1958 and had then gone on, in 1960, to use the prototype Eclair in Paris for *Chronique d'un été*, a film directed by the anthropologist Jean Rouch and the sociologist Edgar Morin.

That same year, for Time and ABC, Drew and Leacock with lightweight Auricons had produced the equally pathbreaking *Primary*.

The film industry apparently saw the application of this new technology as nothing more than (as the *American Cinematographer* put it) 'candid photography' (Bronson, 1964, p. 582). Even television, despite the ABC deal with Drew and company, regarded it as merely a more convenient method of doing traditional newsreel-style coverage. It was only this small band of documentarists and social scientists who went further.

In their view the apparatus had been produced to make good the camera's ability to capture representations of the world in real time with minimal disturbance. Far more was implicitly and explicitly expected of this advance. For Drew and Leacock and those working with them and for the NFBC, the gear represented a chance to liberate the mimetic power of the sound camera for the first time. Now they could really gather evidence, film life as lived, shoot 'events as they happened'. The new equipment did not just bolster and protect documentary's truth claim; it enhanced and magnified it.

26

Documentary as Scientific Inscription: Film as Evidence

In deploying the new technology, this small group of film-makers created a furore that paralleled Grierson's public relations blitz thirty years earlier. The new rhetoric was exciting and uncompromising. It was now possible, at last, to make good on documentary's scientific/legal promise to put 'actuality' on the screen. The equipment was to hand which would allow for reality to be documented in an unmediated fashion. Or so it was claimed.

It was no wonder that at the turn of the 1960s the strongest, most strenuous statements for 'actuality', the documentary as evidence, are found. The original issue of avoiding reconstruction was quite swamped as ever greater truth claims permeated the world of these film-makers and their audiences. So large a gap with the past did these claims make that the new observational work was seen as being not only different from the traditional reconstructed realist documentary but vigorously opposed to it. In North America, it was almost as if the documentary had died and been replaced by something wholly new – direct cinema.

At the time there were two terms, both French, available to describe film-making with the new equipment – *cinéma direct* and *cinéma vérité*. Both were preferred to the nascent English usage, in professional circles, of the word 'candid' as part of some phrase. 'Candid' did not become a term of art for this technology. The French expressions did. Unfortunately, there were also, essentially, two styles of film-making engendered by the new equipment and the French terms were used indiscriminately of both. And, as a final confusion, in the USA and UK, one term (direct cinema) was translated from the French *cinéma direct*) and the other was not. (The bilingual Canadians did better on this front.) Although the Americans at the time preferred the term 'cinéma vérité', here I will use 'direct cinema' to describe their work. Direct cinema was available and used occasionally by them, so I am not being entirely ahistorical. The term 'cinéma vérité' can then be reserved to describe the French applications of the technology which produced a very different style of film (see p. 178).[12]

The observational truth claims made on behalf of the new style immediately caused the film-makers difficulties. The dream of 'simply' filming events proved to be as elusive with the new equipment as it had with the old. To cope with external attacks and internal doubts, direct cinema practitioners (and those who reported on them) developed two overlapping and contradictory rhetorics. One luxuriated in the scientific potential of the form; the other sought to deny it. First, I shall deal with the enthusiasm, then (in the next chapter) with the caveats.

With the new equipment to hand, enthusiasm for its observational possibilities knew few bounds. Just as the thermometer gives 'real' temperatures, so, in the right direct cinema hands, the camera can give 'real' life. Synch portable equipment reduced the need for intervention to the point where scientism, as it were, triumphed. It is the experimental method and the place of the camera as scientific instrument that provides the context in which the film-maker/observer, a veritable fly on the wall, emerges.

Richard Leacock claimed:

Many film makers feel that the aim of the film maker is to have complete control. Then the conception of what happens is limited to the conception of the film maker. We don't want to put this limit on actuality. What's happening, the action, has no limitations, neither does the significance of what's happening. The film maker's problem is more a problem of how to convey it. How to convey the feeling of being there. (Bachmann, 1961, p. 16)

'To convey the feeling of being there' – this was the drive of the Leacock generation.

Peter Graham reflected the general sense of how this technological breakthrough was received at the time when he wrote (1964, p. 34):

With this equipment [direct cinema film-makers] can approximate quite closely the flexibility of the human senses. This opens up whole new fields of experience; they can follow their subjects almost anywhere, and because of their unobtrusiveness (they need no artificial lighting) people soon forget the presence of the camera and attain surprising naturalness.

Very quickly this sort of rhetoric, which implicitly denied the subjectivities of selection and arrangement, took hold. Film-makers were said to be 'concerned with using their technical skill ... to record reality without tampering with or imposing on it' (Haleff, 1964, p. 20). The talk, as film-maker and critic James Blue summed it up (1964, p. 22), was of 'the effort to capture, with portable sound-film equipment, life as it is lived and not as it is re-invented by the traditional cinema'. 'It is life observed by the camera rather than, as is the case with most documentaries, life recreated for it' (Taylor, C., 1971, p. 401).

The result was a new vividness: 'Time and time again, one finds oneself wincing and looking away from the screen because what is coming from it is obviously too real' (Blumer, 1971, p. 571). Louis Marcorelles asserted (1963, p. 16) that these films give 'a sensation of life, of being present at a real event'.

Yet it was not just critics who adopted this position, which traded so simplistically on the scientific connection; film-makers were also happy to make similar claims. Don Pennebaker: 'It's possible to go to a situation and simply film what you see there, what happens there, what goes on.... And what's a film? It's just a window someone peeps through' (Levin, 1971, pp. 235 and 254). Robert Drew: 'The film maker's personality is in no way directly involved in directing the action' (Bachmann, 1961, p. 14). The Maysles brothers were equally emphatic. Al said, 'Dave and I are trying to find out what's going on. We capture what takes place' (Haleff, 1964, p. 23).

Not only that – Al Maysles went so far as wanting to eschew editing; and Pat Jaffe, who with Charlotte Zwerin perfected direct cinema editing, herself allowed that 'when the cameraman is really operating smoothly and moving from one image to another with ease, the footage has the quality and rhythm of a ballet, and whole sequences may be left intact' (Jaffe, 1965, p. 46).

When editing occurred, it could be shaped by what had been obtained unconsciously. Richard Leacock claimed: 'Often we discover a new kind of drama that we were not really aware of when we shot it' (Shivas, 1963a, p. 17). Sometimes the film-makers were surprised at what they had chanced to record: 'The film-makers didn't even know what the girl was saying until later; someone just held a microphone up, and afterwards they found it was a prayer that had been recorded' (Mamber, 1974, p. 83).

Exploiting a different sense of unawareness, while filming Jack Kennedy in his hotel room for *Primary*, Leacock recalled: 'I retired into the corner and got lost, sitting in a big comfortable arm-chair with the camera on my lap. I'm quite sure he [Kennedy] hadn't the foggiest notion I was shooting' (ibid., p. 37).

This became a crucial element in the direct cinema enterprise, the heart of the promise that the material was unmediated. Leacock described 'never asking anybody to do anything' as a 'discipline' (Shivas, 1963a, p. 17). It was essentially this discipline which allowed him to claim, as he did of *Happy Mother's Day* (1963) for instance, 'we were simply observers' (Mamber, 1974, p. 197).

These film-makers were after 'revelation through situation' and it was crucially important for them to be ignored by their subjects. When Leacock was asked if his aim was to get the people he was filming entirely to forget the camera, he replied that 'the story, the situation ... is more important than our presence. ... We don't cheat' (Labarthe and Marcorelles, 1963, p. 26). On one occasion, Leacock began a film, *Nehru* (1962), uncertain whether or not basic permission had been granted. As far as he and his sound recordist Gregory Shuker were concerned, the film turned on Nehru's willingness to ignore them. So they just began working during a reception; and, in Shuker's words, 'Nehru greets his guests but ignores our presence. The deal is on' (Mamber, 1974, p. 86). This sort of non-intervention, with its implied promise of unmediated observation, thus became the prime source of legitimacy for film-makers as observers.

These new observers worked 'believing that the camera finally has only one right – that of recording what happens. They find the events, they don't ask anyone to *do* anything or to say anything' (Shivas, 1963b, p. 14). This is the sense in which the rhetoric was scientific: it positioned 'the camera as an impartial and unobtrusive observer capturing the sight and sound of real life' (Taylor, C., 1971, p. 403). And the people operating the equipment were proved invisible by the emotional intensity of what they managed to film. In fact, they sought situations – crises – in which that intensity was likely to give them the cloak of invisibility. Does a man cry, then the filming is, supposedly forgotten.

Leacock got to his armchair on the crest of a wave of dissatisfaction with standard film equipment. When there, however, a profound change came over him. He was being transformed – from Griersonian artist to fly on the wall. 'An ethic of non-intervention', to use Stephen Mamber's telling phrase (1974, p. 145), was being forged.

The result was that the films, at last, became evidence. 'Using the films as evidence', Mamber could ask (ibid., p. 133), 'what do we [the audience] learn about people in crisis?' 'We [the audience] find ourselves *there*, with the camera. We are observers, but there is no handy guide' (Sullivan, 1979, p. 453). As the film-maker Frederick Wiseman told an interviewer: 'You have to make up your own mind about what you think about the people you're seeing.... as you watch the film, you have to make up your own mind about what is going on. You are not being spoon-fed or told what to think about this or that' (Halberstadt, 1976, p. 301).

So it was suggested that when watching direct cinema films the film-makers' view of the subject matter was unimportant – for all of the above reasons, not just because they eschewed commentary. In general, 'Great stress was placed on the objectivity of the film-maker' (Klughertz, 1971, p. 456). Film-makers claimed to be attempting 'to give evidence about which you can make up your own mind' (Shivas, 1963b, p. 18). You as a member of the audience can read the Book of Nature, watch the dancing needles of the physiograph (as it were), for yourself. You can be a member of the jury. 'And this is a great step forward. If other film makers can follow his [Leacock's] lead, it is entirely possible that a whole new documentary tradition will arise: a tradition of "meeting the reality of the country" in a more intimate, interesting, and humanly important way than any Grierson imagined' (Callenbach, 1961, p. 40).

Others did follow Leacock's lead. Frederick Wiseman was drawn to direct cinema, he said, by 'the idea of using film and film technology to have a look at what's going on in the world' (Levin, 1971, p. 315). Explaining why he made his first film, *Titicut Follies* (1967), he said:

At Boston University Law School [where Wiseman taught in the late 1950s] a lot of students go on to become assistant DAs and DAs and judges in Massachusetts; yet most people working on the prosecution end of things have little idea of where they are sending people. ... So that's how I got to know Bridgewater [the mental institution in *Titicut Follies*], and the idea of making the film grew out of that. (Rosenthal, 1971, p. 67)

Thus, at the outset, the claims of direct cinema were presented as being relatively unproblematic – to be 'recording life as it exists at a particular moment before the camera', to produce a cinema, moreover, which would be, to quote a title of a 1961 article of Leacock's, 'uncontrolled' (Jaffe, 1965, p. 43; Leacock, 1961, p. 23).[13]

A hundred and thirty years or so after François Arago claimed the camera for science, the documentary purists, essentially American direct cinema proponents, implicitly reasserted that claim on behalf of the light-weight Auricon and the Eclair. In such hands the camera was nothing more than an instrument of scientific inscription producing evidence objective enough to be 'judged' by a spectator. The claim was that of science.

The break with the Griersonian tradition, though, was less radical than it seemed at the time. Fundamentally, for all the talk of how different direct cinema was, it was still (indeed, finally) 'actuality' and therefore recognisable as a continuation of the same enterprise. Most significantly, it had the same tendency to run from social meaning. In fact, this tendency was exacerbated by these new techniques. Surface became all as direct cinema tried to avoid those elements of the Griersonian repertoire which, if developed, could perhaps have led to a more analytic style – interviews, commentary, graphics, and 'reflexive' modes (modes which reveal the film-maker's presence).

This is not to say that the films actually lacked interviews and commentary; they did use such elements but the drive was without question to reduce and eliminate them. Instead direct cinema preferred following people around and, strange to say, the fact that such activity tended to yield only footage of the subjects' backs, as it were, was obscured. For the moment, just how limiting this could be was lost in the excitement of the hunt for 'moments of revelation'.

The key film of this first direct cinema wave was *Primary*, about the Democratic presidential primary race between Senators John Kennedy and Hubert Humphrey in Wisconsin in 1960. In this film, there were things never before seen in a documentary – available-light synch talk inside a car, for instance. So overwhelming was this that many 'faked' synch shots – in some crowd scenes, for example – were seen and heard as also being in synch. They were not.

This is true of the film's most famous moment, the *locus classicus* of the direct cinema 'follow-the-subject' shot – a 75-second unbroken take of Kennedy pressing the flesh as he makes his way through a crowd to a stage. The camera is held high over the operator's head and an extreme-wide-angle lens captures the candidate, centre screen, with people reaching to him from either side. Whistling and chatter is heard and snatches of talk: 'Ah! Ah! I can't wash my hands', and the like. Yet this, the classic demonstration of what could apparently be done with the new equipment, is not actually a synch shot. Rather, it demonstrates what Jeanne Hall has called (1991, p. 30) 'a strategy of [direct cinema] self-validation' involving 'the pairing of asynchronous sounds and images for conventionally realistic effects'.

Pennebaker had given Al Maysles a new 5.7mm wide-angle lens for a standard silent Arri. This is the camera he used for this shot. (It was Leacock who had the synch rig. He did not make the shot. Indeed he was waiting on the stage for Kennedy and can be fleetingly seen in the last seconds of it.)[14]

The point is that carrying even a silent camera was unusual enough to get the shot written into the history as a breakthrough. It looked, quite literally, like nothing ever before seen on the screen (Mamber, 1974, p. 38). Less technically flamboyant, the comparatively static cutaway of Jacqueline Kennedy's hands, linked behind her back, in this same location seemed to convey an intimacy with the subject, a candour, which also looked utterly fresh and new.

So fresh and new did all this *look*, few seemed to notice that the film really marked a continuation of the well established Griersonial failure to analyse and inform. The politics of the situation – *Primary*'s subject matter, after all – remain hidden. We learn nothing of the issues, of what divides the candidates, of the significance of the events filmed, except tangentially because the people being filmed happen, as it were, to be concerned with little else. What we hear, however, is largely incoherent with the clearest information coming from bits of radio commentary and the sparse dollops of 'voice of God' commentary. Any understanding we gain of the campaign is a sort of fortunate by-product of our own political and, now, historical knowledge.

Rather than representing a breakthrough in the cinema's ability to illuminate the nature of the 'real' world, *Primary* flags the onset of one of the most significant media failures of our time, certainly in the USA – the failure to control, and effectively explicate, the political image. What looked like the opening of previously closed doors turned out to be no such thing. It was, of course, not apparent at the time but politicians and their staffs were to become as adept at controlling this new level of access as they had been when contact had been far more formal and limited. In taking that walk with the camera running, Al Maysles was not so much liberating his powers of observation as inadvertently setting up his successors for the 'spin-doctors'. It is *Primary* as much as the more extensively discussed Kennedy–Nixon debates of the same election which points the way down this road.

Douglas Gomery and Robert Allen suggest that it was the rhetoric of direct cinema objectivity which helped secure a brief network showcase for these Drew films (while the attendant rhetoric of technological innovation secured sponsorship from Bell & Howell). They see this claim of objectivity allowing network and sponsor to rise above any controversy which the films might provoke (Allen and Gomery, 1985, pp. 229ff.). By this reading ABC and Bell & Howell were merely, as it were, the disinterested purveyors of objective information – and what could be more public-spirited than that?

However, I think the rare use of an outside producer – Time-Life, for which the Drew group worked – also helped in achieving this blameless publisher role. (ABC brought in Time-Life to play 'catch-up' with the rival CBS and NBC news/documentary operations, both of which had strong public service traditions dating back to the radio era, which ABC, being of more recent foundation, lacked.)

In terms of subject matter, direct cinema actually broke little new ground in this earliest Time-Life phase to 1963. Direct cinema primarily sought situations of tension and stress which were not necessarily of much social import but rather allowed the advantages of the new style to be highlighted – a bitter high-school sports rivalry or a single driver's performance in successive Indy 500 motor races, for instance. So much was this the case that Steve Mamber (1974, pp. 115ff.) was able to identify, as the dominant narrative characteristic of these films, a 'crisis structure'. If direct cinema dealt with more salient social issues, then it tended to revisit the established documentary agenda as that had been determined by the television news industry both nationally (for example, the criminal justice system, race relations) and internationally (for example, Latin America).

As this agenda embraced 'difficult' topics, television did not, prima facie, need direct cinema to tackle them. In fact, the deployment of traditional realist documentary resources by the networks' production teams was capable of producing more controversial films than those made by the Drew group. For instance, *CBS Reports'* 'Harvest of Shame', also transmitted in 1960, created a public furore about migrant workers' conditions which has become part of American television history. NBC's 1962 *Battle of Newburgh*, about the inadequacies of the welfare system, caused a similar uproar. (On the other hand, the networks were capable of 'candid' work of less social moment, as in the *CBS Reports* 1961 exposure of an illegal bookmaker shot on hidden cameras.)

As William Bluem pointed out (1975, p. 128), the Drew-Leacock film on race, *The Children Were Watching*, revisited a *CBS Reports*, 'Mississippi and the Fifteenth Amendment', but did not notably improve it. This is despite the undoubted power of some of the sequences in the direct cinema version. Bluem used this example to mount an attack on the efficacy of the entire direct cinema project. He asserted that Leacock, by emotionally involving his viewers in racist tirades and stoic African-American opposition, denies them the opportunity for intellectual contemplation. Bluem's view (ibid., p. 130) was that such an opportunity is 'a virtue which underlies the documentary idea' and that, therefore, the direct cinema films were a species of backward step.

But this is to buy into a Griersonian notion of public education. As I have been arguing, I believe the documentary tradition effectively precluded the opportunity for analysis exactly in favour of emotionalism and aesthetic pleasure. That is what running from social meaning involves. So direct cinema films were not in some way 'less' than their predecessors; it is rather that their faults were the same. Direct cinema practitioners, their first audiences and their earliest critics all ignored this continuation of Griersonian analytic failures because they were prey to 'the magic of pure technique'. 'The drive to be objective ... had led [direct cinema] into the same blind alley – where the subject is all and interpretation nothing' (Klughertz, 1971, p. 456).

In the event, direct cinema was to make only one significant addition to the range of documentary subjects. The roots of this contribution can best be seen in the Leacock-Pennebaker film *The Chair* (1962), and Leacock's *Happy Mother's Day*.

The Chair is a tightly focused study, nearly obedient to the Aristotelian unities, shot over a five-day period as a man condemned to the electric chair awaited news of his last appeal. This is the 'crisis' film *par excellence*. It used two crews, one in the prison and one outside. By the standards of the time an enormous amount of film was consumed, a ratio of 20:1 as against the 4 or 5 that was the old norm. Even *Primary* was less than 10:1 – not least because it was not shot entirely in synch (Mamber, 1974, p. 97).

This technique of continuous shooting over a fixed period of time was to be used, most notably by Frederick Wiseman, to make direct cinema's long march through the institutions. The institution as a subject was not new but, as Wiseman's *Titicut Follies* amply demonstrates, the footage obtained by simply hanging around always ready to shoot, the nudity and bad language for example, was of a different order from that which old-style sponsorship and old-fashioned reconstruction produced.

Eventually this 'wait and watch' technique was to yield a whole new documentary topic. It was used to shoot people not in crisis, or in institutions, but in the private sphere. The possibilities of the filmed documentary portrait were thus transformed and expanded. Private intimacy of a sort that would previously have been thought voyeuristic was put on the screen for the first time in documentary film. The documentary, because of this takeover of the domestic, turns into melodrama.

This is why *Happy Mother's Day* can be seen as a second progenitor of this new topic. *Happy Mother's Day*, to the network's distress, was a study of the rather baleful effect of publicity on Mrs Fisher, an ordinary mother who happened to give birth to quins. The film documents a vivid clash between the public and the private, with Leacock's camera, paradoxically, becoming the mother's co-conspirator in her stoic struggle to deal with the media circus swirling about her and her family. Becoming part of the solution rather than the problem was a considerable feat on Leacock's part. He achieved it, as he was to do again and again in his subsequent work, because of his boundless sympathy for the people before his lens. (In stark contrast, others – the Maysleses and Wiseman, for example – were to use the direct cinema camera mercilessly.)

The next step towards exploring the private sphere can be seen in Pennebaker's *Don't Look Back*, a study of Bob Dylan's 1965 British concert tour. The rock performance/tour movie is, with the historical compilation film, one of the few documentary forms to achieve sustained mass audience acceptance. *Don't Look Back* is the model. In addition to the concert coverage, and like *Happy Mother's Day*, the film focused on the private. Because Dylan, unlike Mrs Fisher, was a public figure Pennebaker reversed, in some sense, Leacock's take – the private side of the normally public subject, rather than the public side of the normally private. However, in both cases it was the focus on the private realm which was new.

Another similarity was that Pennebaker's vision of Dylan was not judgmental – unlike, say, Kroiter's and Koenig's view of Paul Anka in *Lonely Boy*, but again like Leacock's approach to Mrs Fisher. Pennebaker, like Leacock, normally does not deal with people he does not like. This portrait of Dylan, although it does not hide the singer's callowness and callousness, is no exception. (This distinction in film-maker–subject relationships is no minor matter, for all that it has been repressed in the discussion of the documentary. It will return. (See p. 229.))

The new theme was approached by this series of comparatively small steps from the private life of ordinary people caught in the accidental glare of publicity to the private life of extraordinary people to, finally, the private life of ordinary people in ordinary circumstances. It took some time for this point to be reached because direct cinema was initially a journalistic enterprise. Under Time-Life's patronage and Drew's guidance, it was interested in the 'man bites dog' story. Ordinary folk in ordinary circumstances is very much the reverse of that – no 'story' at all as far as a journalist is concerned. The 'ordinary' arrived as an appropriate subject for the documentary on the back of these prior journalistic explorations of the private. 'Actuality' then comes into play again, allowing a sociological legitimation, which could embrace the study of the 'ordinary', to take the place of the original journalistic legitimation.

For *A Married Couple* (1969) the Canadian film-maker Allan King moved into a couple's house for three months, rigging in extra lighting for the duration. For the first three weeks the camera was run empty to get the pair and their son used to the presence of the crew. Then they shot and shot and shot.

The result was a picture of proto-yuppie malaise, never entirely free of the possibility of vamping on the part of the subjects, always teetering on the edge of a somewhat pornographic representation of the private on the part of King. Here was synecdoche writ large – not *What Happened When Allan King and Crew Moved in with Antoinette and Billy Edwards for a Few Months* but *A Married Couple*, implicitly a sociological document. 'The film ... tries to promote selected gleanings into self-evident generalisations', as Molly Haskell perceptively noted at the time (1971, p. 475).

155

That is how documentary synecdoche operates in general, of course. This new subject, the intimate picture of the private, shot in this new way, direct cinema, simply affords the most extreme examples of this synecdoche at work.

Here too is the direct cinema film-maker most obviously and clearly emulating a fly on the wall. Actually, in the case of *A Married Couple*, the crew left bits of equipment stuck to the location's walls like so many enormous swatted flies.

It was this sort of project rather than an increase in range or depth of illumination that supported the claim of a new dawn for documentary. The enthusiasm for the new gear and its fly-on-the-wall possibilities fuelled the rhetoric which claimed that documentary was now on a new footing.[15] The hype concentrated on the new style of shooting, but other production activities were also affected, although this was much less noticed.

For example, the claim to evidence was reinforced by a contempt for research. Research became a suspect activity wherein the film-maker traditionally did (and still could) structure the material to be shot. This was now to be avoided. Sometimes that did not matter much. For instance, although Pennebaker declared himself to be against research, his lifelong interest in popular music allowed him to make films in that area *as if* he had conducted lifelong research into music – which he had. More often, though, the result of this hostility to research was damaging – Leacock went to India to cover Nehru during an election campaign unaware that his man was virtually guaranteed a victory. Journalistically, there was no story; and, in the event, there was as near as makes no matter no film (Mamber, 1974, pp. 86ff.).

Post-production was a different matter. Despite Al Maysles's protestations, these films were edited, mostly with great skill and care. Take, for instance, Pennebaker's parody in *Don't Look Back* of the standard background biographical section in any mainstream documentary on an artist. This sequence uses footage in which Dylan can be seen singing 'Only a Pawn in the Game' to a small group of African Americans. That material is cued by an Afro-Caribbean BBC radio interviewer in London asking him the 'standard question' about how he started. Dylan does not reply but, instead, the cut allows for the song to function as a very unstandard answer. The song footage concludes with a close-up of African Americans' hands clapping, which is cut to a close-up of the clapping hands of the audience at Dylan's first concert on the tour.

The films as a whole luxuriate in such cleverness, whatever claims the rhetoric might have made about their unstudied nature. And it was not only at the level of the cut that this was displayed. Even when a 'crisis' did not dictate it, the overall structure was often very adroit. Wiseman was particularly careful about this: 'When I'm editing I try to work out a very elaborate theory which I set-down as I talk to myself: for example – "Well, this fits this way" and "that fits that way", but in the way I finally get to it I can see that the rationalisation frequently comes after the connection exists' (Graham, 1976, p. 43).

Roberta Pearson and I have argued that these connections occur because Wiseman structures his films according to deeply embedded normative social topoi, such as deviancy (Winston and Pearson, 1982, pp. 12ff.). For instance, in *Hospital* (1969), the sequences are arranged on a rising curve of such deviance – from diagnosis, through gynaecology and medical training to child abuse, drug abuse, violence and death. The film has a classic tease, a glimpse of an operating theatre, incisions in close-up, and a classic coda, set in the hospital chapel. The film's sequences therefore exhibit 'limited [narrative] reversibility by reason of Wiseman's use of (as a basic conditioner of the order of sequences) a notion of social deviancy'. This is the clue, in our view, to the film's effectiveness as narrative.

Obedience to narrative norms had been the mark of the Griersonian documentary. It was to remain so with direct cinema, just as much a key to a documentary's success as it ever had been. But the fact that the films had been so carefully structured was somehow hidden (as hidden as the asynchronicity of the tracking shot in *Primary*). There was, as we have seen, already a propensity to deny that documentaries in general were narratives. Direct cinema's rhetoric of unstructured observation encouraged this.

For instance, Bill Nichols claims (1981, p. 210): 'The overall structure of Wiseman's films is decidedly non-narrative (lacking closure, a diachronic trajectory ...).' Mamber (1974, p. 4) thought that the sequences in Wiseman 'look as if they could be switched around in a variety of permutations. ... the films are mosaic in structure.' But, as the example of *Hospital* suggests, they are not. A chrono-logic of some considerable sophistication is usually at work.

The concept of the mosaic structure elided with and served a more general sense that the films were somehow unmediated by editing. This, in turn, was supportive of the overall idea of direct cinema as evidence since it denied the film-maker's hand yet again.

Despite this reliance on the norms of narrative, largely traditional subjects and the usual synecdoche, direct cinema nevertheless set about putting documentary on its claimed new footing with a great deal of fanfare, ballyhoo and, indeed, aggression. Drew and his associates became 'furious' with people who worked in the older way (Cameron, 1963, p. 20). Drew dismissed virtually all previous work: 'In my opinion, documentary films in general, with very few exceptions, are fake' (Bachmann, 1961, p. 17). Al Maysles felt that the use of narration and music produced 'illustrated lectures' and described much of the documentary work of the NFBC, which was still mainly traditional in form, as 'propaganda' (Haleff, 1964, pp. 22f.).

The traditionalists were in no position to respond. Not only had reconstruction sapped at the foundations of the documentary, but sponsorship, now largely commercial after the Second World War, had also taken its toll. In retrospect some of the older generation of traditional documentarists saw the effects of this clearly. One of them, George Stoney, has written: 'We lost the respect we once had as documentary filmmakers on the part of the intellectual and artistic community. ... For, in truth, the disillusionments of the late 1940s and the intimidations of the McCarthy Period that followed destroyed our political underpinnings' (Ellis, 1989, p. 302). The Griersonians were ripe for attack.

The insistence on direct cinema pre-production and production techniques as the only true path was propounded at a crucial meeting arranged by the French national broadcasting organisation (ORTF) and held in Lyon in 1963 as part of a *Marché International des Programmes et Équipements de Télévision*. The Americans encountered the French and

(Mario Ruspoli aside) each side discovered itself to be divided from the other by more than language – or different cameras. The established American feeling that anything less than an 'automatic' approach could not produce documentary film was expressed vigorously, as a British observer, Mark Shivas, reported (1963b, p. 13): 'Because they could now record actual events and sounds, they believed that anything else, including any sort of rehearsal or post-synchronisation, was immoral and unworthy of a showing at a conference on Cinéma Vérité. If the material was not spontaneous, they said, how could it be true?'

The basic fact was that, for the first time in the history of the documentary, such a position of reduced or non-mediation could be articulated and major claims made for it.

27

This Objective–Subjective Stuff Is a Lot of Bullshit

Such claims were also immediately attacked. 'Among some of the technicians at Lyon a blinkered approach to the new possibilities was evident, the result of an inadequate appraisal of the medium,' reported Shivas (1963b, p. 13). A little later Jean-Luc Godard, writing in *Cahiers du Cinema*, complained (1963, p. 140):

> Leacock and his team do not take account (and the cinema is nothing but the taking of account) that their eye in the act of looking through the viewfinder is at once more and less than the registering apparatus which serves the eye. ... Deprived of consciousness, thus, Leacock's camera, despite its honesty, loses the two fundamental qualities of a camera: intelligence and sensibility.

Godard (who, some five years after these remarks were published, was to use both Leacock and Pennebaker as camerapersons in an unhappy episode) was still looking for 'the ordinary virtues of an art' (Levin, 1971, pp. 204 and 245ff.).[16]

The objections Godard and others raised were grounded in a sense that the Griersonian baby was being thrown out with the direct cinema bathwater. These nay-sayers were most strenuously reinforced by another body of opinion that questioned the degree to which the new style could or could not deliver on its scientific claims. The resultant argument was summed up by Noel Carroll (1983, pp. 6ff.): 'No sooner was the idea ... abroad than critics and viewers turned the polemics of direct cinema against direct cinema. A predictable *tu quoque* would note all the ways that direct cinema was inextricably involved with interpreting its materials. Direct cinema opened a can of worms and then got eaten by them.'

To take an example of a film already cited, people were able, eventually, to contrast Humphrey's treatment in *Primary* with Kennedy's and to see in the difference clear evidence of a preference on the film-maker's part. (Humphrey is seen meeting in a less than crowded hall with seemingly bored farmers, for instance, while Kennedy has an enthusiastic encounter with Polish Americans.) Some began to see more detailed differences in the way the two men were shot, too (Van Wert, 1974, pp. 19ff.). Refutations of direct cinema objectivity became a commonplace in the critical reception of the films.

On occasion, critics would go even beyond the charge that the materials had merely been interpreted. For instance, Molly Haskell (1971, p. 475) thought that the couple in *A Married Couple* 'seem to have been catalysed by the camera into forcing the marriage to a showdown'. Seldom, if ever, was Griersonian reconstruction accused of so massive a manipulation. This sort of accusation, the charge of provocation by the very act of filming, was also to be heard increasingly.

In the face of such objections, direct cinema practitioners and those who reported on them quickly learned to refine their rhetoric, in effect adding a second (and contradictory) strand to it – one that sought to deny the scientific standing of the apparatus altogether.

They soon discovered that the techniques of direct cinema, especially 'the tremendous effort of being there', could encompass the idea of the film-maker's personality, and in ways that did not compromise the 'raw material' claim. An accommodation to a measure of subjectivity could be achieved. This was to be the essential characteristic of this second strand of rhetoric; and, as a result of its deployment, what was said about the films by their makers and by critics would undergo considerable elaboration (and obfuscation) as the decade progressed.

By 1964, Leacock was developing a way of deflecting the criticism that claims made for direct cinema's objectivity were too strong:

> When you make an electrical measurement of a circuit, you do it with a volt-meter. Now the moment you do that, you change the circuit. Every physicist – and I used to be one – knows this. So you design your volt-meter so that very little goes through it. And in a very sensitive situation you need very much less going through it. ... The physicist is a very objective fellow, *but he is very selective*. He's much more selective than we are. He tells you *precisely* and *only* what he wants you to know. All the rest is irrelevant. (Blue, 1965, p. 16)

This stance also had the advantage of re-endowing the film-maker with Godardian 'intelligence' and 'sensibility'.

Drew takes a similar line. For him subjectivity became more or less synonymous with sensitivity. Sensitivity was defined as the quality required in order to know when an event was 'happening'. In other words, personality determined when the machines were switched on. That is why Drew could say, 'The film maker's personality has much more effect in this form of reporting' (Bachmann, 1961, p. 15). Obviously, these admissions and analogies do not compromise direct cinema's explicit claim to authenticity exactly because the film-maker's personality operates only in the context of what is not being filmed, not what is.

By the late 1960s more elaborate rhetorical responses had been built on these early distinctions, essentially allowing for subjectivities to invade the perimeter while preserving the authenticity of the central matter – the uncut footage. Al Maysles:

> We can see two kinds of truth here. One is the raw material, which is the footage, the kind of truth that you get in literature in the diary form – it's immediate, no one has tampered with it. Then there's another kind of truth that comes in extracting and juxtaposing the raw material into a more meaningful and coherent storytelling form, which finally can be said to be more than just raw data. (Levin, 1971, p. 227)

Note here that the raw material is like a diary. This transformation of science (that is, 'raw material' with which 'no one has tampered') into subjectivities ('diary') is the key.

It would be easy to dismiss this sort of sophistry as but the thought of a moment uttered into the interviewer's tape recorder. But such talk was very persistant, unlike some aspects of the early rhetoric which were soon abandoned – for instance, Al Maysles's announced refusal to edit his material. When Leacock told his interviewer Roy Levin this in 1970, Levin dismissed it, saying: 'So David [Maysles] does it.' By this time Leacock too was less certain than he had been that he was involved in a breakthrough that would (as he thought seven years earlier) 'revolutionize the whole industry' (Shivas 1963a, p. 17). The willingness to abandon these other early rhetorical positions is in contrast to the continued insistance in the interviews on Jesuitical arguments about objectivity.

By its second decade, direct cinema had produced an advocate who could create an obfuscating blizzard of such rhetoric off screen, while on screen protecting the central observational premise with a series of apparently uncompromised 'pure' films. Frederick Wiseman was given this role because of the regularity of his output, if for no other reason. By the time of *Titicut Follies*, the second rhetorical strand had been well established and Wiseman was quick to use it. Even as he claimed that *Titicut Follies* was evidence for trainee DAs, he could in the same interview also claim that his films were 'totally subjective. The objective–subjective argument is from my point of view, at least in film terms, a lot of nonsense. The films are my response to a certain experience' (Rosenthal, 1971, p. 70).

Elsewhere Wiseman told Roy Levin that the objectivity claim was 'a lot of bullshit' (Levin, 1971, p. 321). In another interview he dismissed the row about objectivity as 'a real phoney-baloney argument' (McWilliams, 1970, p. 22). This repeated protestation creates a profound contradiction.

The confusions between a direct cinema ambition to acquire evidence of an institutional reality and so vehement a dismissal of the mimetic power of the camera can be easily explained. Wiseman found himself entrapped after making *Titicut Follies* in a series of legal difficulties. These were to condition his whole subsequent approach, both in terms of film-making practice and rhetoric (see p. 213).

Aside from legalistic defences of what he actually did while filming, his main response to those problems has been to articulate a sophisticated and opaque rationale for his work and the 'bullshit' or 'phoney-baloney' issue of objectivity. The Wisemanian formulation, if it can be so described, of the objectivity question becomes very dense. With one interviewer he adopts the original rhetorical stance: 'Which is not to say the films don't have a point of view. But they have a point of view that allows you – or, hopefully, asks you – to think, to figure out what you think about what's happening' (Halberstadt, 1976, p. 301).

On the other hand, with another interviewer, he denies it: 'I don't know how to make an objective film. I think my films are a fair reflection of the experience of making them. My subjective view is that they are fair films' (Levin, 1971, p. 322).

With these confusions – the construction of a questioning viewer behind a smokescreen of double-talk – our hero springs free of the chains of objectivity and escapes to a postmodernist world of open textuality and critical acclaim. And he takes the entire direct cinema movement with him.

In the course of the 1960s, the whole question of objectivity (and with it the underlying scientific legitimation of the direct cinema enterprise) became shrouded in a miasma of such circumlocutions. By the 1970s, Wiseman's pronouncements function as a new testament, come to fulfil the promise of the old (as it had been more haltingly expressed by Leacock and the others).

The films are now both self-expression ('a fair reflection of the experience of making them') while still being objective evidence ('that allows you ... to figure out ... what's happening'). Leacock (1975, p. 148) was taking much the same position by this time:

> The rules of this game are often very strict: never ask a question; never ask anyone to do anything; never ask anyone to repeat an act or phrase that you missed; never pay anyone; etc. If the same people film the material and edit it, the results can be summarised as 'aspects of the observer's perception of what happened in the presence of a camera'.

But they cannot be – nor were they ever – so summarised. The films' titles alone refute that. But more than that, this denial of objectivity is not quite what it seems. Leacock and Wiseman are still, in effect, rendering the film-making process transparent. It is no longer a window on the world, perhaps, but it is still a window:

The films are claimed as objective evidence of the subjective experience of the film-maker – but so sensitive was that experience and so accurate is its recording on film that the audience can supposedly act as judge of the original event. The result is that this rhetorical strand, 'objectivity is bullshit', still in effect makes the same implicit cultural appeal to photography's scientific heritage as does the other strand of the direct cinema practitioners' 'window on what's happening' rhetoric. It is the film-maker's subjectivity that is being objectively recorded. Direct cinema is still evidence of something – the film-maker's 'witness'.

But, of course, the films are more than that. For all the film-makers' denials, they are presented as windows on the world, not windows on the film-makers' experience or even on the film-making. Direct cinema hides its processes as much, if not more, than does Hollywood. The long takes, the lack of commentary, music and post-synch sound effects, the absence of cinematic lighting, the understated titles, even the persistent use of black-and-white stock long after the TV news had gone to colour – what are these if not earnests of objectivity for an audience schooled in the reception of realist images? As early as 1944, James Wong Howe was pointing out to his cinematographer colleagues that the authenticity of war footage was becoming bound up in the audience's mind with shaky black and white shots (Allen and Gomery, 1985, p. 221). In addition to all these markers, direct cinema now added a few further authenticity warrants of its own – the subject's occasional direct gaze at the lens (the exceptional shot that proves the normal rule that the subject was unaware of the camera) and the occasional jump-cut (the guarantee that nothing was repeated for the camera so, of course, Hollywood continuities cannot always be obeyed).

Thus the film-makers might claim that the works are personal as stridently as they like, but in technique they are deliberately and systematically 'objective' – 'unsigned'. As Pauline Kael put it at the time, the style is 'so simple, so basic' (Sullivan, 1979, p. 467). Wiseman reportedly pitched topics to his public television patron in equally simple and basic terms: 'I want to do a juvenile court', or 'I want to do a study of welfare' (Benson and Anderson, 1989, p. 310). The claim of objectivity, as Allen and Gomery point out (1985, pp. 230f.), was a key to network (ABC) and sponsor (Bell & Howell) support for the initial Drew-Leacock series. Most important, the whole technological discussion was grounded in a search for objectivity. As Henry Breitrose wrote at the time (1964, p. 35): 'One often wonders whether the films are made by men using machines ... or by machines alone.'

The anti-objectivity rhetoric turns out to be a smokescreen. It functions, as did Grierson's radical rhetoric, to divert attention from the basic thrust being taken in the films. The failure to escape from the prison-house of objectivity can therefore be most vividly seen on the screen. It is the films themselves that reinforce a continued and unavoidable claim on scientism; that, in effect, give the lie to the anti-objectivity rhetoric of the film-makers.

The reception of the first decades of direct cinema did not depend on the changing rhetorical positions taken by these film-makers. In fact, the reception of the films was in general less conditioned by the film-makers' rhetoric than by these powerful, if unstated, culturally implicit claims of objectivity.

Audiences thirty years ago missed the construction and mediation of the earliest direct cinema films. The misreading of the Kennedy shot in *Primary* is a good example of this, as is the general failure to note how many traditional elements the films used (Hall, J., 1991, pp. 27ff.). Audiences missed all this because of both the particular excitement and enthusiasm engendered by the technological advances in 16mm equipment and the deep-seated cultural position of the photographic apparatus as scientific. For these audiences, as well as producers, networks, and sponsors, and even for the film-makers themselves, five centuries of lens culture and the successful efforts of Arago *et al.* to place the reception of the photograph in the realms of science and of law were not to be thrown aside merely by repeatedly crying 'bullshit!'

28

Kinopravda

There was another way of avoiding being eaten by the worms, whether of the Godardian sort, nibbling at the sensibility issue, or of the *tu quoque* variety, attacking on the mediation front: simply take the position of the other side at the Lyon meeting.

The French cinéma vérité practitioners (as I am calling them, in contradistinction to their North American direct cinema colleagues) took on the objectivity problem directly and tried to solve it by putting themselves into their films. Jean Rouch and Edgar Morin sought something more limited but, as they hoped, rather more incontrovertible than the truth claims of direct cinema. They tried in some way to guarantee the 'truth' of their own observation because we, the audience, could observe them apparently in the act of observing.[17] Rouch's *Chronique d'un été* (1961), the key cinéma vérité film, attempted to close the gap between a rhetoric of subjective witness and the idea of objective evidence by avoiding transparent production practices: 'The direct cinema artist aspired to invisibility; the Rouch cinéma vérité artist was often an avowed participant. The direct cinema artist played the role of an uninvolved bystander; the cinéma vérité artist espoused that of provocateur' (Barnouw, 1974, p. 255).

There was precedent for such provocations. The direct cinema people could look back to the realist documentary, while cinéma vérité's proponents, as this term clearly indicated, could call up a more attenuated but equally venerable tradition. Reflexive documentary (that is, a film-making practice which on the screen reveals rather than hides itself) arose out of Soviet revolutionary experimentation in the 1920s.

In 1924, the year Grierson went to Chicago on his Rockefeller scholarship, Dziga Vertov was working in Moscow on *Kinoglaz: Zhizn' vrasplokh – Kino* (or *Cinema*) *Eye: Life Caught Unaware* (or *Unrehearsed*). He wrote (1984, p. 34) that this was 'the world's first attempt to create a film-object without the participation of actors, artists, directors; without using a studio, sets, costumes. All members of the cast continue to do what they usually do in life.' By this time, Vertov had already issued forty-five *Kinonedelia* (*Cinema Weekly*) newsreels (1918–19) and also, from 1922, nearly twenty 'film-newspapers' under the title *Kinopravda – Cinematruth*, *Cinémavérité* (Feldman, 1973, *passim*).

Vertov's documentary practice, although it preceded Grierson's by some years, was nevertheless far more overtly rigorous and complex. Those who worked on *Kinopravda* were not involved in duplicating the narrative forms of popular journalism and drama (or worrying arcanely and privately about the nature of 'the real'); rather, in the strident manifesto-language of the day and place, Vertov claimed (1984, p. 34) that 'Kinopravda made heroic attempts to shield the proletariat from the corrupting influence of artistic film-drama'. It did this, in part, by seeking to film life unawares (that is, by making documentaries rather than fiction films), but also by making sure that the audience understood the nature of film production even as they watched the screen. Vertov 'wanted his films ... to function not as a mere reflection of reality' (Enzensberger, 1972, p. 102). He hoped 'to break the mesmeric spell of the cinema to ensure its didactic powers' (Fisher, 1985, p. 28).

For Vertov, this involved a trajectory beginning in the newsreels with a willingness to juxtapose materials taken at different times and in different places. As with Muybridge, it also meant seeking revelations, by means of fast and slow motion, and the like, of physical phenomena imperceptible to the human eye. 'The movie camera', Vertov claimed (1984, p. 67), 'was invented in order to penetrate more deeply into the visible world' than could the unaided human eye. (In this he understood it to be, significantly, like the microscope and the telescope.) Any cinematographic trick was acceptable as a way of revealing the film 'fact'. The camera plus the human operator were together a new entity, the 'kino eye'.

Thus in *Kinoglaz*, to illustrate the labour required to make a loaf of bread, there is a sequence of shots from harvest to oven; but they are reversed and in reverse motion, so that the sequence begins with the bread coming out of the oven and finishes with women 'harvesting' the corn (that is, restoring the cut plants). Film, claimed Vertov (1984, p. 84), is 'not merely' the sum of 'facts recorded on film ... but the product, a "higher mathematics" of facts'.

The Man with the Movie Camera was planned as a complex 'symphony of a city' structure (actually to be shot in a number of cities) contrasting, as one major theme, the new Soviet reality with both the lingering remains of the pre-revolutionary society and the consequences of Lenin's New Economic Policy, which was in place at the time (Petric, 1987, pp. 84ff.).

Also included in the scenario was what Vertov described (1984, p. 289) as 'a small secondary production theme – the film's passage from camera through laboratory and editing room to screen'. In line with the attempt to demystify the film-production process for audiences, the theme, in a film dealing with forces of production, ensured that film-making itself was seen as one such force – hence the repeated appearance on the screen of Vertov's cinematographer brother Mikhail Kaufman and his film editor wife Elizaveta Svilova at work. This small, secondary addition had, however, profound effects. It increased exponentially the complexity of the film's 'higher mathematics'. It created nothing less than what Annette Michelson (1984, pp. xxviff.) calls a 'key film text': 'A critique of cinematic representation is united with cinematic production within the construction of a socialist economy by one film-text, which epitomizes and sums up the resources and development of cinematic theory and practice until 1929.'

Michelson reflects the current dominant critical view. Since Vertov's reputation has not always stood thus high, this is a revised position representing a radical re-evaluation of his general importance as well as that of the significance of this one film.

At the time, Vertov's observational claims and his war against narrative form were vigorously called into question. In the USSR, he was attacked on the one hand over his hostility to the fiction film – by Sergei Eisenstein, for example, who wrote (1949, p. 44) that Vertov was 'a film hooligan' producing 'unmotivated camera mischief'. On the other hand, for his willingness to alter and manipulate newsreel materials Vertov was attacked by members of the LEF Arena. For these theoreticians, 'Vertov's thoughtless rejection of the necessity for a scenario in the "unplayed" film is a serious mistake' (Brik and Shklovsky, 1973, p. 15). They castigated him for his cavalier treatment of his 'film facts', accusing him of documentary impurity (Enzensberger, 1972, p. 103). 'Dziga Vertov cuts up newsreel,' wrote Viktor Shklovsky. 'In this sense his work is not artistically progressive' (Taylor and Christie, 1988, p. 152).

Everywhere informed opinion misunderstood and dismissed Vertov's work, a process not hindered by the man's personal abrasiveness. Grierson concluded, in a contemporary review of *The Man with the Movie Camera*, that 'Vertov has pushed the argument to a point at which it becomes ridiculous' (Grierson, 1981, p. 139). Reviewing *Enthusiasm* (*Symphony of the Donbas*) (1930), he claimed that Vertov had failed, 'because he was like any bourgeois highbrow, too clever by half' (ibid., p. 141). A critic in *Close Up* in 1931 wrote: 'Vertov ... has waged fierce, vehement and desperate battles with his materials and his instruments ... In this he has failed' (Leyda, 1960, p. 251). Paul Rotha testified half a century later that this was the received view among the Griersonians: 'Vertov we regarded really as rather a joke you know. All this cutting, and one camera photographing another camera photographing another camera – it was all trickery, and we didn't take it seriously, quite frankly' (Marris, 1982, p. 7).

So dominant was Grierson's vision of the documentary that Vertov's long-form work was seen in the West at the time as being not of the same order at all. When Vertov's films arrived in the West, some positive critics were at pains to point this up and distance the revolutionary Vertovian documentary from the romantic realist one:

> It would be a mistake, however, if the term 'documentary' led one to believe that all Vertov had done was to formulate principles which had already been utilised by directors in all countries and have resulted in works like *Nanook*, *Moana*, etc. The 'documentary' film as conceived and organised by Vertov and his school has no relation whatever to these works. (Moussinac, 1935, p. 7)

Despite this sort of assessment of his significance, Vertov was nevertheless as much marginalised by the documentary film movement and others in the West as by the Soviet film community.

But this is not to say that he has therefore been without influence. Despite all the hostility, even initially and certainly currently Vertov has carried no little weight.

For example, Esfir Shub, an editor of genius, acknowledged her debt to him and considered herself his pupil. This was despite the apparently inevitable 'disputes and disagreements' (Petric, 1987, p. 19, fn.). Shub was among the first to seek the 'incontestably and absolutely true' filmed history dreamed of by Matuszewski nearly thirty years before. She pioneered the compilation documentary with *The Fall of the Romanov Dynasty* (1927), which used the Tsar's home movies as well as newsreel footage (Leyda, 1964, p. 15).

Unlike Vertov, reproached by his comrades for 'betraying the document', Shub was 'beyond suspicion' in this regard (Yampolsky, 1991, p. 161). That is why she could be set in opposition to him by Vertov's LEF critics, her work being read as marking a move away from 'construction' towards a period of artistic enterprise in which 'raw material' would be dominant (ibid., pp. 162ff.).

On the other hand, unlike Matuszewski, but in a sense like Vertov, she had a refined and sophisticated conception of the implications and limitations of what she called 'authentic material'. For instance, the radical cliché of contrasting newsreel shots of rich and poor is done in *The Fall* as follows: the imperial family is on a cruise aboard a battleship when a dance is held. In the next shot, peasants dig a ditch. The dance is introduced with the intertitle 'Their Honours Were Pleased to Dance with Their Highnesses'. The shot is interrupted by the intertitle 'Until They Perspired'. As the shot continues and the dance ends, the women are seen wiping sweat from their faces. Cut to ditch diggers. A worker, centre screen, vigorously scratches himself in an echo of the gestures in the previous shot before spitting on his hands, grasping his pick and continuing to dig.

Coverage of whole events can be equally elegantly transformed by one brief title: a long open-air public religious parade and ceremonial, for instance, is recast as evidence of 'The Priests' Moscow'.

It is clear that Shub had no illusions about the 'absolutely true' nature of the documentary/newsreel shot. She understood that the 'higher mathematics' of these film 'facts' (in the sense that the found shots were actually existing pieces of celluloid) could be revealed by juxtapositionings and her own careful sense of structure and flow. The counter-revolutionary images, especially those made by the Tsar's private camera operators, could therefore be of service to a revolutionary film, although at some cost to their 'authenticity'. In her autobiography she wrote:

> The intention was not so much to provide the facts but to evaluate them from the vantage point of the revolutionary class. This is what made my films revolutionary and agitational – although they were composed of counter-revolutionary material. ... Each of my compilation films was also a form of agitation for the new concept of documentary cinema, a statement about unstaged film as the most important cinematic form of the present day. (Petric, 1984, pp. 24 and 37)

It is in this last belief that she stands with Vertov.

As sorry as has been Vertov's reception in the West over the years, it is, at its worst, better than the treatment accorded Esfir Shub – perhaps unsurprisingly given her gender. Except for snippets, her writings have yet to be translated into English and she is scarcely a presence in the Western vision of the cinema's development. None of her films has been canonised. Rotha, as late as the third edition of *Documentary Film* (1952, p. 91), dismissed Shub as follows: 'Before leaving the Russians, there should be reference made to Esther Shub, who has edited a considerable footage of news-reel materials. None of her work has been presented in England.' Only Vlada Petric, Jay Leyda and Mikhail Yampolsky have endeavoured (in English) to draw our attention to her importance as a theoretician, holding the ring in the great arguments Vertov engendered in Soviet film circles.

This is all the more extraordinary because, unlike Grierson, Lorentz, and their like, Shub developed a documentary form which has actually had a wide measure of public acceptance. (This popularity is shared only by the rock performance documentary.) Shub's compilation film, as Jack Ellis points out (1989, p. 36), has become a documentary staple – from the left independents' 'synthetic documentaries' in the 1930s through *Why We Fight* in the 1940s to 'countless compiled documentaries made for television since the great success of *Victory at Sea*' (1952–3).

The Shubian compilation film is not the only legacy of this period. Vertov and Shub are also the real models for the *engagé* film-maker. Such things as the alternative left film tradition in the 1930s (not just its propensity to recycle newsreel footage), the radical turn in Ivens's career, the rebirth of the revolutionary newsreel in the 1960s are all, in this sense, Vertovian (or Shubian). There are even traces of Vertov's formalist 'giddy heights' in *Land Without Bread* or *A propos de Nice* (which was, after all, shot by his youngest brother, Boris Kaufman) (Bordwell, 1985, p. 41).

Today the dialogue on documentary theory occasioned by the work of Vertov and Shub can be seen as the most pregnant element in this inheritance.

Echoes of the arguments in Moscow were heard in the West at the same time as Vertov travelled to Paris and London. Translations of his writing appeared in *Filmfront No. 3* in 1935 (quoted above) and his films were seen. On occasion his work forced a Western critic into a theoretically richer response than did the Griersonian cinema. For example, in the first issue of *Film* in 1933, Robert Fairthorne wrote:

> In Dziga Vertov's *The Man With The Movie Camera* the cameraman himself is shown at work, a scene as factitious as anything in a *spielfilm*. This part of the theory, the Kino-Eye, can never be carried into practice, for 'real' material is inevitably manipulated by the very process of obtaining it. Which side of the lens the manipulation takes place is a matter of indifference. (Macpherson, 1980, p. 171)

But then the *œuvre* and the responses it provoked were, to all intents and purposes, forgotten. This level of debate was eclipsed by Grierson's public relations blitz and such delicate and critical issues were not to be raised again for thirty years.[18]

Eventually, though, the 'higher mathematics' of Vertov's documentary practice forced itself back into collective consciousness, and with considerable effect. Not only were the writings diffused, the debate recovered and the films studied; the practice was also revived – most significantly by Jean Rouch.

Rouch, as a sophisticated social scientist, saw in the new equipment (over the development of which he, like Leacock, had exerted an influence) a fresh possibility for a 'kino eye'. The new gear could perhaps allow for the Vertovian dream of 'not "filming life unawares" for the sake of the "unaware", but in order to show people without masks, without makeup, to catch them through the eye of the camera in a moment when they are not acting, to read their thoughts, laid bare by the camera' (Vertov, 1984, p. 41).

For Rouch, such films were not to be made by a film-maker emulating a fly on the wall, nor yet by her or him becoming confused about the effects of observation on the observed. Rather, the project was to be accomplished by entering into the spirit of Vertov – with the understanding of an ethnographer.

Rouch told Levin: 'I'm one of the people responsible for this phrase [cinéma vérité] and it's really in homage to Dziga Vertov' (Levin, 1971, p. 153). In embracing Vertov, however, Rouch was rejecting the tradition of anthropological film-making of which he had been a leading exponent. His contribution to the development of the documentary cannot be understood without a history of this, the other main influence on him.

29

Film as Ethnography

Although this is not to say much, anthropology more than any other science, natural or social, has employed film as a tool. Ethnographic film-making has kept almost exact step with the realist documentary and its precursors from the very beginning of cinema. *Poterie crue et origine du tour* was a series of images of a Berber woman making a pot. It was shot at the Colonial Exposition in Paris in 1895 by an associate of the cinematographic pioneer Jules-Étienne Marey, Charles Comte, and a physician-turned-anthropologist, Félix-Louis Regnault. Regnault was to go on to make a number of similar records of African men and women in motion or sitting (*à la* Muybridge or, better, Marey) and to suggest that such materials could constitute a valuable archive (De Brigard, 1975, pp. 17ff.; Sorenson, 1967, p. 444).

There were also early films of fieldwork. Movies were made by an expedition to the Torres Straits in 1898, and on field trips to south-west Africa in 1907 – but film did not establish itself even as well as did photography as a normal part of ethnography (De Brigard, 1975, p. 16).

This can be explained in part by the expenses involved in cinematography and the difficulties of the technology, although it should be remembered that photography, full-plate, was scarcely 'user-friendly' at this time, either. The emergence of the *documentaires romancés*, a genre which afforded Curtis a model, did nothing to enhance the cinema's already fragile reputation for seriousness of purpose. It would take but little prejudice in anthropological circles to dismiss a technology at once so popular and so capable of producing the worst type of unscientific sensationalism. Certainly the cinematograph was a scientific instrument and as such it could not lie; but could it tell an anthropological truth? That Curtis's idea for the documentary was, as I have argued, both anthropological and commercial, and that this 'spin' was clearly picked up by Flaherty, did not therefore help.

Nevertheless, Regnault's point was not completely lost and the possibility that in trained hands film could be ethnographically valuable was to be explored. The scientific status of the camera demanded as much.

Franz Boas, the key American ethnographic pioneer, had been working in the Pacific north-west from 1885 on. He knew of Curtis's activities among the Kwakiutl since Boas's field colleague George Hunt had facilitated Curtis's 'old-fashioned Indian dressed photographs' (as Hunt called them in a letter to Boas). Later Boas tried, gently, to wean Theodore Roosevelt from supporting Curtis, but to no effect (Public Broadcasting Associates, 1980, pp. 8 and 12).

Boas was concerned with ethnographic techniques. For example, he pushed for researchers to learn the languages of the peoples they were studying and to develop non-Indo-European frames to describe the grammars involved. This interest in technique led him to revisit Regnault's example in connection with his study of Kwakiutl dance. His eminence affording a sort of protection from the anthropological establishment, he was able to use film to study Kwakiutl dance kinesics. Jay Ruby: 'Boas believed that the camera gave him a superior way of understanding behavior ... so he begins something – a tradition – which is with us today ... an important means of studying human behavior' (ibid., p. 12).

Unlike Curtis's 1914 'drama' with its specially made totem poles, house façades, clothes and canoes, Boas's 1930 Kwakiutl dance footage appears to be 'evidence'. The men dance in jeans and European shirts. The footage has been given no shape; it records an activity without a context, without a frame of any kind. It is, in the terms of Grierson's definition, 'untreated' actuality, shapeless reproduction indeed. David MacDougall, not only a major ethnographer but also a thoughtful commentator, calls this sort of ethnographic filming 'record-footage' (Macdougall, 1969, p. 29).

Research film of this type was taken in Australia in 1932 and 1935. The series made on Bali by Margaret Mead and Gregory Bateson between 1936 and 1938 on *Character Formation*, which includes 'Bathing Babies', also has something of the same quality (ibid., pp. 18ff.). It is perhaps significant that the Mead-Bateson films were shot on 16mm, available by then for more than a decade, while most ethnographers continued to use 35mm, just as the documentarists did (De Brigard, 1975, p. 20).

The field-note record-footage use *per se* was not widely taken up and filming did not, therefore, become a regular technique in the ethnographers' repertoire. Nevertheless, fragmentary footage of this kind did insert itself into the practice of anthropology as a teaching (rather than as a research) tool. This classroom context lessened, but did not entirely remove, the need for the ethnographer to engage the film's student audience by using the essentially fictionalising patternings established for the documentary.

Nor was this educational function and occasional research use the end of the matter. There were always Curtis, Flaherty, Cooper, Schoedsack and all the other commercial purveyors of dramatised ethnographic exotica for the film-making anthropologist to emulate. The practice of anthropology is itself not cheap. Ethnographic documentaries made by trained anthropologists were a potential source of funding and a public relations technique for encouraging support. In theory at least, these advantages could more than compensate for the additional difficulties filming entailed, including costs. So beyond the classroom, ethnographic films came to be, at least on occasion, publicly distributed. Yet the effectiveness of such films in creating support for fieldwork did not mean that, at the same time, prejudice or hostility among non-film-making anthropologists towards the moving image would be removed or reduced. On the contrary. ...

The price of public acceptance is that the films be accessible; and, even if the ethnographer avoids sensationalism, such works must obey documentary narrative, and therefore fictional, norms. The film ethnographer has thus become victim of a species of double-bind where the wherewithal for filming in the field could depend in part on a public appetite for conventionally narrativised ethnographic movies; yet these very movies then reduced the status of such footage in any form as serious ethnographic evidence.

The Hunters (1958) was made among the !K'ung of the Kalahari for the Film Study Center at the Peabody Museum by Robert Gardner and John Marshall (who was later to film *Titicut Follies* for Wiseman). Let us leave aside the fact that this film (and all social anthropology of the time) presents the !K'ung as a 'Stone Age' people living in sophisticated symbiosis with an incredibly hostile environment. This is, in Keyan Tomaselli's words (1992, p. 208), 'a denial of history', since the !K'ung had been driven into the desert over many centuries by hostile neighbours, both white and black, and forced to adapt to it to survive.

The Hunters, shot over a period of some years and culled from 250,000 feet of footage, is about giraffe hunting. Actually, the film presents a coherent story of just one giraffe hunt. It is therefore 'treated', just as Flaherty 'treated' his footage.

It is perhaps no accident that hunting, the most dramatic activity of the !K'ung to Western eyes, was the chosen subject. More problematic is just how dramatic this film makes that activity. David MacDougall is not unreasonable when he asks (1975, p. 110): 'Could one accept that this was how the !K'ung conducted long hunts, given the fact that the film was compiled from a series of shorter ones?'

Beyond that, hunting was a secondary activity for the !K'ung, less significant than gathering, but the film does not make this clear. Nor does Robert Gardner. In 1969, he described the film as being definitively about a 'primitive hunting society' (Gardner, 1969, p. 25). Gardner did intend to make further films in the series, including one to be called *The Gatherers*, but these were not realised (Gardner, 1957, p. 351).

So *The Hunters* misrepresents the culture it is trying to document, denying its history, while fictionalising an actual, if exceptional, activity in that culture.

Marshall turned away from such films as being 'over-ambitious and dominated by Western structural conventions' (MacDougall, 1969, p. 24). He went on instead to produce record-footage fragments about the !K'ung for use in the introductory anthropology course at Harvard.[19]

Gardner, on the other hand, began 'to think in terms of [a film] about an agricultural group'. He arranged an expedition from the Peabody to the Dani of Dutch New Guinea (West Irian). 'The goals were to produce a major film, a scientific monograph, a general book, a book of photographs and a comprehensive series of sound recordings' (Gardner, 1969, p. 25). In the event the film, *Dead Birds* (1963), is not about agriculture but about the far more attractive topic (in public exhibition terms) of warfare.

Gardner was very lucky. As Margaret Mead wrote in the introduction to the 'general book', 'Only a month after the major part of the filming was completed, and most of the expedition had left, the Kurelu region where the expedition worked was pacified' (Mead, 1974, p. ix). Gardner gives a different impression. His account of violence among the Dani is, as his film also inevitably must be, in the present tense. 'The Dani are warriors because they have wanted to be since boyhood. ... They are ready to fight whenever their leaders decide to do so' (Gardner and Heider, 1974, p. 135). Mead presents the enterprise as salvage. Gardner claims it as a picture of practice.

Contrast Richard Sorenson's work during this same period across the border in Papua New Guinea with the Fore: 'Warfare was considered a curse by most Fore, and although their accounts have elements of excitement and bravado, I have yet to hear a Fore nostalgically or enthusiastically recall it. It ceased almost spontaneously with the distant arrival of the first Australian (Sorenson, 1976, p. 41).

Colin Young complained that, in *Dead Birds*, Gardner '*tells* us on the sound track information not substantiated by the image' (MacBean, 1983, p. 32). For instance, over the shot of a boy watching men at work we hear: 'He watches, thinking of the day when he himself will be a farmer.' Again, David MacDougall's question (1973, p. 110) seems very fair: 'In Robert Gardner's *Dead Birds*, how could one know that the thoughts attributed to the subjects were what they might really have been thinking?' One cannot even know that all the incidents are as they are presented; but one does know (for instance) that footage of peaceful co-operative activities was edited out (Collier, 1988, p. 83).

Sorenson also filmed on his side of the Irian–Papuan border, but in record-footage mode. His practice was particularly strict, with all footage remaining in the order in which it was shot, uncut, with the track offering voice-over annotation (Sorenson, 1967, p. 448). (To Sorenson's suggestion that such methods should become standard, Timothy Asch added that synch sound with translation track was equally important (ibid., p. 462).) Sorenson's twenty-five Fore films typically detail single incidents, such as a medical examination or a wedding.

Sorenson's sense of film's uses 'in the study of man' was more complex than most. For him the narrativised public documentary is the 'demonstrative film'. Record-footage he divides into two categories. The 'cinema as a research aid' begins with Regnault's Berber potter but is primarily a medical film-making tradition – studies of human motion (1916), high-speed cinematography of somatic motor disturbances (1921) or reflex actions (1936) and the study of babies (1934–49) among other observations (ibid., pp. 443ff.). 'Cinema Research Records for the study of non-recurring or exceptional phenomena' is his term for fieldwork research footage.

Much of his own filming was of these types, being concerned with kuru, a neurological childhood disease, which was being eradicated at the time. Even when he was shooting more typical material such as feasts, though, he made few concessions to the 'demonstrative'. Not even the titles would fit a distributor's catalogue or a public television schedule, for example: *SOUTH FORE Children IV: Waisa village, Eastern Highlands, East New Guinea, December 16, 1963* (Sorenson, 1976, pp. 260f.).

Some anthropologists supportive of film, such as Karl Heider, felt Sorenson's suggested procedures to be too expensive ever to be used – but then Heider was Gardner's partner on the Dani expedition, which produced, in *Dead Birds*, a very dramatic 'demonstrative film' indeed.

While Gardner and Sorenson were in New Guinea (the former working, supposedly in contrast to the latter, in what Heider calls 'the more restricted realm of the possible'), the direct cinema revolution was getting under way. Aware of the importance of language, film-makers like Marshall were pushing for synch even before this time, just as Leacock had been.[20]

Gardner's trilogy of films about basic ecologies is completed with a study of the nomadic Nuer of the Sudan and Ethiopia, which was shot for him on the new equipment by documentarist Hilary Harris. The synch is deployed in a fairly strict direct cinema fashion so, although the important step of giving the tribal people a voice is accomplished, they are not heard to be saying much. Instead, *The Nuer* aestheticises the tribe completely – Gardner thought them 'handsome', 'elegant' and 'among the world's most graceful people' (Gardner, 1971, pp. 12ff.). Harris rendered them as Giacometti-like stick-figures in a sombre landscape of browns.

Once again, the film as a whole leaves much unsaid. There are particular omissions; for instance, the tribe was suffering from a smallpox epidemic at the time of the filming but that is not allowed to mar the visual pleasure of *The Nuer*. It was edited out. More generally, and more significantly from the ethnographic point of view, *The Nuer* is quite literally a picture of only half the Nuers' existence. Gardner hoped that 'somehow the other half of the Nuer life, the rainy season, can become another film' (Gardner, 1971, p. 14). It never did.

This trilogy thus documents a gathering people hunting; a pastoral people, now pacified, fighting; and a nomadic people stationary.

Gardner then turned to India, where his luck continued to hold. In 1975 he filmed an ancient Brahman ritual, the *agnicayana*, in Panjal, Kerala State. His partner in this enterprise, Frits Staal, writes: 'This event, which lasted 12 days, was filmed, photographed, recorded and extensively documented. From 20 hours of rough footage, Robert Gardner and I produced a 45-minute film, *Altar of Fire*. ... Vedic ritual is ... the oldest surviving ritual of mankind (Schechner, 1981, p. 7).

The problem is that, contrary to the impression given by the film, the ritual is not an actual living one. The previous *agnicayana* had taken place some time in the 1950s, the last of a series going back maybe three thousand years or, as Richard Schechner points out in a searing analysis of the movie's production circumstances (ibid., p. 8), 'maybe not':

Were it not being filmed, photographed, and recorded the agnicayana would not have been performed. The impetus for the 1975 agnicayana came from America, not India, and most of the funding originated outside India. I doubt that various agencies would have responded with cash to pleas by Nambudiri Brahmans for support of a ritual that was too expensive for them to mount unaided. In fact it was the threat of extinction, the sense that 'this is the last chance to record this event', that created the event.

Staal was concerned to base a whole theory of ritual on the animal sacrifice he thought was involved in the *agnicayana*. Unfortunately for him, the local authorities, communists, determined that animal sacrifice was barbaric. The Brahmans had to substitute rice wrapped in leaves for the goats the Americans originally wanted them to provide.

The deficiencies of these films are not to be explained by claiming that they arise from the practice of the particular ethnographers involved. This would carry the implicit, and unfair, implication that others could do better; but they could (and have) not. Rather these shortcomings reveal that there are intrinsic flaws in the concept of the demonstrative ethnographic film itself, flaws which are grounded in the limitations of the camera as a scientific recording device. Demonstrative film is no more able to deliver on its promise of scientific evidence than the Griersonian documentary can avoid running from social meaning. And this is not just a question of narrativising. Even at the level of the raw and uncut record-footage these promises cannot be met.

In so far as the anthropological establishment countenanced film-making, record-footage was preferred. Margaret Mead, in spite of her public support of demonstrative movies like *Dead Birds*, spoke to this preference in the 1970s (1974, p. 10):

> Those who have been loudest in their demand for 'scientific' work have been least willing to use instruments that would do for anthropology what instrumentation has done for other sciences – refine and expand the areas of accurate observation. At the present time, films that are acclaimed as great artistic endeavours get their effects by rapid shifts of the cameras and kaleidoscopic types of cutting. When filming is done only to produce a currently fashionable film, we lack the long sequences from one point of view that alone provide us with the unedited stretches of instrumental observation on which scientific work must be based.

Alan Lomax's plea (1973, p. 477) for an 'urgent anthropology' on film specified that film-makers should avoid close-ups, should shoot synch and, 'above all, take long sequences; three minutes should be the minimum'. Despite his disagreements with Sorenson, Heider also suggested that 'the attributes of ethnographicness' ought to include synch, long takes, framing which displays whole bodies and shots which include whole acts, all of which Sorenson also favours (Biella, 1988, p. 48).

But the problem was not to be solved so simply. Such techniques do not guarantee the Griersonian promise of 'actuality'. This is because the whole idea of record-footage brings us into direct and unavoidable contact with the scientific, probabilistic question of evidence. For film to be evidence, as anthropologists such as Heider seem to assume it can be, requires, according to Peter Biella, an 'indefensible' reductionist belief that equates perception with truth and knowledge of reality. For an anthropologist such as Heider, ethnographic material is said naturally to exude order and meaning. Sorenson, although not going quite this far, claims that record-footage can be 'programmed sampling' and therefore capable 'of almost endless scientific and historical inquiry' (Biella, 1988, p. 49). This is less naive than Heider but Biella suggests (ibid., p. 50) that, despite Sorenson's careful practice, such expectations cannot be met: 'Behind Sorenson's vocabulary of natural science lies the fact that, for *most* "scientific and historical inquiry", his sample data are necessarily inappropriate and statistically insignificant. At best, they are suggestive and interesting.'

The result is that it has been just as easy to distort the fragment – record-footage – as to manipulate the whole demonstrative film. Even Boas's Kwakiutl footage of 1930–3, for instance, is suspect: 'By 1930 Kwakiutl culture was far too altered to have provided [Boas] with ceremonies of the complexity and grandeur he had witnessed 40 years earlier and, thus, all the sequences here are re-enactments of parts of rituals, games or technological processes' (Walens, 1978, p. 204).[21]

Napoleon Chagnon and Timothy Asch offer in the *The Ax Fight* (1974) a classic example of these inevitabilities. Although less strict than

Sorenson, Asch's work tends to be more of the record-footage than finished-film type. *The Ax Fight* consists of various presentations of twelve shots hurriedly taken as a fight broke out at about ten past three on the afternoon of 28 February 1971 in the Yanomamö village of Mishimishiböwie–Teri in Venezuela. (This information is provided in the film by captions or voice-over.)

The film is in six parts. First, there is an introduction with two maps. Over the maps is a supered intertitle: 'The fight began when a woman was beaten in the garden ...'. On the soundtrack we hear the details of time and place and a second voice says, as the supered title and then the second map fade to white, 'Two women are fighting with each other. ... Bring your camera over here, it's going to start.'

The second part begins with two flash shots, followed by a stable wide shot of a hut. Over this is supered: 'You are about to see and hear the unedited record of this seemingly chaotic and confusing fight just as the field-workers witnessed it on their second day in the village.' The title fades and this third shot continues. It constitutes the longest single element in the rushes, including, in extreme and obscured long shot, most of the action of the scuffle that is *The Ax Fight*. There follow three shots taken in among the men during the aftermath, the last of which concludes with some men laughing, seemingly about the fight. Then there are two shots of a boy, somewhat mysteriously, who appears to be drawing a line in the earth with a long pole. Finally there are three more shots of women at the hut. The first of these, after some confusion, resolves itself into a medium shot of a woman whose screamed insults are subtitled. There is then a general shot of the hut followed by a second shot of the same woman in close-up who continues to shout insults, which are again subtitled.

The third part is a sound-only conversation between the anthropologists over a blank screen. 'Sound reel 14, wife beating sequence,' says one voice. 'Wife beating my foot,' says a voice (Chagnon's, one assumes). 'It was a club fight.' He then reveals that he had been told the fight was because an incestuous relationship between a mother and son had been discovered. 'No kidding,' says another voice.

The informant who produced this juicy explanation was, however, 'kidding', according to the fourth part. This begins with an intertitle which states: 'First impressions can be misleading. ...' Over an edited version of the footage, complete with slow motion and superimposed arrows to point out the main figures. Chagnon in voice-over explains what had really happened. Mohesiwä, an ex-villager who has returned with Nanokawa, his leader, for a visit, has beaten Sinabini because she refused (while gardening) to give him food. First her brother, Uuwä, then Mohesiwä's brother, his sister and his mother, then Sinabini's husband and her brother-in-law, Këbowä, become embroiled. Finally Nanokawa, the leader, steps in to prevent serious bloodshed.

The fifth part shows, in diagrammatic form, how these various parties are related. Chagnon explains that there are three lineages living in two villages. Mohesiwä is a member of the first lineage, Këbowä and his brother (Sinabini's husband) are of the third, while the others all belong to the second. Thus the fight, according to Chagnon, threatens to divide the second lineage and split the village.

The last part offers a cut version of the incident. The narrative line outlined in the third and fifth parts is now quite clear. The flash shots (shots

176

1 and 2), the laughing men and the boy (shots 7, 8 and 9) and the wide shot of the hut (shot 10) are not used. But the cut still has eleven shots because the early part of the row in shot 3 has now been cross-cut with the screaming woman of shot 9, while other parts of shot 3 have been tightened.

Despite this exhaustive presentation of the material, the value of the footage as evidence can be questioned in several particulars. First, there are the obscurities of the filming to consider.

In the third part, despite the arrows, a number of key incidents are simply not captured by the camera. Këbowä's critical blow to Mohesiwä with the axe (blunt side) is obscured at the edge of the frame. His felling of Mohesiwä's brother with, again, the blunt side of the axe is not seen at all. In fact we are in extreme long shot at that point (if point it be), with a mass of people between the action and the camera.

The brother's response to this attack is in turn to attack Këbowä. He is described by Chagnon as hitting Këbowä repeatedly but we see only one blow land. The sister is said to be shouting vicious insults at Uuwä but she is clearly screaming at Mohesiwä most of the time. Can she really be hurling insults at her brother? In the fourth shot, the brother is described as lying on the ground and slowly regaining consciousness, but in fact he is sitting up and seemingly wide awake. (There is at least one still photograph in which somebody can be seen flat out on the ground, but no figure appears in that position in the film) (Sandall, 1978, p. 219).

Beyond these specifics, there are the more general interpretations made by Chagnon. For instance, at the end of the third shot the people are described as 'enraged'. Certainly some are clearly and unambiguously very irate. However, most, despite grabbing long staves, which we are told are their weapons, seem to be bystanders. Over the tenth shot, Chagnon says: 'Some of the women, dissatisfied with the outcome, continue to provoke the situation.' There is, beyond the vigorous language of the woman of shots 9 and 11, no evidence of this. I do not know that Nanokawa's people can even hear her so I do not know whether she is provoking them or not. The whole tirade might be therapeutic. Finally, over the diagram, Chagnon confidently explains what would have had to happen if the fight had escalated.

Of course, I am not suggesting here that the events in these shots are other than as Chagnon and Asch present them, or that Chagnon's interpretations are anything other than informed and accurate. I am just pointing out the degree to which I have to take these explanations, even at the mimetic level, on trust. Strictly viewed, Chagnon's commentary is altogether more tangential and suggestive than might be expected in such an enterprise. It reveals this research footage to have much in common with mainstream documentary where such a tangential relationship between sound and picture is something of the norm. Scientific imaging could be expected to produce a less ambiguous, more mimetic affinity where the audio track is strictly limited by the visuals.

These questions arise before I adopt the pose of Bruno Latour's obstinate dissenter. Such a sceptic would want more evidence than this film provides. Why, the dissenter could ask, should we believe that the women were dissatisfied with the outcome? What evidence is there that, as Chagnon claims, they had been fighting among themselves and 'had scores of their own to settle'? Why should we believe the informants who told us the tale of returning villagers wanting to be provided with food but who were unwilling to garden themselves? Why not believe the informant with the incest story? Why not find other informants with other stories?

And as for the three lineages, let me (the obstinate dissenter might say) remind you of the possibility that this is an imposed monological organisation coming from Chagnon. Perhaps the Yanomamö and Chagnon see the relationships differently. Perhaps Yanomamö women see them differently from Yanomamö men, or the old see them differently from the young. Perhaps they have kept their vision of how relationships work a secret. Claude Lévi-Strauss has written of varied and contradictory descriptions of village structures and relationships typically obtained by anthropologists, all of which could be 'different ways of describing one organisation too complex to be formalised by means of a single model' (Lévi-Strauss, 1968, p. 134).[22] We have to hand only Chagnon's account legitimated by the fact that the Yanomamö are 'his' tribe by dint of much fieldwork in their midst.

Chagnon's basic vision of the Yanomamö is that they are 'A Fierce People', as he called his popular 1968 ethnography of them. It has been suggested that he might be overstating this view of them. Other Asch footage and other written ethnographic accounts suggest that the Yanomamö are gentle and warm (Collier, 1988, pp. 84ff.). It is even possible to read *The Ax Fight* as evidence of a society well able to handle even extreme conflict. After all, the men use only the blunt sides of the axes and yield to virtually unarmed authority – Nanokawa apparently has only to pick up a club to compel peace.

Although, with the one exception noted, the shots are not long, the people are not framed as a whole, the action is incomplete and the synch is largely tenuous, nevertheless Asch is prepared to claim (1988, p. 25) that Sorenson-style inquiry into this footage is possible.

Most record-footage can be similarly critiqued. Let me say again, I am not disputing for a moment that the incident in *The Ax Fight* is as the anthropologists describe it. I am simply pointing up how little support for that description actually rests with the footage. For all its scientific inheritance, the camera was simply not yielding 'evidence' at a compelling level.

There was one other avenue being explored at this time. A few anthropologists had thought that film could be used for a quite different ethnographic purpose, neither to make finished films nor to record in the field. The media professor Sol Worth and the anthropologist John Adair had asked (1972, p. 3): 'What would happen if someone with a culture that makes and uses motion pictures taught a people who had never made or used motion pictures to do so for the first time?'

Funded by the US National Science Foundation, they did just this with a group of Navajo in the summer of 1966. The resultant films were analysed by Worth and Adair as being significantly different from Western practice and, more speculatively, indicative of a specific Navajo *Umwelt* – the world seen 'Through Navajo Eyes', as their well received book was called. John Adair explained: 'We wanted to fulfil Malinowski, the famous anthropologist of the twenties, who said that the first duty of the ethnographer is to see the culture through the eyes of the natives themselves, to see their world through their own eyes' (D'Agostino, 1980, p. 61). Worth and Adair believed that the films showed they had achieved this ambition (Gross, 1980, pp. 3ff.).

For instance, much of the films was taken up with walking; there was a very extreme reluctance to use close-ups; conversely there was a tolerance for jump-cuts. These were seen by Worth and Adair 'as the "truest" reflections of Navajo perceptions of reality' (Eaton and Ward, 1979, p. 118).

However, what the investigators saw as evidence of the Navajo mental frame for comprehending the world can be explained far more prosaically – the lack of close-ups, for instance:

> Such close-ups would be in flat violation of the Navajo taboo against direct looking in the face – which is an unpardonable rudeness that all Navajo avoid with consistency every day of their lives, and could hardly be expected to indulge in just because they are looking through a viewfinder. (Callenbach, 1973, p. 62)

So the lack of close-ups is evidence of the way in which the Navajo behave, but it reflects a social code, not a difference in perception.

As to the walking shots: it is often difficult for people unfamiliar with film to judge, against established screen codes, which activity is worth covering at what length. Commonly, failures of judgment by these norms are, with shaky camera movements and a tolerance for jump-cuts, exactly the difference between amateurs and professionals in our culture. Anyway, there are many reasons why a film might have a lot of walking in it, most of them without much deep cultural significance, especially in a society where people still walk a lot.

And the jump-cuts? As Worth, a teacher of film production, could well understand, the Navajo were no more adept at coverage and film editing than most beginning film students. That they see the world in some fragmented way may or may not be the case. The jump-cuts are no evidence of it, either way.

One can explain the Navajo films, then, as being made by amateurs just as readily as one can explain them as being made by aliens to Western culture. That the Navajo produce movies which look, more or less, like other non-professional (that is, amateur) films should come as no surprise. After all, they are North Americans with ready access to the media. Being asked to make films would not pose a problem in terms of the deep conflict between this imposed culture and their own traditional ways; it would simply be part of the imposed culture – like car driving.

The results are no more persuasive if the equipment is given to people whose experience of the West is more limited. A series of experiments was conducted in New Guinea by Edmund Carpenter, who wanted to 'observe what happens when a person – for the first time – sees himself in a mirror, in a photograph, on films; hears his voice; sees his name'. This he did, with a curious disregard (in one so aware of media and their effects) for the potential damage that might ensue. He also provided Papuans with movie cameras. In Port Moresby people used them but to make static images as if they were still-cameras. With tribal peoples in the country, 'when we left cameras behind for them to use, they were generally ignored'.

Despite this, Carpenter obtained about seventy films made by indigenous Papuans, but only one seemed to him to have anything of a non-Western approach.

Western audiences delight in stories about natives who use modern media in curious ways, their errors being both humorous & profound, suddenly illuminating the very nature of media themselves.

Even when these stories are true, I think their importance is exaggerated. Surely the significant point is that media permit little experimentation & only a person of enormous power & sophistication is capable of escaping their binding power. (Carpenter, E., 1973, p. 184)

Gardner is clearly correct about the difficulties involved.

The error made in these experiments was to assume that the apparatus was in any way culturally neutral. This is especially true of Worth and Adair. It is curious that anthropologists, trained after all to understand human cultures as constructs, should fail to see the camera as a culturally determined artefact. Instead, they seem to have regarded the apparatus as a scientific instrument and to have seen scientific instruments as being somehow acultural. The entire Worth-Adair experiment depended on believing in 'the culturally unbiased vision of the camera' (MacDougall, 1969, p. 25). John Adair: 'It seemed to me that the camera was an ideal way of doing this [seeing the world through native eyes], as one could so to speak, jump into the eyes of the natives by way of the camera' (D'Agostino, 1980, p. 61). But the camera is not a product of Navajo culture and nothing it produces can be anything other than Western, whoever operates it. These experimenters wanted the film-maker to be culturally biased while ignoring the cultural bias of the camera manufacturer.

Although influenced a millennium ago by Arab scientists, for the last five hundred years the lens has been a prisoner and a product of the West. It is ground to produce images with single-vanishing-viewpoint perspective according to Western representational codes. The camera to which it is attached has a viewfinder so small that it works (is focused, for example) most easily if individual faces are privileged. Indeed, David MacDougall has pointed out that filming interactions is quite difficult, especially if you are as low as you need to be to shoot most non-Western domestic scenes. The machine is produced by Western individuals to photograph Western individuals.

And, as I have documented elsewhere, colour film stock and the TV colour system are designed by white people to photograph other white people. They are, literally, biased chemically or electronically against persons of colour (Winston, 1985, *passim*). No amount of sophistication, it seems to me, will allow a non-Western operator to produce anything but moving images almost entirely conditioned by or, at best as Carpenter suggests, in struggle against the West. That is all the machine can do – even in the hands of culturally powerful non-Westerners such as the Japanese.

One of the Navajo, Sam Yazzie, asked Worth and Adair, 'Will making movies do the sheep good?' On being told that it would not, Yazzie asked, 'Then why make movies?' (Worth and Adair, 1972, p. 4).[23]

This was a very good question indeed, and one that could be put to all sorts of ethnographic film-makers. Some were even beginning to put it to themselves. Foremost among these was Jean Rouch.

30

Film as Truth

Jean Rouch trained as a engineer and his first jobs were in Africa during the Second World War. His interest sparked by native peoples, he returned to Paris to study anthropology under the two leading French scholars in the field, Marcel Griaule and Marcel Mauss. It was they who suggested that Rouch take a film camera with him when he returned to Africa in 1946.

One of Griaule's earliest exploits had been a major expedition in the course of which he gathered some 3,500 African objects which eventually constituted a major collection of the Musée de l'Homme in Paris. He was also the pioneer of French ethnographic film, producing shorts from material shot on two fieldwork trips to the Dogon of Mali in 1935 and 1938 (Clifford, 1988, pp. 55ff.; Rouch, 1985, p. 33). Griaule drew the usual distinction between finished films ('works of art' which were documentaries in a recognisable Griersonian sense) and record-footage ('notes of inquiry'). The ones he made were 'works of art', though, with titles, narration, music and commercial distribution.

Rouch's understanding was that Mauss also made this distinction. Rushes were 'a visual memory which could record the totality of a phenomenon' (Eaton, 1979, p. 2). Works of art were something else. Rouch saw the commercial sponsorship of Griaule's work as producing 'travesties' and much preferred the apparent freedom to be scientific (by creating visual 'notes of inquiry') that American university funding had bestowed on Mead and Bateson (Rouch, 1975, p. 88).

Rouch made a series of short films on various ceremonies among the Songhay and Sorko of Niger and the Dogon during his field trips. In 1952 an International Committee of Ethnographic and Sociological Film was founded, headquartered at the Musée de l'Homme. Rouch became its secretary-general.

In 1957 a 36-minute short on a controversial cult, *Les Maîtres fous*, which Rouch had shot some years earlier, was commercially released in France with Bergman's *Sawdust and Tinsel*. The film itself was as controversial as the cult it depicted, many seeing it as exploitative – with its scenes, for example, of men in trance plucking bits of dog from a boiling cauldron. But Rouch had been approached by the cultists to film the ceremony; and his commentary sought to show the ceremony as nothing but a response to the irrationality and alienation of colonialism because the cultists in trance become white authority figures. Yet these factors did not serve to defend him or the film from attack.

This release did not mean that he had begun making commercial

'travesties', however. On the contrary, the film was resolutely anthropological. What could be made of it, even by an informed anthropologist,
remained in doubt. 'The main trouble – and this is not intended as a criticism', wrote a scholarly critic some years after the event, 'stems from the
fact that it is almost impossible to fully understand and hence appreciate a
film that concerns religion and symbolism' (Muller, 1971, p. 1472). None
of this criticism, informed or otherwise, quite overwhelmed the power of
the film. It did not prevent the film's winning the prize for the best documentary at Venice in 1957. Nor did it stop the same producer from
putting five earlier Rouch shorts, shot in 1952, together in the compilation
feature, *Les Fils de l'eau*, released in 1958.

Despite all this Rouch did not begin to film with a view to satisfying
such exhibition possibilities. Instead he resisted the temptation and developed what might be described as a research agenda into the issues of
authenticity and the validity of the documentary idea. Whatever else this
programme was, it was certainly not designed for commercial success.

At the centre of Rouch's emerging concerns was the use of fictional
techniques. He had started exploring this possibility before the release of
Les Maîtres fous. In a film begun in 1954 (and completed in 1967 as
Jaguar) Rouch tested how the 'real' people with whom he was working
might respond in some fictional settings. He wanted thereby to illuminate
something otherwise not filmable – their mental states.

He conceived another project designed more thoroughly to explore the
inner life of modern Africans, to show them firmly as citizens of independent countries, and to reveal them as urban. In 1957 he directed *Moi, un
noir* about a group of slum dwellers who worked as casual labourers in
Abidjan, Ivory Coast. For these people the weekend was, in Rouch's
words, 'a sort of mythical Eldorado, based on boxing, the cinema, love
and money' (Eaton, 1979, p. 8). These became the film's subject.

The people Rouch involved all have nicknames taken from the movies.
One of them, Oumarou Ganda, 'Edward G. Robinson', narrates the film
(which Rouch shot silent). Rouch said, 'Fiction is the only way to penetrate reality – the means of sociology remain exterior ones.'

Moving even further towards using the camera as a provocation, in
1959 he made *La Pyramide humaine*. When he discovered that he could
not film the relationship between the black and white students in the
Abidjan lycée (because, essentially, the two groups did not mix), he
arranged 'a plot' – in both its general and technical sense. A new girl,
white, insists on getting to know the black students. Rouch then filmed
the resultant encounters – some of them with a blimped tripod-mounted
Cameflex weighing over 100 lb. Rouch also screened the rushes to the
participants in *La Pyramide humaine* and filmed their responses. The
equipment, however, reduced spontaneity.

Before *La Pyramide humaine* Rouch, like most users, had not exhibited
much interest in the technology. He had always tended to shoot in 16mm
and never on a tripod. A mythopoeic anecdote has it that he lost his tripod
in a river on the first expedition in 1946 and, having been forced to work
without it, always thereafter handheld the camera (Eaton, 1979, p. 2). He
was essentially an ethnographic film-maker of a somewhat strict record-
footage type. In fact, it was not until his material was prepared for
commercial release as *Les Fils de l'eau*, some ten years after he had begun
film-making, that he encountered film editing as a technique. 'Rouch at

first thought that an editor was superfluous (like a camera operator) but was pleased with the results when editing the films with Suzanne Baron, who had worked with Jacques Tati and later worked with Louis Malle' (ibid., p. 5).

Like many ethnographers, he had been convinced of the importance of sound but not to the point where he pushed for technological innovation. It was not for him, as it was for Drew and Leacock, 'une exigence fondamentale' (Marcorelles, 1963, p. 14). A non-synch soundtrack recorded on a clockwork- driven tape-deck had contributed to the controversy over *Les Maîtres fous*. *Moi, un noir* had been shot silent. However, the experience of *La Pyramide humaine* showed him how crucial synch sound was. A technical element was added to the experimental agenda which was anyway pushing Rouch out of Africa and back to France. In the summer of 1960, using the prototype self-blimped Eclair 16mm camera, he directed a film in Paris.

Chronique d'un été is, at one level, nothing more than a reversal of the normal ethnographic film, with 'the strange tribe that lives in Paris' as its subject and even a young African (Landry, who had appeared in *La Pyramide humaine*) playing the part of the great (white) explorer/ethnographer (Morin, 1985, p. 13). It was made at the behest of the sociologist Edgar Morin. He was interested, from an engaged far-left political perspective which is never quite revealed in the film, in the state of France at that particular moment and the degree to which film could be used to illuminate it.

At the time, such a project sat well with Rouch, with the general rising concern with scientific epistemology, with the state of French anthropology – and with its major institutions, such as the Musée de l'Homme, which was to be the site of the film's climactic sequences. Anthropology was experiencing something approaching a crisis, especially in France, occasioned not least by the collapsing legitimacy of fieldwork in general and the ethnographers' monological authority in particular. For example, the classic texts on the Dogon, created by Marcel Griaule, were being subjected to increasing questioning about their authenticity. There was now a presumption that his informants had actively distorted the information they had given him over a long period. That he never learned the Dogon language and had to rely on translators was no help (Clifford, 1988, pp. 58ff.).

As an anthropologist connected to the museum and numbering Griaule as one of his teachers, Rouch was not untouched by these developments. As we have seen, Rouch's own work had not been immune from attack. It was a time to deal with these questions – the politics of anthropology ('the eldest daughter of colonialism', as Rouch was to call it (Eaton, 1979, p. 26)); the limitations of participant observation ('You distort the answer simply by asking the question' (Georgakis, 1978, p. 22)); the usefulness of film as a 'note-taking tool' (Eaton, 1979, p. 33).

In France, Rouch and Morin also had a rather different documentary tradition in which to work. It was the impressionistic filmed essay rather than the sociological public education text in the Grierson mode which dominated the French documentary tradition – although it shared that dominance with engaged political work to a greater degree than was true of Britain and America.

This impressionistic tradition begins with city symphony feature documentaries popular in the 1920s, such as *Rien que les heures* or *Berlin:*

Symphony of a Great City. At a smaller scale, but in the same mode, were Ivens's first films, elegiac studies of a railroad bridge (*The Bridge*, 1928) and a city in *Rain*.

Emblematic of the persistence of this European tendency to relative abstraction was *Pacific 231*, Jean Mitry's 1949 hymn to the steam engine, enriched by a score written for the film by Honegger. (From Holland, Bert Haanstra's *Glas* (1958) became the most widely distributed of such films. It won an Oscar. This sort of work was standard art-house supporting-programme material.)

In France, the post-war documentary was generally and unambiguously, in the terms used by Griersonians, poetic, aesthetic and personal. It was also protected by French law, which prohibited double features until 1953 and thereafter awarded prizes to meritorious films (Goretta, 1956, p. 156). (These were exactly the sort of measures Grierson had failed to establish in Britain, where cultural issues were never an element in film legislation.)

The 1953 decision in favour of double features was largely rendered a dead letter, in part because the documentarists organised themselves into a pressure group, the *Groupe de Trente*, to resist it. Among these film-makers were Alain Resnais and Georges Franju, both documentary 'poets' rather than 'observers'. For Resnais, a Holocaust death camp is aestheticised, becoming a realm of *Nuit et brouillard* (*Night and Fog*, 1955); the Bibliothèque Nationale contains *Toute la memoire du monde* (*All the Memories of the World*, 1956). For Franju, the abattoir is aesthetically awash with *Le Sang des bêtes* (*The Blood of Beasts*, 1949). Robin Wood has pointed out (1973, p. 44) that, far from these being 'a kind of prelude to their fictional features', they are rather 'the best of ... their most personal work'.

Perhaps even more pertinently for Rouch and Morin, Chris Marker, a colleague of Resnais, was overtly and insistently in the first person in a number of major documentaries made during the second half of the 1950s. His *Letter From Siberia* (1957) is constructed as just that: 'Je vous écris d'un pays lointain', the commentary begins (Marker, 1961, p. 41). Marker was to deal with one international current affairs topic after another – the USSR, China, Israel, Cuba. But each time the stuff of the Anglo-Saxon journalistic documentary – the 'facts' and the 'figures' – was to be turned into irony, buried in a collage of images played against a poetic and personal text: 'Ses arbres calcinés, ses plaines désertes ne me sont pas moins chers que ses rivières et ses fleurs. On l'appelle la Sibérie' (ibid., p. 79).

There are real differences between Marker on the one hand and Rouch and Morin on the other. Marker was a great deal more sceptical in general than they were about the possibility of discovering 'truth' through the tools of social science such as interviews. So Marker's insistence on the voice-over and avoidance of interviews, as Genevieve Van Cauwenberge argues persuasively (1992, *passim*), marks more than just a stylistic divergence. Nevertheless, Marker does share one crucial technique with them – he puts himself into the film.

It is not to belittle the extent of Rouch and Morin's experiment in *Chronique* to say that their decision to do likewise and put themselves into the film – the critical mark of cinéma vérité – is less drastic, given the context of a personal tradition in the French documentary, than it would have been for even the most sophisticated of Anglo-Saxon film-making social scientists. Clearly Rouch and Morin were less bound than the direct cinema people to Grierson's legacy of 'objectivity' and personal detachment.

Chronique d'un été begins with Rouch and Morin asking, on camera, a woman whom we come to know as Marceline (Marceline Loridan) whether or not she would mind being filmed:

> JR: What we're asking of you, with great trickery, Morin and I, is simply to talk, to answer our questions. And if you say anything you don't like, there's always time to cut. ... (Feld and Ewing, 1985, p. 38)

We are introduced to a seemingly random group of people, in fact basically Morin's friends and anti-Stalinist political allies, and we see them discussing the issues of the day, largely over meals. That is the substance of this chronicle.

It was halfway through the summer that Michel Brault arrived from Canada and picked up a prototype of the new self-blimped camera from Coutant. The mode of the film was transformed from what Morin called 'commensality' (filming on a tripod 'excellent meals washed down with good wines') to something new – 'pédovision', Rouch's equally jocular term for handheld shooting (Morin, 1985, pp. 7 and 11). Rouch understood how important Brault's contribution was: 'It was Brault who brought us new shooting techniques, which we didn't know and which we have been copying ever since. ... We have to admit that everything we have done in French cinéma vérité derived from the Canadian National Film Board' (Rohmer and Marcorelles, 1963, p. 17).

But this generosity is somewhat overstated. The underlying interventionist and reflexive method of the film remained unchanged after Brault's arrival although the new technology did lead to moments of pure exuberance similar to the follow-the-subject shots in *Primary*. For example, Brault follows Marilou, a secretary at *Cahiers du Cinema*, holding hands with her boyfriend (the philosopher – unidentified – Régis Debray) down a Parisian staircase, worthy of Max Ophuls's attention, from garret to street.[24]

But most of the time the film is as far from *Primary* as it can be. It is at constant pains to remind us that filming is in progress. For instance, just before the above example of 'pédovision', Morin is seen closing a window, and thereby revealing the reflection of a light, prior to questioning Marilou.

Rouch and Morin manipulate and condition the film at every turn, most importantly by insisting that the topics they think significant are dealt with by the other participants. If something was being missed they arranged a meal and, again on camera, bullied the others into discussion:

> JR: We've reached the point where the film, which up to here has been enclosed in a relatively personal and individual universe, opens up onto the situation of this summer of 1960.
>
> VOICES: Yeah, yeah....
>
> JR: So, shall we go ahead?

EM: Yes, but I'd really like to know what they think.

JR: Let's go!

EM: Okay, Let's go ... here we go, here we go ... here we go ... I don't know, but if I were a student ... y'know... right now, the men in particular. I mean old enough to do military service, I'd be thinking about events in Algeria. ... You don't give a damn about this issue, about the war in Algeria, do you? (Feld and Ewing, 1985, p. 56)

Finally, as Rouch had done in *La Pyramide humaine*, all the participants were filmed watching a rough cut in the cinema at the Musée de l'Homme. They heatedly debate the truthfulness of the revelations in the film. Was Marceline, a Jew, acting when she remembered being deported during the war and reunited with the remnants of her family afterwards? Was Marilou 'immodest'? As a coda, shot by Brault handholding the camera while seated on a makeshift dolly, Rouch and Morin are seen walking to and fro in a gallery of the museum debating the same issues.

JR: So, Edgar, what do you think of the screening?

EM: Well I think it's interesting because, all things considered, everything that has been said can be summed up in two things: either the characters are reproached for not being real enough ... or else they are reproached for being too real. (Feld and Ewing, 1985, p. 69)

Rouch and Morin had, then, quite different ambitions for, and understandings of, the new apparatus. As anthropologists and sociologists, rather than physicists, journalists and lawyers, they had perhaps the advantage of a more sophisticated concept of the difficulties raised by participant observation and other fieldwork problems. It is this awareness that drove *Chronique*'s (and cinéma vérité's) reflexivity.

Rouch's Anglo-Saxon opposite numbers were seemingly unaware of the issues with which he was grappling. The direct cinema group was not sympathetic to *Chronique*. In fact, they were as critical of cinéma vérité as they were of more traditional realist documentaries. *Chronique*, they claimed, was less powerful than their texts because it 'seemed to have been manipulated arbitrarily both in shooting and editing' (Freyer, 1971, p. 438). Leacock said the film 'bothered me very much' (Levin, 1971, p. 216). Leacock's concern centred on the fact that in *Chronique* the event was the filming. He felt that the camera affected people 'since the only thing that's happening to them is the fact they're being filmed. There's nothing else to think about. How can they ever forget it?' (Shivas, 1963a, p. 18).

This is, of course, to miss the point. Rouch and Morin were beyond the simplicities of direct cinema where 'manipulation' (or, rather, the supposed lack of it) was the be-all and end-all. On the contrary, cinéma vérité accepted the *tu quoque* charge of mediation with enthusiasm. Moreover, it could not be accused of denying the film-makers' intelligence and sensibility, either.

I have always found it easier to sympathise with Rouch's positions than with the direct cinema group's – despite the humanism often seen in

Leacock's and Pennebaker's films. Rouch is insightful, provocative, original and, it seems to me, unconfused. His candour is very winning.

For example, he told a major ethnographic film conference: 'Every time as film is shot, privacy is violated' (Rouch, 1975, p. 92). Or, even while he praised Vertov's work to Roy Levin he acknowledged: 'It was a cinema of lies' (Levin, 1971, p. 135). Indeed, whenever he is interviewed, he always unfailingly produces such good copy. Among the things he said to Dan Yakir in 1978, for instance, were:

It is ineffectual to continuously assert your own opinions. ...

I plan to make a cine-portrait of Margaret Mead. For me, she is what we call in anthropology a 'totemic ancestor,' so we're already in the imaginary. ...

The objectivity of the lens is ... an incredible stimulant for the observed as well as the observer. (Yakir, 1978, pp. 3, 6 and 7)

He told Marcorelles: 'It's impossible to make a film with the people concerned in your film if you stop contact with them when the film is finished' (Eaton, 1979, p. 4). With James Blue he shared the thought that 'this extremely strange game we were playing may also be extremely dangerous' (Blue, 1967, p. 23). Rouch deploys an ironic self-awareness which stands in attractive contrast to direct cinema tendentiousness.

However, despite this appealing personal style and despite the seductiveness of *Chronique*'s reflexive practice, despite the lack of tendentiousness in the film's rhetorical positioning, despite one's sympathies for the oppositional political and anthropological impulses involved – despite all this, the film still embraces science and the possibility of the image as evidence.

At the time, at the Lyon meeting, for example, *Chronique* was received as being diametrically opposed to *Primary*, with Rouch and Morin in opposition to Drew and his colleagues. But how deep was this chasm really? Notwithstanding their on-screen presence, how far are Rouch and Morin with their 'research' from, say, Wiseman with his 'voyages of discovery'/'spoor collection'?

Chronique, Morin wrote (1985, p. 6), 'is research. ... This research concerns real life.' Their on-screen appearances and this rhetoric, even allowing for the slightly different and less deterministic concept of 'research' in French, had the desired effect. Critics understood this to mean that *Chronique* was an experiment in the realm of the uncertainty principle. Bohr and Heisenberg were both invoked in the *Cahiers* review, for example. The experiment was authenticated because Rouch and Morin knew that 'it is also necessary to isolate the observer from his apparatus of observation. ... They are honest enough to enter the arena, to put themselves onto the stage (and into the question). ... They set before us all the conditions of the experiment' (Fereydoun, 1963, p 249).

But, unavoidably, cinéma vérité turns out to offer its audience data – evidence – just as direct cinema does. It too trades on the scientific inheritance of the camera.

Chronique eschews the transparency of an invisible direct cinema filmmaker to offer us another transparency, that of Rouch and Morin in the shot. The scientific status of the image is therefore still in play – as was understood by Lucien Goldmann (1979, p. 66):

> The cinema has no autonomy in relation to equivalence with reality except in so far as it wishes to be seen as a means of aesthetic creation. Which is to say that at the same time as acknowledging the value of experience and testimony represented by Morin and Rouch's film, we are afraid that right from the start it is very close to the limits of this kind of film, and that scientific truth, cinematic realism and aesthetic value are precisely beyond these limits.

At the end of *Chronique*, walking the halls of the Musée de l'Homme, Morin sums up by saying: 'Nous sommes dans le bain' – 'We're implicated'.[25] And they are – just as much as any direct cinema film-maker.

Direct cinema (for all its caveats) aspired to be a 'fly on the wall'. Cinéma vérité, as Henry Breitrose notes (1986, p. 47), wanted to be a 'fly in the soup ... visible for all to notice'. Cinéma vérité might luxuriate in revealing its processes, allowing for a claim that the work is personal, 'signed' and mediated in an open and above-board fashion. But the gesture becomes hollow because the spirit of Arago yet hovers over the enterprise urging us to believe that what we see is evidence, evidence of documentarists making a documentary.

31

The Principles of Visual Anthropology

It is now necessary to examine how, after the Lyon meeting, these two very different strategies for the new documentary developed – to chart the influence of both direct cinema and cinéma vérité on a whole variety of film-makers from the socially engaged independent to the mainstream television producer. To begin, let us stay with the anthropologists to see how the new equipment affected the practice of ethnographic film-making.

As the 1960s progressed, the possibilities of the new technology putting ethnographic film on a new and firmer foundation were explored but in a less vigorous way than Rouch was suggesting in *Chronique*. This exploration was led primarily by Colin Young and his students in the Ethnographic Film Program at UCLA because other film-using anthropologists were not particularly quick to take up the new equipment (Wright, 1976, p. 336). When these students, David and Judy MacDougall and others, began to film with the new gear in the field, their model was to be a direct cinema style heavily inflected with Rouchian sensibilities.

Although the new cameras and recorders looked like the 'perfect' record-footage machines, such as Sorenson might have described if he had been more technically sophisticated, that is not the way they were primarily deployed by these younger anthropologists. They were too well educated for that. The noisy debate in documentary circles about the scientific claims of the new apparatus, in which they had played a not insignificant role, had alerted them to the limitations and dangers of such a rhetoric. Instead, in anthropology, they used the new gear to build a bridge across the chasm between record-footage and demonstrative films, producing what Young had began to call 'observational cinema'. MacDougall noted (1969, p. 16):

> Ethnographic film-making occupies a curious place between the art of film and the social sciences. It has long lacked the full support of either, yet it has the capacity to achieve a truly humanistic kind of perception embracing them both. Recent interest in the ethnographic film, spurred by the accelerating disappearance of traditional cultures, may now enable it to fulfil its promise.

There seemed to be some reason for David MacDougall's optimism. At first sight, the films of this new generation appeared to avoid many of the traditional pitfalls; for instance, MacDougall's own *To Live with Herds*

(1972), which was shot among the Jie of Uganda, deploys synch exactly to enhance the humanity of the subject. By using interviews as well as direct recording, MacDougall and his sound recordist Judy MacDougall gave the Jie an individuality Harris (and indeed most pre-1970s ethnographers) denied their subjects.

To avoid making the hitherto unavoidable choice between record-footage and a structured product, the MacDougalls developed the concept of 'the unprivileged camera style' – the opposite of the 'privileged camera angle' which in Hollywood terminology means a camera position impossible in everyday life.

Although they shot the action within the Jie compound from more than one angle, they found in the editing room that they did not want to cut in footage from the second position.

> At first when we asked ourselves what had happened, we blamed the technical framing of our shots. Later we began to see that wasn't the real problem. ... We were trying to give a sense of being in a Jie compound ... – to counteract the prevalent representations of 'exotic' people, to express the realities of field work, to record informal aspects of culture, to allow individuals to emerge rather than types – and a number of things made it possible: our subjects' acknowledgement of our presence, our long and static camera takes, and the very low energy of much of what we filmed. We were not singling out dramatic subjects for attention so much as opening the film up to a kind of anti-subject-matter. ... By intercutting shots from two or more camera positions we found we were taking away from that immediacy by invoking a style of fictional film making. ... We were aware that the conventions of fiction had considerably influenced documentary films, but we had under-estimated the extent to which we and other film-makers had been taught to accept them as appropriate. (MacDougall, 1982, p. 8)

The result of such insights was not direct cinema. On the contrary, here was no crisis and much intervention – interviews, intertitles and other material provoked by the film-maker. For example, the world of the Jie is established in a single shot – a slow 360° pan in which Logoth, the central figure in the film, points out the geography of the area, an apparently featureless plain, to the camera; and, sector by sector, David MacDougall photographs that horizon, keeping his informant always in the foreground.

As for record-footage, MacDougall had been taught that that was only 'a scientific application of technology rather than true film making'; and he wanted to be doing 'true film making' (MacDougall, 1969, p. 19). So in *To Live with Herds* the attempt is made to meld the two, creating an overall structure without losing the record-footage quality of any single sequence. The MacDougalls are not entirely successful in this only because in the end structure, as ever, wins. Although there is indeed much in the record-footage mode – enough for Jean Rouch (curiously) to complain to Colin Young that *To Live with Herds* 'wasn't really a MOVIE' (Young, 1975, p. 73) – there is also more which shows the MacDougalls as consummate film-makers. For instance, the way in which they slowly reveal how the Jie interact with the modern world would not disgrace a feature director.

In its structured (demonstrative) mode the constant omission in most ethnographic documentary is just this interaction. Even if there is no conscious attempt to re-create the past in the manner of a Curtis or a Flaherty, there has still been a tendency until very recently for such film-makers to offer pictures of uncontaminated cultures and to disguise their own presence. Such films ignored the effects of contact and suppressed evidence of the ubiquity of the West.

The first section of *To Live with Herds* is like this, presenting a picture of traditional African life – drawing blood from a cow for sustenance, herding, life in the homestead, and so on. Only a fleeting shot of a toddler playing with a piece of printed paper gives any hint that the Jie are in touch with the outside world. The second section begins with a reference to the British in an intertitle and some shots of a primitive water pump. The homestead children play a guessing game by hiding objects in their hands. The things include a yellow fruit, goat dung, a stone. Then one child reveals that his hidden plaything is a piece of plastic bag.

Cut to the nearby town, and thereafter see the Jie's way of life in the context of an independent African state. The Jie are shown to live in a political world and have political opinions – some fairly outrageous to liberal Western ears, as when regret for the passing of British rule is remarked on.

To Live with Herds finishes with an equally well structured closure. At the film's climax, Logoth determines to check on his herds, which are pastured some way to the west. In the film's last shots we see him at this cattle camp. In the gathering dusk, he greets his fellows: 'Hail to the cattle camps. Hail to my greeting to you. May you grow old and walk with a stick. Hail with thanks. To cows. To our seeing each other again.... May you always live with herds.'

Chaplin danced down no sunset-lit road to greater effect. Despite the record-footage obtained with their unprivileged camera style, the MacDougalls have in fact made a movie. Record-footage does not as a general rule win the Venezia Genti prize at the Venice Film Festival. *To Live with Herds* did, in 1972.

The MacDougalls' agenda, though, went beyond this attempt to create a synthesis between demonstration film and record-footage to embrace other issues; in fact, as the 1970s progressed, they were moving 'Beyond Observational Cinema' (as David MacDougall had entitled a 1975 paper) altogether, more and more towards a Rouchian position. A critical issue had now become the pretence of non-presence on the part of the observer. Having the subject acknowledge the presence of the film-maker was, despite Rouch, still something of a direct challenge to anthropology's basic assumptions about 'science'.

Established ethnographic opinion, Rouch aside, held to a fairly straightforward notion of inscription. For example, Edmund Carpenter, on being hired as a communications consultant by the government of Papua New Guinea in 1969, conducted a number of experiments to see what difference awareness of the camera made: 'For New Guinea, the record is clear: comparing footage of a subject who is unaware of the camera, then aware of it – fully aware of it as an instrument for self-viewing, self examination – is comparing different behaviour, different persons' (Carpenter, E., 1973, p. 139).

MacDougall had now come to distrust this orthodoxy. On the contrary, he felt, as had Rouch previously, that, hidden cameras perhaps apart, the assumption that the film-maker could be ignored itself vitiated the possibility of accurate ethnography. So the MacDougalls' practice became increasingly reflexive. In *Lorang's Way* (1978), that questions are being put is highlighted by having them in the form of intertitles. Lorang refers to Judith MacDougall by name. The camera car appears. (The absence of Land Rovers in *The Hunters*, where surely they would have been needed to transport the film-makers, was the thing that struck me most forcibly the first time I saw the film.) There is never any question but that we are looking at a film made about an African by a white ethnographer.

MacDougall is an extremely sophisticated practitioner. These attempts to synthesise ethnographic film-making's two antithetical modes or to solve the problems of participant observation were not much emulated. On the other hand, giving tribal people their voice – subtitling tribal speakers talking in their own languages in synch – was a great breakthrough and one widely copied. As increasing sensitivity to paternalism and racism have coloured our perceptions of the dangers of such moviemaking in general, letting the subjects speak was perceived as combating, at least in part, the alienating exoticising of tribal life that used to be the norm.

Now even a popular series such as Granada TV's *Disappearing World*, of which twenty-three episodes were made between 1970 and 1978, regularly allowed tribal people to speak in synch. Some of these films also went a long way to avoid the exotically dramatic and sensational. In the first of a trilogy on the Mursi of Ethiopia (1974), for instance, Leslie Woodhead the director and the anthropologist David Turton concentrated on shooting the meetings which illuminated the tribe's democratic decision-making procedures. That was what the film was about, the Mursi being one of the few peoples on earth not to have chiefs and leaders. But, to make a film about this topic, Woodhead and Turton had virtually to ignore the 'war' with the neighbouring Bodi which was provoking the debates they were filming (Woodhead, 1985, pp. 3ff.). (That they managed to do so in the context of a television film is to be applauded.)

Synch equipment has been used in these films to transform the *National Geographic* stereotype of the grunting native. The grunts turn out to be language. For instance, to take a less 'popular' example, in Gary Kildea's *Trobriand Cricket: An Ingenious Response to Colonialism* (1973), the image of 'Stone Age' New Guinea people is systematically destroyed not least because the language of the rituals is both translated in the subtitles and explained by the participants.

The synch and the subtitles reveal the Trobrianders as witty and eminently reasonable. The film shows how the dances associated with Trobriand cricket were copied from the marches of the more than one million American servicemen who passed through the islands in the Second World War. It also explains how the missionaries' rules for cricket have been improved on. The Trobrianders felt limiting teams to eleven players each was unnecessary and they allow all the village men to play; they felt the bat was too narrow; the rule about straight-arm bowling was clearly very curious and could be abandoned with advantage. As one who suffered agonies at school being forced to play this game, I found myself in enthusiastic agreement on these last points with the Trobrianders.

Did all this then – sophistication, synch, sensitivity – allow ethnographic film finally 'to fulfil its promise'?

During the 1970s there was a series of meetings which can be used to chart the degree to which this happened. In 1973, the Ninth International Conference of Anthropological and Ethnological Sciences gathered in Chicago. An International Conference on Visual Anthropology, funded by the US National Endowment for the Arts, was part of the proceedings. These were confident and coherent enough to yield a volume entitled *Principles of Visual Anthropology* (Hockings, 1975). In the enthusiasm of the aftermath Alan Lomax called for an urgent world-wide ethnographic film-making programme which could 'vastly benefit the human race' as it headed towards 'a less varied future' (Lomax, 1973, pp. 474–5).

Five years later, in 1978, an International Ethnographic Film Conference was held in Canberra. It was hosted by David and Judy MacDougall, who were at that time the resident directors of the Film Unit of the Australian Institute of Aboriginal Study. The agenda was dominated by Colin Young and his ex-students, the MacDougalls among them; but the conference was marked by vigorous disputes (Sandall, 1978, p. 217). It was, in contrast to Chicago, a volatile and somewhat acrimonious meeting. One major reason for the less than even tenor of the event was that the subjects, tribal people, were also participants – and they made it clear that they were not best pleased with what the ethnographers had done to them over the years. Another reason was that the veteran documentarist George Stoney screened his then new film about how Flaherty had made *Man of Aran* in the early 1930s.

> *Man of Aran: How the Myth Was Made* (1978) had popped the lid off all the distortions and omissions in Flaherty's highly romanticised depiction of life on the Aran Islands.... Many in the audience at the conference's premier screening of Stoney's revelatory documentary had been incensed at what they now saw to be Flaherty's falsification of the life he purported to be documenting. (Macbean, 1983, p. 33)

By some strange accident Stoney's ancestors had come from Aran Island where Flaherty shot *Man of Aran*. In 1976, Stoney returned to the island with Jim Brown to make a film dealing in part with his own history, in part with Flaherty's attitude to Aran and in part with the effect of *Man of Aran* on those involved and on the community generally.

Stoney was of the generation which most directly bore the brunt of direct cinema's aggressive rhetoric. For instance, his classic 1952 midwifery training film, *All My Babies*, was a breakthrough in the sympathetic representation of African Americans on the screen. It was so far from the run of ordinary training films that it had been selected for the Edinburgh Film Festival (Ellis, 1989, pp. 166ff.). But none of this impressed direct cinema's Young Turks. The film was synch and, in that era, this meant that it had to have been scripted and therefore reconstructed and was therefore dismissible.

In response, Stoney remained stoically appreciative of the strengths of the older tradition of documentary film-making. Against what MacBean calls 'Flaherty's genius for poetic imagery', Stoney saw the current generation of film-makers fretting 'about the veracity of details' (Macbean, 1983, p. 33; Stoney, 1978, p. 1). *How the Myth Was Made* was conceived as a defence of 'the power and poetry of earlier films' and a specific justification for Flaherty. It is, the film says, Flaherty's strength (his poetic eye) that causes him to ignore the socio-political realities of Aran life.

Although I find this unpersuasive, nevertheless *How the Myth Was Made* is a remarkable film. It is a rare document in its concern for the effect of filming on the people filmed and those around them. Moreover, it offers evidence of Flaherty's omissions and suppressions even if Stoney himself did not choose to use them to damn the man!

In the context of the Canberra meeting, *Myth* gave further evidence to the native peoples present and their partisans that Western documentary film-making was a mendacious and exploitative enterprise.

In November later that same year, 1978, the third International Meeting on the Scientific Applications of Audio Visual Media took place in Paris. No less than three days were devoted to screening films about the Yanomamö. As the largest unacculturated tribe in South America, they have been much filmed. The conference watched record-footage taken by Jeanne Liedloff in 1961–2 which is the earliest known film of the tribe, the Asch work which began in 1968 and was still in progress, and television films made by the French, the Yugoslavs and the Japanese as well as some of the 40 hours of material shot by New York avant-garde video artist Juan Downey during an eight-month sojourn with the tribe. One observer noted:

> Objectifying the Indians, none of the film or video makers communicated a feeling for a Yanomamö as an individual. ... It is also surprising to note the similarity of information presented in these documents. The same limited material is covered in many of the films over and over again leaving the audience with many questions on other aspects of Yanomamö life. For instance, the role and activities of women is one subject touched on by the Japanese but on the whole overlooked by the all-male film crews and anthropologists from other countries. Personal interactions between and within family groups is also virtually ignored. (Sloan, 1979, pp. 22–3)

The Yanomamö archive as it stood in 1978 indicated that, at least as far as the most filmed tribe in the world was concerned, MacDougall's enthusiasm had been misplaced and the prospects for ethnographic film were less rosy than he had thought. The pitfalls of previous ethnography were proving not so easy to avoid after all.

First, the films were still questionable as scientific evidence. For instance, *Trobriand Cricket* was in fact as much set up as *Altar of Fire*, although at the behest of the participants. As Annette Weiner, who has done considerable fieldwork among the Trobrianders, points out (1977, p. 506): 'The film is a *reconstruction* of a cricket match (a point curiously deemphasised by the film makers) specifically enacted for the camera team by the members of a local political movement who at the time of the filming (1973) were seeking an ascendant role in Trobriand politics.' In other words, the film is a political campaign commercial. Weiner suggests that the film itself is 'an example of an "ingenious response" to the potential of Western media'.

Weiner also demonstrates (1978, pp. 754ff.), using a film by a Japanese anthropologist, Yusuko Ichioka, how anthropological preconceptions are dangerously prone to govern all such films. Weiner happened to be in the same Trobriand village when Ichioka arrived to continue a project: 'The filming focused primarily on the actual filling of the yam house, an activity that was visually exciting to record. But for the villagers, the most significant events of the day surrounded the distribution of pork which were not part of the filming schedule.'

So the question of omission/selectivity would not go away – even with synch, even with native instigators, even with anthropologists and filmmakers aware of and sensitive to the need not to misrepresent tribal people.

Disappearing World, for example, seldom really directly addressed itself to why the world it filmed was disappearing (Macbean, 1983, p. 35). The series's premises was that enough remained in these cultures of precontact life to warrant filming. The producers insisted that the modern world was so far absent as to negate the union's crewing agreement. The shop, though, had a clear understanding that such a claim was fraudulent quite a lot of the time (Brown, 1978, pp. 88ff.). This mistrust eventually led the union to demand full crewing, a financial and ethnographic impossibility. André Singer, series producer at the time, describes *Disappearing World* as being put 'into cold-storage because of incessant union/management squabbles over crewing' (Singer, 1988, p. 376). But more was at issue than a Western labour relations problem. What the dispute addressed was, in an oblique way, the persistent omissions of demonstration ethnography.[26]

Omissions also remained unavoidable even in the record-footage style of ethnographic work, no matter how hard the film-maker tried. Take a later film by Gary Kildea, *Celso and Cora* (1983), about a young couple in a Manila slum barely surviving as street vendors. Kildea meticulously fades to black at the end of each shot so the film is, largely, uncut. Despite this strategy, when he screened it for my class at New York University in 1984 my students were eager to know about one series of shots in which the couple had obtained money which they used for buying a sick child medicine. Where had they got the cash? Kildea revealed that, of course, he had given them the money. Outrage as to why this was not in the film! Such questions about omissions were becoming a commonplace after Canberra.

In short, the new equipment had no more solved ethnographic film-making's problems than it had finally delivered on the promise of the Griersonian documentary.

Special to ethnography were the difficulties of anthropology as a whole. Mike Eaton and Ivan Ward argue (1979, p. 114) that it is not enough to acknowledge anthropology as a 'handmaiden of colonialism'. Rather it is a branch of zoology extended to include man.

The new equipment did not of itself help correct this orientation. If anything, anthropology's dubious ideological thrust was aided by the voice ethnographic film now gave to native peoples. Allowing speech might have encouraged empathy by providing a more fully rounded and human image of the 'other', but that was not necessarily any better than previous modes which had long been accused of encouraging racial scorn and disgust in part by denying the voice.

Thus my response to the Trobriand rules revision of cricket – that I was invited by the film to see the Trobrianders as the *same* as me – is held suspect. *Disappearing World* is full of such moments – as when participants in a ceremonial are filmed saying that they are embarrassed and confused by what they are required to do. The trouble is that, as David Turton has argued (1992, p. 291), '*our* behaviour legitimates *theirs*'. The trick is 'how to demonstrate the humanity we share with the people we study without privileging our own, or, as James Faris [another leading ethnographic film-maker] puts it, how to "obliterate otherness while preserving difference"'.

But, for Eaton and Ward, this cannot be done, certainly not as long as 'a naive conception of film as a neutral record [is] accepted' (Eaton and Ward, 1979, p. 115). It follows that other justifications – the recording of threatened cultures, even the creation of archives for the native peoples themselves – are all equally suspect.

As a first step to getting beyond this impasse, Annette Weiner suggests (1978, p. 757) that any 'theory of ethnographic film must address itself to the issues of film as "construction" rather than film as "truth"'. But in the last decade this step has scarcely been taken although some anthropologists, James Faris for example, are ready to acknowledge that 'the status of film as document is no longer persuasive' (Faris, 1992, p. 172).

If this is so (as I believe it is), the full implications are today being side-stepped so that ethnographic filming, which has received another techno-logical boost from the introduction of video, can still go on. However, filmed visual anthropology's ambitions are much reduced from twenty years ago.

At conferences now, such as the one held in 1990 in Manchester in con-junction with the Granada Centre for Visual Anthropology, papers from which I have been quoting, it can once again be claimed: 'As for their anthropological value, however, films are not on equal terms with ethno-graphic writing.' In the view of this anthropologist, Kirsten Hastrup, ethnographic films are (in Geertzian terms) 'thin'; written ethnography is 'thick' (Hastrup, 1992, p. 21). James Faris, at the same conference, admitted that ethnography remained a 'problematical, undertheorized and obstinate set of endeavours' (Faris, 1992, p. 179).

All this is a long way in tone from Margaret Mead's heady charge (1975, p. 6), made at the height of enthusiasm for the new 16mm equip-ment, that anthropology's neglect of film was 'criminal', a 'gross and dreadful neglect'. The distance is the measure of how handheld synch failed ethnographic film. Because such film-making made the strongest claims to science, stronger than the implied sociology of most documen-tary, this failure was most grievous. The evidential pretensions of the new equipment fell harder and further in anthropology.

32

Flies in the Soup: The Influence of Cinéma Vérité

There was one final option available to anthropologists.

In Australia, land claims, whereby Aborigines sought considerable damages in the courts for the seizure of their lands, were becoming a major political issue by the mid-1970s. The usefulness of media exposure in such cases was more and more obvious to the Aboriginal communities involved. Douglas and Judy MacDougall themselves were caught up in the most controversial and extensive of these disputes, that of the Aurukun Aboriginal community.

The Borroloola, another community involved in a land claim, decided that making a film might help their case. They also had in mind that it would help recall for themselves and their children the history of their struggle against white Australian authority in both its police and welfare modes. But some Borroloola had attended the Canberra meeting on anthropological film in 1978 and were therefore well aware of the failings of ethnography. They needed film-making help but they knew they wanted collaborators rather than directors and technicians. They found them in ethnographers Caroline Strachan and Alessandro Cavadini, who had previously made a film in collaboration with the Palm Island Aborigines.

The Borroloola project, *Two Laws* (1981), was a very distinct enterprise. It was well beyond 'observational cinema', and, although it bore some resemblances to the Navajo film exercise in that it was made 'through native eyes', it also differed from that in a number of crucial regards.

Two Laws was instigated at the behest of the native people and it had overt political purposes, not some rather arcane formalist concern about the nature of image making. These purposes, unlike those of the participants in *Trobriand Cricket*, are foregrounded. *Two Laws* exemplifies what MacBean says of this Aboriginal film-making movement in general – it was designed to '*express* rather than merely *observe* Aboriginal culture' (MacBean, 1983, p. 39). As a secondary theme, *Two Laws* also answered, *en passant*, the sort of question Adair and Worth had asked in their Navajo project. For instance, after a period of film tests, the Borroloola determined that they preferred the wide-angle lens. Wide-angles allowed people to make statements and have others in shot confirm or contradict them and also avoided conferring a spurious authority on individuals through the close-up. The film is therefore shot entirely in wide angle and largely in long takes.

They also had very distinct ideas about how to represent their history on film. *Two Laws* includes reconstructions of past events, most notably a forced march suffered in 1933. These reconstructions are discussed and rehearsed on camera prior to being finally enacted. Both rehearsal and final enactment are included in the finished film.

All these techniques are deployed with the very clear purposes of the Borroloola always in focus on the screen. The result is extremely important: 'All in all, the film *Two Laws* is a breakthrough of major significance in ethnographic film' (MacBean, 1983, p. 43).

Certainly, the anthropologists and the native people involved in *Two Laws* are far from having 'a naive conception of film as a neutral record'. The only problem is that this acute awareness of the ideological underpinnings of Western image making takes the project so far from anthropological film as to destroy, in effect, that form. *Two Laws* involved abandoning the entire ethnographic enterprise of using film as evidence. Because of its reflexivity, it became instead an example, one of the best to date, of how cinéma vérité's influence came to be played out in the world of documentary film-making in general.

For it was not only Aborigines who wanted to reflect media practice in their media production. Western film-makers also began to choose the media as their subject. As they did so, they became more reflexive.

How the Myth Was Made, for example, has Stoney himself on camera explaining how he came to make the film. This was to become a not uncommon sight in documentary, especially when the film did not quite work out as planned – Michael Rubbo documented his failure to get to Castro in *Waiting for Fidel* (1974). Jill Godmilow has similar trouble getting to Poland for a film about Solidarity in *Far From Poland* (1984), while Michael Moore achieved a rare and unexpected US theatrical hit with *Roger and Me* (1989), a film about Moore's sterile attempts to persuade Roger Smith, then Chairman of General Motors, to visit Flint, Michigan.

This is quite different from the general use of on-screen reporters in television current affairs because these figures are all drawing attention to the film-making process. TV reporters are in part disguising that process either by, with one degree of effectiveness or another, explicating evidence or by covering narrative gaps in the footage.

It also became possible to make documentaries about image production or media representation in a more general way. Such a combination went beyond the Rouchian danger, which all the above films share to a certain extent, that cinéma vérité was a sort of *reductio ad absurdum* because the only possible film was one about how that same film was made.

It would be technologically determinist to suggest that the equipment was responsible for this more general strand of work. It is rather that some film-makers learned the lessons of *Chronique* in the context of a particular rediscovery of Vertov and a generally rising Marxian awareness about the importance of media as model ideological state apparatuses. These film-makers melded a critique of image production as an ideologically charged practice with a more general radical critique of society – an enterprise that invoked the name of Brecht just as often as that of Vertov.

Nightcleaners (1975), a study of the plight of the women who clean London's offices during the night, is a clear example of such work. Made by the Berwick Street Collective, at one level it both documents the struggle for better conditions and intervenes in that struggle as a potential organising tool. The 'secondary production theme' involved a simultaneous deconstruction of such texts using a full panoply of Vertovian techniques. Clapperboards, editing tables, repeated takes and slow motion are all deployed in support of this task. The film is a most rigorous example of both 'accusatory aesthetics' and Vertovian self-referentiality.

Unfortunately, this breakthrough was to little purpose. In the case of *Nightcleaners*, the collective's concerns with the nature of image production, while neither unimportant nor trivial, looked impossibly sterile and irrelevant when yoked with the raw plight of a group of exploited women trying to organise a strike against the advice of their union. The result was to reduce the deconstructionist agenda to a bathetic formalism. The film was received with much hostility by most viewers and the collective's response to this was simply callow:

> The film doesn't fulfil the messianic functions the organized Left – the Communist Party, the International Socialists, the International Marxist Group, etc. – require of a film. Our struggle is in a sense as much with the Left as it is with the film making tradition we come from ... for we have to struggle with the Left's notion, for example, of what the working class will understand, what they mean by understanding. If somebody doesn't understand something, and if in the middle of a viewing someone gets up and says, 'I'm bored to tears with this', we the film makers have to be there to discuss it. The film isn't meant to be shown with everybody unanimously understanding it, it offers itself to be argued with. (Waugh, 1984, p. 210)

Arguing with *Nightcleaners* was not the issue for audiences unschooled in, or conditioned to dislike, avant-garde work. At best the filmed bored; at worst, it got in the way of the nightcleaners' struggle.

Nevertheless, Claire Johnston and Paul Willemen (1984, p. 204), not necessarily incorrectly, assumed that *Nightcleaners*, 'if we take it seriously ... could provide a basis for a new direction in British film making'. In the event, this was a road not taken even by those on the left more ready and able to deal with the realities of the communication process than was the Berwick Street Collective. The combination of the politics of representation and an examination of the things represented was, however, taken up elsewhere in a less overtly avant-garde and radical form.

Ilan Ziv's television series *Consuming Hunger* (1987), for instance, documented how the First World is sold, via the media, Third World famine as a charitable opportunity. Even after I declare my interest in this series (I was one of his 'media experts') I think it is fair to say that he melds critically important topics (stereotyping the Third World, famine as a sociopolitical construction, and so on) with the issues raised by the image making that attends these themes. Bill Nichols thinks (1991, pp. 11ff.) the films 'extraordinary' and on a par with Berger's pathbreaking (but equally traditionally shot and constructed) television series about painting and advertising, *Ways of Seeing* (1972).

There were other, perhaps even more tangential, consequences of the rising sophistication heralded by cinéma vérité practices. The access television movement, which was designed as a species of political empowerment, shared with Rouchian cinéma vérité an overt rejection of the objectivity assumptions of the Griersonian tradition (including direct cinema) – and, of course, of TV news and public affairs broadcasting. Most of access television is only accidentally reflexive in the sense that attention is drawn to production norms because they are not being met. But this 'use of media by citizens' organisations', facilitated by the introduction of the first cheap portable video (the Sony ½-inch reel-to-reel Portapak in 1968), was sometimes more overtly concerned with the ideology of image making and the issue of objectivity (Ellis, 1989, p. 275). The model for this lay with the Canadian National Film Board.

The Griersonian agenda for social amelioration, with which the Board normally worked, had become institutionalised in a Federal programme, Challenge for Change/Société nouvelle, which started in 1966. This production strand had been inaugurated with Tanya Ballentine's direct cinema study of urban poverty, *Things I Cannot Change*. The film is close enough in subject matter to the tradition for Grierson to claim, with some justice, that it was modelled in some sense on *Housing Problems* – albeit shot with the new equipment.

To take Grierson's point here does not mean that one needs also to support a wider argument he and his colleagues from the 1930s were to be heard making increasingly at this time – that there was no innovation going on because they had done it all before (Gillespie, 1975, p. 43). In 1970, for instance, Grierson wrote (1970, p. 293) that Challenge for Change was merely following 'decently in the original cinema-verite [*sic*] tradition which the English documentary people associate with *Housing Problems* (circa 1936)'. Sponsorship, technology and technique render this broader claim spurious.

Beyond these obvious differences is an even more significant cinéma vérité consideration. The TV transmission of *Things I Cannot Change* brought the family in the film, who had revealed the details of their poverty, much local humiliation. This made the NFBC think about the moral implications of the Griersonian victim tradition (Engelman, 1990, pp. 7ff.). As a result NFBC film-makers concluded that their responsibilities *as film-makers* were very different from those of Grierson's artists. They came up with a protocol which involved the people they filmed in a pre-screening or test-screening process before completion, as Rouch had done in *Chronique*, so that these subjects could both have some influence on the final work and be prepared for what trials exposure might bring (Watson, 1970, p. 18). All this is a very long way from the GPO. It is even distant from Flaherty's practice of sharing his rushes, which he did but without any sense that his artistic and editorial control would be affected.

Even that was not the end of the matter.

Exhausted by the orgy of promotional documentary production occasioned by the World's Fair Exposition in Montreal in 1967, some Film Board personnel sought projects within the Challenge for Change rubric that would return them to more socially relevant subject matter. Colin Low went to Fogo Island, off Newfoundland, where the community was under threat of destruction because of the collapse of its fishing industry. The Newfoundland government had determined that a structured withdrawal was in order. The Fogo islanders, divided among themselves, were unable to resist. Low found himself making short, modest films to explain the islanders' case to their government and to help them discuss and resolve their differences with each other. A targeted audience, the government, had been added to the process of involving the subjects in the film-making process. This combination became the mark of Challenge for Change projects.

The next logical step was to begin to train people to make these films themselves, which was what George Stoney did with a group of Mohawk and Iroquois people when he took over the directorship of the project in 1968 (Star Blanket, 1968, *passim*). There was a row going on about the closure, by the Canadians, of a bridge vital to a Mohawk reservation's communication system. The recently trained Native American film-makers organised a protest which they (and NFBC personnel) then filmed. The resultant movie, *You Are on Indian Land* (1969), was used to bring about meetings of the tribe with local whites and, eventually, the Federal Government in Ottawa. The bridge was allowed to remain open (Ellis, 1989, p. 274). The film was also a critique of the mainstream media's misrepresentation of the event as a violent confrontation.

The introduction of the Portapak videotape recorder, the use of which was pioneered at the board by Dorothy Todd Henaut and Bonnie Klein, facilitated this sort of direct-action use of image making. Under them and Stoney Challenge for Change further metamorphosed. It became a programme not to produce films or tapes at all but rather simply to distribute VTRs to activists and others and support their work with them. Henaut (1970, p. 8) described professionals in such a role as 'facilitators of communication'. What happened, at least with the first group of social activists to be trained in video by Henault and Klein, is the subject of a conventionally shot but necessarily extremely reflexive film, *VTR St. Jacques* (1969) (Engelman, 1990, pp. 12ff.). Anstey's claim that *Housing Problems* was the slum-dwellers' own film was unsustainable: *VTR St. Jacques* demonstrates how such claims for the subject-as-author could be made good.

But in effect, in this move to use video to 'foster government–citizen dialogue to address social ills', Stoney and his colleagues had written the role of the professional documentarist out of the script, just as Strachan and Cavadini had virtually written the anthropologist out of *Two Laws* (Engelman, 1990, p. 17). In Canada, the professional was no longer even an advocate; he or she was indeed, as Henaut suggested, now simply a trainer, a facilitator, or a social animator. The National Film Board felt that this was somewhat too strong a challenge, so Challenge for Change died. Stoney returned to the States, where he founded the Alternate Media Center at New York University and educated a whole generation of engaged access programmers for the nascent cable television industry.[27]

The very ubiquity of Portapaks ensured that in many different hands and places access-style work would be done. John Gaventa, for instance, working closely with the reformist group in the United Mine Workers of America, made a series of videotapes to encourage solidarity and break through a hostile media environment in the bitter Harlan County, Kentucky, coalfield strike of the mid-1970s. These tapes were not made by the miners themselves but by Gaventa. All the same, as he was at that time much more of a political scientist than a media professional, his work had the feel of access material. The tapes are very basic technically (although not crude to the point of image and sound impairment), single-minded and specific. Gaventa's purpose was simply to put the miners' case to other workers both within the county and across the county line, thus breaking the mine owners' media monopoly. To see the tapes, the audience gathered round Gaventa's monitor.[28]

Although in North America a steady flow of engaged material is produced for the cable access channels, access, in most situations, was to remain marginalised. The phenomenon is widespread, largely because of the political need of the cable industry for a measure of respectability which such a public service provision affords; but the channels have audiences too small to be measured by conventional ratings techniques. As the proponents of access claim, the programming is often the only outlet for many of the voices involved, but it seems to me that a self-evident strength of the early work is missing.

This is because more is at stake in the Challenge for Change and Gaventa approach than just the involvement of the subject in the production process. Unlike Grierson, whose public education programme required large audiences but who finished up with small ones, Challenge for Change and Gaventa always had from the outset a clearly targeted and very small audience for whom the work was specifically designed. So even if people were to tune into the cable access channels, which as far as can be known very few do, that specificity of audience would still not be delivered.

A final strand of reflexive work comes from an area of overlap where documentary and avant-garde practice mingle – the autobiographical or family-study film where the film-maker and the subject are related. Here too one can see the influence of cinéma vérité at work. However, John Katz, who assembled more than sixty contemporary autobiographical films for an art gallery film season in Canada in 1978, believes that the development of this strand had as much to do with the general *Zeitgeist* as with any formal understanding of the reflexivity issue in cinéma vérité. 'Part of the rise, both in the numbers of autobiographical films and in an audience for them, can be attributed to a heightened interest in self-awareness, personal growth, family background, expanded consciousness and the human potential movement' (Katz, 1978, p. 10). For these documentarists, the proper study of mankind was not any longer man (or, indeed, woman) but, rather, me.

While Katz is clearly correct in attributing this vainglorious impulse to the times, a specific factor in its development nevertheless also had to do with cinéma vérité. The technology with which to facilitate filming the rising obsession with self was at hand. Synch sound added a dimension that moved, say, the personal expression of a Brakhage into a more conventional documentary mode. 'Finally,' announced Ed Pincus (1972, pp. 24–5), 'it has become possible to shoot synch sound films without a crew, just the film maker working alone. ... I have been shooting a film diary about my life and those around me since December of 1971. I plan to continue the project for five years.'

It is not insignificant that the founding text in this mode, as cited by Katz, is in fact the fake (and hilarious) 'documentary' *David Holzman's Diary* (1968). This was made by Kit Carson and Jim McBride exactly as a slap against the new documentary's truth-telling pretensions – what they refer to as 'the blubber' (Carson, 1970, p. viii). 'David Holzman', as played by Carson, is also in and of himself pretty much an indictment of the 'heightened interest in self-awareness' rampant in these decades. 'Holzman' would sooner film than fornicate, or do much else, in his quest for self-understanding via image making.[29]

Pennebaker, walking out of an early screening of *David Holzman's Diary*, told Carson, 'You killed cinéma vérité.' Recalling this incident in his introduction to the published script of the film (1970, p. xiii), Carson commented that Pennebaker was wrong: 'Truthmovies are just beginning.' He was right.

As the decade progressed, film-makers expanded their obsession with self somewhat and began to make films encompassing other members of their families. For instance, in 1974, an eighteen-year-old, Jeff Kreines, made a 47-minute synch film about his brother, *The Plaint of Steve Kreines as Recorded by His Younger Brother Jeff*, on the basis of which he got (albeit briefly) to MIT and Leacock. In that same year Amalie Rothschild released an intergenerational study of her mother, her grandmother and herself, *Nana, Mom and Me*.

Deviancy was not precluded. Having a mentally challenged cousin could result in an Oscar-winning film – Ira Wohl's *Best Boy* (1979). As Wohl explains in voice-over, his cousin Philly, fifty-two at the time of the filming, has been 'mentally retarded since birth'. He goes on to describe how about three years prior to making the film he became aware that Philly, who lived at home, was going to be in a difficult position when his aging parents died. Wohl intervened to ensure that Philly would be independent enough to cope with this crisis and documented that intervention in his movie. Philly's father died during the filming; his mother, according to a credit, shortly after.

There is no question that Philly was indeed fortunate to have a cousin as concerned and as able and effective as Ira. It is equally true that Ira was indeed fortunate to have a cousin as photogenic as Philly in a situation as emotionally satisfying as the one Ira plotted for him.

Even if one takes this admittedly cynical view of *Best Boy*, the film nevertheless speaks in an uncomplicated way about altruism, both that of Philly's parents and of Wohl himself. It is sensitive to the family's dignity. Other family-study films have been more remorseless. Cinéma vérité, in these instances, became a species of therapy. The classic case-text (as it were) is Maxi Cohen's *Joe and Maxi* (1978), a study of the film-maker's vexed relationship with her cancer-ridden and dying father. Cohen writes:

> Very soon after we began filming, I began to 'see' my father. He was no longer the omnipotent hero. The more I saw and understood his vulnerability, his shortcomings, more importantly his fears and needs, the more I learned about myself and my past. The process of getting to know him was really about separating from him. And in the editing of the film, my perceptions and perspective kept for ever changing as I watched my behaviour, as I observed my father, as I got to understand the dynamic, the truth, the pain and the patterns of my relationship with this first man in my life. (Katz, 1978, p. 47)

Film-making, Joe tells Maxi, is what she does instead of having a real job, like a secretary. But his sexism should not mask the reasonableness of his objection to the enterprise expressed later in the film when he complains that 'I am not a document. I'm a person'.

Despite these various types of activity – taking media representations as a topic, giving subjects access, making portrait films – all in all, the Anglo-Saxons did not take to cinéma vérité. The new technology did not particularly encourage film-makers to put themselves into their films, except in the circumstances I have just been noting. These were exceptional. The influence of cinéma vérité was contained. Instead the norm was to use the new gear to pretend to a new level of self-effacement. It was direct cinema that won the battle for the soul of the documentary in the American and British heartlands of the realist tradition.

33

Flies on the Wall: The Influence of Direct Cinema

The first point to note about this triumph was that the upheavals of the 1960s did not encourage among direct cinema film-makers a more theoretical and sophisticated discussion about their work. On the contrary, direct cinema was presented as the Griersonian equivalent of 'the end of history'. All the problems that were said to have plagued documentarists were now deemed to have been solved.

The film-makers were encouraged in this view by the fact that direct cinema also triumphed as far as the public perception of documentary was concerned. It came so to condition the received idea of what a documentary should be that traditional-style films, including the Griersonian classics, were often seen as not being documentaries at all – because of reconstruction, commentary, and so on.

Direct cinema made the rock performance/tour movie into the most popular and commercially viable documentary form thus far. These were for many the only sort of documentary they saw and responded to positively. The coverage of the Beatles' first US tour and *Don't Look Back* had established the form. Pennebaker himself was still making them twenty-five years later – *Dépêche Mode 101* (1989). In the rock documentary the event being filmed seemed unambiguously more important than the filming; the lack of commentary was more acceptable than the paternalistic voice of God; the behind-the-scenes candour (and/or clowning) appeared to be more compelling as evidence than the reconstructed encounters of the classic documentary.

This appearance of greater 'truth' was also attached to direct cinema's ability to penetrate the private. Studies of death, especially by cancer, became something of a commonplace in documentary output. Marital discord and family strife (as in *A Married Couple*) were covered more than once. Craig Gilbert chronicled family break-up in *An American Family* (1973), a twelve-part series which was shot by Alan and Sue Raymond and Joan Churchill. Not only was there divorce but one of the children revealed his homosexuality. 'My instructions', wrote Gilbert (using a more revealing phrase than he perhaps realised, 'were that they [the Loud family] were to live their lives as if there were no camera present.' The British copied this exercise with *The Family* made by Paul Watson for the BBC the following year. Since that series began transmission before the shooting was over, *The Family* became, somewhat curiously, a documentary about an 'average' family whose private life is repeatedly exposed on national television.

The move to videotape from 16mm synch sound, which is still under way, was perfectly in line with the technical requirements for coverage of these intimate domestic topics. Video was introduced to documentary without much fanfare and has thus far had a far less radical effect on production norms and aesthetics than did the move from older methods to 16mm synch. The first networked documentary using small-format video was broadcast in the USA in 1974. (This was TVTV's *The Lord of the Universe*, made under the auspices of WNET's experimental Television Laboratory in New York (Merjan, 1978, p. 7).)

Video aids the essentially intrusive nature of direct cinema in two main ways. First, tape, compared with film, is so cheap that the limitation on shooting becomes the time available in post-production to process footage rather than the cost of such footage in terms of raw stock and negative processing. The flies can stay on the wall far longer than they could when they had film cameras.

Second, they can also see in the dark more easily. For instance, an early video documentary, also made at the TV Lab, was the Raymonds' *The Police Tapes* (1977). The dim streets of the South Bronx and the ill-lit hallways of the projects and tenements were seen in a new level of available light, because a special low-light camera was used. So sensitive was it that a police car's flasher registered with the intensity of a theatrical follow-spot focused on a star (Marjan, 1978, p. 12). To give the impression that a scene is light when it is, in fact, dark is a new sort of distortion.

The idea that direct-cinema-style studies of these kinds were the essence of documentary was further reinforced by the much-fanfared (and virtually annual) transmission in America of a new Wiseman film.

Wiseman was not only unique among modern American documentarists in achieving this sort of regularity, but his ever-growing *œuvre* was also the only one to be noticed widely. For instance, Michael Arlen gave Wiseman the cultural kudos of long pieces in the the *New Yorker*. By 1980 Arlen was comparing him to, of all people, Vertov (Arlen, 1980, p. 96). Wiseman has now made twenty-three films and is the subject of five books – including Liz Ellsworth's *Frederick Wiseman: A Guide to References and Sources*. In the early 1990s it was still possible for one of these authors, Barry Grant, to treat the films as unproblematic evidence – in fact, *Voyages of Discovery* (1992), as his title asserts. The context for all this attention makes it even more extraordinary for, as Bill Nichols points out (1991, p. ix), in the fifteen years to 1989 there was not one single-authored volume on documentary in general and very little other work either.[30]

A final paradoxical proof of the potency of direct cinema as the dominant model for contemporary Anglo-Saxon documentary comes from the reception of *Roger and Me*, a film made in a somewhat different self-referential cinéma vérité mode. So far had the 'pure' direct cinema idea of the documentary as an evidential reflection of the world triumphed in the public mind that *Roger and Me* was criticised, for instance, because the order of the filming was not the order of the film.[31] That no direct cinema practitioner ever made such a lock step part of their practice is neither here nor there. Rhetoric, Al Maysles's for example, and the (supposedly 'mosaic') films themselves are responsible for such naive expectations.

Thus by its third decade direct cinema appears to have won the battle begun at Lyon for the right to determine what is and is not a documentary. So what did the mature direct cinema film look like at its best?

Early in 1982, the Institute of Contemporary Arts in London mounted a retrospective of the work of Roger Graef to coincide with the transmission on BBC 1 in prime time (just) of his latest multi-part documentary, *Police*. Graef is an American theatre director who came to Britain in 1962 and began his career as a film-maker in 1964. By 1970 he was working in a very austere direct cinema mode. Over the next decade and more he made several documentaries and documentary series, more than thirty films in all, which together certainly rival Wiseman's *œuvre* for extent and far outstrip it, in my view, in seriousness of intent.[32]

It must not be thought that Graef's achievement was the result of enlightened support on the part of British television. This was really little better than its American counterpart. Documentary had been confined into a TV ghetto nearly as narrow as it was in the States. Nevertheless, documentary was part of the television schedule with its leading practitioners, Denis Mitchell, for example, still maintaining a strong Griersonian vision. Mitchell was an important innovator who in the late 1950s and early 1960s sought to go against the grain of the technology by – for instance – experimenting with full-scale outside-broadcast TV units for the making of domestic documentaries. Despite the very different technology, he was, like Leacock, looking for a more direct form (Corner, 1986, *passim*).

But when a little later direct cinema techniques proper began to be imported from the USA, others less visionary treated them as a threat to the Griersonian tradition. Richard Cawston, for instance, a man best known for his pathbreaking 1968 'informal' portrait of the Queen, was then head of BBC documentaries. He and his senior staff promulgated in 1972 the 'Principles and Practice in Documentary Programme' policy document. This made it clear that the BBC, at least, was more interested in 'eternal', rather than cinema, verities: 'A documentary explores a factual subject in depth. It not only shows, it illuminates. It attempts not merely to inform, but to provoke deeper thought and understanding than a cold presentation of facts would do' (Cawston *et al.*, 1972, p. 5).

Dai Vaughan (1974, p. 74) offers a damning analysis of this windy rhetoric. He points out that Richard Cawston and his fellows appeared to believe, *inter alia*, that, in Vaughan's words:

1 A shot of someone speaking is more truthful than a shot of someone listening.
2 Someone who is aware of the camera is aware of the television audience.
3 People's considered adaptation to the camera is more real than their spontaneous response.
4 What the director sees when the camera is absent is what would be happening if he himself were absent.

Even if the booklet were produced as much, if not more, for political consumption rather than for practical application, it is still illuminating. As far as Graef's sort of film-making was concerned, for instance, Cawston *et al.* stated clearly (1972, p. 11) that 'even the purest piece of "*ciné vérité*" [sic] can never be – and indeed should never be – totally free of the day-to-day business of directing'.

This curious document was being circulated just as the BBC was transmitting Graef's first major series, *The Space Between Words*, in which he flouted many of these rubrics. The goal of the series was to document how communication worked as a process in various settings – work, school, diplomacy, politics and family. Shot at a ratio of 30:1, *The Space Between Words* not only established Graef's matured working method but also pointed to what was to develop into the major difference between him and almost every other documentarist in the direct cinema field.

Interested in how institutions function, Graef was not to be seduced into attempting to illuminate the ordinary. Instead he began here in three of these films, 'Work', 'Politics', and 'Diplomacy', to avoid the private domain altogether and thereby the pitfalls of the dominant 'victim' documentary. In doing this he moved direct cinema away from what had become an obsessive concentration on the victim towards studies of the powerful.

For the rest of the decade Graef was to work largely for Granada Television, the producers of *Disappearing World*. His first film there, *The State of the Nation: A Law in the Making* (1973), documented the arguments going on between ministers, MPs, civil servants and pressure groups over a four-month period as the Fair Trading Bill was drafted. In 1975, he observed the same sort of processes at work in the headquarters of the European Commission in Brussels in another *State of the Nation* film. In 1976 there were three studies made of how a major decision is reached by each of three different complex organisations, British Steel, Occidental Petroleum and the London Borough of Hammersmith. In 1978, Graef watched the British Communist Party, at its Thirty-Fifth Congress, laboriously hammer out a new-look Eurocommunist policy.

These portrayals do not treat power as if it were deviancy – which is the way Graef's direct cinema colleagues for the most part tend to treat poverty and other misfortunes. Rather, he has substituted the *frisson* to be had from watching normal but usually secret behaviour for the *frisson* of watching deviance.

Graef uses the purest of direct cinema modes. However complex the topic, he eschews interviews and narration. In the hands of his long-time collaborator the cinematographer Charles Stewart, the style of these films is minimally interventionist. Graef's day-to-day business, in defiance of BBC Documentary Department assumptions, has been to minimise the crew's disruption to the point where he would often absent himself from the room in which the shooting was taking place.

He claims to be making 'films of record'. These can be attempted only if very limited canvases are tackled with considerable filmic resources. Graef delineates the canvas by observing, within the complexities of an organisation, just one small singular activity, one issue. Often he is not in at the very beginning, but he always has enough time to wait for a resolution. The crew asks to be informed of all developments relevant to the one issue agreed upon as the film's subject. They bind themselves to secrecy until the film is made. The subjects are allowed to view a fine cut for the purpose of checking accuracy only.

Graef thus came to occupy a position in the UK not entirely unlike Wiseman's in the USA – one of a small group of documentarists who commanded enough serious critical attention to be fundable. Nevertheless, it was significant that his return to the BBC in 1981 for the *Police* series was engineered not by the Documentary Department in London but by John Shearer, an executive from the very different BBC world of Current Affairs working in BBC West. The trust was deserved since *Police* achieved a then rare 'hit' ratings success for documentary.

Police perfectly reflects the dilemma of modern British police, caught between a traditional self-image of public guardian and a more contemporary vision of a besieged defender of law and order facing a rising sea of barbarism. It was perhaps this schizophrenia that allowed the senior officers of the Thames Valley force to agree to Graef's system of film-making and to permit transmission of the results.

In all the thirteen episodes of the series, no film better catches the essential tension between old and new than the one devoted to the work of a recently created 'flak' team. A drunken phone call threatening violence to a dog was enough to bring out them out. As the team's superiors, two senior policemen, walked into the range of their own guns to talk the supposed offender out of his lair, the radio mikes picked up their wry comments on the dangers of friendly fire and with it all the implied problems of 'modernising' a previously unarmed service. The strain between the old and the new was also expressed in glances, the looks the ordinary policemen gave each other when faced with the tactics of the armed force now recruited to their ranks. Catching such minutiae, and *Police*'s thirteen hours are full of little else, is not only direct cinema's greatest strength, it is also the strongest basis for its claim to authenticity.

I can think of few texts on the realities of class in Britain better than another episode in *Police* in which the CID lie in wait for a band of expected thieves at the Duchess of Marlborough's country house. One officer, a cockney, took most of the film to get to the correct form of address. His first try, 'Lady Marlborough', was curtly corrected to 'It's the Duchess of Marlborough actually'. Thereafter he tried the odd 'Madam' and even 'Er, er, Duchess' before he finally achieved 'Your Grace'.

However, I justify my choice of *Police* as the casebook example of direct cinema's best in its third decade not just because of the excellence of its observation or the fact that it was the then rare phenomenon, a documentary popular with the public. It also illustrates the power of direct cinema as *evidence*.

One episode, 'A Complaint of Rape', had three officers interrogating a woman who claimed to have been raped. The entire encounter was filmed from over the woman's shoulder, concealing her identity. The style of police questioning – hostile, overbearing and insensitive to a painful degree – caused a public outcry. In this it was no little aided by the fact that the Prime Minister, Margaret Thatcher, was already in full voice about a series of judicial decisions letting rapists off with scandalously light sentences. The impact of the film was immediate. Officers were demoted and reforms promised, including a special rape unit staffed by women police.

In all this there was never any question but that this was a film of record. Critical response suggests that, for many, Graef's films are quite simply evidence. This reception marks him off from other documentarists. Rows over his movies, which are not infrequent, turn as in this case on the substance of the events filmed rather than on the filming.

This is not true of most documentaries. Whenever films become involved in controversy this usually turns, as with the example of *Roger and Me*, on the integrity of the film itself as evidence. Nor is direct cinema immune from this, as the various rows about Wiseman's films attest. He is often accused of misrepresentation by selection at both the filming and the editing stage. Indeed, one major complaint against *Titicut Follies* was exactly that only the most sensational aspects of life in the hospital were filmed. The same was true of his *High School* (1969) (Benson and Anderson, 1989, pp. 144ff.). The Loud family, stars of *An American Family*, complained that, despite twelve hours of transmitted coverage, Craig Gilbert had failed to film their good moments but had concentrated on tension and disaster (Gilbert, 1983, p. 192). Examples of this sort of objection are endless.

With Graef, however, this tends not to be a problem because he focuses down so finely. Had he offered a picture of, say, activities at the police station and come up with a film containing only this one interview/interrogation, no doubt he would also have been attacked for distortion. As it was, he offered only a record of the interview and that was accepted as such. The one caveat expressed suggested that the police might have been modifying their behaviour for the camera, but this view did not prevail.[33] 'A Complaint of Rape' is therefore that rarest of things, a realist documentary which actually had an easily demonstrated effect in the world.

Graef thus appears to fulfil direct cinema's promise to deliver actuality. That is why I propose *Police* as the *ne plus ultra* of direct cinema. But all this is not to say that direct cinema was triumphant in that documentaries in general were now all made in this way and had these sorts of effects in the world. Most direct cinema films, such as Wiseman's, had no such effects, of course; but even the stylistic influence of direct cinema needs to be carefully examined. In fact, direct cinema was a model more honoured by pastiche than emulation.

For Graef is in many ways exceptional. His practice is very much at odds with the norms as, for instance, they are enunciated in the BBC's 'Principles and Practice'. Most important of these are rubrics that affect the economics of documentary film production. Graef was a very expensive film-maker, as were all direct cinema documentarists who used film. He was not bound by the standard ratios of the day, the 11:1 or 12:1 proposed by Cawston *et al.* (1972, p. 12), but used about three times as much stock. 'His prodigality in the use of film stock enables him to deny himself a number of established practices in constituting a film and eschew most of the injunctions in *Principles and Practices*' (Collins, 1986, p. 135). Graef's 'prodigality' is no small (or even great) economic thing. It is the heart of the matter.

Direct cinema depends on high ratios. All else flows from this. That Graef could be considered exceptional in this regard says nothing more than that direct cinema also remained exceptional as a production style for documentary. It was not a success as a model and only a few documentarists, such as Graef and Wiseman, were allowed to practice in this 'pure' (that is, high-ratio) mode.

This is not to say that direct cinema therefore had no effect on the run of documentary production. On the contrary, the effect was profound; but it came to be primarily expressed through the creation of a third style – neither cinéma vérité nor direct cinema proper, but what I call (following professional UK usage at the time) 'vérité'.

Vérité is an ersatz style developed by television on both sides of the Atlantic, a bastard form which reduces the rigour of direct cinema practice to an easy amalgam of handheld available-light synch shooting and older elements. Vérité films (and tapes) contain direct-cinema-style material, but can also use commentary, interviews, graphics, reconstruction and the rest of the realist documentary repertoire. As a consequence, shooting periods and ratios are reduced to levels close to traditional norms. Thus it is that the current dominant documentary style is not direct cinema itself, but is rather a derivative of it.

This result stems from the fact that, from the middle-to-late 1960s on, the new 16mm synch equipment was accepted into mainstream production and slowly became the industry norm. Thus cameras that *could be* handheld and film stocks that *could be* used for available-light shooting became ubiquitous. This is not to say they were so used, for this was an era when camera personnel demanded whether directors wanted something shot 'properly' (that is, on a tripod) or in 'wobblyscope' (handheld), and sound recordists audibly queried the acceptability of mumbles. But this happy season soon passed and technicians mastered the new capabilities of the machines. So the vérité handheld take became another element in the documentary film style – the mark not of a wholly fresh approach to documentary film but of a grudging and economically viable application of the new gear's potential.

However, vérité meant much more than this. It was not simply a question of long handheld takes, actuality sound and a certain looseness with the rules of continuity cutting, because vérité caused 'damage' to all the older elements.

Most important, vérité had the effect of reducing the structural vigour of the classic realist documentary film by encouraging film-makers to place too great a reliance on happenstance. Because of the influence of direct cinema, they do not research documentaries and write feature-style scripts for them as they used to. Research can often now become simply a question of doing the deal to get inside whatever door needs to be opened. However, instead of lurking behind the door for months, doing the research as part of the shooting as direct cinema people do (or claim to do), the vérité film-maker then spends as little time with the camera as did the old-style fully researched documentarist.

Moreover, the rhetoric of direct cinema is used to limit the manipulation once thought necessary to make a coherent and dramatic statement. Now all we have is 'the tremendous effort of being in the right place at the right time' (Bachmann, 1961, p. 15). This became 'the major creative task'. This search for 'the highly charged atmosphere' results in a certain undervaluing of structure (Klughertz, 1971, p. 456). Much work is confused and ill thought out, essentially because film-makers have been duped by the seeming randomness of direct cinema.

It is a paradox that direct cinema has, at its best, never fallen into this trap, as I have demonstrated above in discussing the care with which film-makers such as Pennebaker and Wiseman edit (see p. 152). This again is in part a function of time since direct cinema purists are not held to television post-production schedules. On the other hand, vérité produces less footage to edit. Nevertheless, the careful structuring of direct cinema, in part necessitated by the need to find a narrative without the help of commentary, interviews and other mainstream devices, was not absorbed as part of the vérité package.

Middletown, an American PBS series of the same year as *Police* but transmitted three months later, reveals the typical results of vérité. As such it was a far better indicator of the influence of direct cinema as that stood three decades after its introduction than is *Police*.

The six segments of the *Middletown* series (only five of which were publicly seen) looked at first sight like nothing so much as reruns of direct cinema's first subjects. Here, as in *Primary*, was the close-up of the political campaign. Here, as in Lipscomb's *Mooney v. Fowle* (also known as *Football*) (1961), was the high school sports event. Here, as in Wiseman's *High School*, was the teenage subculture. By the early 1980s it seemed as if direct cinema had exhausted America. It was now doomed, as with a grade school essay entitled 'What I did on my visit to the Midwest', to endless repetitions.

In its overt sociological ambition, *Middletown* also revisited *Sixteen in Webster Groves*. The series too claimed to be grounded in sociology. Each *Middletown* episode contained an opening credit 'From the Middletown Studies', referencing the classic *Middletown* by Helen and Robert Lynd, published in 1929 and added to, as *Middletown in Transition*, in 1937. The television series thus implicitly purported to be an updating of this work, which was celebrating its fiftieth anniversary, even as it was transferring it to another medium.

'Middletown', as the Lynds were at pains to hide but as is now well known, is Muncie, Indiana. Thanks in part to them, this is now a town so average that a large sign on an approach highway proclaims it as 'Modeltown, America'. The film series grew out of a further work of revision to the original sociology undertaken by academics at the Center for Middletown Studies, which is housed in Muncie's main university, Ball State. However, these scholars were unable to keep control of the film-making. Of course, they constituted the necessary academic board needed to give the project the respectability PBS and other American funders demand; but their power melted in the face of the artistic and journalistic privileges claimed by the film-makers. Their accounts of how this happened constitute a most valuable and rare insight into the micro-politics of documentary film-making (Vander Hill, 1982, pp. 48ff.; Hoover, 1987b, 1993, *passim*).

The result was that these consultants were so thoroughly ignored that the series became totally unmoored from its central premise. Illustrating the ongoing work of the Center would have necessitated, of course, the deployment of the whole range of traditional documentary techniques, including the use of archival material. Instead, in four of the six episodes, the series producer, Peter Davis, opted for the happenstance of vérité. Thus *Middletown* does not really revisit classics of direct cinema, because, two films apart, it was not really direct cinema at all.

Middletown is a particularly compelling example of vérité's traps because it cannot be dismissed as the work of second-rate people. In fact, it demonstrates how limiting vérité is on even the most practised of film-makers. Peter Davis enjoys a very distinguished reputation. At the time of the *Middletown* project he was interested in small towns and had made a research visit to Muncie as a result of which he had met the Ball State academics (Hoover, 1987a, p. 164). He was eventually to publish his own book-length study of small-town life in Hamilton, Ohio (Davis, 1982); but the sociologists knew him as a film-maker, an Emmy winner who had been associated with some of the most famous documentaries of the time.

Davis was a veteran of the CBS Documentary Department, where he had worked on the classic *CBS Reports* 'Hunger in America' (1968) and had produced the controversial 'Selling of the Pentagon' for the same series in 1971. 'Hunger', like 'Complaint of Rape', was another of those rare films which had some demonstrable effect in the world. It had contributed to the debate about reforming the dole system which led to the establishment of the food stamp programme (Hammond, 1981, p. 175). 'Selling' was about how the Pentagon marketed itself, via a massive public relations enterprise, to the American public. For two screenings an exceptional audience of nearly 24 million was claimed. The film occasioned an uproar culminating in a congressional inquiry (*FLQ*, 1971, pp. 10ff.; Hammond, 1981, pp. 176ff.).

After leaving CBS, Davis directed for theatrical release one of the most widely discussed Vietnam documentaries, *Hearts and Minds* (1974). Charles Hammond, the historian of this period of US TV documentary production, describes David as 'a rare talent'. Of these films, Hammond says (1981, p. 179), Davis 'has written three of the best American news documentaries of the sixties and seventies'. It is no wonder that the Center for Middletown Studies was 'dazzled' by his reputation (Hoover, 1987b, p. 55).

In none of this work had Davis shown himself to be a direct cinema filmmaker. Constrained by CBS formulae, he had used all the paraphernalia of the realist documentary, but even given the freedom of a film for theatrical release he still eschewed direct cinema techniques. *Hearts and Minds* is an exhaustive and somewhat inchoate account of the war. It consists largely of interviews interspersed with archival and newsreel materials, including some stills and some specially shot handheld sequences.

There was no reason, therefore, to suppose that faced with *Middletown*, an anniversary project which implies the need for a similar range of techniques, Davis would not use them. But instead he opted for direct cinema for some episodes and, to conserve resources, for others he chose the usual accidents and happenstances of vérité – that is, short filming periods using handholding and adding only interviews. By so doing he destroyed any credible claim to be reflecting and updating the original sociological work.

The result is a series which is non-representational in any sociological sense, consisting of two direct cinema and four vérité programmes, one of which was shot on tape. They are by and large predictably personal and idiosyncratic but they have been forced to assume, because of the title, a weight which they can in no way carry.

Middletown piles synecdoche on synecdoche. Not only do the individuals in the six segments stand for those classes of individuals, but 'Middletown' itself stands for America. The actual programmes take second place to the sustaining rhetoric, the context created by the public television channel, its documentary slot and, above all, a title which establishes for the viewer exactly what sort of work is intended. Thus calling a series of documentaries after a classic sociological study makes explicit the usually hidden sociological legitimations of such films and invites comparison between the screen and the book.

In this case, without prejudice to the value and limitations of positivist sociology, the comparison is disastrous to the films. In short, the books tell us much and the films tell us little. The books are interested in documenting the ordinary, what happens in an average day to average folk.

They are exercises in probabilistics. The basic understanding of the town achieved by five decades of follow-up sociological study was how stable attitudes and behaviour patterns were across this half-century. That was what the Ball State academics were trying to sell to PBS.

The film-makers preferred their received understanding of American society as a place of change and upheaval. The 'news', if you will, about social continuity apparently was, as ever, too 'new' for the media folk to grasp. Moreover, the films are actually concerned with the journalistic, the exceptional, the 'Man Bites Dog'. This culturally determined preference means that for the *Middletown* shows Davis looked for the extraordinary, or unexceptional people in exceptional circumstances – the moments of crisis. Then and only then were the ordinary lives touched by the film-makers deemed to be sufficiently dramatic to sustain a documentary film.[34] It was this, not the 'Middletown' studies (which were not even required reading on the project), which conditioned the choice of subjects.

The result of this is that one can learn more of 'Middletown' from the Lynds' footnotes than one can from the whole transmitted *Middletown* series: such things as what a school dance cost, how you had to take the girl to that dance in a taxi only if you were too poor to have a family car, whose kitchen lights were on at 6 a.m. of a winter's morning, and so on.

Trapped by vérité, Davis failed totally to find a way of dealing with such Lynd topics as 'Food, Clothing and Housework'. Instead, we have the rites of passage – marriage, the big sports game, impending bankruptcy, graduation, an election, interracial sex, faith healers – the 'sexy' bits which, almost accidentally, are made to correspond to the Lynds' sections on such topics as work, education and religion.

The Lynds found two classes in 'Middletown' – the business class and the working class – and of the 43 per cent of the inhabitants who worked, seven out of ten were employed workers and three belonged to the business class. This is where the Lynds start, with what they call 'the long arm of the job'. In the *Middletown* series, this aspect of life is covered in 'A Family Business'.

'A Family Business' chose to exemplify the town's industry with a study of an extrovert former Marine officer and his eight children tottering on the brink of bankruptcy running a pizza parlour. Although the film was the best received of the series, it was economics as farce. At the climax one son says that Dad can close up the place without worry because, hell, they can all find jobs. Whether they can or not in the severely depressed Midwest of the early 1980s is simply never dealt with.

The Lynds had almost totally ignored small businesses to concentrate on the town's industry in their studies – perhaps an error. 'A Family Business' did the opposite; but then it was the flamboyance of these characters, not the sociology of work, which was central to the film. Dwight Hoover, one of the Ball State sociologists whose idea the series was, has explained (1987b, p. 60) that, had there been a strike going on in Muncie at the time, that would have been filmed by Davis. As it was, faced with industrial peace, the series ignored industry.

Nor does the employment situation figure in the episode devoted to the town's politics. This, 'The Campaign', covers a mayoral election, concentrating almost entirely, in the American fashion, on personalities; and, in that fashion, it manages to miss most of the political point of what is being filmed (cf. *Primary*). The vérité crew were not familiar enough with the situation in the town to understand and document the only interesting story (from their journalistic point of view) in the election, a schism in the Democratic ranks:

> As a result, *The Campaign* focussed upon surface events without explaining their deeper meaning. A good example of how misleading such a focus could be is the rally which was the grand finale of Carey's [the Democratic candidate's] campaign. Scenes from this rally appearing in the film convey a sense of excitement and enthusiasm which bespoke of [a] Carey landslide. Even the film makers were caught up in Carey's charisma and crowd appeal. Yet a scrutiny of the participants by an informed observer would reveal Carey's weakness as only Carey Democrats attended the rally. (Hoover, 1987b, p. 57)

There is no space in such a film, even if done to better journalistic standards, for the careful analysis of the political structure of the town and how it is inflected by class. Nevertheless, this film, which was the first to be made, was apparently well enough received by the funders to elicit money for the rest of the series.

As with work and politics, so with the personnel. The segment about love and marriage became 'Second Time Around' about the marriage of a couple, both divorced. The sociological problem is that we know from the Ball State academics that people in Muncie were marrying at about the same age as they had fifty years earlier – twenty-three for males and twenty-one for females – and the divorce rate, this being conservative Indiana, was also largely and surprisingly unchanged since the 1920s. The couple chosen were older divorcees and thus not typical Middletowners. Beyond this, vérité did not permit the crew to obtain a picture of the underlying relationships involved. The film isolates the couple from their backgrounds and reduces their decision to marry to a particularly magazine-story inconsequence told through the filming of a series of set-piece activities.

Education was covered in two episodes. One, 'The Big Game', was shot on tape. (The other, 'Seventeen', is discussed below.) About a third of 'The Big Game' is nothing more than coverage of a supposedly critical high school basketball game with voice-over commentary taken from the local radio station. This segment reveals for the only time in the publicly seen episodes that 'Middletown' has an African American community, but, despite the use of interviews, their situation is not examined.

These episodes all had big crews – seven production assistants on the 'The Big Game'; a grip, a gaffer, a best boy and four production assistants on 'A Family Business'. But on the screen distinguishing vérité from direct cinema is not always easy, unless the production circumstances are known or can be deduced. The subtlest deception always occurs when, as with the four vérité shows in *Middletown*, only interviews are added to the mix. The impression is then given that direct cinema, implying months of filming, huge amounts of footage shot, minimal direction of subjects, is being used; but in fact vérité is at hand – which means something closer to the usual visiting TV professional firemen in the usual four-star hotels, interviews, and careful harbouring of resources so that only certain moments in any given situation are shot. It comes as no surprise to learn that so disdainful were these film-makers of Muncie that they even imported their own New-York-based Chinese chef (Hoover, 1993, p. 70).

Direct cinema might have promised more than it could ever deliver, but vérité debases that promise by playing an even greater trick on the audience – which is not to say, however, that direct cinema was the answer to the challenge of the *Middletown* project.

Davis hired Leacock and some of his ex-students to work on the other two *Middletown* films. In contrast to the vérité crews, Leacock had but one assistant, Marisa Silver, and they both moved into Muncie and made their film there. Leacock was assigned religion and his film, 'Community of Praise', deals with the practice of fundamentalist Christianity. The film contains acknowledgments of the camera's presence and some interview material, but is largely still in the classic direct cinema style which he had pioneered more than twenty years earlier.

By the terms, both explicit and implicit, that should have governed *Middletown*, this segment must stand for religion in Muncie, yet the family Leacock chose was atypical, even within fundamentalism. Speaking with tongues, trance-like falls and the like are not widely encountered except on the very fringe of American Christian practice. So in a town full of churches, as are all American towns, religion is represented by the activities of a group so marginal that they are discovered praying in a veterinarian's surgery.

That Leacock thought more mainstream churchgoers to be largely hypocritical and that that is why he insisted on focusing on the supposedly more sincere fringe, I learn from Dwight Hoover, one of the academics, not from the film. That the family belonged to no church at the time of filming and were not even from Muncie but had come there to pray after being expelled from another community, I also learn from Hoover (1987b, p. 61). That the family was less stereotypical than the film suggests, because, for instance, the mother had a big-city background and a degree, I learned from Leacock himself, not from his film.

As ever, the real strength of the film is Leacock's self-evident liking for his subjects. He proceeds throughout with the air of a man who can now say, 'Some of my best friends are holy rollers.' In so far as television frames the religious fringe as a place of bigotry and scandal, and portrays those who believe in it as dupes, 'Community of Praise' usefully goes against that grain. However, this counter-effect is diluted by Leacock's inevitable direct cinema attention to surface, and only to surface. The family might be nice folks in an interview, but Sundays they go off to vomit up the devil. We are given no context, no real insight into what has made them into the sort of people who do such things.

So compare 'Community of Praise' with the Lynds' account of religion in 'Middletown'. Fundamentalism of the sort Leacock concentrates on takes its place amid the thirty-four organised religious groups the Lynds discovered. Their approach to the question of religious practice also related attendance and belief to class. But class, as I have been indicating, no more surfaces in the transmitted episodes of *Middletown* than it does in Hollywood prime-time drama.

'Seventeen', the other picture of high school life, does implicitly deal with class and with race but, perhaps significantly, it became the centrepiece of a complex row and was not transmitted. Joel DeMott and Steve Kreines, normally based in Alabama, like Leacock (whose students they had been) moved to Muncie for the duration of the project. They work, turn and turn about, solo. Theirs is the 'purest' direct cinema film in the series.

The Xerox Corporation, the series's underwriter, did not like 'Seventeen' and neither did the executives of the American public television system. The Muncie establishment, alerted to the content of the show by the local PBS station manager, did not like it either. DeMott and Kreines finished up at war with all these parties and Peter Davis. The film was banned (Hoover, 1987c, p. 172). The usual charges of reconstruction, intervention and incitement were hauled out. But the film-makers, lacking Graef's elaborate work code and dealing with a broad topic which took them to a variety of people and settings, could not easily rebut such accusations.

In 'Seventeen', working-class kids are seen using foul language, goofing off, smoking grass and talking about sex. Apparently Xerox, PBS and Muncie's great and good wanted it understood that the teenagers only behave like this in the presence of a camera when encouraged to do so by passing film-makers. Or, if that is a little far-fetched, an alternative scenario has the film-makers themselves seeking out that extremely small minority of youngsters who do these things.

Hoover, who was not one of those seeking to ban the film, complains that the sociology showed how little Muncie teenagers' attitudes had changed since the Lynds surveyed them whereas 'Seventeen' dramatically suggests they had changed enormously – the same basic charge he makes about the series as a whole (1987a, p. 63). However, this is the only time funders and others took this basic point. They made sudden demands for accurate representation and urgent appeals to the court of the typical in justifying the ban.

But it was not the film's supposed misrepresentation of Muncie's teenagers that caused the trouble. Nor was it the language which ostensibly exercised some objectors. (Except for one sequence which could easily have been cleaned up for transmission, the language was no worse than that heard on some other shows. Anyway, bad language is not unknown on public television in America.) In reality, 'Seventeen's' major sin was that it did capture one aspect of teenage life which, apparently, some thought would best be kept hidden – interracial dating.

During the course of the filming, the chief protagonist, a white girl, started going out with an African American. Of course, the powers that forced the film off the screen could not admit, without revealing their own racial prejudices, that this is what was really concerning them so the public debate that ensued was notable chiefly for its hypocrisy.

The irony was that, atypical or not, alone of the *Middletown* series 'Seventeen' had any 'documentary value' at all. As with *Police*, the film represented the best of direct cinema, being the only segment to have the insight of the Lynds' footnotes, even if the overall sociology was skewed. One learned, for instance, on the micro level, that teenagers in Muncie held beer parties of utter raucousness under the supervision of their parents. On the macro level, the potential for interracial relationships in a Midwestern high school was also surprising, as was the response to the cross burned on the young woman's lawn. The whole family took that, to my surprise, more or less in their stride. This was well beyond the Midwestern clichés of the rest of the series.

All this is not to say that I offer 'Seventeen' as a 'good' film in contradistinction to the other 'bad' films in the *Middletown* series; much less that direct cinema as a whole be seen as 'good' while vérité is 'bad'. The only point here is that in the English-speaking world direct cinema triumphed, as regards influence, over cinéma vérité but was absorbed into mainstream documentary production in an ersatz form, vérité, which diluted and endangered such observational strengths as it could claim.

At the outset of this phase of documentary's development, the problems confronting the Griersonian film were seen to be entirely technical and the solutions were said to lie in the creation of appropriate equipment. I believe that this was a false agenda. The problems were not merely a matter of reconstruction and the like. Rather, they related to the Griersonian claim on the real and the ethical implications that such a claim brought in its train. Fulfilling the technology agenda, which is what cinéma vérité, direct cinema and vérité all did, achieved nothing more than the stark revelation of the persistence of these other more fundamental difficulties.

In effect, the technological problem, always nothing more than a smokescreen, was removed. This is why 'Seventeen', *Police* and direct cinema cannot be considered 'good' and *Middletown* and the run of vérité TV work 'bad'. Both sides are afflicted with problems which arise from precisely the areas which the technologising of the Griersonian agenda ignored.

For instance, ethics.

34

What Constraints?

We last saw the Griersonian documentarist as ethicist, in the person of Paul Rotha, buying beer for unemployed miners in East Shotton, Durham, with his Gaumont-British expense money (see p. 45). I there suggested that the crucial move to the victim documentary, which was being engineered at that time by Rotha and others, occasioned little ethical debate. Nor, it can be added, did the move to cinéma vérité and direct cinema thirty years later do much more, except at the National Film Board. However, greater ease of access to the subject, if nothing else, exacerbated this particular problem.

Calvin Pryluck published an article on documentary ethics in 1976 but so repressed was the topic that this pioneering piece sparked virtually no debate.[35] Instead, as Pryluck points out (1976, p. 256), the same increasingly facile response was always made on the rare occasions the issue surfaced: if the subjects consent, where is the difficulty? I will call this stance 'the consent defence'. Direct cinema film editor Ellen Hovde puts it like this: 'I think people are aware in our society of what a camera is and very aware of what they ought to be doing in front of it' (Rosenthal, 1980, p. 382).

Man of Aran: How the Myth Was Made speaks, among other things, to the profound effects a documentary could have on a whole community, even unto the second and third generation. The original *Man of Aran* is 'the historic benchmark by which most older Islanders measure their existence' (Stoney, 1978, p. 2). For the 'stars' it was clearly the defining event of their whole lives. Forty years after the event, Maggie Dirran could vividly recall with obvious pleasure every last move Flaherty asked her to make. On the other hand, the two males, Coleman 'Tiger' King, who played her husband, and Michaleen Dillane, the 'son', 'found they couldn't live on Aran as former film stars'. Barbara, the daughter of Pat Mullen, Flaherty's local 'fixer' and interpreter, married John Taylor, Grierson's brother-in-law and a crew member, and became a famous character actress in Britain. Two others work in the Irish theatre. The money some earned from the film company was the deposit for a house or the stake for a business.

To this day, the film is regularly screened on Aran for tourists, and for islanders involved in that industry it remains a source of profit, but not necessarily of pride. Many 'resent [Flaherty's] making of their Islands a world-wide symbol for desperate poverty'. On the other hand, the Aran Islands, unlike the not-too-distant Blaskets, are still inhabited. George Stoney suggests that this is, perhaps, in part because of the tourism the film has encouraged. Stoney called his note on the making of *Myth* 'Must a Filmmaker Leave his Mark?' Given the pervasiveness of the 'consent defence', it is not surprising that he is one of the few documentarists ever to raise such a question.

There is as yet no generally agreed framework for sorting out the complexities involved in the ethics of documentary film-making. I propose making a start by concentrating on the everyday documentary. This means that I am not concerned here with the ethics of putting people into straightforward physical danger, as Flaherty did for *Man of Aran*. That case is simple. Flaherty said rhetorically that he should have been shot for what he asked them to do. In my view, rhetorically of course, he should have been. Yet this is not particularly a documentary issue since the sequence in question, a fishing trip in dangerous seas, was specially staged for the cameras. It is a fictional sequence and, had there been an accident, it would have been of a feature-film type. The Aran people's 'consent', like a film actor's, was bought for cash.

It follows that I am not concerned either with cases such as that of the volunteer self-employed labourer who died in 1986 rehearsing a stunt for one of the BBC's more inane efforts, *The Late, Late Breakfast Show*. Escaping from an exploding crate suspended 120 feet in the air was going to be 'the adventure of a lifetime', he was reported as saying twenty-four hours before the fatal accident (Absalom et al, p. 3). In all such disasters the normal standards of legal negligence, balancing the contribution of the victim against various levels of misfeasance by the perpetrator, apply.

Finally, I am not concerned with the more complex factors at work when subjects knowingly put themselves into danger for a greater good – as when a dissident speaks out on camera about a repressive regime in whose power the speaker will remain after the film crew departs. This is not because I consider cases of this type, or the others mentioned, as unimportant but, rather, that they are rarities and I want to deal with the everyday ethical problems which are raised by the more routine activity of documentary film-making.

Let us start by considering the legal position of documentary film-making under the common law. There are two essential legal relationships which in effect create the frame for everyday ethics. First is the relationship of the film-maker to the participants in the film. This turns upon the concept of consent. Second is the relationship of the film-maker to the film or tape, which turns upon copyright. Let us consider consent.

It has been well established in science that the *informed* consent of human subjects involved in experiments requires that it be obtained freely and without coercion, that the procedure and its effects or potential effects be fully understood by the subject, and that the subject be competent to give consent. The most exhaustive protocols along these lines were developed out of the Nuremberg trials of those Nazis who conducted scientific experiments on concentration camp inmates:

> The voluntary consent of the human subject is absolutely essential. This means that the person involved should have legal capacity to give consent; should be so situated as to be able to exercise the free power of choice, without the intervention of any element of force, fraud, deceit, duress, over-reaching, or other ulterior form of constraint or coercion; and should have sufficient knowledge and comprehension of the

elements of the subject matter involved as to enable him [*sic*] to make an understanding and enlightened decision. This latter element requires that before acceptance of an affirmative decision by the experimental subject there should be made known to him [*sic*] the nature, duration and purpose of the experiment; the method and means by which it is to be conducted; all inconveniences and hazards reasonably to be expected; and the effects upon his [*sic*] health or person which may possibly come from his [*sic*] participation in the experiment. (Reynolds, 1982, p. 143)

Consent in film-making has never been held to these standards because they go beyond what the law requires for the legal concept of 'consent'. As a legal term, 'consent' is part of, and essential to, the contracting process. Legally, consent in documentary is simply seen as a form of contract, an implicit or explicit agreement for services between the film-maker and the subject of the film. It exists within a culture which values a fundamental freedom to make such agreements. The scientific protocols for informed consent, except for competence, are not therefore enforceable as such.

The legal concept of consent as a bargain then affects the legal concepts of 'coercion' and 'understanding'. Coercion is very narrowly defined in the common law. There is some question as to whether or not it can embrace more than actual or threatened physical force. 'Understanding' is also narrowly construed so that it excludes as being incapable of understanding very few classes of persons (for example infants and lunatics) in order that the making of contracts in society be facilitated.

However, over the past century a concept of 'undue influence' has developed in the courts to bring some equity to situations where there is no question of physical duress but where, nevertheless, one party to a bargain is at a real disadvantage – as when a senile person remakes a will at the behest of a second party (Atiyah, 1989, pp. 292ff.). There is also another century-long series of cases which protects 'poor and ignorant' parties from making contracts in sales, for example, where the goods are seriously undervalued and no independent advice is at hand (*Fry v. Lane (1888), pp. 312ff.*; Cartwright, 1991, pp. 197ff.).

Although these cases might all seem to have some bearing on the situation of persons who make bargains with film-makers to give interviews or the like, nevertheless it is unlikely that they could be of use in a legal action. For one thing, undue influence cases tend to assume a specific, normally familial, relationship between the parties. For another thing, they seek to redress easily determinable economic damage. Should the subject of a documentary be able to prove loss of this sort, other courses of action – defamation, for instance – would be available to him or her.

So the fact that, for instance, Flaherty offered an irresistible sum of money, a fortune in their eyes, to the Aran fisherman was neither coercive nor any other sort of unequal bargain. It was merely an agreement made between free agents (one of whom was further justified by freedom of expression).

Understanding is assumed unless the contrary can be demonstrated. This legal assumption is blind to the actual circumstances in which consent is obtained for film-making. Usually, obtaining consent is part and parcel of the general confusion and excitement of the film-making process – a process unfamiliar and glamorous for most people. Here is that process in action. The following example is untypical, I would submit, only in that it is being dissected in a court of law. The example is taken from the legal transcript of the case of *The Commonwealth of Massachusetts v. Wiseman*, which arose from the *Titicut Follies* affair:

Q [Counsel]: Now I direct your attention to an interview between a young man and a doctor which takes place in an early sequence of the film and in which, in the course of the interview, the young man reveals to the doctor that he has violated his daughter and has been masturbating through the years. ... Now, when this scene was filmed, did you come in with your tape recorder?

A [Wiseman]: Yes, sir.

Q: And did you have a release form that has been admitted in evidence here?

A: Yes, sir.

Q: And did you give this man the release form before the filming started?

A: I don't remember whether it was before or after the filming started. ...

Q: Wasn't it your general practice to have a release there and get the signature on it before the filming started?

A: Sometimes it was and sometimes it wasn't. ...

Q: Did you tell this young man in any form of words that his features would be clearly identifiable in this picture?

A: Yes, sir. The man signed a release.

Q: Did you tell this young man in any form of words that his features, identifiable in connection with an admission of molesting his own daughter, would be shown in a commercial movie house?

A: I didn't put it in those words, sir, but the man knew his features were going to be shown in the film and he encouraged us to take his picture.

Q: And indicated that he was willing to have his own daughter see him making that confession?

A: He didn't say anything about that, sir.

(Anderson and Benson, 1991, pp. 115ff.)

The only untypical thing here is that the circumstances surrounding the signature on the release are being examined, exactly because the mental competence of the young man is in question. Normally the signature closes the matter as far as the law is concerned. Indeed, consent might not even involve pausing for a signature, but simply making a record in some way or another. Wiseman, after this experience with written consent forms, now simply asks the people he films to speak into his mike, recording consent on the tape. He explained to Pryluck that he says something like 'We just took your picture and its going to be for a movie, it's going to be shown on television and maybe in theatres. ... Do you have any objections?' (Pryluck, 1976, p. 256).

This is because the American courts do demand that some record be made. The need for written – or, at least, recorded – consent in the USA had been established in a 1961 case (*Durgom v. CBS*) where CBS was successfully sued by a person who was represented in a dramatic reconstruction of a real-life incident. It had been made with his consent and advice but without written permission. The court held the last to be necessary.

The professional assumption, the 'consent defence', is that everybody in our society knows what a camera is and understands how to behave in front of it. But this is a palpable nonsense. People do not necessarily know how to behave even when not in front of a camera. To help those who need to appear (politicians and business chief executives, for example), there is a profitable and flourishing trade in teaching them the necessary tricks. Contrary to this professional assertion, the fact is that almost all documentary subjects do not know these tricks – and if they did, the documentarists' claim of authenticity would be seriously jeopardised. Moreover, having never been on the screen and knowing few people who have either, they must be assumed to be largely unaware of potential consequences. The inescapable fact is that a significant number, if not a majority, do not then give informed consent.

This is not to say that the law will tolerate any sort of Faustian bargain about consent. As I have said, there are some limitations as to competence. Consent has been deemed to be unobtainable from minors (Pember, 1972, pp. 224ff.). In *Commonwealth of Massachusetts v. Wiseman*, quoted above, it was finally held that consent had not been obtained from all the participants in the film *Titicut Follies* and this was one ground for restricting its exhibition. Of the sixty-two mental patients seen in the film most were not competent to sign releases and only twelve such forms were completed and those in the circumstances described in court (Anderson and Benson, 1991, pp. 23ff.).

On the other hand, Wiseman took the view that the inmates of the prison hospital, if not mentally competent, were wards of the state:

> I had permission from the superintendent. I had permission from the commissioner of correction. I had an advisory opinion from the attorney general of Massachusetts, and I had the strong support of the then lieutenant governor. However, some of these men turned against me when the film was finished, with most of the trouble starting two or three months after the superintendent and the attorney general had seen the film. (Rosenthal, 1971, p. 68)

The degree to which these various parties had actually knowingly given these permissions or assumed that permissions had been given by others of them has been vigorously disputed in the courts of Massachusetts for nearly a quarter of a century. In fact, this very argument constituted another ground for restricting the film (Anderson and Benson, 1991, pp. 10ff. and 68ff.).

Of more general significance is the contention that these officials turned against the film because they realised that it would reveal the conditions pertaining in Bridgewater. Hostility was then a collective defence to the film as evidence of their administrative misfeasance. It is not unusual for a professional film-maker to see things in this way. Authorities are so blind to their misdeeds or to the way in which those misdeeds will 'play' in public that they fully consent to filming; it is only when they see the reactions of outside audiences and critics that their danger, as it were, is revealed to them and they begin to complain of improperly obtained consent, inaccuracy, misrepresentation, and so on. For the film-maker that row then becomes a witness to the value of the film as evidence.

I shall return to the 'right to know' implications of such an argument below (see p. 218), but, for the moment, let us just consider Wiseman's account from the informed consent standpoint. Reading this change of mind (if that is indeed what it was) by the Massachusetts authorities in the *Titicut Follies* case in this way necessarily implies that even these competent persons were not able to meet the standards of scientific informed consent; that is, they were unable to understand the procedures involved in making a film and predict its possible outcomes. *Titicut Follies* is rare only in that it reveals two levels of failure of informed consent – many of the participants were incompetent to consent and those who were competent to consent on their behalf did not understand the consequences of so doing either for the incompetents or for themselves.

There is a further point which affects the film-makers' 'consent defence'. Informed consent implies an understanding of potential damage to the subject, including psychological damage down to the level of distress. Here again the law takes a different tack. If the only (as it were) damage caused is psychological – distress – then the common law is unconcerned unless such damage can be proved to affect human performance or the material quality of life. Being upset is not enough. Being repeatedly upset is not enough either. One way to contemplate distress legally is to assume a prior right to be undistressed in the form of being undisturbed – that is, a right of privacy.

Although the notion of privacy is part of the United Nations Declaration of Human Rights and the European Convention on Human Rights, in the common law it is seen as a potential constraint on freedom of expression. The common law, of course, acknowledges that physical invasion of privacy – trespass – is actionable. For people who feel that their privacy has been invaded in other ways the remedies of nuisance, defamation and even, on occasion, copyright are also available, and there are statutory protections covering misuse of computer data banks and, in some countries, a legal right to access government information, protection of rape victims' names, and so on. But media intrusion via the disclosure of private facts in general remains unactionable in almost all circumstances except where commercial speech (that is to say, advertising) is involved.

And, of course, most documentary situations involve consent which automatically implies an abdication of privacy claims on the part of the person granting the consent. There has been no tort of invasion of privacy in the common law tradition. Were that now to change, it would likely have little effect on documentarists who would remain simply bound by consent in contract and nothing else.

The common law therefore lays few duties on documentary film-makers beyond the need to obtain bare consent from their subjects. On the other hand, the film-maker's rights are better defended. This brings us to the second element in everyday ethics, the relationship of the film-maker to the film or tape. Grounded in a property right – copyright – the documentarist's first right is the right to be in business.

At the outset, in the 19th century, the positioning of the camera as a scientific instrument worked against conceptualising photography as creative work. This meant that it was not afforded legal protection. The earliest legal view of photography in some jurisdictions was that it was so mechanical as to be beyond the protection of copyright. (This is a further proof of the power of the scientific rhetoric surrounding photography.)

Bernard Edelman persuasively argues (1979, pp. 44ff.) that photography 'startled' French law, despite the concept of intellectual property which had a firm foothold from the Revolution on. The initial position was that mechanical reproduction conferred no rights and that photographs could therefore be copied and otherwise used without limitation; but the massive growth of the photographic reproduction industry necessitated that this be revisited. Unlike the common law, which held that the rights in a photograph belonged to whoever supplied the film (not to the taker of the image), French law solved the problem it had created for itself by elevating the photographer to the level of artist and thereby transformed the photograph into a species of intellectual property like other art work.

However, Edelman makes clear that this was done not because the courts in France developed a sudden interest in aesthetic issues. On the contrary it was because 'the aesthetic was subordinated to commerce' (ibid., p. 50).

> It is an amazing 'paradox' that the 'reality' whose image is reproduced by the negative always belongs to someone. And the paradox of the paradox is that if what I reproduce ... is part of the public domain – streets, rivers, territorial waters – it will become my property only on condition that I reappropriate it. (ibid., p. 38)

The history of the strip of 8mm film of Kennedy's assassination taken by Abraham Zapruder is a vivid example of this paradox in action. Zapruder sold his rights in the film to Time-Life, who stand ready to slap injunctions on anybody using those frames. The company (in *Time Inc v. Geis*) has even tried to stop drawings based on the frames from being published.[36]

The result of such paradoxes is the basis of the *business* of documentary – how a Fred Wiseman, say, makes a living. In the materialist common law tradition, Wiseman's stock-in-trade (literally) is the celluloid and audiotape he buys and has exposed and records. This physical film exists in the law almost without reference to the pre-existing physical objects captured by the exposure, the circumstances in which the exposure was made and the subsequent circumstances of the circulation of the exposed material (Porter, 1978, pp. 94ff.). As such the legal paradox meshes with the artistic rhetoric of the documentary which Grierson inherited from Flaherty. Together, the law and the Griersonian concept of 'creativity' allow Wiseman to say, 'I couldn't make a film which gave someone else the right to control the final print' (Rosenthal, 1971, p. 71). Does a man fall at his feet, as they do quite literally in *Titicut Follies*, Wiseman's responsibility is only that he should faithfully witness the 'actuality' of the fall and his reward for that witness is the ownership of the image, a right of creation and of authorship.

Wiseman appropriated the image of the criminally insane and their guards and immediately started to market the resultant film, entering it for international competition and the like (Benson and Anderson, 1989, pp. 29ff. and 32ff.). The prison was now, in some sense, 'his' to do with what he willed; and so are the high school, the hospital, the monastery, Neiman-Marcus, Central Park, Aspen and the rest of the places and people he went on to film.

Wiseman, needless to say, exercises his legal rights over his stock-in-trade vigorously. At the outset he would only lease, not sell, a print in order to keep 'control' (Halberstadt, 1975, p. 308). Today, he will not release a right to copy the images he has culled, even for scholarly purposes. Scholars perceived as hostile, as Tom Benson and Carolyn Anderson explain in the introduction to *Reality Fictions*, their full-scale study of Wiseman's work, are refused and reduced to using crude drawings of the frames (following the decision in *Time Inc*, the Zapruder film case). Supportive scholars, like Grant, get permission to use frame enlargements – more than forty of them (Benson and Anderson, 1989, pp. xii and 113ff.; Grant, B., 1992, *passim*).

Normally, if I, without consent, capture the image of any person with my camera in public, I will implicitly appropriate the consent of the person even as I appropriate the image (Hirst and Kingdom, 1979, p. 138). Only on those comparatively rare occasions when common law courts have distinguished between advertising and news have they accepted an argument that the person photographed still has a residual property right in her or his image and therefore another should not profit *directly* out of its use. But, in public or private, even this is given up if consent is obtained. The bottom line is that the ownership of the image is legally significant; the ownership of the thing imaged is not. This then becomes the fundamental fact in media relationships as far as the law is concerned.

Jane Gaines, in *Contested Culture* (1992), has most ably pointed out the rich echoes of postmodernist confusion the case law in this area throws up, where real people take second place to constructed media images; where voices can be stolen but not 'looks'; where cartoons have greater legal rights than live actors; where, in short, the things signified take second place to signifiers. But there is a simple reason for this which does not speak to a world of melting real forms in which only the symbolic circulation of signs matters. The reason is cruder, more basic and more, dare I say, ideological than that: the law is looking for property to protect. The confusions arise because the property is incorporeal and can be constructed in various mutually exclusive ways.

For instance, the search for property rights to protect is why the law has begun to acknowledge a distinction between the famous and the ordinary. As with the difficulties photography initially threw up in France, so too with the phenomenon of publicity in America a century or so later. In both cases the law has been 'surprised'. Initially American courts held that fame *reduced* even the limited protection afforded the meek, plodding stay-at-home ordinary citizen. But the massive trade in baseball cards, and other proliferating means of profitable image circulation, put a stop to this line of argument – just as the massive trade in photographs forced the French law to come up with a way of copyrighting them.

In response to this burgeoning American trade, a 'right of publicity' has been emerging in a series of decisions beginning in 1953 when a judge held (in *Haelan Laboratories*) that baseball players had such a right which they could sell to third parties. This 'right of publicity' became part of the Californian Code in 1985, the so-called 'Celebrity Act'.

Copyright can thus be a two-edged sword, certainly protecting the right of the film-maker to possession of the image but also extending rights to an admittedly small group of potential subjects so that filming (and other image making) can be restricted.

However, against this powerful tendency the film-maker can assert yet another right – the underlying principle of freedom of expression. Freedom of expression, as we have seen, has operated to restrain the development of a broad-based common law privacy tort. It does this through two overlapping subsidiary rights: a right to publish (that is, to speak); and, less clearly, a public right to know (that is, to hear).

The First Amendment to the American Constitution lays down that 'Congress shall make no law ... abridging freedom of speech or of the press'. In this it follows the thinking of the English jurist William Blackstone, whose *Commentaries* were part of every legal library carried across the Atlantic in the late 18th century and whose words on the matter of free expression are still to be found in the standard British work on media law by Geoffrey Robertson and Andrew Nicol. Blackstone stated: 'Every freeman has an undoubted right to lay what sentiments he pleases before the public; to forbid this is to destroy the freedom of the Press' (Robertson and Nicol, 1992, pp. 19ff.).

This is not, of course, an unfettered right even in the USA. One can be constrained by the torts of trespass and nuisance; one's rights of commercial speech are limited; one can be limited by consent and other contractual obligations. Moreover, one is shackled by defamation, obscenity and specific legislation (such as that protecting the secrets of the state or the names of rape victims in some jurisdictions).

In Britain, free expression is less than this, not even strictly speaking a qualified legal right, since it has never been enacted (Robertson and Nichol, 1992, p. 1). In addition to the American constraints, in Britain one's speech as a broadcaster is also regulated and there are many more restrictions in blasphemy, Official Secrets, rules against breaches of confidence, and so on.

Nevertheless the eighteenth-century presumption of press freedom and the concomitant presumption of freedom from censorship, however battered (in Britain) and unpopular (in both Britain and America), remains. Blackstone summed up the balance between these freedoms and the operation of other laws thus: 'The liberty of the Press is indeed essential to the nature of a free State; but this consists in laying no *previous* restraints on publications, and not in freedom from censure for criminal matter when published' (ibid., p. 19). This we still believe (for all that in Britain the growing use of the injunction gives the prohibition against prior constraint too much the lie in practice) (Barendt, 1989, p. 331).

Less certain is the other side of this coin, a public right to hear these expressions, a right to know. This right arises specifically against the government in the form of freedom of information and computer database legislation. In such a context it is but the handmaiden of press freedom and a necessary protection of the ordinary citizen in a computerised and bureaucratic society.

However, the concept of a public right to know more generally also occurs in those theories which led Blackstone and his contemporaries to value free information as a necessary prerequisite to a free society. Although more of a political than a legal principle, the right to know glossed as the public interest enters (or could enter) the court in media cases in response to claimed privacy rights. In such cases it brings (or could bring) limitations on privacy so that freedom of expression in the news media shall not be inhibited.

All these – the right of speech, the freedom of the press, the right to be uncensored, the public's right to know – lie at the root of the documentarist's right to make films and tapes. This is so by virtue of the fact that documentaries, as a species of 'actuality', share the same protected legal position as other news media. The general everyday proof of this is highlighted by a major and dramatic exception.

The distribution of *Titicut Follies* was limited by the Massachusetts courts, significantly on the grounds of breach of contract between Wiseman and the prison authorities and invasion of the inmates' privacy by Wiseman.

Equally significantly, Wiseman grounded his rebuttal of these charges as an abridgment of his First Amendment rights as a constitutionally protected speaker. He told Alan Rosenthal that 'this was the first time in American constitutional history, so far as my lawyers have been able to discover, whereby a publication of any sort which has not been judged to be obscene has been banned from public viewing' (Rosenthal, 1971, p. 68).

Wiseman could also defend himself against any charge that the scientific standards of consent had not been met in his filming at Bridgewater by an appeal to the public's right to know. He claimed at the outset, in his initial approach to the Bridgewater authorities, that 'the purpose of this film is to give people an understanding of these problems' – that is, the problems of the state in dealing with the criminally insane (Anderson and Benson, 1991, p. 12).

Wiseman could also use the right-to-know justification to rebut any implications that he had misrepresented himself to the authorities, which he anyway denied, because it was for the greater public good. In the course of *Commonwealth of Massachusetts v. Wiseman*, a member of his legal team went so far as to state this as the obverse of the common sense notion of privacy. This lawyer said, in Wiseman's defence:

> That the right of privacy, your honour, is often stated in terms of a right to be let alone. It is our position that those people so unfortunate as to be in Bridgewater have a right not to be let alone, in other words, that they have been abandoned by society, in effect, and ——
>
> THE COURT: That would be the most monstrous proposition I have ever heard.
>
> (Anderson and Benson, 1991, p. 94)

The point is that, because of a combination of state power and subjects incapable of consent, *Titicut Follies* became the one film that was banned. It follows that all the other films were not. If the subjects can consent, which is the presumption, then duty is discharged and rights can be exercised. So, while society is deemed to be prepared to run the 'risk' of limiting experimentation on human subjects for the sake of informed consent, on the other hand limitations on freedom of expression are not acceptable on the same grounds. This is why Anderson and Benson (ibid., pp. 7ff.) can go so far as to talk of 'the *myth* of informed consent' for the documentary (my italics).

The common law sees documentary film subjects as contractors with documentary film-makers, nothing more and nothing less. It sees documentary film-makers as producers of a commodity, the film or tape, in which they have all rights. These rights, though, do not make the film or tape commercial speech. The law cares almost nothing for invasion of privacy for such 'non-commercial' products. It takes little cognisance of non-material damage such as distress. It sees the film-maker as a protected speaker who utters for the public good.

Wiseman understands this full well, despite his unfortunate experience with his first film. Like all documentarists, he normally works unfettered by constraints, his rights quite overwhelming his duties. 'What constraints?' he said in a recent interview. 'There are no constraints. I get the money and I make the films. What constraints?' (Anderson and Benson, 1991, p. 3).

35

The Repressed in Documentary Film Studies

The legal framework is too loose to compel or even much encourage ethical practice in documentary film-making. Given the dominance of the victim as the realist documentary subject, this is cause for some concern, for it does not mean that the ethical difficulties faced by the realist film-maker go away – only that they can be ignored. We are therefore on our own, as it were, in determining what should and should not be acceptable.

I propose raising three questions occasioned by this repressed topic of documentary ethics. What evidence is there that documentaries have consequences for participants? Can the public right to know compensate for such consequences? Can public information and private costs be balanced by altering the terms of the relationship between film-maker and participant?

The background to all these questions is that direct cinema was particularly prone to being exploitative. Paradoxically, because the new equipment made filming so much less intrusive than it had been, the finished films were far more so. Richard Drew described the goal of such work in its first 'crisis structure' phase:

> What makes us different from other reporting and other documentary film-making, is that in each of these stories there is a time when a man comes against moments of tension, and pressure, and revelation, and decision. It's these moments that interest us most. Where we differ from TV and press is that we're predicated on being there when things are happening to people that count. (Mamber, 1974, p. 118)

It must be said that in the first year at Time-Life the ethical difficulties of this approach were not that apparent since the journalist Drew kept the nascent direct cinema enterprise in the public sphere. But when, as in the 1930s, the more fruitful strand turned out to be the powerless and the everyday, the technology allowed a degree of intrusion into ordinary people's lives which was not previously possible.[37]

It was even able, on occasion, to offer glimpses of that most hidden of all worlds, showbiz power in operation. The unattractive face of show business was explored in *Showman* (1962), *Meet Marlon Brando* (1965) and, often, in the performance films – slightly, for instance, in *Don't Look Back*.[38]

These films apart, this era in general is a golden age for the victim documentary. For instance, in *Salesman* (1969), the Maysles choose to concentrate on a loser. When the salesman tries to explain his sales record, his boss jokes ominously: 'Permit me to offer my own alibi (laughter). Any man that's not good at selling should be able ... should be good at making excuses.' Not only was their central figure a failure but his product, enormously expensive bibles, was presented as absurd and his clientele, the poor, were scarcely seen as dignified either.

The Maysles cannot be accused of finding victims and failure among the lower orders only. In *Grey Gardens* (1975), they similarly expose the foibles, eccentricities and inanities of a pair of reclusive American aristocrats. Is that the subjects were Bouviers, relatives of Mrs Onassis, the justification for the public's right to know?

What is 'sexy' in these movies, what gets them funded and shown, is exactly their voyeuristic freak-show quality. This is true also of the 'family' films, those patterned after *A Married Couple* – although what legitimates them is their supposed typicality, the very opposite of freakishness. In the event, the public display of the private realm seems automatically to turn the private into a freak show – which is exactly what happened with both *An American Family* and the BBC copy of it.

So, what evidence is there that documentaries have consequences for participants?

It is rare that this question is even raised. That there might be consequences is not usually in the forefront of the film-maker's concerns. I recall seeing an NYU student project which took a man recovering from compulsive gambling to the track to see how well he was doing and to provide the film with a climax. The student, understanding the tradition he was learning very well, saw no problem with this.

Kreines and DeMott told me at the time that the young women featured in 'Seventeen' had all, by the date of the planned transmission, moved away from Muncie. Hoover (1987c, p. 65) paints a different picture – of early marriage, almost instant divorce and no removal. The row over the film had the effect of a self-fulfilling prophecy, creating in advance of transmission exactly the furore that was supposed to be the danger if the show went out. The local station worked hard for this to happen, calling in the teenagers for cross-examination and generally making sure that all concerned in 'Seventeen' would regret their part in the venture. As a result, one of the young women went so far as to claim that she was mesmerised into behaving the way she did by the film-makers (Hoover, 1987a, p. 172).[39]

Harold Williamson contributed to the BBC *Man Alive* series which, from 1965 on, came closer, in my view, than any other during that era to importing the standards of the yellow press to British television on a regular basis. Despite this context, Williamson had a deserved reputation as a most sensitive interviewer, especially of children; but his subjects did not benefit from his touch. He had the idea of approaching some of them again, as he reported in *The Listener*: 'For a long time after the programme went out – sometimes for years afterwards – they had been got at by neighbours, or family, or colleagues who, for one reason or another, were angered, outraged, ashamed, envious or offended by their television broadcast to the nation' (Williamson, 1983, p. 8). He tells of fear, loss of jobs, forced house moves. On the plus side, though, he has a rector who turned his crypt into a pub and was visited by the Queen Mother.

Paul Watson, on returning to 'his' family for another documentary fourteen years after the first (*The Family: The After Years*, 1988), found that they had a similar tale to tell. This did not inhibit Watson, who appears on camera in this follow-up film, one iota. For instance, he raises with one of the daughters – to her clear distress – the question of her husband's adultery. When she demands in anger, 'Who told you that?' his reply is a jocular 'I can't remember'.

There are, of course, exceptions to this sort of crassness. Leacock, as I have pointed out, became the ally of the quins' mother and the fundamentalist family and has always tended to find people to film with whom he could empathise – as has Pennebaker. Of course, in the direct cinema mode, evidence of this quality of relationship might often not be on the screen.

Most times what can be more clearly discerned is the opposite, a filmmaker wittingly or unwittingly exploiting the subject to one degree or another. The exploitative potential of the equipment coupled with unfettered freedom of expression has this effect. It is often the case now that the whole history and theory of the form, from the Griersonian legacy of public education to the legitimation of the concept of the right to know, is forgotten or even consciously set aside in a sensationalising scramble for funding and ratings. It is a rare documentarist who can withstand such pressures. For the average participant ridicule, contempt, or, at a minimum, disruption is the likely result of a brush with direct cinema, even if – as I believe is usually the case – none of these outcomes is intended by the film-makers.

Being a cinéma vérité subject can change and disrupt one's life just as much. Oumarou Ganda, the central figure in *Moi, un noir*, became one of Africa's premier film-makers. Marceline Loridan, the first person we meet in *Chronique*, became a sound recordist. Eventually she was working with Joris Ivens as a producer.

On the other hand, attempts to film a worker, known only as Angelo, at the Renault factory resulted in him being dismissed. Angelo explains on camera what happened after Rouch and Morin had filmed him at the factory: 'I went back to work after you left. They came up and they said, "They want you in the office". ... The boss says, "So we're making movies now"' (Feld and Ewing, 1985, p. 61). Subsequently, and unfilmed, he lost his job. He also lost the job Rouch and Morin then found for him at Billancourt Film Studios, because, according to Rouch, he organised a union (Morin, 1985, p. 21; Yakir, 1978, p. 9).

Angelo was not very happy about his entire experience in the world of documentary. In a follow-up questionnaire he wrote that, if he were asked to participate in another film, he 'would try to see to it we [the workers] were the ones who took charge of the operation, and not the sociologists' (*Feld and Ewing*, 1985, p. 76).

So it is clear that being filmed can have consequences and they might be profound. All this is exacerbated by the fact that documentaries dealing with ordinary people can have extended and perhaps nearly indefinite lives.

Paul, the failed salesman in the Maysles film of that name, is constantly exposed as such wherever documentary film classes are taught or Maysles retrospectives are held. The anonymous Midwestern boy who spews his heart up as a result of a drug overdose in Wiseman's *Hospital*, spews away every time the film is screened. Should it be played in the community where he is now (one hopes) a stable citizen there is nothing he can do about it. For the film is not a lie; is not maliciously designed to bring him into either hatred, ridicule or contempt; and, therefore, he has no action for libel. And the film was taken with his consent, presumably obtained subsequent to his recovery.

Nearly a quarter of a century after *Titicut Follies* was made, those who participated in it were still involved with the film because Wiseman was still trying to get it generally released. One of the inmates who had been an illiterate at the time of his admission has earned two master's degrees since his discharge from the prison hospital. Indeed, he had the experience of having to watch the film in a university class of which he was a member. He has stated that he had 'lost many jobs behind this film' (Benson and Anderson, 1989, pp. 112ff.). Nevertheless, now appropriately educated to the norms of his society, this participant on balance supported the wider showing of the film on public right-to-know grounds. Some other ex-inmates were even more enthusiastic about lifting the restrictions on the film. However, the young man whose release form was so closely examined and his family, including the daughter he claimed to have abused, vigorously protested against the lifting of the ban on general exhibition. The point is that decades later the film was still having some effect on their lives.

Autobiographical and family portrait films are also durable (Katz and Katz, 1988, pp. 127ff.). *An American Family* is the most extreme case. Seven years after transmission, the *New York Times* began a story, 'Of course you remember Pat Loud'.

> If you watched public television in 1973, you saw Pat Loud and her family every week for three months, living ... what purported to be their daily 'real' lives.... In one episode you saw Pat Loud tell Bill Loud that she was divorcing him. In another you saw her visit her son Lance ... who was flaunting his campy homosexuality at the Chelsea Hotel.... you saw money. Four months ago, she started her own literary agency, using her notoriety, at first, to command attention. (Harrison, 1980, p. C2)

The mother of Watson's family became in her way as famous as Mrs Loud with, briefly, a calendar of public engagements opening fêtes and the like, a newspaper gossip column and a book. But during Watson's return visit to her, she reveals that she, like Angelo, has learned something about the making of documentaries. On camera she says, 'Anybody who is going to do a documentary – you stick out and get as much as you can get.' 'Margaret,' he replies, offering us perhaps a glimpse of his negotiating techniques, 'you just put the licence fee up about 500 per cent.'

Pat Loud had previously speculated that her children 'may never be able to live [the television series] down, or get away from it' (Pryluck, 1976, p. 260). That would seem to be a reasonable prognostication. Here am I writing about them in 1993, for instance.

Documentarists can explain and justify all of the above by claiming the 'consent defence' and a public-right-to-know legitimation. I have already indicated that the former is something of a myth, for all that it is legal, and the latter is not legal at all. But, as a second point in this repressed topic, can we find any non-legal justifications for the public-right-to-know concept? Can it be made to compensate for the consequences of film-making?

Professionals seem happy to affirm that it can. For instance, Williamson (1983, p. 8) managed to persuade some *Man Alive* victims to work with him again: 'They all needed coaxing to tell their stories but, in the end, they decided to trust television again because, all of them said, someone might benefit from their experiences.' Watson takes the same line in his interview with Margaret of *The Family* when he says: 'I think that everyone would have welcomed being allowed to intrude – if that was the right word – into your lives.' 'Intrude' is clearly the right word.

But let us examine the fundamental assumption, that there is a public benefit to such intrusions, more closely. For professionals such as Thomas Shachtman the road from private exposure to public benefit lies through audience response:

> Looked at in a broad way, social documentaries are almost always about the pain of living. Sometimes we [the film-makers] have to open the wound a bit, though contributing to pain is always itself painful. ... I can remember a moment when I needed to ask Sammie [a juvenile delinquent] what he experienced at the so-called training school where he had been kept ... From the fear mushrooming up behind his eyes as I asked the question, I already had the answer before a word was spoken. But to get that answer on film where everybody could witness it and get angry at what happened to Sammie, I pressed on shutting my eyes to pain in order to open the camera's eye. (Shachtman, 1977, p. 29)

Shachtman is to be complimented for his sensitivity and more for airing the problem in print, but this is unconvincing – naive, even.

For why would Sammie's story be taken as evidence? (I might think he was lying.) And, if taken as evidence, why would it necessarily anger? (I might think he deserved punishment.) And, if it stirred a reaction, why would that necessarily affect the juvenile justice system? (How could my response be translated into action?)

Films on the juvenile justice system are liable to cause comment – each and every time they are made. *Billy*, *Jimmy* and *Aycliffe* were three British television documentaries which occasioned an uproar in 1977. The films, straightforward portraits of two delinquents and their institution, were then remarkable for the picture of amoral violence they presented. Critics such as Dennis Potter went for the jugular of Michael Whyte, the film-maker, suggesting that 'the violence and disaffection of delinquent, working class youth provides exactly the kind of pungent offal which attracts the flyblown eyes of those who work in television'.

Michael Whyte responded: 'Was it as open to misinterpretation as that by someone as intelligent as Potter? ... What chilled people and made them react was the fact that my films [unlike coverage of Vietnam] are nearer home.'

Felicity Grant, from whose report on the furore in the trade magazine *Broadcast* I take these comments, said: 'I'd like to suggest that Whyte's films have not only made available a significant understanding of the problem of violence, they have also made a worthy contribution to the exploration of documentary techniques.'

These responses are inadequate. The notion that Potter was 'chilled' is absurd. And even if my understanding of violence was improved, to what end? It also will not do for film-makers to blame the audience for not understanding their movies or, more to the point, their motives. And who cares if technique benefited?

The public right to know is easy to claim but hard to define; and even where it can be more clearly discerned the ethical problem of cost to the participants remains vexed.

Sixty Seconds of Hatred (1977) concerns a man who killed his unfaithful wife and went virtually unpunished for the crime. The public interest was that the film focused on how this light punishment reflected the sexist conclusion of the court that the crime was in some way justified. It was, therefore, a good example of the sexism of the system.

As a working TV critic, I was invited to screen the movie, on the eve of transmission, and found, among the other critics and film-makers present, the killer and the teenage son of the marriage who was a child when the crime was committed. There was no doubt that the man was eager to relive the incident; but, beyond a careful decision not to include the boy in the film, nobody had further considered what such a public retelling of the tale might do to and for him.

And, finally, there is still a cost to the participants in those even rarer cases where the public interest can be not only discerned but proved – in the sense that the film results not just in a putative rise in understanding, but in action.

In *Police*, Graef's usual focus on the powerful involves 'victims' as the police 'props', as it were. The rape victim, her identity carefully concealed by a crew who never filmed her face, was discovered, no doubt at some expense, by the *News of the World*. According to that paper's account the woman was upset by the cameras, although the language she used in the newspaper interview seemed to me sufficiently at odds with her utterances in the film to call into question the trustworthiness of this testimony. Nevertheless, she was there to be found by the press. The film-makers' justification is that the treatment she was seen receiving at the hands of representatives of the state was vital for the public to know. This is only persuasive because of the uproar caused by the film and the actions taken to correct the situation by the police.

But, despite this, a moral issue does remain for the film-makers, who after all did not know that this would be the outcome. Although the woman was clearly a victim of the police about which we the public had a right to know, she was also, in some sense, a victim of the crew. She was, as I have pointed out, available to be found by the papers.

The problem of balancing the right to know against costs to participants is rendered particularly complex because, in its most journalistic investigative mode, documentary *wants* participants to pay costs. The purpose of the enterprise in such cases is precisely to expose misfeasance or worse and exact, if not punishment, then at least strong reaction. This end is deemed automatically to justify the means, even if the means include subterfuge.

Here is director Mort Silverstein dealing with a farmer while trying to set up a film on migrant workers:

While I was waiting outside with the film crew ... a truck pulled up in front of us and a burly guy clambered out and started yelling, 'What the hell are you guys doing here? You're trespassing, and get the hell off my property'. This was Chudiak, president of the farmers' co-op, but I didn't know it at the time and had to figure out, first, who is this guy; second, what do I say to prevent the whole show from disappearing then and there; third, how can I prevent him from learning what I'm really doing but still tell him a sufficient amount so that I won't feel forever guilty of having lied; and fourth, how can I keep the trust of the migrants, the crew chief, and gain the confidence of this guy, all at the same time. (Rosenthal, 1971, p. 108)

The public interest in the plight of migrants offers a ready justification for subterfuge and disturbance. In fact, that is what prevents the documentarist from feeling guilty about lying.

The history of such film-maker behaviour can be traced back to the 1930s. Watt described conning vicars while making his *March of Time* about church tithes:

Being film people, we'd take advantage. We used to go to sweet vicars living in a twenty room house and with a congregation of ten, mostly old women. And I'd say, 'What a beautiful house and beautiful church. May I photograph?' Of course, I was showing that he was living in this enormous house and having ten parishioners. The church was very annoyed about the whole thing, but it was just what *March of Time* wanted. (Sussex, 1975, p. 89)

And this was an old technique in Watt's day. Journalistic partial representation (or even misrepresentation) where only miscreants are manipulated was pioneered fifty years earlier by the first investigative reporters.

With all due respect to these film-makers, such cases are morally easy. They reveal the documentarist in a traditional journalistic role as protector of the powerless and fearless challenger of the powerful. Mendacity is balanced, and indeed outweighed, by a specific public interest. It is not only that our general understanding of the plight of migrant workers or the extravagance of the church is increased; it is that these topics are deemed to be real agenda items in the political debate. Normally, it is only when the public right to know works in this way that one hears anything about the film-maker–subject relationship.[40]

The public right to know, then, is automatically and implicitly claimed as compensating for the consequences of film-making, should there be any. There is a general unwillingness to confront the question of costs, except when it is a question of exposing evildoers. There is a converse tendency simply to assume a benefit from public knowledge but this assumption obviously does not require any demonstration that an actual benefit has occurred.

Demonstrating an ameliorating effect in the world is difficult. In fact there are few areas where the factual film can be said to have produced more than occasional and ephemeral social effects – for example, exposing crooked businesses, normally small-time, or, more significantly, correcting miscarriages of justice. The BBC series *Rough Justice* and the theatrical documentary *The Thin Blue Line* (1988) would be good examples of the latter. Otherwise, the underlying assumption of most social documentaries – that they shall act as agents of reform and change – is almost never demonstrated.

It will be objected that any expectation of documentaries changing the world is unfair, if not absurd, and is certainly simplistic. However, the public right to know implies that more is involved than just a matter of entertainment or even influence. The public right to know *requires* effects. The entire tradition of the Griersonian documentary is predicated on its having effects. And, finally, documentarists are quick to claim the honour of having effects should they occur (as with the films on miscarriages of justice or the exposures of fraud in investigative current affairs). So the matter of demonstrating effects cannot be sidestepped.

Let us return to Aycliffe Children's Home. The issue is, what did the filming do for Jimmy, Billy and the institution? I have long considered this a necessarily open question as I had no knowledge of the institution beyond these films; but, as I was completing this book, fifteen years after the series, once again Aycliffe was in the news as 'Britain's toughest children's home was accused of abusing teenagers' rights yesterday' (Hugill and Moory, 1992, p. 4). Despite the enormous row in 1977, the *Observer*'s 1992 exposé revealed that the situation had changed not one iota.[41]

In fact, controversy over a documentary is no guarantee of its effectiveness. For instance, Hillary Clinton's first summer job in Washington was checking on the plight of migrant workers a decade after the uproar occasioned by the classic *CBS Reports* 'Harvest of Shame' (Wills, 1992, p. 8). The plight remained.

If this is true of the exceptional documentary, how true is it also of the majority of run-of-the-mill work that causes no uproar? The gap between implicit intention as to outcome and actual outcome forms part of the hidden professional discourse of factual television. For instance, six months after a Granada documentary on the dangers of overprescription of antibiotics, sales of the worst drug jumped 21 per cent. A CBS exposé on *Sixty Minutes* of a crooked politician did not prevent him from getting over 80 per cent of the vote at the next election.[42]

The record suggests that the media in general and the documentary in particular are actually not powerful *instigators*. Their power resides in their ability to amplify. Thus issues already under consideration within the body politic, situations upon which the whistle is being blown, are more likely to produce films which have an after-effect than those dreamed up by the flyblown-eyed documentarists themselves.

There seems to be a sort of isomorphism between pre-existing context (as opposed to simply pre-existing situation) and post-transmission importance. For instance, CBS's *Hunger in America* was instrumental in helping the move from dole to food stamps within the welfare system, but this was because such a reform was already formulated and being pushed.

This was also true of 'A Complaint of Rape'. An external factor, as in this case with the accident of all those rape stories in the papers, is needed to make the film 'work' in this way – and even then it is a rare occurrence.

In Kirwan Cox's survey for the NFBC of documentaries 'that changed the world' (see note 42), precious few titles were forthcoming, even after the question was glossed to exclude *world-wide* change. To get any sort of list at all, 'change' had to be changed to 'influence', a very different thing when the justification for a public right to know is in question.

In the context of change-making, the most interesting film in this list, cited by a number of Cox's interlocutors, is a Thames Television documentary on the shooting by special forces of three Irish citizens on the

Rock of Gibraltar (*Death on the Rock*, 1988). The film helped blow apart the official story of the incident and, according to rumour, cost Thames its licence. It could be said therefore to have had some effect, but more on the television company that made it than on British policy towards Northern Ireland.

While this list can no doubt be extended, the fact remains that the number of documentaries that have had any demonstrable effect is very small. For a form which for sixty years has justified its practices by claiming social amelioration as its objective, this constitutes pretty measly pickings. It is my contention that a demonstrable effect happens so seldom as to vitiate the blanket deployment of the public-right-to-know rhetoric. If the public right to know cannot be translated into action, then it becomes more the documentarist's right to exploit and profit. This casts considerable doubt on the efficacy of the whole Griersonian tradition, including the current direct cinema/vérité phase.

There is another way of looking, then, at Basil Wright's remark about how conditions had not changed much in British schools between *Children at School* (1937) and his interview with Elizabeth Sussex in 1974. Why should this be so? The persistence of the social problems that these films are, at a fundamental level, supposed to be ameliorating is never discussed.

The right to know, in the final analysis, offers flimsy justification for the costs incurred by participants. So a third question in the repressed topic of ethics is whether or not, investigative mode aside, a better balance between rights and costs can be achieved by altering the traditional relationship of film-maker and participant. Shachtman (1977, p. 66) addresses the question in connection with another of his subjects, a young girl: 'Would I be her friend after it was all over? My answer was and is, yes. Do I see her often? No. I am not in her life to stay, and I know it. It hurts me not to be, but I have to go on to other things.'

The film-maker has a living to make and, as a result, the concerns of the people whose co-operation is crucial to her have little place in professional discourse. Indeed, the nearest documentarists come to considering this issue is often in terms of the subjects' potential role as censors. By and large they take an aggrieved view of that possibility because, in their relationship with their subjects, they want the artistic privileges of 'creativity' and the journalistic privileges of 'actuality'.

As Wiseman has said: 'Sometimes after films are completed people feel retrospectively that they had a right of censorship, but there are never any written documents to support that view' (Rosenthal, 1971, p. 71). Wiseman's attitude is, I would argue, the typical one. Interference of any kind is a clear breach of the film-maker's freedom of speech and, as such, is to be resisted.

But we should also remember that the NFBC came to a rather different conclusion after *Things I Cannot Change* and that some film-makers have made it a habit to share their rushes with the participants, not just so that they can see them, as Flaherty always arranged, but so that they could gain a measure of control over their own images. Video, where the images can be replayed immediately, makes this a lot easier, should the film-maker want to do it.

Allowing participants to see a final cut was becoming slightly less uncommon. Rouch's procedure in filming the subjects' reaction to the final cut has also occasionally been copied. For instance, this occurred in *Six American Families* (1977), a series made by Arthur Barron, the Maysles and others for Group W and the United Church of Christ and the United Methodist Church. 'Unlike the now famous Louds of *An American Family*, the families comprising the series will not find it necessary to appear on TV talk shows to set the record straight' (Egan, 1978, p. 5).

But this remains exceptional, such a procedure being seen as an abdication of editorial responsibility rather than as an ethically justified practice. For instance, Philip Donnellan's series *A Moment to Talk* (1982–4) was devoted to shop-floor conversations. The people involved were given videocassettes of the rushes and transcripts. They were also invited to the cutting room for comment at the outset of the editing process and then shown rough cuts. But Donnellan allows that this process had to be conducted virtually in secret as far as the BBC, the producer, was concerned.

There is a further dimension which we must not ignore. Ethics in documentary film-making can also be a two-way street. Exploitation can be met coming the other way.

For instance, what happens if participants in some way ensnare film-makers in their own agenda? This can occur in documentaries as it does with the news, where politicians certainly routinely manipulate the media and political activists are often accused of so doing.

Perhaps this sort of manipulation was in part the case with the killer in *Sixty Seconds of Hatred*. His eagerness to bask once more in publicity then becomes a by-product of the public's need to know of English legal sexism.

It becomes very easy for the public interest to disappear, as Eric Barendt points out (1989, p. 189), in favour of what simply interests and excites the public. Such circumstances leave the film-maker trapped in a sensationalist net of manipulations. What, for example, of the transsexual exhibitionist who allows a documentary crew to film him dressing? It is difficult to see how the documentarists in such instances are different from the producers and hosts of American talk-show television where, for instance, a married graduate student, captioned 'Turned Off By Sex', can feel her appearance was 'empowering'. Her husband, who was disappointed that he was not invited to join her on air, told the *Boston Globe*: 'Being on national television is a kind of a trip' (Golden, 1988, pp. 51 and 17ff.).

At its most extreme the trip can become a nightmare when the documentarist is turned upon physically by the subject. This does not need a war zone. Barbara Kopple, for example, was harassed and shot at on the picket line while making *Harlan County, USA*. In that same part of Kentucky a Canadian, Hugh O'Connor, who had co-produced a much-admired show at the Montreal Expo, had been filming rural Appalachian poverty in 1967. The occupants of the shacks he was photographing had all agreed but the owner of the land had not. Enraged, this person arrived and shot O'Connor dead. After the trial, the prosecuting attorney said that people around Harlan held the general view that the killer '*should've* killed the son of a bitch. ... They oughtn't to make fun of mountain people. They've made enough fun of mountain people' (Trilling, 1985, p. 9).

So as the factual film approaches its centenary a number of factors combine to make the ethical position of the documentarist vexed. There is the example of the amoral Victorian artist. There is a technology that positively encourages voyeurism and incorporeal trespass. There is a legal system more interested in property rights than in individuals. There is a political concept of free expression which privileges journalistic communication over other principles of social responsibility. Above all, there is the authority of science which documentarists claim because of their concern with the 'actual'.

Such a concern closes off any potential argument that this sort of film-making is basically beyond the moral realm, a business for which the existing limited legal constraints are sufficient (Christians, Rotzoll and Fackler, 1983, p. 29). The fictional film industry, after all, operates on principles of 'amoral efficiency' (Christians and Rotzoll, 1985, pp. 229 and 235). Without 'actuality' that could also be the world of the documentarist; but, because of 'actuality', it is not. Yet exercising one's rights of freedom of expression within a moral realm is, as we have seen, very tricky.

Freedom of expression does not allow for the extensive application of a formal ethical system, whether derived from Aristotle, Kant and Mill or from some contemporary thinker such as Rawls (Christians, Rotzoll and Fackler, 1983, pp. 9ff.; Merrill, 1989, pp. 44ff). On the contrary, such systems seem unrealistic in practice and their wholesale application to media situations threatening to free expression. There are other problems with them as well.

When applied to the media worker, for instance, such systems tend to assume the writer or film-maker to be a free agent when in fact most function within a complex net of industrial restraints (Merrill, 1989, p. 38). These systems also yield contradictory guidelines to practice and none of them is generally accepted (ibid., pp. 48ff.).

Therefore, in the increasingly extensive debate on ethics among American journalists, there is a tendency to favour situationist solutions, a modern relativist view which eschews absolutes and encourages treating each case on its merits. But the danger then is that, across a number of situations, principles disappear.

Nevertheless, the journalism ethicists do have something to say to the documentarists. John Merrill, one of the most thoughtful of them, has written (ibid., p. 214): 'What I recommend is an individual and rational ethics, one that will centre moral judgement and responsibility on a personal level, that will help sustain ... authenticity and integrity, and that will combine a respect for tried and tested moral principles with a rational flexibility.'

Merrill's recommendation holds good for documentarists because, like journalists, they too are dealing with 'actuality'. In the long term the 'consent defence' and vague appeals to the public interest are dangerous for factual film-makers. Such ideas leave them primed to exploit the powerless and vulnerable to being manipulated by the powerful and the deviant. Worst of all, these facile concepts debase, in the name of free expression, both the right to speak and the right to hear.

Merrill acknowledges that in such an ethic, what the individual does 'cannot be justified scientifically. There are no empirical tests that can be used' (ibid., p. 165). But this, perhaps at base nothing more than a call for an ethical consciousness, an appeal for responsible behaviour (especially a concern for others), is the best we can do. It certainly supports the view, which I come more and more to believe, that the attitude and sensitivity of the film-maker to the subject and the relationship they establish is the clue to ethical film-making.

In practice, though, this 'best' is likely not to be very good, given that most documentarists are beholden to a system which is unlikely to be as ethical as they might want it to be. Can that system be made more ethical? Not very easily, because external constraints are not, in my view, an option, given the overriding requirement of freedom of expression. Thus, between the Scylla of amoral behaviour and the Charybdis of legal constraint, the only acceptable and safe pattern for ethics has to be self-imposed. The media system as a whole has to demonstrate a commitment to ethical behaviour and be willing to police it itself. All one can say at this stage of development is that the level of self-awareness among individual professionals about ethics is currently too low. These must rise if the rules of conduct are to be, as they must be, both self-imposed and effective.

There can be no question that the rules must be self-imposed rather than imposed. I had previously thought otherwise – that, in fact, the ethical problems of the Griersonian documentarist might be solved if a duty of care to the subject was created via an expanded notion of consent along the lines used for scientific experiments on human subjects. I was primarily concerned with protecting the Griersonian victim (Winston, 1988, pp. 52ff.). Now I believe that any attempt to elaborate consent by bringing it more into line with the scientific protocols would be clearly dangerous to the principle of free expression.

It was events over the past decade, especially in Britain, that led me to realise that my stance was wrong. Perhaps some limited revision of trespass to prohibit surveillance could be contemplated; but, given the pressures against free expression from both government and, alarmingly, the public's increasing hostility to the concept, I now see that a redefinition of consent would certainly be used as a threat against the right to speak. The chilling effect would be exactly the same as that of a privacy tort.

And allowing a privacy tort, with or without a defence of public interest against it, would be to run the considerable danger that freedom of expression would again be seriously curtailed. In the absence of any constitutional guarantees of a right to speak, as in Britain, this is especially probable.

If the media system as a whole constantly tries to walk away from ethical issues, the result is to put these issues on the legislative table. As was happening in Britain in 1992–3, the calls for the imposition of an ethical system imposed by law become importunate. The flow of the debate in Britain supports the view that 'the press is never really free unless it accepts a pattern which protects it from the perils of self-destruction' (Marnell, 1973, p. 212).

My point is that documentarists, because of 'actuality', are not immune from these perils either.

I raise the question of ethics not just because it has been repressed in documentary studies and practice. It was also one of the two major issues which the coming of the new technology failed to address. It was thought – at the 1963 Lyon meeting, for instance – that the new technology had put all the problems facing the Griersonian documentary to rest. As we have seen, ethical difficulty was far from being thus set aside but, on the contrary, was exacerbated in the direct cinema/cinéma vérité era. But there is another even more radical problem which was now becoming ever more clearly exposed.

36

On The Battlefields of Epistemology

There was an irony at the 1963 Lyon meeting which was hidden from most at the time. Both parties offered an enhanced vision of Griersonian 'actuality', the direct cinema people doing so with particular vehemence. But this vision was within a couple of decades shown to be false.

It was to become clear that direct cinema/cinéma vérité, come to fulfil the old Griersonian testament, had revealed Grierson's project as being, more or less, incapable of performance. The realist documentary in all its guises had not only largely failed as a medium of public education; it had also run from social meaning, being obsessed, as it was, with surface. And it had left film-makers in a confused and ambiguous position not only as regards the status of their images but also as regards their personal moral position vis-à-vis those they filmed. The problems of the documentary had not been technological after all. Rather, they had been grounded in Grierson's essentially confusing attempt to claim artistic and scientific legitimations at the same time.

By the mid-1970s it was increasingly apparent to some critics (as well as a few of the more thoughtful film-makers themselves) that the new equipment and techniques were no more capable of 'actuality' than were the old machines and the business of reconstruction. But without 'actuality' what could the documentary be? Claiming the real was both its essence and its bane.

It was a bane because at this time – and specifically around the issue of representing reality – the whole intellectual landscape seemed to be undergoing a fundamental change.

We, as a society, have been hitherto addicted in our representational preferences to a realism which 'offers a fixity in which the signifier is treated as if it were identical with a pre-existent signified' (Tagg, 1988, p. 99). This addiction shaped and informed all the Western plastic arts for half a millennium. It is most potently sited in the lens culture that generated photography; indeed, it is the realist addiction in the arts that conditioned the applications of optics to produce first lenses and, eventually, photography. Ideological power then flows from making a hierarchy of images exactly according to their supposed relationship to the real. The police identification photography is perhaps but the rawest traditional expression of this power (Sekula, 1986, pp. 26ff.; Tagg, 1988, pp. 66ff.).

Despite this, today there are many who would now dispute this hierarchy and with it all assertions that 'the world is in a strong sense independent of our possible representations, and may well extend beyond them' (Nagel, 1986, p. 91). Instead, they would hold that:

It is no longer possible to maintain the old economy of truth and representation in a world where 'reality' is entirely constructed through forms
of mass-media feedback, where values are determined by consumer
demand (itself brought about by the endless circulation of meanings,
images and advertising codes), and where nothing could serve as a
means of distinguishing true from merely true-seeming (or ideological)
habits of belief. (Norris, 1990, p. 166)

Even though Thomas Nagel and Christopher Norris would want to resist
such views, without question they are fashionable and have had a most
dramatic impact on our thinking about the mimetic media.

Stuart Hall points out (1982, p. 75) that once 'the real world was both
origin and warrant for the truth of any statement about it'. This was
particularly so of visual (that is, photographic) texts, but he is of the party
that believes this no longer holds. Hall gives television as an example of
how this 'origin' and 'warrant' yoking ought now to be seen:

It would be more appropriate to define the typical discourse of this
medium [TV] not as naturalistic but as *naturalised*: not grounded in
nature but producing nature as a sort of guarantee of its truth. Visual
discourse is peculiarly vulnerable in this way because the systems of
visual recognition on which they depend are so widely available in any
culture that they appear to involve no intervention of coding, selection
or arrangement. They appear to reproduce the actual trace of reality in
the images they transmit. (ibid.)

Hall is in no doubt as to how improper this appearance of naturalism is.
He concludes: 'This, of course, is an illusion – "the naturalistic illusion"'.
The 'ontological agnosticism of deconstructive criticism', in Julianne
Burton's phrase (1990, p. 361), has become a truism, at least in certain
circles.

The epistemological move to a postmodern scepticism throws the whole
documentary idea into question. The fact was that neither party at Lyon
could 'scape whipping because of this shift in the intellectual ground.
Realism itself was now becoming suspect.

Postmodernist concern transforms 'actuality', that which ties documentary to science, from a legitimation into an ideological burden. It
problematises objectivity for direct cinema and renders cinéma vérité's
reflexive gestures moot. An observation of Noel Carroll's best throws into
relief the enormous extent of this change of terrain.

Carroll (1983, p. 8) is dismissive of 'arguments against objectivity in
nonfiction films ... unless their proponents are prepared to embrace a
rather thoroughgoing scepticism about the prospects of objectivity in general. The defence of such a far-ranging sceptical position would, of course,
have to be joined on the battlefields of epistemology rather than in the
trenches of film theory.'

But it is exactly on the broader epistemological battlegrounds that postmodernism was joining the issue. Carroll's field-position was already
being attacked. Postmodern sceptics were charging it at full tilt.

Even the empirical sciences were coming under fire. Latour's reduction
of 'science in action' to series of inscription practices, cited above, is nothing but a dispatch from this same epistemological war (see p. 131). The

previously impregnable hegemonic identification of knowledge with science was being seriously disputed (Habermas, 1972, p. 4).

It was the din of this very battle which led critics to question the possibility of a documentary objectivity and their scepticism could not be more thoroughgoing. After all, similar questions were being posed in congruent fields. For instance, in anthropology some claimed that 'it is no longer possible to salvage Western rationality or its totalising potential from the clutches of context by ahistorical claims to a superior theoretical and methodological armament' (Nencel and Pels, 1989, p. 83). The suspicion now aroused by the practices of Rouch's teacher Griaule cited above (see p. 177) is a good example of the fall-out of such attacks.

The battle necessarily also swept over photography's evidential claims. Not only was it ever more widely agreed that 'every time we look at a photograph, we are aware, however slightly, of the photographer selecting that sight from an infinity of other sights' (Berger, 1972, p. 10) but more generally photographic objectivity was suspect. Pierre Bourdieu: 'In stamping photography with the patent of realism, society does nothing but confirm itself in the tautological certainty that an image of reality that conforms to its own representation of objectivity is truly objective' (Krauss, 1984, p. 57). And what Bourdieu says specifically of photography as a system of representation, postmodernism says in general of representation in general: A representation is a representation is a representation. The real has nothing to do with it.

And as if that were not enough, there was also a further attack on the basic way in which we look at the world.

Although the camera and the projector emerge out of the work of Arab astronomers, photography was now seen as a specific culturally determined phenomenon of the West. This cultural specificity was extended by historians and theoreticians to embrace not just the development of apparatus but also human sight itself. Some now argued that sight, a particular 'way of seeing', was also culturally specific to the West. This way of seeing was embodied in the photographic apparatus and lens culture. That it was not universal was proved by reference to the specific Western central (single vanishing point) perspective code.

Codes for creating the illusion of three-dimensionality on flat surfaces had been actively explored from ancient times (Doesschate, 1964, pp. 95, 101 and 108ff.). The reimposition of central perspective as the dominant one from the early 15th century limits the exploration of other options and marks the triumph of 'a narrow conception': 'Renaissance perspective adopted vision as the sole basis for representation: every perspective picture represents its subject as it would be seen from a particular point of view at a particular moment' (Galassi, 1981, p. 12).

This locking of a spectator into a single viewing position was deemed to be of ideological significance. The perspective code creates a 'powerful abstraction ... whereby the painter compelled the viewer to see nothing but what he wished him to see' (Gadol, 1968, p. 25).

Such thinking converts the camera from a self-inscribing scientific instrument whose images are evidence of an external reality into a repressive tool imprisoning the viewer in the photographer's Western totalising vision.

It is against this intellectual background that the development of direct cinema/cinéma vérité occurs. It is somewhat ironic, then, that just as documentarists finally obtained the equipment to illuminate, as they sup-posed, the real world of externally verifiable data, that world was denied them. 'Actuality' was on the lam. Their tools were faulty. Their films were, inevitably, in Nichols's felicitous phrase (1981, p. 172), 'ideo-logically complicit'. So when film-makers claimed that their presence had no effect, as when Craig Gilbert dismissed his critics' point that 'the mere fact of observation has an influence on the observed' as 'sheer nonsense', it now sounded like mere braggadocio (Gilbert, 1983, p. 299).

The documentary sceptics have proved to be more than happy to take on Carroll's objection and deny objectivity across a broad front. These sceptics were ready to identify the whole realist aesthetic as the specific bourgeois code of representation *par excellence*.

> Realism's claim to authenticity, its insistence on a language which func-tions largely as a signifier of objects – the knowledge of things … all these characteristics set it apart as the appropriately bourgeois mode of representation. … The power of realism, then, resides in the appearance that its ideology *isn't there*, and that its derivation from bourgeois modes of thought is irrelevant since its version of reality is true. (Fiske and Hartley, 1978, pp. 164–5)

There are no exceptions to this association of realism with all modes of representation that claim a 'truth'. The 'desire for a mimetic relation with nature' is, according to Jurgen Habermas (1975, p. 78), one of the crucial distinguishing elements of bourgeois art. It is a perfect example of the ineffability, as Roland Barthes saw it, of bourgeois ideology: 'Bourgeois art has become a refuge for a satisfaction, even if only virtual, of those needs that have become, as it were, illegal in the material life-process of bour-geois society. I refer here to the desire for a mimetic relation with nature' (Barthes, 1973, p. 142).

Therefore any form of realist representation displays the same ideo-logical complicity. For instance, certain types of late-seventeenth-century theatrical presentations or written narratives in England are properly to be connected with the rise of the bourgeoisie. The new social order emerging at that time, Raymond Williams suggested (1981, p. 164), gave rise to a drama with new, more realistic quotidian subject matter. He quotes:

> Stripp'd of Regal Pomp, and glaring Show
> His muse reports a tale of Private Woe,
> Works up Distress from Common Scenes in Life,
> A Treach'rous Brother, and an Injur'd Wife.

By the next century, drama had become contemporary and inclusive of all ordinary social ranks and it eschewed regal or supernatural elements.

From this viewpoint, then, the radical artists of the 19th century wrecked their new theme of work and workers exactly because by using a realistic aesthetic to present it they also referenced these bourgeois devel-opments. This aesthetic was bourgeois and their art was thus co-opted, whatever they (and, ironically, their bourgeois critics) might have thought to the contrary.

The same error was then made by the realist documentarists who so closely followed them. The common scenes in life had become the essence of documentary but they now stood revealed as a particularly bourgeois theme. Documentary's distinguishing mark, 'the ontological claim on the real', was revealed as the warning sign of a particularly bourgeois enterprise. Documentary film-makers used realism which was now seen as a particularly bourgeois aesthetic. When documentarists promised to show us 'truth', we now understood that they were only hiding behind the scientific claim of 'actuality'. In fact, they were part of the culture which, as Adorno and Horkheimer had long before pointed out (1977, p. 363), 'perpetually cheats its consumers of what it perpetually promises'.

From the perspective of the Frankfurt School the ideological effects of documentaries could be no different from those of fiction: 'The sound film, far surpassing the theatre of illusion, leaves no room for imagination ... hence the film forces its victims [its audience] to equate it directly with reality. ... In films, those permanently desperate situations which crush the spectator in ordinary life somehow become a promise that one can go on living' (Adorno and Horkheimer, 1977, pp. 354 and 373).

The Griersonians were exactly in the business of having audiences equate images with reality and converting desperate real-life situations into promises of a better tomorrow. Nevertheless, these film-makers presented themselves as a species of saviour for Adorno's crushed media victims. Rotha said (1952, p. 47):

On frequent occasions we have heard it alleged that the enemy of social consciousness among the people is amusement. But it would surely be more accurate to say that it is rather the shape and style which, for various reasons, manufacturers give to amusement that is one of the real hindrances to the general ripening of social and civic responsibility.

Yet from the standpoint of those theorising a consciousness industry the documentarists (should they have thought about them) were arguably the worst enemies of social consciousness because of their overt and shameless aspirations to be public educators.

It will not do to dismiss the Frankfurt objection on the grounds that Adorno and his like were elitists with little understanding of the popular and no conception of the powers that mass audiences could bring to bear in reinterpreting hegemonic media messages in their own interests. Griersonian documentaries were not popular. Their hegemonic meanings were not ambiguously buried in and below popular narrative forms but foregrounded, the *raison d'être* for the work. The films look like evidence inviting judgment but they are ruthless in their positioning of the spectator. Of all film forms, documentary is the least able to resist Adorno's criticism.

This is why Wiseman's objection to the 'bullshit' objectivity argument (which can, of course, be read as a postmodernist *cri de cœur*) will not so serve his turn. As I have said, direct cinema films are too grounded in the traditional scientific claim on the real for that position to be tenable. Modern documentarists cannot have their postmodernist cake and eat it – not even when they claim to offer an objective account of their own subjective experience in making the film. As far as Pierre Bourdieu, say, is concerned this is still a realist enterprise tautologically conflating a representation of objectivity with objectivity.

And that is true of Rouch's strategies as well, as Lucien Goldmann suggests. Some commentators now bridled at Rouch's use of the word 'vérité', even as a self-conscious reference back to *kinopravda* (Eaton, 1979, p. 50). The slightest desire to achieve any species of 'film truth' was, inescapably, 'ideologically complicit'.

So, while the influence of critical theory is of major importance to film theory, in the realm of the documentary it is something more. In fact its development marks nothing less than a crisis of legitimation for the documentary idea as Grierson conceived of it and as the direct cinema/cinéma vérité generation sought to work with it and as film-makers today use it.

If the postmodernists are right that would then be the end of the matter – the realist documentary would be, if not dead, then at best a zombie-like creature, a simulacrum of a living film form. The real cannot be captured and therefore documentaries are films like any other, their claims of evidence spurious. There is no 'difference that makes a difference', as Nichols puts it (1991, p. 7), and there cannot be.

But, of course, time marches on.

The postmodernist charge itself begins to falter. The possibility of there being an external reality reasserts itself as the exceptionalist claims of postmodernism come under increasing scrutiny.

After all, this is an old war, between those who see only a world veiled by appearances where forms impenetrable mask unknowable realities and those who do not – between Bishop Berkeley and Dr Johnson, for instance. Here, in the Berkeley role, is Jean Baudrillard (1988, p. 27) who believes that 'For us there is an increasingly definitive lack of differentiation between image and reality. ...'

And here is Christopher Norris, playing Johnson, refuting him *thus* (1990, p. 182):

> It just does not follow from the fact that we are living through an age of widespread illusion and disinformation that *therefore* all questions of truth drop out of the picture ... Baudrillard's mistake is to move straight on from a descriptive account of certain prevalent conditions in the late twentieth century life world to a wholesale anti-realist stance which takes those conditions as a pretext for dismantling every last claim to validity or truth.

Now here is a bugle call that could mean that a rescue for the documentary is getting under way. Say the tide of battle perhaps now begins to swing back, and the wholesale anti-realists run the danger of being defeated: what are the prospects then for documentary film? Can the documentary film, or more generally the evidential status of the photograph, hope to be in the victory parade? Will the documentary have survived the attack?

PART FIVE

DOCUMENTARY IN THE AGE OF
DIGITAL IMAGE MANIPULATION

37

Towards a Post-Griersonian Documentary

How might this rescue work?

Noel Carroll would counter-attack, hard. He demonstrates (1988, pp. 114 and 97), with some thoroughness, that these 'psychosemiotic Marxists', as he calls the postmodernists, are the 'victims of their own metaphors'. On this basis he attempts to maintain the documentary's legitimacy in a straightforward classic sense. He argues (1983, pp. 14ff.) that it is confusions and misuses of language which have caused us to conflate various senses of 'objectivity' with each other and with 'truth'.

We have also been wilful in our use of the word 'illusion' in connection with realism, thereby implying that the realism inevitably involves a 'deception of a disempowering kind'. The idea of 'illusionism', Carroll states (1988, pp. 90ff.), has been made, by postmodernists in the last few decades, into a cognate with realism, which has thereby been reduced to 'the deceptions of a magician'.

Untangling all these, he suggests, would allow for a recuperation of the mimetic power of the camera along Bazinian lines. Indeed, what calls forth some of Carroll's most effective scorn is exactly the hypocrisy (as it were) of his intellectual enemies in denying Bazin's vision of cinematic realism for themselves, while assuming that it works so well for 'ordinary spectators' that they can no longer distinguish image from reality.

In so far as this mimetic power is generally sustained in the culture, then, for Carroll, a documentary form which took advantage of it by 'being still responsible to established standards of objectivity' could exist without difficulty (Carroll, 1983, pp. 31ff.).

This is a brave and bold foray but the old scientific certainties are unlikely to be re-established in so unproblematic a way as to allow for Carroll's objectivity standards, at least as far as photography is concerned. For one thing, the illusionism–realism equation is not quite so much the creature of the postmodernists as Carroll seems to suggest. It is far older. It occurs at the very outset of lens culture. There is, for instance, an obscure reference to Alberti's camera, if indeed camera it was, to suggest that his viewers 'questioned whether they saw painted or natural things' (Irvins, 1973, p. 16). Illusionism and realism, however much Carroll may regret it, go together particularly where lenses are involved, and always have.[1]

Photography's scientism may have disguised that for a century and a half but this old connection is unlikely to be so effectively hidden from view in the future. The basic fact is that we can no longer look at photographs as windows on the world whose panes have been polished to a preternatural transparency by the glazier/photographer. Our sophistication now is such that we will always see the marks on the glass. So, even if Norris is correct and 'every last claim to validity and truth' is not destroyed by postmodernism, photography's evidential status is still unlikely to survive the epistemological battle. Carroll's efforts simply to return to the *status quo ante* seem unlikely to carry the day. But this does not mean that other strategies cannot be more successful.

Bill Nichols (1991, pp. 7 and 109) proposes a more complex tactic which seeks to sap postmodernism by accommodating its 'intriguing ... assertions', even though he does not agree with them. He does this primarily by admitting a constructed historical world: 'Documentary offers access to shared historical construct.' But then he goes on to privilege this construct: 'Instead of *a* world, we are offered access to *the* world.'

It is not the sharing that is critical here. After all, we 'share' the world depicted in any Western but that does not make it a representation of *the* world, the historical reality. It is not even that there are a multiplicity of fictional worlds but only one documentary one. Rather, what is important for Nichols is the distinction which he draws between the way in which the cinema treats this difference. On screen one finds 'a *story* and its imaginary world and an *argument* about the historical world. ... Argument treats the historical world as the ground for the figure of its documentary representation' (ibid., pp. 11 and 126).

The result of the story/argument distinction is that: 'Narrative [i.e. fiction] as a mechanism for storytelling seems quite different from documentary as a mechanism for addressing nonimaginary, real life issues' (ibid., p. 6).

> Both narrative and documentary are organised in relation to the coherence of a chain of events which depends on the motivated relationship between occurrences (taking 'motivation' in the formal sense of justification or causality). ... In documentary as in fiction, we use material evidence to form a conceptual coherence, an argument or story, according to the logic or economy proposed by the text. (ibid., p. 125)

The differences, however, are because of the different relationship to the world. A story about an imaginary world is just a story. A story about the real world (that is, a documentary) is an 'argument'.

Nichols bolsters this by suggesting (1991, p. 19) that documentary editing then reflects this difference:

> Documentary film structure generally depends on evidentiary editing in which the classic narrative techniques of continuity editing undergo significant modification. Instead of organising cuts within a scene to present a sense of a single, unified time and space in which we can quickly locate the relative position of the central characters, documentary organises cuts within a scene to present the impression of a single, convincing argument in which we can locate a logic.

Some of this is unpersuasive. On editing, for example, I would argue that it is the *failure* to modify classic narrative editing which is significant. The documentary director's need to intervene or to reconstruct is driven exactly by editing requiring multiple viewpoints and so on to permit matching – in short, a drive for narrative coverage with, exactly, 'unified time and space' as the prime objective in most circumstances.

Similarly, the distinction between the fictional mechanisms for story-telling and the documentary ones for dealing with 'real life issues' cannot be analysed on a textual basis as Nichols tacitly admits – they only 'seem' to be different. This is not to deny that Nichols is correct to point out that documentaries on the whole require rather more organisation by the narrative voice than does fiction (where the characters perform much of this work). But his concept of the 'argument' does not go much beyond this in that it is not readily distinguished from narrative 'story' – except in one crucial regard.

And this is the rub – the point at which Nichols makes contact with the rescue column. The whole issue is not one of such formal differences on the screen at all. What prevents a documentary from being a 'fiction like any other' is rather 'what *we make* of the documentary's representation of the evidence it presents' (Nichols, 1991, pp. 108 and 125; my italics). It is audiences who can tell the difference between a fictional narrative and a documentary argument.

In other words, it is a question of reception. The difference is to be found in the mind of the audience.

The irony is that it has always been a question of reception. As I have already noted, Robert Fairthorne saw this quite clearly sixty years ago: '"Actuality" is not a fundamental property, but a relation between film and audience' (MacPherson, 1980, p. 171). Grounding the documentary idea in reception rather than in representation is exactly the way to preserve its validity. It allows for the audience to make the truth claim for the documentary rather than the documentary implicitly making the claim for itself.

For this to happen, though, the entire Griersonian project must be abandoned.

The Griersonian idea of 'actuality' depends on an assumption of a particular naivety in the audience. Without such naivety, the audience could not believe that anything of the real would survive 'creative treatment'. For 'actuality' to overcome the contradictions of Grierson's definition required that the camera be seen not only as a scientific instrument but as one more like a thermometer than not, one that gave a 'reading' of reality which was unmediated (or less mediated) than other readings. But it is exactly this strong case for the instruments of science which now most seems naive, even if postmodernist scepticism is otherwise rejected.

Thus, even if the presence of the photographer is acknowledged, the camera in her hands still points at a world most people persist in believing is in some way real. The camera can, and inevitably *must*, 'lie' – but the world is 'out there' none-the-less. The only compromise possible is to acknowledge the photographer so that the relation of image to imaged depends not on the image's intrinsic quality guaranteed by science but on our reception of it as an image of the real guaranteed by (or corresponding to) our experience.

This renegotiation of photography's claim on the real means that the audience relation to documentary can embrace an understanding of the inevitable mediations of the film-making process. What then is left for documentary is a relation to actuality which acknowledges the normal circumstances of image production but is at the same time consonant with our everyday experience of the real.

The cost of this changed relation is that the documentary image now represents a reality no more and no less 'real' than the reality presented by the photographic image of, say, Michelle Pfeiffer or Gérard Depardieu. The benefit is that even though photography thus loses what Maya Deren thirty years ago (1960, p. 155) could still call 'the innocent arrogance of an objective fact', we in the audience can yet process 'the documentary's representation of the evidence it presents'.

The abandonment of the Griersonian position would bring in train other benefits. If documentary drops its pretension to a superior representation of actuality, promises of non-intervention will no longer need to be made because they are beside the point. Objectivity, whether scrambled in meaning or elegantly redefined, can either way be abandoned also. Actuality can be an earnest of little more than the physicality of the plastic material before the lens. (At least for the moment.) Most important, since the audience's understanding that what is on offer is indeed a truly subjective interaction with the world – one, unlike direct cinema's, unburdened by objectivity and actuality – what is on offer can be really 'creatively treated'. Documentary style could then be liberated.

The distinction between the subjectivity I am suggesting and that claimed by the direct cinema practitioners becomes a question of aesthetics. The pretension to a superior representation of the real is deeply encoded in the dominant documentary style. Handheld, available light, available sound, long take, jump-cut, direct gaze, minimal graphics – all these signify 'evidence'. This signification is the reason why direct cinema film-makers can *say* they are being subjective, but their aesthetic practice *says not*. (The reflexivity of cinéma vérité is no better in this regard: those film-makers *say* they are being subjective, but their signification practices, exactly similar to direct cinema's, also *say not*.)

To abandon the claimed Griersonian privilege in favour of an honest subjectivity therefore means abandoning this style, at least in its 'purest' forms. Such 'purity' is now as much a mark of duplicity as reconstruction was thirty years ago. The 'real nitty-gritty', as Henry Breitrose then called 'actuality', has gummed up the works.

If documentarists in general were not to claim a privileged relation to the real then their films or tapes could start to look, for instance, more like Errol Morris's *The Thin Blue Line* (with its deployment of film noir conventions in a miscarriage-of-justice documentary) than inevitably and rigidly looking like Frederick Wiseman's six-hour prizewinning voyeuristic and stultifying intrusion into death and grief, *Near Death*, which was also made in 1989.

This new subjective, stylistically much more varied documentary could then seek a broader audience. The clue to succeeding in that search is tone. Documentary must abandon its limited, and always serious, tone. It must cease to be always and only one of Nichols's 'discourses of sobriety' (Nichols, 1991, p. 3).

The perennial unattractiveness of many documentaries, certainly many unvoyeuristic ones, to audiences must be acknowledged. This means, in effect, acknowledging the connotations of 'public education'. Audiences know full well that Grierson's public education purpose, however much glossed and disguised, is a virtual guarantee of boredom. For sixty years documentaries have gained nothing from being a 'discourse of sobriety' except marginalisation. It is possible to gloss Metz's remark (1974, p. 4) that 'One is almost never totally bored by a movie' by adding 'unless it be a Griersonian documentary!'[2]

The pretension to public education needs, like the pretension to an enhanced claim on actuality and the limited stylistics of direct cinema, to be abandoned. After all, one of the two truly popular documentary forms, the rock performance film, has gratifyingly little public education sobriety about it. The use of film noir as a style source in *The Thin Blue Line* does not detract from Morris's seriousness of purpose. He is just not being grim-visaged about it. Even more, the use of a satiric tone in *Roger and Me* or *Cane Toads* (1987) (the story of an environmental disaster shot like a comedy horror/sci-fi movie) does not destroy the quality of their social commentary. On the contrary.

I would argue that Grierson killed off a line of biting social satire for documentary which could be seen in embryo in *A propos de Nice* and *Land Without Bread*. *Roger and Me* and *Cane Toads* not only revive that tradition, they demonstrate that it is possible to make it popular. It is only Grierson's heritage that stands between us and a documentary form that could be, on occasion, satiric, irreverent and comic.

And committed.

Of course, the committed documentary is established but, from the time Grierson mounted his attack on the film-makers to his left, commitment has been seen as a species of deviancy, a falling off from the 'objectivity' that was supposedly the norm of the Griersonian documentary. But why should commitment be seen as deviant? In so far as documentary is of a piece with journalism, thus far is advocacy permitted. Advocacy is a legitimate journalistic activity. The burden Grierson laid on the documentary was to pretend that his films were reports on the news pages, as it were, when in fact they were editorials for the established order. The time has come to liberate documentary from this spurious position and admit it as a species of editorialising *in its essence*. Clearly this can be accomplished more easily once the 'actuality' claim, the style and the sober 'public education' tone have all been laid aside.

There can be no doubt how burdensome the tradition is. For instance, the radical newsreel film-making occasioned in the USA by the Vietnam war in the late 1960s was seriously inhibited by the dead weight of the Griersonian heritage (as the more cynical might suggest it was supposed to be). John Hess points out (1985, p. 139) that the reception of such work was curtailed in part 'because of the education context in which we come to know [the documentary] in the first place'. In other words, the Griersonian documentary, despite the rock performance film, had inserted itself so effectively into the public mind as boring that there was no easy way within the counter-culture to move people away from that perception.

Commitment leads to new subjects. Radical film-makers, for example, found that some audiences had not lost their taste for the other sort of popular documentary (apart from the rock performance film) – the historical compilation.

Television's continued use of this form had not killed off the possibility of turning it to Esfir Shub's original purpose. Independent films have been made in America recovering the lost history of the left whether before the Second World War (*Seeing Red*, 1983, by Julia Reichert and James Klein and *The Good Fight*, 1984, by Noel Buckner, Mary Dore and Sam Sills) or during the Vietnam war (*The War at Home*, 1979, by Barry Brown and

Glenn Silber). The archive of cold-war propaganda films was recycled for satiric effect in *The Atomic Cafe* (1982) by Jayne Loader and Kevin and Pierce Rafferty.

Of course, all these films are subject to attack for failing Griersonian standards of 'objectivity' and seriousness, that is for being *in their essence* committed. Why wasn't the plight of other left-wing groups in Spain included in one? (Georgakis, 1978, p. 47). Why didn't another deal with Soviet foreign policy? (Rosenthal, 1988, p. 14). Why, by failing to be sober, have the makers of *The Atomic Cafe* ('a shockingly entertaining film') 'painted a one-sided view of fifties America'? (Boyle, 1982, pp. 39 and 41).

Out of this revival of radical film-making, specifically out of the news-reel network, came a full-scale and sustained (if still more marginal than deserved) women's documentary movement. Over the past two decades, sometimes in styles owing little to the dominant documentary cinema, a solid body of achievement has accumulated.

One strand of this can be seen in Julia Reichert and James Kleins's earlier film *Union Maids* (1976), in Ann Bohlen, Lyn Goldfarb and Lorraine Gray's *With Babies and Banners* (1978) and in Connie Field's *The Life and Times of Rosie The Riveter* (1980). These labour history films, like those recovering the general history of the left, sometimes parallel and sometimes rely on previously gathered oral testimony (see Lynd and Lynd, 1973; Berger Gluck, 1987). They are about women in and around the labour movement and the world of work, and they 'offer new and forgotten images of history, of women's work and of the women's world' (Erens, 1981, p. 9).

But here again one can see the baleful influence of the tradition. In so far as they were within the mainstream, the films were also liable to be faulted. For instance, it was noted that *Union Maids* displays a 'lack of clarity' about the communist affiliations of its subjects which exactly mirrors a similar fudging in *Chronique* (Gordon, 1985, p. 156). (This was not a problem, of course, with Reichert and Klein's *Seeing Red*, a history of the American Communist Party during its heyday.)

But some would go beyond these supposed sins of omission to claim that these films in general 'take the form of a humanist historicist mode with a universalising populist tendency and, surprisingly, fit quite closely Brecht's description of the operation of bourgeois theatre' (King, 1981, p. 12).

It seems to me that such criticisms (even after we leave aside the impossibility of ever getting completely to the left of some commentators) inevitably arise because the films are within the Griersonian tradition sufficiently to be read and criticised as such. (*Rosie the Riveter* actually won the John Grierson award at the American Film Festival in 1981.) The film-makers, I would add, had no option but to work within this tradition because it was the only one deemed acceptable to their sponsors and their intended audiences. But the dangers of this strategy were well understood.

In 1975, Eileen McGarry noted how direct cinema tended to perpetuate female stereotypes and, although others (notably Julia Lesage) suggested that the documentary form itself could be subverted, attempts began instead to break down the boundaries between documentary, fiction and experimental film (McGarry, 1975, pp. 50ff.; Lesage, 1978, pp. 507ff.; Erens, 1988, p. 561).

For instance, as Patricia Erens notes (1981, p. 7), 'Self-image and photographic image are important themes in women's documentaries' often giving them a reflexivity not necessarily expressed in a cinéma vérité mode. Michelle Citron's *Daughter Rite* (1979) is a good example. It mixed childhood home movies with a conversation shot in a direct cinema style, but which was in fact enacted. The film's reception would have been much less vexed were Griersonian dominance removed.

In looking beyond Grierson, there is another point to be made. This book has been almost entirely limited to the documentary of the English-speaking world. I am, therefore, as guilty as Jacobs, Barsam and Barnouw, who stand rightly accused, by Julianne Burton, of marginalising other work and traditions, such as those of Latin America (Burton, 1990, pp. 7ff.). It could well be the case that the documentary, differently conceived, differently inflected and, above all, differently positioned politically could have a force that I believe it has never had in the countries on which I have been concentrating.

Burton (ibid., pp. 6ff.) makes such an argument for Latin American documentary:

Documentary provides: a source of 'counterinformation' for those without access to the hegemonic structures of world news and communications; a means of reconstructing historical events and challenging hegemonic and often elitist interpretations of the past; a mode of eliciting, preserving, and utilising the testimony of individuals and groups who would otherwise have no means of recording their experience; an instrument for capturing cultural difference and exploring the complex relationship of self to other within as well as between societies; and, finally, a means of consolidating cultural identification, social cleavages, political belief systems, and ideological agendas.

I note how many of these functions are alien to the Griersonian tradition and how in the homelands of the realist documentary either they are thus delegitimated or, as I have just been suggesting, they constitute a terrain of struggle for oppositional documentary practice. Burton understands this when she writes (ibid., p. 7): 'These functions go far beyond conventional conceptions of documentary as an educational medium.'

Indeed, all the circumstances of documentary in these countries can be very different. It is, for instance, one thing for a direct cinema film-maker in America to claim, on no ground whatsoever, that the audience has a new relationship to the screen when viewing his work; it is quite another for Fernando Solanas and Octavio Getino to make a similar claim for members of their audience. 'This person was no longer a spectator' if he or she chose to attend a screening of *La Hora de los fornos* (*Hour of the Furnaces*, 1968). This was true if only because such attendance was illegal and subject to extreme repression (Solanas and Getino, 1976, p. 61). That is scarcely the situation of a person choosing to watch a direct cinema movie transmitted on an American public television station.

For another thing, it could well be that such political situations, or even slightly less extreme variations on them, allow for

certain cases ... where the here-and-now of the shooting became not a naive assertion of [direct cinema] techniques as an unmediated explanation of the world and its deep logic, but a piece of 'authentication' inserted into a broader rhetoric that sustains its force on the legitimate referential weight of what is presented on the screen. (Xavier, 1990, p. 363)

Again, it is hard to imagine how such a film-making opportunity could occur in cultures where the Griersonian writ still runs; or even, should it be removed, where it so recently ran.

Nevertheless, in arguing for change, it is clear that the post-Griersonian documentary ought to be open and receptive to such different traditions as a source of inspiration and reinvigoration. So, despite my having come so late and so cursorily to them, these alternatives to our conventions are another major source of enrichment.

In all of this I have allowed Grierson's concept of creativity to keep its place; but I have already indicated that, under the influence of cinéma vérité, there have been moves to renegotiate the function of the documentarist away from the model of the Griersonian artist. In a sense this is the ultimate commitment for the post-Griersonian documentarist, to transform oneself from creator into facilitator.

This is critical to the most crucial reform needed, namely that documentary should get beyond the Griersonian obsession with the victim. One easy way of effecting this for the film-maker is to become just such a facilitator.

Thus far this has involved following the line of those advocacy films and tapes discussed above as being made under the influence of cinéma vérité. The attempts – from *Challenge for Change* in Canada, to the access movement in the States, to *Two Laws* in Australia – which give the victims of the Griersonian tradition the camera obviously transform them. Advocacy *by* the subject means the end of the documentarist as artist but, perhaps just as significantly, it also means an end of the victim *as* subject – a necessary development if the ethical mess is to be cleared up.

This, finally, is the most important point. Advocacy ensures that the film-maker respects the rights, needs and aspirations of the people being filmed. I would want to argue that such respect is crucial to the post-Griersonian documentary in general. It certainly must not be limited to advocacy films alone.

For the post-Griersonian documentarist working in any mode, abandoning the all-powerful position of the artist is a necessary prerequisite for ethical filming. Once the film-maker is liberated from implications of actuality and creativity, then ethical behaviour becomes even more crucial than it was previously. Free of the need to be objective and with the amorality of the creative artist cast aside, there is no reason why such a documentarist could not put the relationship with participants on the pedestal where once these other concepts were enshrined.

To hide behind science or aesthetics is not just illogical, it is unethical. The documentary needs to break free. In this way, breaking the Griersonian claim on the real brings in train a liberation from the restrictions of creativity, as the tradition conceived of it, and from the dangerous illusionism of actuality. The post-Griersonian documentary should be as various in its forms as is the fiction cinema. The post-Griersonian documentarist should be constrained only by the needs of the relationship of film-maker and participant.

38

The Innocent Arrogance of Objective Fact

At a time when anti-realist intellectual forces are being counter-attacked and British prime-time documentary and American fact-based programming are enjoying something of a vogue, it is perhaps odd to be demanding that the entire documentary enterprise be rethought. Nevertheless, rethought it must be if it is long to survive the coming of the digital image.

Unlike the challenge posed by postmodernism, the challenge of digitalisation cannot be resisted. Digitalisation destroys the photographic image as evidence of anything except the process of digitalisation. The physicality of the plastic material represented in any photographic image can no longer be guaranteed. For documentary to survive the widespread diffusion of such technology depends on removing its claim on the real. There is no alternative.

As I indicated at the outset of this book, the impact of digitalisation over the course of the next half-century is likely to be profound. That is why it is not, in my view, too soon to move the basis of documentary difference from representation (where nothing can be guaranteed) to reception (where nothing need be guaranteed).

Of course digital uncertainty will certainly affect the changed approaches I am proposing as a necessary condition of the documentary's further development, but that is the best we can do. My point is that, in such a technological situation, Grierson's original strong claim on actuality will stand no chance at all. As it collapses, it will bring down the entire documentary edifice. The only hope is for documentary to shift to a new site where, paradoxically, because less is claimed, more might be sustained.

In all this one thing only is certain – the edifice of 'creative', 'treatment' and 'actuality' which Grierson built is going to collapse, bulldozed by a force more thorough than any dreamed of by any postmodernist. Claiming the real in the old sense is rapidly becoming untenable.

ENVOI

Esfir Shub in 1927:

The whole problem is what we must film now. As soon as that is clear to us, then the terminology won't matter – fiction or non-fiction. (Tretyakov *et al.*, 1971, p. 34)

Notes

Part One
The Creative Treatment of Actuality

1 Such competitions, all based on manipulating news photographs, were becoming an established tabloid feature. For instance, *The News of the World* was running a non-royal series from 1992.

2 I regret very much that my 1978 article was being reprinted by Rosenthal (1988, p. 21) as I was discovering how wrong was my opening phrase there: 'It all begins with this, "Moana ... has documentary value".' Another regret about this piece is noted on p. 264.

3 Boleslaw Matuszewski was born in Pinczow, Poland, in 1856. He worked in St Petersburg as a cinematographer, possibly with the Lumière operation there, covering political events.

   Daniel Kazimierski has speculated (private correspondence) that one such occasion might have given Matuszewski the idea of film as documentary evidence. In January 1898, the President of France visited Russia and Bismarck protested that the Frenchman had failed to salute a march past in his honour. Matuszewski's 'living pictures' of the event proved otherwise. An 'incident' was averted!

   Une Nouvelle Source de l'histoire, subtitled 'Création d'un dépôt de cinématographie historique', was published the same year. In it Matuszewski calls for a 'cinematic museum or depository [for materials] of documentary interest' (Barnouw, 1974, p. 26), making him the father of film archives, a fact acknowledged in 1955 by FIAF (the International Federation of Film Archives). The pamphlet was followed up by *La Photographie animée*, cited in the text.

   In this second document, he spoke of the reactions of audiences to 'what other nations, lands, ceremonies, folk law and big national rallies look like'. He locates the specific importance of the cinema in its ability to capture 'scenes from life'. Subsequently in his career he filmed surgical operations. Two issues of *Cultures* (Paris, UNESCO, vol. 2 no. 7, 1974, and vol. 6 no. 7, 1979) have further materials on him. I am grateful to Kazimirski for expanding my knowledge of Matuszewski and providing the quotation given above.

4 Since the restoration also has one new shot, a number of questions as to its efficacy must be raised. It seems to me that adding shots is an obviously absurd thing to do. Adding an anthropologically accurate soundtrack, while of interest to anthropologists no doubt, is equally unfortunate from the cinematic point of view.

5 Williams also warned against the ideological partialities of the *OED*. I use it here, then, with this caution in mind.

6 Wright was not alone in remembering Grierson's remarks so clearly. The Griersonians all disparaged the word 'documentary' and cited the 'creative treatment of actuality' as the standard definition (Hogenkamp, 1989, p. 18 fn.).

263

7   'Travelogues' as a term in English relating to the cinema was coined by Burton
     Holmes in 1908 (Barsam, 1988, p. 15). Hogenkamp (1989, p. 18) reports that
     'documentaire' was a term of art in the Dutch film trade for any non-fictional
     film by 1920.

8   In the 1979 abridged edition of *Grierson on Documentary*, Forsyth Hardy
     announced that the abridgment concerned only some film reviews which he then
     hoped would find their way into another volume, which they have – Grierson,
     1981. However, there are considerable differences between the 1979 abridgment
     and earlier editions (1946, 1966). Many pieces have been omitted which were
     not film reviews, namely 'The Creative Use of Sound', 'Films and the
     Community', 'A Scottish Experiment', 'Metropolitan', 'Films and the ILO',
     'Edinburgh and the Documentary Idea', 'The Malaise of Disillusionment' and
     'A Mind for the Future'.

        Hardy also rewrote his introduction since he was republishing the original
     material, largely biographical information about Grierson, in vastly expanded
     form in his full-scale biography (Hardy, 1979).

        The phrase 'creative treatment of actuality' then slips between these two
     stools of abridgment and biography. The phrase is attributed to Grierson in the
     introduction to the first edition of *Grierson on Documentary* without citation. It is
     similarly attributed to him by Rotha (1952, p. 70), again without citation.

Part Two
Creative: Documentary as Art

1   Watt made this observation in an interview in *Man of Aran: How the Myth Was
     Made*, George Stoney's 1977 documentary on the Flaherty film. Barsam (1973a,
     p. 143) argues that the basking shark sequence was not really dangerous because
     the fish fed on plankton. However, elsewhere (1988, p. 64) he admits that there
     was an element of danger. The point is that the real exploitation occurs in the
     two sequences I cite in the text, not in the shark hunt with its somnolent animals
     and its obviously faked close-up harpoon shots.

2   Ricky Leacock has stated (in private correspondence): 'When in 1975, some fifty
     years after the filming of *Moana*, Monica Flaherty and I visited the village where
     she, aged five, had learned to swim, we saw every single thing that you see in the
     film still taking place, including several young men who had been tattooed just as
     Moana was.'

3   There is another curious echo of nineteenth-century painterly practice in
     Grierson's insistence on location and its superiority over studio: 'We believe that
     the cinema's capacity for getting around, for observing and selecting from life
     itself, can be exploited in a new vital art form. The studio films largely ignore this
     possibility of opening up the screen on the real world' (Grierson, 1979a, p. 36).

        The painters had the same dislike of the studio, the same belief in the
     increased authenticity that comes from location work, whatever the subject.
     English Pre-Raphaelites also stressed the importance of location work. Ford
     Madox Brown's *The Last of England* was painted (he stated) 'for the most part in
     the open air on dull days, and, when the flesh was being painted, on cold days'
     (Nochlin, 1966, p. 94). Holman Hunt painted *The Light of the World* by night:
     'For my protection from the cold, as far as it could be found, I had a little sentry-
     box built of hurdles and I sat with my feet in a sack of straw' (Nochlin, 1966,
     p. 107).

        Grierson's comment (1979a, p. 64) surely covers these endeavours as well as
     his own: 'Where the artist is not pursuing entertainment but purpose ... the

technique is energized inevitably by the size and scope of the occasion. How much further it reaches and will reach than the studio leap-frog of impotent and self-conscious art!'

4   Nevertheless, Courbet's reputation by this time did cause the authorities to fear him. His presence in the Place Vendôme on 16 May when the column was demolished by the mob was used as an excuse for his arrest and prosecution (Foucart, 1977, p. 93). However, Clark states (1982a, p. 49) that 'Courbet was never more *quarante-huitard* than when he explained his own dazed abstention from the revolution'. Julian Barnes has written (1992, p. 3): 'For all his Proudhonism and anti-establishment beliefs, his genuine desire to cleanse the mucky stables of French art, there was more than a touch of Yevtushenkoism about him, of the approved rebel calculating how far he can go, and knowing how to turn outrage to his own advantage.'

Thus, although the realists were on both sides of the barricades in 1848 (and on the fence), I feel justified in suggesting Courbet as the model for Grierson (about whom Barnes's words could equally well apply). After all, Courbet did boast, 'In '48 there were only two men ready: me and Proudhon' (Clark, 1982a, p. 47).

5   The soundtrack was added as part of the deal Grierson secured for the theatrical release of 'The Imperial Six' of which *Industrial Britain* was a part. Hardy suggests that Grierson was forced to accept Calthrop because the EMB had no sound equipment of its own and the distributor supplied the voice with the mixing studio. The script, however, is unmistakably from Grierson's hand.

6   This same year, 1935, the British Commercial Gas Association also bought itself a film called *The Romance of a Lump of Coal*.

7   Pronay is to be much complimented on the fact that he is one of the very few to have worked with Grierson and remained 'unenchanted'.

8   There were two jobs in the yard for sister ships, one slightly more advanced than the other. Rotha was able to reduce the time he spent in Barrow by shooting both, 'because in the final film you couldn't tell the difference between the two ships' (Orbanz, 1977, p. 27; Rotha, 1973, p. 100).

9   One can mount much the same argument about a supposed move to a greater degree of whimsy under Cavalcanti. Len Lye was hired by Grierson in 1935 and in the following year it was Grierson who discovered Norman McLaren. McLaren arrived in January of 1937 (see also p. 91). So Cavalcanti was simply continuing a policy of Grierson's when he in turn hired Lotte Reiniger and Richard Massingham. Whimsy, therefore, scarcely increases and was anyway present so early – *Pett and Pott* dates from 1934 – as to be an integral part of the movement. It was the part that had unabashedly to do with selling the GPO's services.

10   In another incident Caroline Lejeune attacked 'The Documentary Fetish' in the pages of *The Observer*, calling Grierson 'a dangerous influence'. This celebrated and well argued change of mind about the documentary film movement was quite disgracefully and sexistly attributed by Grierson to Lejeune's personal animosity (he said it was because he had fired her husband) (Hardy, 1979, p. 68).

11   In the light of all this, it is more than a little unfair that Grierson, while head of the National Film Board of Canada – to which he went after leaving the GPO – should become involved in a red scare spy case in 1946 which rocked the Canadian government. He was implicated via his secretary but, needless to say, he was totally uninvolved, as was she (Beveridge, 1978, pp. 198ff.). On cross-examination during these proceedings, he announced that he would be delighted to answer the classic cold war question, 'Are you a communist or a

[*sic*] communistically inclined?': 'I have been a public servant now for a matter of 18 years. I was trained in the classical Whitehall School. ... Now, that meant in the Whitehall sense that you have no party affiliations' (Evans, 1984, p. 252).

Despite Grierson's exoneration, hostile Canadian politicians used the incident to bolster their attacks on the Film Board and Grierson left the country under something of a cloud. Wright suggests (1950, p. 43) that the commercial film lobby wanted to break the NFB's 'dangerous monopoly', and encouraged the political attack. Grierson's US visitor's visa was also not renewed. It was not restored until 1962.

12   Anthony Aldgate and Jeffrey Richards point out that the civil servant responsible at the outset was a Tory party professional publicist, Sir Joseph Ball, who had carefully cultivated the newsreels in the pre-war period. They also suggest that the documentarists would be against him politically. Yet the movement had always easily embraced reactionary sponsors. Swann's analysis of Grierson's poor performance as a civil service team-player could be factored in here as an element explaining Whitehall's hostility, although Grierson himself was out of the picture and, under Cavalcanti, the unit itself had settled down. I would argue that the most important consideration for the MoI was not the documentary movement's perceived radicalism but the realities of the unpopularity of documentary film with the audience. This would be sufficient to account for the MoI's initial position of support for the newsreels without these other considerations coming much into play.

13   There are other estimates. The films made by the gas industry alone, it was claimed in 1938, had been seen that year by a million people. At a conference of librarians in 1939, one of Grierson's associates claimed 10 million annual audience (Swann, 1989, pp. 103 and 16). By 1943, Grierson himself was claiming an audience 'of progressive millions' outside the cinema. Two years later he was to fix this number at 6 million, all involved in a 'highly specialized and highly scientific circulation system' outside the cinema. The following year, 1946, Grierson asserted: 'It is a common observation that there is more seating capacity outside the theatres than there is inside the theatres.' The audience in these non-theatrical settings had reached 27 million by this time, he wrote in this piece; or, perhaps, as he claimed in 1949, only 20 million. Whatever the size, Grierson felt in 1949 that 'We should aim at 50 millions in the next three years' (Grierson, 1979a, pp. 152, 170, 185 and 201).

14   William Alexander suggested that Hurwitz, Steiner and Strand (and some others who joined them in left film-making activities) did not have the 'native, instinctual inheritance' of Pare Lorentz or Willard Van Dyke since they were Jews and the sons of immigrants 'who had chosen exile from their native lands' (Alexander, 1975, p. 27; 1981, p. 207). The political and anti-Semitic stereotyping of this assertion (leftists descending from those 'who had *chosen* exile') is unfortunate – not least because Hurwitz and Steiner both attended Ivy League universities and Strand, whose father had his own business, was able to travel widely, including trips to Europe before the First World War.

Alexander seems to be reflecting an attitude floating around Lorentz's productions. There is, perhaps, a further echo of it in Campbell's mind when he also references (1978, p. 238) the fact that these film-makers 'were, for the most part, first generation American'. In the Van Dyke letter quoted in my text, Van Dyke remembers Lorentz as reporting that he, Lorentz, had told his wife he had found in Van Dyke 'a young *gentile*, a youngster who wanted to work' (Van Dyke, 1965, p. 45 – my italics). Alexander acknowledges this remark to be 'sinister' (Alexander, 1981, p. 136). It is – as is his quoted above.

15 She denied this to a tribunal in 1947. And as late as 1971 she is still denying that she ever received official recognition from the Nazis (Hitchens, 1973, pp. 99ff.). She did so again during a promotional tour for the English translation of her autobiography in October 1992.

16 Riefenstahl was in Spain engaged in preproduction work on her feature film *Tiefland*. Principal photography on this was not begun until 1941 and the film was shelved in the following year. It was completed after her de-Nazification was finalised and she was allowed to work again. *Tiefland* was finally released in 1954. For it, she used 60 Romany extras whom she cast in 1941 and 1942 at a small holding concentration camp, the Maxglan Lager, near Salzburg. After being used without pay in the film, the Romanies were returned to the camp system and all but two families were exterminated. Nina Gladitz located these survivors for her documentary *Time of Darkness and Silence*. Riefenstahl's response to this vivid evidence of her complicity in the Holocaust was to take Gladitz to court. Gladitz's accusations were upheld in 1987 (Reutschler, 1989, p. 48, fn. 2). This same article contains further evidence of her complicity at p. 66.

17 'Workers' was rapidly dropped from the leagues' titles in both countries (Hogenkamp, 1986, pp. 105ff.; Alexander, 1981, pp. 4ff. and 65ff.). The numbers and names of the organisations involved in production and distribution proliferated. Macpherson (1980, p. 212) lists over thirty in the UK alone.

   The complex institutional history of these activities in various countries – UK, USA and beyond; the relationship of such activities to the work of Comintern (in general) and Willi Muenzenberg's WIR organisation (based in the USSR and Weimar Germany until 1933) in particular; and the exacerbating problems of political and personal differences among the film-makers can be found in Alexander, Buchsbaum, Campbell, Hogenkamp, Jones, Macpherson, Murray and Wegg-Prosser.

18 I should add that Hemingway is no help to the film. 'This is the true face of men going into action. It is a little different from any other face you will ever see,' he says over shots of soldiers who are clearly doing no such thing and exhibiting no such emotions. Ivens's dramatic footage of the civilian dead in Madrid and his coverage of an air raid do not need this hyperbole.

   On the other hand, in the short stories *Night Before Battle* and *Under the Ridge* Hemingway used the filming experience as an effective framing device, in the process illuminating the making of the film: 'Our heaviest attacks were made in the afternoon, God knows why, as the fascists then had the sun at their backs, and it shone on the camera lenses and made them blink like a helio and the Moors would open up on the flash' (Hemingway, 1987, p. 437). Ivens did not make much impression on him, though. He is just 'the tall one'.

19 Ralph Bond's Workers Film Society was a response to these high fees. It should be noted that the authorities allowed the LFS audience to view *Potemkin* while prohibiting screenings by societies, like Bond's, which charged less for admission (Macpherson, 1980, pp. 108ff.).

20 For instance, Aitken claims (1990, p. 181) on the authority of Ralph Bond that Grierson 'launched' the London Workers' Film Society with him. Although Bond names Grierson as one of a group responsible for this, Grierson's role in either the founding or continuing activities of the Workers' Film Society was not sufficiently significant in his life for it to figure in his biography (Bond, 1979, p. 247).

21 Rotha too might have joined himself and his people to the ACT, he claimed in the 1980s, but he disliked its 'politics' (Marris, 1982, p. 18). In this he sounds just like every other anti-union film producer the ACTT encountered.

22   To read the reality of this relationship through the eyes of Ralph Bond, in my experience an unfailingly courteous and good-natured man, is to run the risk of erasing real differences from the record.

23   Bevan made these remarks in 1948. A decade had passed and the texture of the Depression was already becoming a thing of memory. A half-century on, the texture is even more threadbare. Revisionist efforts are underway to rewrite the whole history of the decade as one where rising material well-being rendered these social tensions moot (Jones, 1987, pp. 5ff.).

Part Three
Treatment: Documentary as Drama

1   These counts refer to a Films Incorporated print of the 1976 restoration (by David Shepard) with a specially composed soundtrack for modern classical sextet added (see Ruby's note in Rotha, 1983, p. 29). A fuller history of the various versions of *Nanook*, including a description by Shepard of his work, can be found in Steve Dobi, 1977, pp. 7ff.

2   In the endless debate about Flaherty's 'reconstruction' of a romanticised Inuit past, this essentially improbable plot point – celebrating the arrival of the Arctic winter by taking a trip – is overlooked. Formulated in this way, the plot of *Nanook* seems somewhat unlikely, but this is indeed what Flaherty explicitly tells us is happening. In its way, though, the taking of the trip is no more unlikely than the fact that the Arctic winter does not apparently alter the light conditions. Winter comes but not the Arctic dark – for obvious reasons. Of course, substituting another title for 'Winter Comes' would solve these problems.

3   Today most of the species of non-fiction film recognised by Grierson, by industrial practice or by scholars are conflated and subsumed under an extended non-fiction genre – 'documentary'.

4   Grierson grudgingly admits to Sussex that Jennings was a minor poet (Sussex, 1975, p. 110). The documentary movement really did not like Jennings. Grierson became characteristically opaque when commenting on him: 'Jennings was a very stilted person. ... He hasn't got this inner feeling for movement that Basil Wright has. ... The word is that he didn't have a sense of smell' (Sussex, 1975, p. 110). Whatever this might mean, one thing is certain: Jennings really was a published poet, albeit posthumously. It can be added that Jennings reciprocated the animosity. In a letter he could refer to 'Rotha and other of Grierson's little boys' (Jennings, M.-L., 1982, p. 27).

5   Riefenstahl's skill as an editor is much praised by her admirers and there is no sense in this reception of her that she is being canonised because of her avantgarde contempt for normative practices. On the contrary, it is exactly her supposed talent as a mainstream editor which is being praised. Yet in this film, despite multiple cameras covering each event. Riefenstahl breaks every editing rule. She hacks pan to pan, she reverses action (crosses the line), she jump-cuts synch action. Much of this also applies to *Olympia* (1938), except in the diving sequence, where all these 'mistakes' are turned to advantage. But this one exception does not mean that her reputation as an editor is deserved.

6   The film Dudley Andrew is discussing is Babert Schroeder's biographical documentary *General Idi Amin Dada* (1975). Andrew suggests that Schroeder was 'under little compunction to achieve formal closure' because it was not only a documentary but also a biography of a living subject. But first-person narratives, eyewitness accounts (which begin in the European tradition with Odysseus's story – significantly – of his journey, told to the Phaeacians), always had this problem.

268

Such personal stories, which came to include both Dante's *Commedia* and Cellini's *Vita*, nevertheless become 'the natural form of the mimetic narrative' (Scholes and Kellogg, 1966, pp. 73 and 250). As such, they are certainly capable of achieving formal closure; so much so that even the *in medias res* last words of Cellini ('da poi me n'andai a Pisa') work as a Barthesian 'final stroke' (Barthes, 1990, p. 188). I cite this observation of Andrew's as an example of how, *en passant*, documentary narrative difference is (almost) taken as read by film scholars.

7   To take a random example: In *Oh What a Morning* (1992), produced by Russell Lyne for HTV, the Aberfan disaster (in which a coalmine tip slid to engulf a Welsh village school) was remembered on its twenty-fifth anniversary by survivors (teachers and pupils), rescuers and others in the community. The film is framed by a villager recalling the disaster, standing above the valley. This colour shot cross-fades into the same camera position in black and white filmed on the day of the disaster. The result is a subjective flashback. Much the same effect can be seen in most oral history films. Stephen Peet's long-running BBC series *Yesterday's Witness* (1969–80) was particularly adept at using archive footage in order to illustrate specific memories.

8   The films Vaughan discusses are Georges Franju's *Hôtel des Invalides* (1952) and Adrian Cowell's *The Tribe that Hides from Man* (1970). Specifically in *Hôtel* Vaughan queries the documentary status of a sequence in which a young woman in the museum looks through a periscope of the sort used in First World War trenches to see playing, magically, First World War archive footage taken through such a device. The second film deals with a failed expedition to find an Amazonian tribe. The story is told in flashbacks, some of which involve re-enactments. Neither of these cases invalidates my examples and neither is a warrant, in my view, for Branigan's general statement about the impossibility of subjectivity in the documentary. This is another example of the assumption of documentary difference.

9   In general, Guynn offers an application of Metz's syntagmatic system to a variety of documentaries. This allows him to make an argument (1990, pp. 48ff.) as to how many narrative as opposed to non-narrative syntagmas are present in a variety of classic documentaries. The persuasiveness of this obviously depends on the degree to which one is persuaded in the first place by the efficacy of Metz's approach.

10 In my original analysis I suggested, on the basis of the different patterns of light behind the speakers, that more might have been reshot in Berlin (Winston, 1981, p. 105). Peter Nowotny has pointed out to me that the *Völkischer Beobachter* reported that speakers could signal the lighting engineer from the rostrum to alter the lighting. I am grateful to Dr Nowotny for this correction.

11 Also in Britain the post-war terrain was different; not so much 'feature versus documentary' but rather 'cinema versus television'. Rotha's brief sojourn as the head of the BBC television Documentary Department (1953–5) confirmed that in this new dichotomy the old documentarists were part of the cinema (Bell, 1986, p. 70). The original institutional scheme at the BBC was to make a tripartite division between a news service, a news feature production unit (known initially as Talks and subsequently as Current Affairs) and an independent Documentary Department. By 1955, Talks, with its magazine journalism culture, had absorbed Documentary. The subsequent protoplasmic movements and combinations of these units and others (including the re-emergence of a Documentary Department) accurately reflect the changing BBC perception of the status of audiovisual 'fact' within the culture as well as the more mundane power battles of the television executives involved.

269

Part Four
Actuality: Documentary as Science

1   Even before photography, this use of the *camera obscura* was being suggested:

> An occurrence originated in a Camera Obscura exhibited here during the Fair week [Glasgow, August 1824], which shows the important use to which this amusing optical apparatus may be applied. A person ... beheld [through the *camera*] the appearance of one man picking another man's pocket. Perfectly aware of the reality of this appearance, he opened the door, and recognising the culprit at a short distance, ran up and seized him. ... From this circumstance, the utility of placing such apparatus in all places of public amusement and exhibitions must be obvious. (Jennings, H., 1985, p. 164)

2   To say again, this entire argument is without prejudice to Aitken's insights as to the specialised philosophical understanding Grierson might have had of the term 'actuality'. However, I am assuming that such a restricted meaning would be of little significance in general. I am here trying to map what *in general* 'actuality' might have meant. My case is that the absorbed scientific *Umwelt* is a better clue to this reception than the rarefied discourse of neo-Kantian philosophy.

3   To take one example of the effects of this change: insurance had for centuries been akin to gambling despite the attempted application of statistics linking, for instance, life premiums to mortality bills in the 17th century. Nevertheless, life insurance, seen as a wager, was illegal in most European countries until the 19th century. Even in Britain, where life was insurable, in the 18th century the Privy Council held that attempting to reduce 'chance of mortality ... to a certain standard ... is mere speculation'. Within a century, because of probabilistics, this 'speculative' activity had become actuarial science (Daston, 1987, pp. 237ff.).

4   Barron seems to have been somewhat burned by this experience (and the trouble he had with his previous film *The Berkeley Rebels*, 1965) of trying to make the realist documentary live up to its promise in some way. Within two years he was complaining bitterly about network failure to produce engaged documentary films:

> I think that the reason is that we live in an uptight society. I think we are afraid of honest emotion ... at the networks, it's business as usual. They're working on next year's list of films at CBS: a film on the legal profession, on Japan, on the affluent Negro [*sic*], on tax exempt foundations and so on and so on. Happy viewing! (Barron, 1968, p. 23)

> His contribution to that year's (1968–9) happy viewing was a film about Johnny Cash and a three-parter on the great American novel. He then headed the film programme at his Alma Mater. Of course, today at CBS there is no longer any list of documentary production plans because there is no longer a proper schedule of documentary production.

5   Peirce classed photographs as indexical: 'Photographs ... were physically forced to correspond point by point to nature. In that aspect, then, they belong to the second class of signs [indexical], those by physical connection' (1965, p. 159). As a result of this technological naivety, a whole generation of contemporary scholars insists on following Peirce in describing the photographic image as indexical when in fact it is rather, in his own terms, iconic: 'Anything whatever, be it quality, existent individual, or law, is an Icon of anything, in so far as it is like that thing and used as a sign of it' (p. 143). This confusion can perhaps best be solved, for the time being at least, by using the term mimetic rather than either iconic or indexical to describe the realist image.

6   Elsewhere this film-maker, Frederick Wiseman, has spoken of his work in terms of natural history, specifically, 'spoor collection' (see Rosenthal, 1971, p. 70; and McWilliams, 1970, p. 22).

7   The jury has its origins in the need of a party at trial to augment the veracity of his or her oath with the oaths of others, compurgators, who would themselves swear as to the truth of the party's own oath. This was also a form of ordeal, albeit with the pain (in case of perjury) delayed until the afterlife (Harding, 1966, pp. 25ff.).

8   Despite its new-found current confidence in its evidential procedures, as Jonathan Cohen points out, the common law actually does not feel the need to back this up by using modern scientific or mathematical bases for testing probability in a systematic way. Cohen argues (1977, p. 51), somewhat controversially, that a non-mathematical inductive approach to probability, which he characterises as 'Baconian', is possible but allows that it is insufficiently developed for the law to use instead of the eschewed mathematics. Balancing probabilities and assuaging reasonable doubt remain, legally at least, very imprecise activities.

9   Not uncoincidentally, this is also the period when the shocking (to some) newspaper practice of paying correspondents, and thus turning them into 'journalists', was becoming commonplace (Baker, 1986, pp. 3ff.; Schudson, 1978, p. 24).

10 There was something corrupting about this development, something not quite proper, in the opinion of many, especially in Europe (Schudson, 1979, p. 2). Before interviews, newspapers were filled with accounts and opinions. Opinions in the form of editorials had crept in slowly, first as essays addressed to the editor, then (in at least one instance) in italicised columns and finally in their modern format in about 1800 (Mott, 1962, p. 102). Originally it was thought that the proper place for such personal expression was in pamphlets; but as the 18th century wore on, the pamphlet yielded pre-eminence as a platform to the paper. Editorials were the first element within the pages of a newspaper to be, as it were, generated by the newspaper itself rather than occasioned by reflexive response to outside events. Interviews were the next.

11 The breakthrough phase, as it were, was now over. For a fuller account of these developments see my *Necessities and Constraints* (London: BFI, 1995).

12 This approach is now becoming the norm in documentary film studies. See, for example, Ellis, 1989, pp. 223ff.

13 For a sense of the persistence and strength of this naive view of direct cinema's evidential claims, see Ali Issari and Paul's annotated direct cinema filmography published as late as 1979 (pp. 179ff.).

14 Richard Leacock, private communication. The tracking shot is often credited to Leacock (for example Rouch, 1975, p. 93).

15 I remember Dick Fontaine's enthusiasm when, while in the *World In Action* screening room watching rushes shot for him by the Maysles on model Jean Shrimpton's first trip to New York in the summer of 1964, I remarked that it seemed to me that she had 'cheered up a bit' in the course of the day's shooting. His point was that only direct cinema footage could have allowed me, as somebody not present during the filming, to make such a judgment. The incident sums up for me how naively we treated this material initially even within the industry. (I should add that it was Fontaine who had argued with Granada TV the previous February that the Maysles should be hired to cover the Beatles' first US trip. The footage was used in a *World In Action* ('Yeah, Yeah, Yeah') and subsequently shows up as a Maysles production, without any credit to Fontaine, *What's Happening?: The Beatles in the USA* (1964), the Maysles having negotiated US rights to the material in lieu of a fee.)

16   Al Maysles also worked for Godard but rather more happily. In January of 1965 he shot 'Montparnasse-Levallois', Godard's segment of *Paris vu par ...* (Taylor, C., 1971, p. 405).

17   This is reminiscent of the instructions in a current British police photography manual recovered by John Tagg: 'In producing photographs to court, the police photographer must state on oath the time, day and date he took the photographs' (Tagg, 1988, p. 97).

18   After the contemporary translations referred to, Vertov's writings again began to attract attention in the 1960s. Some pieces, translated by Brody, who had been active in New York radical film-making circles in the 1930s, were republished in *Film Culture* in 1962. Fragments also appeared in *Le Cinéma soviétique par ceux qui l'ont fait*. These were then further translated into English in 1973 as 'Kino-Eye: The Embattled Documentarist' (Schnitzer, Schnitzer and Martin, 1973, pp. 77ff.). By this time, there was not inconsiderable activity including 'The Vertov Papers' (Carynnyk, 1972, pp. 46ff.) and 'The Factory of Facts and Other Writings' (O'Brien, 1979, pp. 110ff.) as well as extensive writings on Vertov. The process culminates in 1984 with Michelson's editing of Kevin O'Brien's translation of a Russian collection (done by Sergei Drobashanko and published in Moscow twenty-four years previously).

        By comparison, Shub's work has been neglected. Not only are her films difficult to obtain and untaught; the documentary literature, except as noted and in Barnouw (1974, pp. 66ff.) and as one of the LEF quartet translated in Jacobs (1971, pp. 34ff.), still tends to ignore her as much as Rotha did. For instance, she does not appear in *Cinema in Revolution* (Schnitzer, Schnitzer and Martin, 1973). She rates but a sentence in Barsam (1973a, p. 24).

        Two more points: Shub came to documentary with a new vision of the role of the film-maker. In the opening titles of (and on the posters for) *The Fall* she took only the modest credit 'Work by E. I. Shub' (Leyda, 1964, p. 25).

        And finally, a counter to this story of neglect in the West: it should be noted that in the USSR Shub had a long career with the Soviet newsreels, eventually becoming chief editor of *Novosti Dyna* (News of the Day). She wrote two books and figures apparently appropriately in Soviet film literature (Petric, 1984, p. 31).

        Vertov also worked on *Novosti Dyna* for the last decade of his life but this, and the comparatively regular additions to his documentary *œuvre* in the 1930s, mask the fact that already with *Three Songs of Lenin* (1934) the experimental fire was being extinguished by the Stalinised film industry. (But not quite, since *Three Songs* contains, *inter alia*, synch interviews with workers a year before *Housing Problems*.) Michelson (1984, p. lxi) sums the career up thus:

> We may easily sense Vertov's claim, as the revolutionary founder of a cinema that offered the Communist Decoding of the World, to the title of the Lenin of Cinema. Everything – and most of all, his sustained commitment to the construction of socialism in one country – conspired to prevent him from acknowledging that he had instead become cinema's Trotsky.

        Vertov died in 1954, Shub in 1959.

19   *Titicut Follies* was shot on Marshall's equipment. On the day when he heard about the first injunction being obtained against the film, Marshall and his wife Heather resigned from the production company. Timothy Asch was also briefly involved in the filming (Anderson and Benson, 1991, pp. 19, 62 and 20).

20   It would be wrong to suggest, though, that anthropology as a field was well up with technical developments on the documentary side. For instance, an extensive

survey article on 'Visual and Sound Recording Apparatus in Ethnographic Fieldwork' published in 1970 reduces a decade of massive technological development to a footnote:

> Several light but very expensive 16mm single-system sound cameras have recently been manufactured for television film production. They would be ideal for use in the field. (Polunin, 1970, p. 11)

Single system (Bach-Auricon) by this date was no longer the industry standard and had not been for at least five years.

21   One use of the Boas footage was to inform the creation of 'very innovative diorama' for the Museum of Natural History in New York. Jay Ruby points out that this process, whereby the museum's artists took the footage as a template for making figurines, turned Boas's images, in which the Native Americans wear their everyday (Westernised) dress, into a vision of pre-contact Kwakiutl life. Thus, at least as far as the public presentation in the museum of this aspect of his research was concerned, the museum put native peoples back into their own supposed pasts just as much as Curtis and Flaherty did.

22   On the other hand, Roger Sandall reported that at least one tribal person, an Australian Aboriginal, liked the kinship chart in *The Ax Fight* particularly. 'In that chart he recognized his own world' (Sandall, 1978, p. 220).

23   Sam Yazzie was about eighty years old and suffering from chronic tuberculosis. He had no sheep at the time. It is, I acknowledge, a crude thought but finding out if the Navajo would make Navajo-ish movies seems to me to be a fairly irrelevant if not vexatious activity, given the economic and political situation of the Navajo nation.

24   However, as with *Primary*, it is as well not to get too carried away in the presence of the new technology. Brault did not use the proto-Eclair all the time. There are production stills of him with a standard Arri St (Feld and Ewing, 1985, p. 54).

25   In 'I Think We Are in Trouble' (Winston, 1978) I used the last subtitle of a version which mistranslates 'Nous sommes dans le bain' in this way. This is the second error I wish to correct in connection with this piece (see p. 253).

26   I should perhaps point out that, despite the presence of anthropologists on *Disappearing World*, other anthropologists remained dismissive: 'As television documentaries', wrote Timothy Asch (1988, p. 17), 'these films were of high standard, but I know of no case in which they had value for research, and their use in teaching anthropology was limited.' Certainly, even without crewing difficulties, Granada could not afford to let people stay on location for the length of time that might be more usual in anthropology. On the other hand, Asch's comment has a self-fulfilling quality about it.

27   Again, the challenge for change was a little too strong and, within a decade, the work of the Alternate Media Centre was redirected to the safer tasks of telecommunication policy analysis and corporate communications training in new technologies. Stoney was ousted from its leadership.

28   All this is in marked contrast to Barbara Kopple's Oscar-winning documentary about the same strike, *Harlan County, USA* (1976). This is a well intentioned but romantic film which, lacking serious analysis, nearly managed to run from all social meaning in the approved Griersonian fashion. As a sympathetic critic put it, '*Harlan County, USA*'s strength is not in its analysis but in its passion' (Biskind, 1977, p. 4). It was saved from the usual irrelevance only by the naked and unrepentant violence of the coalfield managers towards the strikers and the film-makers. Being shot at and threatened at gunpoint gave the film one of its most dramatic reflexive moments (Rosenthal, 1980, pp. 306ff.). There can be no

question of the reality of the danger Kopple and her crew faced. At least one film-maker has been killed by a local resident in Appalachia in circumstances far less tense than these (see p. 230). So this sequence also speaks to Kopple's considerable personal commitment to the miners' struggle, from which this critique is not intended to detract. (As has been said: 'Any critical reading of *Harlan County, USA* falls silent in the face of authorial good intention' (King, 1981, p. 7).) Kopple, who had worked with the Maysles on *Salesman*, won another Academy Award in 1991 for *American Dream* (1990), about another bitter labour dispute, this time at the Hormel meat-packing plant in Austin, Minnesota.

29   By the 1980s, the 'me' thing had penetrated American society so deeply that film-makers could revisit *David Holzman's Diary*, specifically his preference for filming over fornication, for real (as it were) in Ross McElwee's documentary *Sherman's March* (1986); or as melodrama in the feature film *Sex, Lies and Videotape* (1989).

McElwee had been a student of Pincus's and he had also studied with Leacock and shot material on the !K'ung for Marshall (MacDonald, S., 1988, pp. 14 and 16).

30   Nichols claims none, but Vlada Petric's study *Man with a Movie Camera* was published in 1987. This notwithstanding, his point is otherwise well taken, at least as regards North America.

But such a silence is less evident in Great Britain. Here, in the 1980s, Roger Silverstone published his study of BBC documentary production methods (1985), Bert Hogenkamp the summary of his pioneering work recovering the history of left film-making in the UK (1986), and (as I have already mentioned) Dai Vaughan his undeservedly underrated book on the film editor Stewart McAllister (1983). (Vaughan's is, in my view, not only the best book available about the nature of collaboration in film-making, it is also the most succinct de facto rebuttal of the auteurist fallacy I know.) The 1990s have thus far seen Aitken's evaluation of Grierson (1990) and Peter Loizos's 1993 survey of the ethnographic film between 1955 and 1985.

I should also note that in the last few years there has been a change in the United States, too. Since Ellis broke the silence in 1989, not only has Nichols's work appeared but dissertations by Swann (1989) and Guynn (1990) have also been published.

31   It is possible that these same critics were not so absurdly naive as this suggests but were simply trying to blunt the withering attack on Reaganite capitalist enterprise which *Roger and Me* mounts. On the other hand, conservative students at the university where I was then working genuinely felt that chronological manipulation vitiated the film's truth claims and made it 'not a documentary'. Carl Platinga (1990) has documented how widespread this reading was.

32   Wiseman's cameramen, Richard Leiterman (*High School*, 1968) and Bill Brayne (from *Law and Order*, 1969, to *Sinai Field Mission*, 1977) were part of the same loose group as Graef's collaborators, notably his cameraperson Charles Stewart. They were all freelancing in and around Allan King's London operation, AKA (Bateman, 1986, pp. 7ff.).

33   It is just as likely that the police officers concerned were doing no such thing. Indeed, the most obnoxious of the three detectives involved kept dismissing the woman's fears of reprisal from her attackers with the phrase 'This is not *Starsky and Hutch*'. I thought his manner, and the manner of all the 'modern' officers in *Police*, was very much *Starsky and Hutch*.

34   For *Hometown* (1982), his book, Davis legitimated his choice of Hamilton, Ohio, as location for his study of an absolutely typical Midwestern town by reporting

that an official of the Census Bureau directed him to it. Nevertheless, the tale he told of life there is far from average. Hamilton, as Davis reported it, had much of David Lynch about it – certainly enough illicit sex and violence to justify a trade book.

35   The literature on documentary film ethics is minimal. Aside from Pryluck, see Blumberg, 1977, Sobchack, 1984, and Gross, Katz and Ruby, 1988.

36   Vincent Porter quite correctly points out that Edelman does not understand all the nuances of the common law tradition, specifically the distinction between underlying idea and expressive form. Gaines supports this criticism (Porter, 1979, pp. 144–5; Gaines, 1992, p. 266). However, I do not think this detracts from Edelman's importance, if only because a number of the issues with which he deals are increasingly pertinent to the common law. The idea of the law being 'surprised' by new technology is not unknown to the Anglo-Saxon tradition. Apart from celebrity rights there are other examples. For instance, US Supreme Court cases in the 1970s refused to allow that algorithms were patentable because they were too close to basic principles and concepts. It took legislation to correct this and create the necessary property rights (Nichols, 1988, pp. 39ff.). Second, there are certain basic continental legal ideas of the sort with which Edelman deals, such as an artistic moral right in ownership, which are being incorporated into the common law (Porter, 1978, p. 99; Docherty, 1988, pp. 156ff.).

37   Aesthetic as well as technical trends also favoured the victim as subject. It is received opinion that television demands close-ups but it is no part of profession-alisation, in my experience, to stress any such thing. The industry tends to avoid the big scene because of the expense such shots involve as much as because they are considered unreadable by the audience, which, palpably, they are not. A number of other factors lead to the close-up. One is the fact that, against light backgrounds, receiver tubes (for at least twenty years after the war) tended to over-modulate and reduce all darker areas to silhouette. By moving into the face this could be avoided. Another is that the very small eyepieces of 16mm reflex cameras (and, latterly, lightweight video equipment) again encourage the close-up as being more easily focused than longer shots. The prevalence of the 10:1 zoom lens, which can only be properly focused at the long (that is, close-up) end of its range, has the same effect. Without prejudice to other cultural consider-ations, all these technological constraints favour the close-up, which emerges as the dominant shot in the modern documentary.

38   *Madonna: Truth or Dare* (1991) is likely to become a classic text in this small subset, if only for the prayer meetings Madonna holds before each concert.

39   The station, presumably, thereby maintained its distance from the network so that its local fund-raising efforts would not be endangered.

40   None of this means that the acute limitations of that right should be forgotten. While all the Maysles' films about the powerless are freely available for hiring, the two films they made about powerful figures, Marlon Brando and Joe Levine, were not to be seen for years, because both were padlocked in their vaults by high-powered lawyers acting for the subjects concerned. Even without a right to publicity, the powerful could still control their images vis-à-vis the documentarist.

41   The filming did nothing for the seven young protagonists of the series. In a follow-up documentary Polly Bide for *Cutting Edge* discovered what one critic called 'a trail of human wreckage, pain and untimely death'. The programme, John Naughton said (1992, p. 48), 'left one numb with despair'.

42   These results were reported by Maxine Baker and Phil Sheffler, respectively, to Kirwan Cox of the NFBC. As part of its planning for the celebration of the

cinema's centennial in 1995, the NFBC commissioned him to produce a canon of documentary work, specifically, 'the ten documentaries that changed the world'. Some forty-eight film-makers and academics were interviewed, including the author. I am very much in debt to Kirwan Cox and Dennis Murphy, executive producer Documentary (Studio C) of the NFBC in Toronto, for permission to see and quote from Cox's report.

Part Five
Documentary in the Age of Digital Image Manipulation

1   A similar point can be made about bourgeois ways of seeing.
     That realism is a dominant characteristic of bourgeois art forms cannot be disputed – but that it is a characteristic of bourgeois art forms *only* can. For instance, as I have said, perspective has a longer history than does the bourgeoisie. There are references in Pliny to illusionist paintings and a fairly coherent tradition of such work can be discerned intermittently between the ancients and the Renaissance (Doesschate, 1964, p. 85). Not all such illusionism, therefore, occurs in the bourgeois period. The tendency to inscribe central perspective as a species of bourgeois invention with the visually imprisoned viewer as a type of exploited subject under capital is clearly, whatever else it might be, ahistorical.
2   This gloss, though, perhaps would not apply to Metz himself. He was reported as 'loving' *Harlan County, USA* (King, 1981, p. 7).

276

Bibliography

Adorno, Theodor, and Horkheimer, Max (1977), 'The Culture Industry: Enlightenment as Mass Deception' (abridged), in Curran, Gurevitch and Woolacott, q.v.

Advertisement (1955), 'Presenting Auricon Filmagnetic', *Journal of the SMPTE*, December.

Agee, James (1966), *Let Us Now Praise Famous Men* (New York: Ballentine).

Aitken, Ian (1990), *Film and Reform: John Grierson and the Documentary Film Movement* (London: Routledge).

Aldgate, Anthony (1979), *Cinema and History: British Newsreels and the Spanish Civil War* (London: Scolar).

Aldgate, Anthony, and Richards, Jeffrey (1986), *Britain Can Take It: The British Cinema in the Second World War* (Oxford: Blackwell).

Alexander, William (1975), 'Frontier Films, 1936–1941: The Aesthetics of Impact', *Cinema Journal*, Fall.

—— (1981), *Film on the Left: American Documentary Film from 1931 to 1942* (Princeton, NJ: Princeton University Press).

Ali Issari, M., and Paul, Doris (1979), *What Is Cinéma Vérité?* (Metuchen, NJ: Scarecrow Press).

Allen, Robert, and Gomery, Douglas (1985), *Film History: Theory and Practice* (New York: Knopf).

Alpers, Svetlana (1983), *The Art of Describing: Dutch Art in the Seventeenth Century* (Chicago: University of Chicago Press).

Anderson, Carolyn, and Benson, Thomas (1991), *Documentary Dilemmas: Frederick Wiseman's Titicut Follies* (Carbondale: Southern Illinois University Press).

Anderson, Lindsay (1954), 'Only Connect: Some Aspects of the Work of Humphrey Jennings', *Sight and Sound* vol. 23 no. 4, Spring (reprinted in Jennings, M.-L., 1982, q.v.).

Andrew, Dudley (1984), *Concepts in Film Theory* (New York, OUP).

Arlen, Michael (1980), 'The Air: Fred Wiseman's "Kino Prava"', *New Yorker*, 21 January.

Arnheim, Rudolph (1957), *Film As Art* (Berkeley: University of California Press [1933]).

Arts Council, The (1947), *The Factual Film* (London: PEP/Geoffrey Cumberlege at the OUP).

Asch, Timothy (1988), 'Collaboration in Ethnographic Filmmaking', in Rollwagen, q.v.

Atiyah, Patrick Selim (1989), *An Introduction to the Law of Contract* (Oxford: Clarendon Press).

Atkins, Thomas (1974), 'The Films of Frederick Wiseman: American Institutions', *Sight and Sound* vol. 43 no. 4, Autumn.

277

——— (ed.) (1976), *Frederick Wiseman* (New York: Monarch Press).

Atkinson, Paul (1990), *The Ethnographic Imagination: Textual Constructions of Reality* (London: Routledge).

Avis, Peter (ed.) (1983), *Action: Fifty Years in the Life of a Union* (London: ACTT).

Bach, Walter, Berndt, E. M., Brown, A. N., and George, R. L. (1956), 'Magnetic 16mm Single-System Sound-on-Film-Recording Camera Equipment', *Journal of the SMPTE*, November.

Bachmann, Gideon (1961), 'The Frontiers of Realist Cinema: The Work of Ricky Leacock', *Film Culture* vol. 19–23, Summer.

Baddeley, W. Hugh (1963), *The Technique of Documentary Film Production* (London: Focal Press).

Baker, Robert (1986), 'A Historical View of the Journalist', in D. Weaver and C. Cleveland (eds), *The American Journalist* (Bloomington: Indiana University Press).

Barendt, Eric (1989), *Freedom of Speech* (Oxford: Clarendon Press).

Barnes, Julian (1992), '"The Proudest and Most Arrogant Man in France"', *The New York Review of Books*, 22 October.

Barnouw, Erik (1974), *Documentary: A History of the Non-Fiction Film* (New York: OUP).

Barr, Charles (ed.) (1986), *All Our Yesterdays: Ninety Years of British Cinema* (London: BFI).

Barron, Arthur (1968), 'Towards New Goals in Documentary', *Film Librarians Quarterly* vol. 2 no. 1, Winter 1968–9.

Barsam, Richard (1973a), *Nonfiction Film* (New York: E. P. Dutton).

——— (1973b), 'Leni Reifenstahl', *Film Comment* vol. 9 no. 6, November–December.

——— (ed.) (1976), *Nonfiction Film: Theory and Criticism* (New York, E. P. Dutton).

——— (1988), *The Vision of Robert Flaherty: The Artist as Myth and Filmmaker* (Bloomington: Indiana University Press).

Barthes, Roland (1973), *Mythologies* (trans. A. Lavers) (London: Paladin).

——— (1981), *Camera Lucida* (trans. R. Howard) (New York: Hill & Wang).

——— (1990), *S/Z* (trans. R. Miller) (Oxford: Blackwell).

Bateman, Amanda (1986), 'AKA Clocks up its First 25 years', *Film and Television Technician*, ACTT, January.

Baudrillard, Jean (1988), *The Evil Demon of Images* (Sydney: Power Institute Publications), quoted in Nicholas, 1991, q.v.

Bazin, André (1967), *What Is Cinema?* (trans. H. Gray) (Berkeley, University of California Press).

——— (1971), *What Is Cinema?* vol. 2 (trans H. Gray) (Berkeley: University of California Press).

——— (1973), *Jean Renoir* (trans. W. W. Halsey and W. Simom) (New York: Simon & Schuster).

——— (1981), *French Cinema of the Occupation and Resistance: The Birth of a Critical Esthetic* (trans. S. Hochman) (New York: Frederick Ungar).

Bell, Elaine (1986), 'The Origins of British Television Documentary: The BBC 1946–55', in Corner, 1986, q.v.

Benjamin, Walter (1969), *Illuminations* (trans. Harry Zohn) (New York, Schocken Books).

——— (1972), 'A Short History of Photography', *Screen* vol. 13 no. 1, Spring.

Benson, Thomas A., and Anderson, Carolyn (1989), *Reality Fictions: The Films of Frederick Wiseman* (Carbondale, Ill.: Southern Illinois University Press).

Berger, John (1972), *Ways of Seeing* (Harmondsworth: Penguin).

——— (1980), *About Looking* (New York: Pantheon).

Berger Gluck, Sherna (1987), *Rosie the Riveter Revisited: Women, the War and Social Change* (New York: New American Library).

Beveridge, John (1978), *John Grierson, Film Master* (New York: Macmillan).

Biella, Peter (1988), 'Against Reductionism and Idealistic Self-Reflexivity: The Ilparakuyo Maasai Film Project', in Rollwagen, q.v.

Bigelow, Melville (1880), *History of Procedure in England: The Norman Period (1066–1204)* (London: Macmillan).

Biskind, Peter (1977), 'Harlan County, USA: The Miners' Struggle', *Jump Cut* no. 14, March.

Black, David (1987), 'A Likely Story: The Witness as Camera', unpublished paper, given at the Society of Cinema Studies, Montreal.

Blue, James (1964), 'Discussion with the Maysles', *Film Comment* vol. 2 no. 4, Fall.

—— (1965), 'One Man's Truth: An Interview with Richard Leacock', *Film Comment* vol. 3 no. 2, Spring.

—— (1967), 'Jean Rouch in Conversation', *Film Comment* no. 4, Fall.

Bluem, William (1975), *Documentary in American Television* (New York: Hastings House).

Blumer, Ron (1971), 'King's *A Married Couple*', in Jacobs, q.v.

Blumberg, Richard (1977), 'Documentary Films and the Problem of Truth', *Journal of the University Film and Video Association* vol. 29 no. 1, Fall.

Boas, George (ed.) (1938), *Courbet and the Naturalistic Movement* (New York: Russell & Russell).

Boas, Marie (1970), *The Scientific Renaissance 1450–1630* (London: Fontana).

Bond, Ralph (1979), 'Cinema in the Thirties', in Jon Clark *et al.*, q.v.

—— (1980), 'Love At First Sight', *Film and Television Technician*, February.

Bordwell, David (1985), *Narration in the Fiction Film* (Madison: University of Wisconsin Press).

Bordwell, David, Staiger, Janet, and Thompson, Kirstin (1985), *The Classical Hollywood Cinema* (New York: Columbia University Press).

Bordwell, David, and Thompson, Kirstin (1990), *Film Art: An Introduction*, 3rd edn (New York: McGraw Hill).

Bourdieu, Pierre (1990), *Photography* (trans. Shaun Whiteside) (Stanford, Calif.: Stanford University Press).

Bowser, Eileen (1990), *History of the American Cinema: The Transformation of Cinema, 1907–1915* (New York: Scribner's).

Boyle, Deirdre (1982), 'The Atomic Cafe' (review), *Cineaste* vol 12 no. 2.

Branigan, Edward (1992), *Narrative Comprehension and Film* (London: Routledge).

Breitrose, Henry (1964), 'On the Search for the Real Nitty-Gritty: Problems and Possibilities in *Cinéma Vérité*', *Film Quarterly*, Summer.

—— (1986), 'The Structure and Functions of Documentary Film', *CILECT Review* vol. 2 no. 1, November.

Brik, Osep, and Shklovsky, Viktor (1973), '*The Eleventh*', trans. in *Screen* vol. 14 no. 4, Winter.

Bronson, Gerald (1964), 'The Candid Photography of "The Fabian Story"', *American Cinematographer*, October.

Brown, Liz (1978), 'The Two Worlds of Marrakech', *Screen* vol. 19 no. 2, Summer.

Buchsbaum, Jonathon (1988), *Cinema Engagé: Film in the Popular Front* (Urbana: University of Illinois Press).

Burton, Julianne (ed.) (1990), *The Social Documentary in Latin America* (Pittsburg, Pa: University of Pittsburgh Press).

Callenbach, Ernest (1961), 'Going out to the Subject II', *Film Quarterly* vol. 14 no. 3, Spring.

—— (1973), 'Through Navajo Eyes' (book review), *Film Quarterly* vol. 17 no. 2, Winter 1973–4.

279

Cameron, Ian (1963), 'William Klein', *Movie* no. 8, April.

Campbell, Russell (1978), *Radical Cinema in the United States 1930–1942: The Work of the Film and Photo League, Nykino and Frontier Films* (Ann Arbor: UMI), dissertation, Northwestern University.

———— (1985), 'Radical Cinema in the 1930s: The Film and Photo League', in Steven, q.v.

Carey, John (1969), 'The Communications Revolution and the Professional Communicator', *Sociological Review Monographs*, January.

Carpenter, Edmund (1973), *Oh, What a Blow That Phantom Gave Me!* (New York: Holt, Rinehart & Winston).

Carpenter, Humphrey (1981), *W. H. Auden: A Biography* (Boston, Mass.: Houghton Mifflin).

Carroll, Noel (1983), 'From Real to Reel: Entangled in the Nonfiction Film', *Philosophical Exchange* (Brockport, NY: State University of New York, Brockport).

———— (1988), *Mystifying Movies: Fads and Fallacies in Contemporary Film Theory* (New York: Columbia).

Carson, Kit (1970), *David Holtzman's Diary* (New York: Farrar, Straus & Giroux).

Cartright, John (1991), *Unequal Bargaining: A Study of Vitiating Factors in the Formation of Contracts* (Oxford: Clarendon Press).

Carynnyk, Marco (trans.) (1972), 'The Vertov Papers', *Film Comment* vol. 1 no. 8, Spring.

Cawston, Richard, Hearst, Stephen, Reid, Robert, de Lotbiniere, Antony, Ralling, Christopher, Jay, Anthony, and Cary, Roger (1972), 'Principles and Practice in Documentary Programmes', London, BBC Television Service, April (issued internally).

Chagnon, Napoleon (1968), *Yanomamö: A Fierce People* (New York: Holt, Rinehart Winston).

Chatman, Seymour (1990), *Coming to Terms: The Rhetoric of Narrative in Fiction and Film* (Ithaca, NY: Cornell University Press).

Christians, Clifford, Rotzoll, Kim, and Fackler, Mark (1983), *Media Ethics: Cases and Moral Reasoning* (New York: Longman).

Christians, Clifford, and Rotzoll, Kim (1985), 'Ethical Issues in the Film Industry', in Bruce Austin (ed.), *Current Research in Film* (Norwood, NJ: Ablex).

Clark, Jon, Heinemann, Margot, Margolies, David, and Snee, Carole (1979), *Culture and Crisis in Britain in the 30s* (London: Lawrence & Wishart).

Clark, T. J. (1982a), *Image of the People: Gustave Courbet and the 1848 Revolution* (London, Thames & Hudson).

———— (1982b), *The Absolute Bourgeois: Artists and Politics in France 1848–1851* (London: Thames & Hudson).

Clay, Walter (1969), *The Prison Chaplain: A Memoire of the Rev. John Clay, B.D.* (Montclair, NJ: Patterson Smith).

Clifford, James (1988), *The Predicament of Culture: Twentieth Century Ethnography, Literature and Art* (Cambridge, Mass.: Harvard University Press).

Cockburn, J. S. (1972), *A History of English Assizes* (Cambridge: CUP).

Cockburn, J. S., and Green, Thomas (1988), *Twelve Good Men and True: The Criminal Trial Jury in England 1200–1800* (Princeton, NJ: Princeton University Press).

Cohen, Bernard (1987), 'Revolutions, Scientific and Probabilistic', in Kruger, Daston and Heidelberger, q.v.

Cohen, Jonathan (1977), *The Probable and the Provable* (Oxford: OUP).

Cole, Sidney (1989), 'Ralph Bond – Obituary', *Film and Television Technician*, July–August.

Collier, John, jr (1988), 'The Future of Ethnographic Film', in Rollwagen, q.v.

Collins, Richard (1986), 'Seeing Is Believing: The Ideology of Naturalism', in Corner, 1986, q.v.

Colls, Robert, and Dodd, Philip (1985), 'Representing the Nation: British Documentary Film, 1930–45', *Screen* vol. 26 no 1, Spring.

Commonwealth of Massachusetts v. Wiseman, 365 Mass. 251 N.E. 2nd 610 (1969); certiorari denied, 398 US 960 (1970); rehearing denied, 400 US 954 (1970).

Corner, John (ed.) (1986), *Documentary and the Mass Media* (London: Edward Arnold).

———— (ed.) (1991), *Popular Television* (London: BFI).

Crawford, Peter, and Turton, David (eds) (1992), *Film as Ethnography* (Manchester: Manchester University Press).

Curran, James, Gurevitch, Michael, and Woolacott, Jane (eds) (1977), *Mass Communication and Society* (London: Edward Arnold).

Curran, James, and Porter, Vincent (eds) (1983), *British Cinema History* (London: Weidenfeld & Nicolson).

Curtis, Edward (1972), *Portraits from North American Indian Life* (intro. by A. D. Coleman and T. C. McLuhan) (New York: Outerbridge & Lazard).

D'Agostino, Peter (1980), 'Visual Anthropology: An Interview with John Adair', *Wide Angle* vol. 4 no. 3.

Danzker, Jo-Anne Birnie (ed.) (1979), *Robert Flaherty: Photographer and Filmmaker* (Vancouver: Vancouver Art Gallery).

———— (1980), 'Robert Flaherty/Photographer', *Studies in Visual Communication* vol. 6 no. 2, Summer.

Daston, Lorraine (1987), 'The Domestication of Risk: Mathematical Probability and Insurance 1650–1830', in Kruger, Daston and Heidelberger, q.v.

Davis, Peter (1982), *Hometown* (New York: Simon & Schuster).

De Brigard, Émilie (1975), 'A History of Ethnographic Film', in Hockings, q.v.

DeGreef, Willem, and Hesling, Willem (eds) (1989), *Image, Reality, Spectator: Essays on Documentary Film and Television* (Louvain: Acco).

Delahaye, Michel (1965), 'Leni et le loup: entretien avec Leni Riefenstahl', *Cahiers du Cinéma*, September.

Delmar, Rosalind (1979), *Joris Ivens: 50 years of Film-Making* (London: BFI).

Deren, Maya (1960), 'Cinematography: The Creative Use of Reality', *Daedalus* vol. 89 no. 1, Winter.

Diamond, Edwin (1991), *The Media Show: The Changing Face of the News 1985–1990* (Cambridge, Mass.: The MIT Press). 1991

Dickinson, Margaret, and Street, Sarah (1985), *Cinema and the State: The Film Industry and the British Government 1927–1984* (London: BFI).

Dobi, Steve (1977), 'Restoring Robert Flaherty's *Nanook of the North*', *Film Librarians Quarterly* vol. 10 no. 1–2.

Docherty, David (1988), 'Director's Rights and Copyright', *Sight and Sound* vol. 57 no. 3, Summer.

Doesschate, G. Ten (1964), *Perspective: Fundamentals, Controversials, History* (Nieuwkoop, B. De Graaf).

Durgom v. CBS, 214 NYS 2nd 1008 (1961).

Dusinberre, Deke (1980), 'The Avant-Garde Attitude in the Thirties', in Macpherson, q.v.

Eaton, Mike (ed.) (1979), *Anthropology – Reality – Cinema* (London: BFI).

Eaton, Mike, and Ward, Ivan (1979), 'Anthropology and Film', *Screen* vol. 20 nos. 3–4, Autumn–Winter 1979–80.

Edelman, Bernard (1979), *Ownership of the Image: Elements for a Marxist Theory of Law* (trans. E. Kingdom) (London: Routledge & Kegan Paul).

Eder, Joseph Maria (1972), *History of Photography* (trans. E. Epstean) (New York: Dover).

Egan, Catherine (1978), 'Six American Families and How They Reacted to their Portrayals', *Film Librarians Quarterly* vol. 11 nos 1–2.

Eisenstein, Elizabeth (1983), *The Printing Revolution in Early Modern Europe* (Cambridge: CUP).

Eisenstein, S. M. (1949), *Film Form: Essays in Film Theory*, trans. Jay Leyda (New York: Harcourt-Brace).

Eldridge, John (ed.) (1993), *Getting the Message: News, Truth and Power* (London: Routledge).

Ellis, Jack (1989), *The Documentary Idea: A Critical History of English Language Documentary Film and Video* (Englewood Cliffs, NJ: Prentice Hall).

Empsom, William (1935), 'Proletarian Literature', *Scrutiny* vol. 3 no. 4, March.

Engelman, Ralph (1990), 'The Origins of Public Access Cable Television: 1966–1972', AEJMC Monograph no. 123, October.

Enzensberger, Masha (1972), 'Dziga Vertov', *Screen* vol. 13 no. 4, Winter 1972–3.

Erens, Patricia (1981), 'Women's Documentaries as Social History', *Film Library Quarterly* vol. 14 no. 1–2, Spring–Summer.

——— (1988), 'Women's Documentary Filmmaking', in Rosenthal, 1988, q.v.

Evans, Gary (1984), *John Grierson and the National Film Board: The Politics of Wartime Propaganda 1939–1945* (Toronto: University of Toronto Press).

Faris, James (1992), 'Anthropological Transparency: Film Representation and Politics', in Crawford and Turton, q.v.

Featherstone, David (ed.) (1984), *Observations: Essays on Documentary Photography* (New York: Friends of Photography).

Feld, Steven, and Ewing, Anny (1985), 'Chronicle of a Summer' (transcript), *Studies in Visual Communication* vol. 11 no. 1, Winter.

Feldman, Seth (1973), 'Cinema Weekly and Cinema Truth', *Sight and Sound* vol. 23 no. 1, Winter.

Fereydown, Hoveyda (1963), 'Cinéma Vérité ou réalisme fantastique', *Cahiers du Cinéma* vol. 125, November; trans. in Jim Hillier, *Cahiers du Cinéma in Translation II* (London: RKP, 1986).

Field, R. D. (1938), 'Naturalism in English Painting', in G. Boas, q.v.

Fielding, Raymond (1972), *The American Newsreel, 1911–1967* (Norman, Okla.: University of Oklahoma Press).

——— (1978), *The March of Time: 1935–1951* (New York: OUP).

Film Archive of China and the Editorial Department of New World Press (1983), *Joris Ivens and China* (Beijing: New World Press).

Fisher, Walter (1985), 'The Narrative Paradigm: In the Beginning', *Journal of Communications* vol. 35 no. 4, Autumn.

Fiske, John, and Hartley, John (1978), *Reading Television* (London: Methuen).

Flaherty, Francis Hubbard (1937), *Elephant Dance* (New York: Scribner's).

——— (1960), *The Odyssey of a Film-Maker* (Urbana, Ill.: Beta Phi Mu Chapbook).

FLQ (1971), 'Peter Davis on *The Selling of the Pentagon*', *Film Library Quarterly* vol. 4 no. 4, Winter.

Forman, Denis (1952), *Films 1945–1950* (London: Longman, Green/British Council).

Forman, Helen (1982), 'The Non-Theatrical Distribution of Films by the Ministry of Information', in Pronay and Spring, q.v.

Foucart, Bruno (1977), *G. Courbet* (New York: Crown).

Freund, Gisele (1982), *Photography and Society* (Boston, Mass.: David R. Godine).

Freyer, Ellen (1971), 'Chronicle of a Summer – Ten Years After', in Jacobs, q.v.

Fry v. Lane (1888), 40 Ch.D.

Gadol, Jean (1968), *Leon Battista Alberti* (Chicago: University of Chicago Press).

Gaines, Jane (1992), *Contested Culture: The Image, the Voice and the Law* (London: BFI).

Galassi, Peter (1981), *Before Photography* (New York: Museum of Modern Art).

Gardner, Robert (1957), 'Anthropology and Film', *Daedalus* vol. 86 no. 4, October.

—— (1969), 'Chronicles of Human Experience: Dead Birds', *Film Library Quarterly* vol. 2 no. 4, Winter.

—— (1971), 'The Making of "The Nuer"', *Film Library Quarterly* vol. 4 no. 3, Summer.

Gardner, Robert, and Heider, Karl (1974), *Gardens of War* (Harmondsworth: Penguin).

Genette, Gérard (1980), *Narrative Discourse: An Essay in Method* (trans. J. Lewin) (Ithaca, NY: Cornell University Press).

Georgakis, Dan (1978), 'Malpractice in the Radical American Documentary', *Cineaste* vol. 8 no. 4.

Gilbert, Craig (1983), 'Reflections on *An American Family*', *Studies in Visual Communication* vol. 36 no. 3, Spring; reprinted in Rosenthal, 1988, q.v.

Gillespie, Gilbert (1975), *Public Access Cable Television in the United States and Canada* (New York: Praeger).

Glasgow Media Group (1980), *More Bad News* (London: Routledge & Kegan Paul).

Godard, Jean-Luc (1963), 'Richard Leacock' (trans. P. Graham), *Cahiers du Cinéma* nos 150–151, December 1963/January 1964.

Goethe Institute (1984), *German Newsreels 1933–1947* (Munich: Goethe-Institut).

Golden, Daniel (1988), 'Confessional TV: Why Are So Many People Telling Us their Trouble?', *Boston Globe Magazine*, 10 July.

Goldmann, Lucien (1979), 'Cinema and Sociology: Thoughts on *Chronique d'un été*' (trans. J. Higgins), in Eaton, q.v.

Gomes, P. E. Salles (1971), *Jean Vigo* (Berkeley: University of California Press).

Gordon, Lynda (1985), 'Union Maids: Working-Class Heroines', in Steven, q.v.

Goretta, Claude (1956), 'Aspects of French Documentary', *Sight and Sound* vol. 26 no. 3, Winter 1956–7.

Graham, John (1976), 'Interview with Frederick Wiseman', in Atkins, 1976, q.v.

Graham, Peter (1964), 'Cinéma-Vérité in France', *Film Quarterly*, Summer.

Grant, Barry (1992), *Voyages of Discovery: The Cinema of Frederick Wiseman* (Urbana: University of Illinois Press).

Grant, Felicity (1978), 'The Whyte Trilogy: Intrusion or Socially Conscious?', *Broadcast*, 22 January.

Green, Thomas (1988), 'A Retrospective on the Criminal Trial Jury', in Cockburn and Green, q.v.

Greene, Graham (1980), *The Pleasure Dome: The Collected Film Criticism 1935–40*, ed. J. Russell Taylor (Oxford: OUP).

Gregory, Richard (1981), *Mind in Science* (Harmondsworth, Mx: Penguin).

Grierson, John (1970), 'Decentralizing the Means of Production', in Beveridge, 1978, q.v.

—— (1979a), *Grierson on Documentary*, ed. Forsyth Hardy (London: Faber).

—— (1979b), *John Grierson's Scotland*, ed. Forsyth Hardy (Edinburgh: The Ramsay Head Press).

—— (1981), *Grierson on the Movies*, ed. Forsyth Hardy (London: Faber).

Griffith, Richard (1953), *The World of Robert Flaherty* (New York: Duell, Sloan & Pearce).

Gross, Larry (1980), 'Sol Worth and the Study of Visual Communications', *Studies in Visual Communications* vol. 6 no. 3, Fall.

Gross, Larry, Katz, John, and Ruby, Jay (eds) (1988), *Image Ethics: The Moral Rights of Subjects in Photographs Film and Television* (New York: OUP).

Guynn, William (1990), *A Cinema of Nonfiction* (Rutherford, NJ: Fairleigh Dickinson (Associated Universities) Press).

Habermas, Jurgen (1972), *Knowledge and Human Interest* (trans. J. Shapiro) (London: Heinemann).

—— (1975), *Legitimation Crisis* (trans. T. McCarthy) (Boston, Mass.: Beacon Press).

Hacking, Ian (1987), 'Was There a Probabilistic Revolution 1800–1930?', in Kruger, Daston and Heidelberger, q.v.

Haelen Laboratories, Inc, v. Topps Chewing Gum, Inc, 202 F.2d 866 (2d Cir. 1953)

Halberstadt, Ira (1976), 'An Interview with Fred Wiseman', in Barsam, 1976, q.v.

Haleff, Maxine (1964), 'The Maysles Brothers and "Direct Cinema"', *Film Comment* vol. 2 no. 2.

Hall, Jeanne (1991), 'Realism as a Style in Cinéma Vérité: A Critical Analysis of *Primary*', *Cinema Journal* vol. 30 no. 4, Summer.

Hall, Stuart (1982), 'The Rediscovery of "Ideology": Return of the Repressed in Media Studies', in Michael Gurevitch, Tony Bennett, James Curran and Janet Woollacott (eds), *Culture, Society and the Media* (London: RKP).

Hambourg, Maria Morris (1984), 'Atget, Precursor of Modern Documentary Photography', in Featherstone, q.v.

Hammond, Charles (1981), *The Image Decade: Television Documentary* (New York: Hastings House).

Hampton, Benjamin (1931), *A History of the Movies* (New York: Covicim Friede); republished as *A History of the American Film Industry: From its Beginnings to 1931* (New York: Dover, 1970).

Harding, Alan (1966), *A Social History of English Law* (Harmondsworth, Mx; Penguin).

—— (1973), *The Law Courts of Medieval England* (London: Allen & Unwin).

Hardy, Forsyth (1979), *John Grierson: A Documentary Biography* (London: Faber).

Harrison, Barbara Grizzuti (1980), 'Hers', *New York Times*, 17 April.

Haskell, Molly (1971), 'Three Documentaries', in Jacobs, q.v.

Hass, Robert (1976), *Muybridge: Man in Motion* (Berkeley: University of California Press).

Hastrup, Kirsten (1992), 'Anthropological Visions: Some Notes on Visual and Textual Authority', in Crawford and Turton, q.v.

Hauser, Arnold (1983), *The Social History of Art: Naturalism, Impressionism, The Film Age* (London: Routledge & Kegan Paul [1951]).

Hemingway, Ernest (1987), *The Complete Short Stories of Ernest Hemingway* (New York: Scribner's).

Hempel, Carl (1983), 'Studies in the Logic of Confirmation', in P. Achinstein (ed.), *The Concept of Evidence* (Oxford: OUP).

Henaut, Dorothy Todd (1970), 'Television as Town Meeting', *Challenge for Change Newsletter* no. 5, Autumn.

Hess, John (1985), 'Notes on US Radical Film, 1967–80', in Steven, q.v.

Hiley, Nicholas (1985), '*The British Army Film, You!* and *For the Empire*', *Historical Journal of Film, Radio and Television* vol. 5 no. 2.

Hill, Christopher (1974), *Intellectual Origins of the English Revolution* (London: Panther).

Hinton, David (1978), *The Films of Leni Riefenstahl* (Metuchen, NJ: The Scarecrow Press).

Hinz, Berthold (1979), *Art in the Third Reich*, trans. Robert and Rita Kimber (New York: Random House).

Hirst, Paul, and Kingdom, Elizabeth (1979), 'On Edelman's *Ownership of the Image*', *Screen* vol. 20 no. 3–4, Autumn–Winter 1979–80.

Hitchens, Gordon (1973), 'Leni Riefenstahl Interviewed by Gordon Hitchens, October 11th, 1971, Munich', *Film Culture* vol. 56–57, Spring.

Hoberman, Jim (1978), 'Breadline Eyes: Radical Newsreels of the 1930s', *Village Voice*, 30 October.

Hockings, Paul (ed.) (1975), *Principles of Visual Anthropology* (The Hague: Mouton).

Hodgkinson, Anthony (1975), 'Humphrey Jennings and Mass Observation: A Conversation with Tom Harrisson', *Journal of the University Film Association* vol. 27 no. 4, Fall.

Hogenkamp, Bert (1976), 'Film and The Workers Movement in Britain, 1929–39', *Sight and Sound* vol. 43 no. 2, Spring.

—— (1979), '"Making Films with A Purpose": Film-making and the Working Class', in Jon Clark *et al.*, q.v.

—— (1984), 'Workers Newsreels in Germany, The Netherlands and Japan During the Twenties and Thirties', in Waugh (ed.), q.v.

—— (1986), *Deadly Parallels: Film and the Left In Britain 1929–1939* (London: Lawrence & Wishart).

—— (1989), 'The British Documentary Movement in Perspective', in DeGreef and Hesling, q.v.

Hollins, T. J. (1981), 'The Conservative Party and Film Propaganda between the Wars', *English Historical Review* vol. 96.

Holm, Bill, and Quimby, George Irving (1980), *Edward S. Curtis in the Land of the War Canoes* (Seattle: University of Washington Press).

Hood, Stuart (1983), 'John Grierson and the Documentary Film Movement', in Curran and Porter, q.v.

Hoover, Dwight, (1987a), 'Censorship or Bad Judgement? An Example from American Public Television', *Historical Journal of Film Radio and Television* vol. 7 no. 2.

—— (1987b), 'The Middletown Film Project: History & Reflections', *Journal of Film and Video* vol. 39 no. 2, Spring.

—— (1987c), '"Seventeen": The Genesis of the Idea and the Continuing Reaction', in Ruby and Tuareg, q.v.

—— (1990), *Middletown Revisited*, Ball State Monograph no. 34 (Muncie, Ind.: Ball State University).

—— (1993), *The Middletown Film Project* (New York: Harwood).

Hugill, Barry, and Moory, Graham (1992), 'Mounting Scandal: Hardline Regime of a Durham Children's Home', *Observer*, 9 August.

Hurwitz, Leo (1934), 'The Revolutionary Film – Next Step', *New Theatre*, 1 May.

—— (1975), 'One Man's Voyage: Ideas and Films in the 1930s', *Cinema Journal* vol. 15 no. 1, Fall.

Infield, Glenn (1976), *Leni Riefenstahl: Fallen Film Goddess* (New York: Crowell).

Ireland, R. W. (1984), 'The Presumption of Guilt in the History of English Criminal Procedure', *Journal of Legal History*.

Irvins, William, Jr. (1973), *On the Rationalization of Sight* (New York: Da Capo).

Ivens, Joris (1969), *The Camera and I* (New York: International Publishers).

—— (1983a), 'How I Filmed *The 400 Million*', in Film Archive of China, q.v.

—— (1983b), 'On Reconstruction in Documentary Film Making', in Film Archive of China, q.v.

Jacobs, Lewis (ed.) (1971), *The Documentary Tradition: From Nanook to Woodstock* (New York: Hopkinson & Blake).

Jaffe, Patricia (1965), 'Editing Cinéma Vérité', *Film Comment* vol. 3 no. 3, Summer.

Jennings, Humphrey (1985), *Pandaemonium: The Coming of the Machine as Seen by Contemporary Observers, 1660–1886* (New York: The Free Press).

Jennings, Mary-Lou (ed.) (1982), *Humphrey Jennings: Film-Maker, Painter, Poet* (London: BFI).

Johnston, Claire (1980), 'Independence and the Thirties', in Macpherson, q.v.

Johnston, Claire and Willemen, Paul (1984), 'Brecht in Britain: *The Nightcleaners* and the Independent Political Film', in Waugh, 1984, q.v.

Jones, Stephen (1987), *The British Labour Movement and Film, 1918–1939* (London: Routledge & Kegan Paul).

Katz, John (ed.) (1978), *Autobiography: Film/Video/Photography* (Toronto: Art Gallery of Ontario).

Katz, John, and Katz, Judith (1988), 'Ethics and Perception of Ethics in Autobiographical Film', in Gross, Katz and Ruby, q.v.

Kelman, Ken (1973), 'Propaganda as Vision – Triumph of the Will', *Film Culture* vol. 56–57, Spring.

King, Noel (1981), 'Recent "Political" Documentary: Notes on *Union Maids* and *Harlan County, USA*', *Screen* vol. 22 no. 2, Summer.

Klughertz, Daniel (1971), 'Documentary – Where's the Wonder?', in Jacobs, q.v.

Kracaeur, Siegfried (1973), *From Caligari to Hitler: A Psychological History of the German Film* (Princeton, NJ: Princeton University Press).

Krauss, Rosalind (1984), 'A Note on Photography and the Simulacral', *October 31*, Winter.

Kruger, Lorenz, Daston, Lorraine, and Heidelberger, Michael (1987), *The Probabilistic Revolution: No. 1 Ideas in History* (Cambridge, Mass.: MIT Press).

Kuhn, Annette (1980), 'British Documentary in the 1930s and "Independence": Recontextualising a Film Movement', in Macpherson, q.v.

Labarthe, André, and Marcorelles, Louis (1963), 'Entretien avec Robert Drew et Richard Leacock', *Cahiers du Cinéma* vol. 24 no. 140, February.

Lafferty, William (1983), 'The Blattnerphone: An Early Attempt to Introduce Magnetic recording into the Film Industry', *Cinema Journal* vol. 22 no. 4, Summer.

LaJuene, Catherine (1932), *Observer*, London, 11 August.

Latour, Bruno (1987), *Science in Action* (Cambridge, Mass.: Harvard University Press).

Leacock, Richard (1959), 'La Caméra Passe-Partout' (trans. L. Macorelles), *Cahiers du Cinéma* vol. 94, April.

——— (1961), 'For an Uncontrolled Cinema', *Film Culture* vol. 19 no. 23, Summer.

——— (1973), 'Remembering Francis Flaherty', *Film Comment* vol. 9 no. 6, November–December.

——— (1985), '*Robert Flaherty: A Biography*' (book review) *Field of Vision* no. 13, Spring.

Lee, Rohana (1984), *Master of the Film Medium: John Grierson Pioneered the Documentary Film in Britain and Canada* (Ames, Iowa: The American Archives of Factual Film, Iowa State).

LeftFilmFront (1937), *Bulletin of the Film and Photo League*, no. 1, July 1937 (reprinted in Macpherson, 1980, p. 158).

Lesage, Julia (1978), 'The Political Aesthetics of the Feminist Documentary Film', *Quarterly Review of Film Studies*, Fall.

Levin, G. Roy (1971), *Documentary Explorations* (Garden City, NY: Anchor Press).

Lévi-Strauss, Claude (1968), *Structural Anthropology* (trans. Claire Jacobson and Brooke Grunfest Schoef) (London: Allen Lane, The Penguin Press).

Lewis, Jonathon (1977), 'Before Hindsight', *Sight and Sound* vol. 44 no. 2, Spring.

Leyda, Jay (1960), *Kino: A History of Russian and Soviet Film* (London: Allen & Unwin).

——— (1964), *Films Begat Films* (London: Allen & Unwin).

Lindsay, Vachel (1915), *Art of the Moving Picture* (New York: Macmillan).

Loizos, Peter (1993), *Innovation in Ethnographic Film: From Innocence to Self-Consciousness 1955–1985* (Manchester: Manchester University Press).

Lomax, Alan (1973), 'Urgent Anthropology: Cinema, Science and Cultural Renewal', *Current Anthropology* vol. 14 no. 4, October.

Lorentz, Pare (1975), *Lorentz on Film* (New York: Hopkinson & Blake).

Lovell, Alan, and Hillier, Jim (1972), *Studies in Documentary* (New York: Viking).

Lovell, Alan, Hillier, Jim, and Rhodie, Sam (1972), 'Interview with Alberto Cavalcanti', *Screen* vol. 13 no. 2, Summer.

Lovell, Alan, Wollen, Peter, and Rhodie, Sam (1972), 'Interview with Ivor Montagu', *Screen* vol. 13 no. 3, Autumn.

Low, Rachael (1979a), *The History of the British Film 1929–1939: Documentary and Educational Films of the 1930s* (London: Allen & Unwin).

—— (1979b), *The History of the British Film 1929–1939: Films of Comment and Persuasion of the 1930s* (London: Allen & Unwin).

Lucaites, John, and Condit, Celeste (1985), 'Re-constructing Narrative Theory: A Functional Perspective', *Journal of Communications* vol. 35 no. 4, Autumn.

Lyman, Christopher (1982), *The Vanishing Race and Other Illusions* (New York: Pantheon).

Lynd, Alice, and Lynd, Staughton (1973), *Rank and File: Personal Histories of Working Class Organizers* (Boston, Mass.: Beacon Press).

MacBean, James Roy (1983), '*Two Laws* from Australia, One White, One Black', *Film Quarterly* vol. 36 no. 3, Spring.

MacCann, Richard (1973), *The People's Films: A Political History of the US Government Motion Pictures* (New York: Hastings House).

Macdonald, Gus (1978), 'The Documentary Idea and Television Today', The John Grierson Archive Occasional Papers No. 1: Inaugural Addresses, University of Stirling.

MacDonald, Scott (1988), 'Southern Exposure: An Interview with Ross McElwee', *Film Quarterly* vol. 41 no. 4, Summer.

MacDougall, David (1969), 'Prospects of the Ethnographic Film', *Film Quarterly* vol. 23 no. 2, Winter 1969–70.

—— (1975), 'Beyond Observational Cinema', in Hockings, q.v.

—— (1982), 'Unprivileged Camera Style', *RAIN* no. 50, June.

McGarry, Eileen (1975), 'Documentary, Realism, and Women's Cinema', *Women and Film* vol. 2 no. 7.

Mackie, J. D. (1964), *A History of Scotland* (Harmondsworth: Penguin).

Macpherson, Don (1980) (ed. in collaboration with Paul Willemen), *Traditions of Independence* (London: BFI).

McWilliams, Donald (1970), 'Frederick Wiseman', *Film Quarterly* vol. 24 no. 1, Fall.

Maitland, F. W. (1965), *The Constitutional History of England*, ed. H. A. L. Fisher (Cambridge: CUP).

Mamber, Steve (1974), *Cinéma Vérité in America* (Cambridge, Mass.: MIT Press).

Manvell, Roger (1946), *Film* (Harmondsworth, Mx: Penguin).

—— (1951), *The Cinema: 1951* (ed. with R. K. Neilson Baxter) (Harmondsworth, Mx: Penguin).

—— (1974), *Film and the Second World War* (London: Dent).

Marcorelles, Louis (1963), 'L'Expérience Leacock', *Cahiers du Cinéma* vol. 22 no. 140, February (trans. J. Hillier).

Marker, Chris (1961), *Commentaires* (Paris: Éditions du Seuil).

Marnell, W. (1973), *The Right To Know* (New York: Seabury Press).

Marris, Paul (1980), 'Politics and "Independent" Film in the Decade of Defeat', in Macpherson, q.v.

———— (ed.) (1982), *Paul Rotha* (London: BFI), Dossier no. 16.

Matthews, J. H. (1971), *Surrealism and Film* (Ann Arbor: The University of Michigan Press).

Mead, Margaret (1974), 'Introduction', in Gardner and Heider, q.v.

———— (1975), 'Visual Anthropology in a Discipline of Words', in Hockings, q.v.

Mellin, Joan (1978), *The World of Luis Buñuel* (New York: OUP).

Merjan, Ruby (1978), *A Report on the Television Laboratory at WNET/Thirteen: 1972–1978* (New York: WNET).

Merrill, John (1989), *The Dialetic in Journalism: Towards a Responsible Use of the Press* (Baton Rouge: Lousiana State University Press).

Metz, Christian (1974), *Film Language: A Semiotics of Cinema* (New York: OUP).

Michelson, Annette (1984), 'Introduction', in Vertov, q.v.

Monegal, Emir Rodriguez (1955), 'Alberto Cavalcanti: His Career', *The Quarterly of Film Radio and TV* vol. 9 no. 4, Summer.

Montagu, Ivor (1966), *Film World* (Harmondsworth: Penguin).

Morin, Edgar (1985), 'Chronicle of a Film' (trans. S. Feld and A. Ewing), in *Studies in Visual Communication* vol. 11 no. 1, Winter.

Mott, Frank (1962), *American Journalism: A History 1690–1960* (New York: Macmillan)

Moussinac, Leon (1935), 'Dziga Vertov on Film Technique' (trans. S. Brody), *Filmfront No. 3*.

Muggeridge, Malcolm (1971), *The Thirties in Great Britain* (London: Collins).

Muller, Jean Claude (1971), 'Les Mâitres fous' (film review), *American Anthropology* vol. 73 no. 3, December.

Murray, Bruce (1990), *Film and the German Left in the Weimar Republic: From Caligari to Kulhe Wampe* (Austin: University of Texas Press).

Musser, Charles (1990), *History of the American Cinema: The Emergence of Cinema, The American Screen to 1907* (New York: Scribner's).

Nagel, Thomas (1986), *The View From Nowhere* (New York: OUP).

Nairn, Tom (1977), 'The Twilight of the British State', *New Left Review* vol. 101–102, February–April.

Naughton, John (1992), 'Bare Brass for Old Rope', *Observer*, 20 December.

Neale, Steve (1979), '*Triumph of the Will* – Notes on Documentary and Spectacle', *Screen* vol. 20 no. 1, Spring.

Neale, Steve, and Nash, Mark (1977), 'Film: History/Production/Memory', *Screen* vol. 18 no. 4, Winter.

Nencel, Lorraine, and Pels, Peter (1989), 'Critique and Reflexivity in Anthropology', *Critique of Anthropology* vol. 9 no. 3.

Newton, Kenneth (1969), *The Sociology of British Communism* (London: Allen Lane/Penguin).

Nichols, Bill (1978), 'Fred Wiseman's Documentaries: Theory and Structure', *Film Quarterly* vol. 31 no. 3, Spring.

———— (1981), *Ideology and the Image* (Bloomington: University of Indiana Press).

———— (1986), 'Questions of Magnitude', in Corner, 1986, q.v.

———— (1988), 'The Work of Culture in the Age of Cybernetic Systems', *Screen* vol. 29 no. 1, Winter.

———— (1991), *Representing Reality: Issues and Concepts in Documentary* (Bloomington: Indiana University Press).

Nilsson, Nils (1971), 'The Origin of the Interview', *Journalism Quarterly* vol. 48 no. 4, Winter.

Nochlin, Lynda (ed.) (1966), *Realism and Tradition in Art: 1848–1900* (Englewood Cliffs, NJ.: Prentice Hall).

288

———— (1971), *Realism* (Harmondsworth, Mx: Penguin).

Norris, Christopher (1990), *What's Wrong With Postmodernism: Critical Theory and the Ends of Philosophy* (Baltimore, Md: Johns Hopkins University Press).

Nowell-Smith, Geoffrey (1986), 'Humphrey Jennings: Surrealist Observer', in Barr, q.v.

O'Brien, Kevin (trans.) (1979), 'The Factory of Fact and Other Writings: Dziga Vertov', *October* no. 7, Winter.

Orbanz, Eva (ed.) (1977), *Journey to a Legend and Back: The British Realistic Film* (Berlin: Edition Volker Spiess).

Orbanz, Eva, Tuchtenhagen, Gisela, and Wildenhahn, Klaus (1977), 'Paul Rotha', in Orbanz, q.v.

Orlow, Dietrich (1973), *History of the Nazi Party*, vol. 3 (Pittsburg, Pa: University of Pittsburg Press).

Ormiston, Gayle (1977), 'Peirce's Categories: Structure of Semiotic', *Semiotica* vol. 19 no. 3/4.

Peirce, Charles (1965), *Collected Papers: Volume II* (Cambridge, Mass.: The Belknap Press at The Harvard Press).

Pember, Don (1972), *Privacy and the Press* (Seattle: University of Washington Press).

Petric, Vlada (1984), 'Esther Shub: Film as a Historical Discourse', in Waugh, 1984, q.v.

———— (1987), *Contructivism in Film: The Man with a Movie Camera* (Cambridge: CUP).

Pincus, Ed (1972), 'One Person Sync-Sound: A New Approach to Cinéma Vérité, *Filmmakers Newsletter*, December.

Platinga, Carl (1990), 'Mockumentary, Docucomedy, Documentary, or "Sick Humor": *Roger and Me* Meets the Media', unpublished paper given at the Twelfth Ohio University Film Conference, November.

Polunin, Ivan (1970), 'Visual and Sound Recording Apparatus in Ethnographic Fieldwork', *Current Anthropology* vol. 11 no. 1, February.

Porter, Vincent (1978), 'Film Copyright: Film Culture', *Screen* vol. 19 no. 1, Spring.

———— (1979), 'Film Copywright and Edelman's Theory of Law', *Screen* vol. 20 no. 3–4, Autumn–Winter.

Potter, Harold (1932), *An Historical Introduction to English Law and its Institutions* (London: Sweet & Maxwell).

Pronay, Nicholas (1982), 'Political Censorship of Films in Britain between the Wars', in Pronay and Spring, q.v.

———— (1989), 'John Grierson and the Documentary – 60 years on', *Historical Journal of Film, Radio and Television*, vol. 9 no. 3.

Pronay, Nicholas, and Spring, D. W. (1982), *Propaganda, Politics and Film, 1918–45* (London: Macmillan).

Pryluck, Calvin (1976), 'Ultimately We Are All Outsiders: The Ethics of Documentary Filming', *Journal of the University Film Association* vol. 28 no. 1, Winter; reprinted in Rosenthal, 1988, q.v.

Public Broadcasting Associates (1980), 'Odyssey: Franz Boas (1848–1942)', transcript of documentary (Boston, Mass.: Public Broadcasting Associates).

Quetelet, Adolphe (1984), *Research of the Propensity for Crime at Different Ages* (trans. S. Sylvester) (Cincinnati, Ohio: Anderson).

Raphael, Max (1979), *Proudhon, Marx, Picasso: Three Studies in the Sociology of Art* (trans. I. Marcuse) (London: Lawrence & Wishart).

Ravetz, J. R. (1973), *Scientific Knowledge and its Social Problems* (Harmondsworth, Mx: Penguin).

Reeves, Nicholas (1985), *Official British Film Propaganda During the First World War* (London: Croom Helm).

Renov, Michael, (1986), 'Rethinking Documentary: Toward a Taxonomy of Mediation', *Wide Angle* vol. 8 nos 3–4.

Rentschler, Eric (1989), 'Fatal Attractions: Leni Riefenstahl's *The Blue Light*', *October* no. 48, Spring.

Reynolds, P. D. (1982), *Ethics and Social Science Research* (Englewood Cliffs, NJ: Prentice Hall).

Richards, Jeffrey, and Sheridan, Dorothy (eds) (1987), *Mass Observation at the Movies* (London: RKP).

Robertson, Geoffrey, and Nicol, Andrew (1992), *Media Law* (Harmondsworth, Mx: Penguin).

Rohmer, Éric, and Marcorelles, Louis (1963), 'Entretien avec Jean Rouch', *Cahiers du Cinéma* vol. 24 no. 144, June (trans. in Ali Issari and Paul, 1979, q.v.).

Rollwagen, Jack (ed.) (1988), *Anthropological Filmmaking* (Chur, Switzerland: Harwood Academic Publishers).

Rosenthal, Alan (1971), *The New Documentary In Action* (Berkeley: University of California Press).

——— (1980), *The Documentary Conscience* (Berkeley: University of California Press).

——— (1988), *New Challenges for Documentary* (Berkeley: University of California Press).

——— (1990), *Writing, Directing and Producing Documentary Films* (Carbondale: Southern Illinois University Press).

Rosenweig, Roy (1980), 'Working Class Struggles in the Great Depression: The Film Record', *Film Library Quarterly* vol. 13 no. 1, Spring.

Rotha, Paul (1952), *Documentary Film*, 2nd edn (London: Faber [1935]).

——— (1963), 'Preface' to Baddeley, q.v.

——— (1966), *Documentary Film*, 3rd edn (London: Faber [1935]).

——— (1973), *Documentary Diary: An Informal History of the British Documentary Film, 1928–1939* (New York: Hill & Wang).

——— (1983), *Robert J. Flaherty: A Biography*, ed. J. Ruby (Philadelphia: University of Pennsylvania Press).

Rouch, Jean (1975), 'The Camera and Man', in Hockings, q.v.

——— (1985), 'The Cinema of the Future?', *Studies in Visual Communications* vol. 11 no. 1, Winter.

Rubin, James (1980), *Realism and Social Vision in Courbet and Proudhon* (Princeton, NJ: Princeton University Press).

Rubinstein, E. (1983), 'Visit to a Familiar Planet: Buñuel among the Hurdanos', *Cinema Journal* vol. 22 no. 4, Summer.

Ruby, Jay (1980), 'The Aggie Will Come First', in Danzker, q.v.

Ruby, Jay, and Tuareg, Martin (eds) (1987), *Visual Explorations of the World* (Aachen: Rader-Verlag).

Rupert-Hall, A. (1970), *From Galileo to Newton 1630–1720* (London: Fontana).

Ryan, Trevor (1980), 'Film and Political Organisations in Britain 1929–1939', in Macpherson, q.v.

——— (1983), '"The New Road to Progress": The Use and Production of Films by the Labour Movement, 1929–39', in Curran and Porter, q.v.

Sandall, Roger (1978), 'More Ethnic than Graphic and Often Remarkably Long', *Sight and Sound* vol. 47 no. 4, Winter.

Scannell, Paddy (1986), '"The Stuff of Radio": Developments in Radio Features and Documentaries before the War', in Corner, q.v.

Scharf, Aaron (1974), *Art and Photography* (Harmondsworth, Mx: Penguin).

Schechner, Richard (1981), 'Restoration of Behaviour', *Studies in Visual Communication* vol. 7 no. 3, Summer.

Schnitzer, Luda, Schnitzer, Jean, and Martin, Marcel (1973), *Cinema in Revolution: The Heroic Era of the Soviet Film* (trans. with additional material by D. Robinson) (New York: Hill & Wang).

Scholes, Robert, and Kellogg, Robert (1966), *The Nature of Narrative* (New York: OUP).

Schudson, Michael (1978), *Discovering the News*, (New York: Basic Books).

——— (1979), 'The Interview: History of a Social Form', unpublished paper.

Sekula, Alan (1986), 'The Body and the Archive', *October* vol. 39, Winter.

Shachtman, Thomas (1977), 'The Exploitation Factor', *Media and Methods*, January.

Shapiro, Barbara (1983), *Probability and Certainty in Seventeenth Century England* (Princeton, NJ: Princeton University Press).

Shivas, Mark (1963a), 'Interviews: Richard Leacock', *Movie* vol. 8, April.

——— (1963b), 'New Approach', *Movie* vol. 8, April.

Silverstone, Roger (1985), *Framing Science: The Making of a BBC Documentary* (London: BFI).

Singer, André (1988), 'Choices and Constraints in Filming in Central Asia', in Rollwagen, q.v.

Sloan, Jen (1979), 'Compared Views of the Yanomamö: Paris Conference of Anthropologists and Filmmakers', *Film Library Quarterly* vol. 12 no. 1, Spring.

Snyder, Robert (1968), *Pare Lorentz and the Documentary Film* (Norman: University of Oklahoma Press).

Sobchak, Vivian (1984), 'Inscribing Ethical Space: Ten Propositions on Death, Representation and Documentary', *Quarterly Review of Film Studies*, Fall.

Solanas, Fernando, and Getino, Octavio (1976), 'Toward a Third Cinema', in Bill Nichols (ed.), *Movies and Methods* (Berkeley, Calif.: University of California Press).

Sontag, Susan (1977), *On Photography* (New York: Dell).

Sorenson, E. Richard (1967), 'A Research Film Program in the Study of Changing Man', *Current Anthropology* vol. 8 no. 5, December.

——— (1976), *The Edge of the Forest: Land, Childhood and Change in a New Guinea Protoagricultural Society* (Washington, DC: Smithsonian Institution Press).

Sorenssen, Bjorn (1986), 'The Documentary Aesthetics of Humphrey Jennings', in Corner, 1986, q.v.

Stam, Robert, Burgoyne, Robert and Flitterman-Lewis, Sandy (1992), *New Vocabularies in Film Semiotics: Structuralism, Post-structuralism and Beyond* (London: Routledge).

StarBlanket, Noel (1968), 'A voice for Canadian Indians: An Indian Film Crew', *Challenge for Change Newsletter* vol. 1 no. 2, Fall.

Steven, Peter (ed.) (1985), *Jump Cut: Hollywood, Politics and Counter-Cinema* (Toronto: Between the Lines).

Stoney, George (1978), 'Must a Filmmaker Leave His Mark?', unpublished mimeographed paper, New York, 13 March.

Sufrin, Mark (1955), 'Filming a Skid Row Documentary', *Sight and Sound*, Winter 1955–6.

Sullivan, Patrick (1979), '"What's All the Cryin' About?": The Films of Frederick Wiseman', *The Massachusetts Review* vol 13 no. 3, Summer.

Sussex, Elizabeth (1975), *The Rise and Fall of British Documentary* (Berkeley, University of California Press).

Swann, Paul (1989), *The British Documentary Film Movement 1926–1946* (Cambridge: CUP).

Swijtink, Zeno (1987), 'The Objectification of Observation: Measurement and Statistical Methods in the Nineteenth Century', in Kruger, Daston and Heidelberger, q.v.

Tagg, John (1988), *The Burden of Representation* (Amherst: University of Massachusetts Press).

Tallents, Stephen (1968), 'The Birth of The British Documentary', *Journal of the University Film Association* vol. 20 nos 1–3.

Taylor, Charles (1971), 'Focus on Al Maysles', in Jacobs, q.v.

Taylor, Richard (1979), *Film Propaganda: Soviet Russia and Nazi Germany* (London: Croom Helm).

Taylor, Richard, and Christie, Ian (eds) (1988), *The Film Factory: Russian and Soviet Cinema in Documents, 1896–1939* (London: RKP).

Thomas, Claire (1980), 'Independence and the Thirties', in Macpherson, q.v.

Thompson, E. P. (1972), 'Mayhew and the *Morning Chronicle*', in Yeo and Thompson, q.v.

Thurlow, Richard (1987), *Fascism in Britain: A History 1918–1985* (Oxford: Blackwell).

Time Inc v. Bernard Geis Associates, 293 F.Supp. 130 (1968).

Todorov, Tzyetan (1981), *Introduction to Poetics* (Minneapolis: University of Minnesota Press).

Tomaselli, Keyan (1992), 'Myths, Racism and Opportunism: Film and TV Representations of the San', in Crawford and Turton, q.v.

Tretyakov, Sergey, Shklovsky, Viktor, Shub, Esfir, and Brik, Osip (1971), 'Symposium on Soviet Documentary', in Jacobs, q.v.

Trilling, Calvin (1985), *Killings* (New York: Viking).

Tudor, Andrew (1973), *Theories of Film* (New York: Viking).

Turnbull, George (1936), 'Some Notes on the History of the Interview', *Journalism Quarterly* vol. 13, September.

Turton, David (1992), 'Anthropology on Television: What Next?', in Crawford and Turton, q.v.

Twining, William (1985), *Theories of Evidence* (Stanford, Calif.: Stanford University Press).

Uricchio, William (1987), 'Object and Evocation: The City Film and Its Reformulation by the American Avant-Garde (1900–1931)', unpublished paper given at the Society of Cinema Studies, Montreal.

Vander Hill, Warren (1982), 'The Middletown Film Project: Reflections of an "Academic Humanist"', *Journal of Popular Film and Culture* no. 10.

Van Dyke, Willard (1946), 'The Interpretive Camera in Documentary Films', *Hollywood Quarterly* vol. 1 no. 4, July.

—— (1965), 'Letters from "The River"', *Film Comment* vol. 3 no. 2, Spring.

Van Wert, William (1974), 'Fictional Structures', *Film Library Quarterly* vol. 7 no. 1, Spring.

Vaughan, Dai (1974), 'The Space Between Shots', *Screen* vol. 15 no. 1, Spring.

—— (1979), 'Arms and the Absent', *Sight and Sound* vol. 48 no. 3, Summer.

—— (1983), *Portrait of An Invisible Man: The Working Life of Stewart McAllister, Film Editor* (London: BFI).

Vertov, Dziga (Denis Kaufman) (1984), *Kino-Eye: The Writings of Dziga Vertov* (selected by Sergie Drobashenko, trans. K. O'Brien) (Berkeley: University of California Press).

Van Cauwenberge, Genevieve (1992), 'Chris Marker's *Le Joli Mai*: Reflections on the Camera as Provocator', unpublished paper given at Society for Cinema Studies Conference, Pittsburgh.

Walens, Stanley (1978), 'The Kwakiutl of British Columbia 1930–31 by Frank Boas' (audiovisual review), *American Anthropologist* vol. 86 no. 1, March.

Watson, Patrick (1970), 'Challenge for Change', *Art Canada* no. 142–3, April.

Watt, Harry (1972), 'NFT Programme Notes (n.d.)', *Screen* vol. 13 no. 2, Summer.

Waugh, Thomas (1982), '"Men Cannot Act in Front of the Camera in the Presence of Death": Joris Ivens' *The Spanish Earth*', *Cineaste* vol. 12 no. 2.

—— (ed.) (1984), *'Show Us Life': Toward a History and Aesthetics of Committed Documentary* (Metuchen, NJ: The Scarecrow Press).

Weber, Max (1971), 'Verification in Sociological Analysis', in J. E. T. Eldridge (ed.), *Max Weber: The Interpretation of Social Reality* (London: Michael Joseph).

Wegg-Prosser, Victoria (1977), 'The Archive of the Film and Photo League', *Sight and Sound* vol. 46 no. 4, Autumn.

Weiner, Annette (1977), 'Trobrian Cricket' (audiovisual review), *American Anthropologist* vol. 79 no. 2, June.

—— (1978), 'Epistemology and Ethnographic Reality: A Trobriand Island Case Study', *American Anthropologist* vol. 80 no. 3, September.

Welch, David (1983), *Propaganda and the German Cinema 1933–1945* (Oxford: OUP).

White, W. L. (1939), 'Pare Lorentz', *Scribner's*, January.

Wildenhahn, Klaus (1977), 'Approaches to the Legend', in Orbanz, q.v.

Williams, Raymond (1976), *Keywords* (New York: OUP).

—— (1981), *Culture* (London: Fontana).

—— (1983), *Culture and Society 1780–1950* (New York: Columbia University Press).

—— (1989), *The Politics of Modernism: Against the New Conformists* (London: Verso).

Williamson, Harold (1983), '"Appear on the box again! No, thank you"', *The Listener*, 6 January.

Wills, Gary (1992), 'A Doll's House?', *New York Review of Books*, 22 October.

Winston, Brian (1978), 'Documentary, I Think We Are in Trouble', *Sight and Sound* vol. 48 no. 1, Winter 1978–9.

—— (1981), 'Was Hitler There?', *Sight and Sound* vol. 50 no. 2, Spring.

—— (1985), '"A Whole Technology of Dyeing": Ideology and the Apparatus of the Chromatic Moving Image', *Daedalus* vol. 114 no. 4, Fall.

—— (1986), *Misunderstanding Media* (Cambridge, Mass.: Harvard University Press).

—— (1988), 'The Tradition of the Victim in the Griersonian Documentary', in Gross, Katz and Ruby, q.v.

—— (1990), 'In the Eye of the Beholder', *Harvard Information Technology Quarterly*, Spring.

—— (1993), 'The *CBS Evening News*, 7 April 1949: Creating an Ineffable Television Form', in Eldridge, q.v.

Winston, Brian, and Pearson, Roberta (1982), 'This Fits This Way; Narrative Structure in Wiseman's *Hospital* and *Model*', unpublished paper given at the Society of Cinema Studies Conference, UCLA.

Wolfe, Glenn Joseph (1973), *Vachel Lindsay: The Poet as Film Theorist* (New York: Arno).

Wollheim, Peter (1980), 'Robert Flaherty's Inuit Photographs', *Canada Forum* vol. 13, November.

Wood, Robin (1973), 'Terrible Buildings: The World of Georges Franju', *Film Comment* vol. 9 no. 6, November–December.

Woodhead, Leslie (1985), *In Search of Cool Ground: The Mursi Triology 1975–1985* (Manchester: Granada Television).

Worth, Sol, and Adair, John (1972), *Through Navajo Eyes* (Bloomington: Indiana University Press).

Wright, Basil (1950), 'Documentary: Flesh, Fish or Foul?', *Sight and Sound* vol. 19 no. 1, Spring.

—— (1956), 'The Documentary Dilemma', *Hollywood Quarterly* vol. 5 no. 4, Summer.

—— (1976), *The Long View: An International History of the Cinema* (London: Paladin).

Wyver, John (1982), *Nothing but the Truth: Cinéma Vérité and the Films of the Roger Graef Team* (London ICA/BFI).

Xavier, Ismail (1990), '*Iracema*: Transcending Cinéma Vérité', in Burton, q.v.

Yakir, Dan (1978), '*Ciné-transe*: The Vision of Jean Rouch', *Film Quarterly* vol. 31 no. 3, Spring.

Yampolsky, Mikhail (1991), 'Reality at Second Hand', *Historical Journal of Film, Radio and Television* vol. 11 no. 2.

Yeo, Eileen (1972), 'Mayhew as Social Investigator', in Yeo and Thompson, q.v.

Yeo, Eileen, and Thompson, E. P. (eds) (1972), *The Unknown Mayhew* (New York: Schocken).

Young, Colin, (1975), 'Observational Cinema', in Hockings, q.v.

Index

295

297

298